Lecture Notes in Computer S

T0238186

Commenced Publication in 1973
Founding and Former Series Editors:
Gerhard Goos, Juris Hartmanis, and Jan van Leeuwen

Masami Hagiya   Philip Wadler (Eds.)

Functional and Logic Programming

8th International Symposium, FLOPS 2006
Fuji-Susono, Japan, April 24-26, 2006
Proceedings

 Springer

Volume Editors

Masami Hagiya
University of Tokyo
and NTT Communication Science Laboratories
Department of Computer Science
Graduate School of Information Science and Technology
E-mail: hagiya@is.s.u-tokyo.ac.jp

Philip Wadler
University of Edinburgh
Department of Informatics
James Clerk Maxwell Building, The King's Buildings
Mayfield Road, Edinburgh EH9 3JZ, UK
E-mail: wadler@inf.ed.ac.uk

Library of Congress Control Number: 2006923563

CR Subject Classification (1998): D.1.6, D.1, D.3, F.3, I.2.3

LNCS Sublibrary: SL 2 – Programming and Software Engineering

ISSN   0302-9743
ISBN-10   3-540-33438-6 Springer Berlin Heidelberg New York
ISBN-13   978-3-540-33438-5 Springer Berlin Heidelberg New York

Springer is a part of Springer Science+Business Media

springer.com

© Springer-Verlag Berlin Heidelberg 2006
Printed in Germany

Typesetting: Camera-ready by author, data conversion by Scientific Publishing Services, Chennai, India
Printed on acid-free paper   SPIN: 11737414   06/3142   5 4 3 2 1 0

Preface

This volume contains the proceedings of the 8th International Symposium on Functional and Logic Programming (FLOPS 2006), held in Fuji-Susono, Japan, April 24–26, 2006 at the Fuji Institute of Education and Training.

FLOPS is a forum for research on all issues concerning functional programming and logic programming. In particular it aims to stimulate the cross-fertilization as well as the integration of the two paradigms. The previous FLOPS meetings took place in Fuji-Susono (1995), Shonan (1996), Kyoto (1998), Tsukuba (1999), Tokyo (2001), Aizu (2002) and Nara (2004). The proceedings of FLOPS 1999, FLOPS 2001, FLOPS 2002 and FLOPS 2004 were published by Springer in the *Lecture Notes in Computer Science* series, as volumes 1722, 2024, 2441 and 2998, respectively.

In response to the call for papers, 51 papers were submitted. Each paper was reviewed by at least three Program Committee members with the help of expert external reviewers. The Program Committee meeting was conducted electronically for a period of 2 weeks in December 2005 and January 2006. After careful and thorough discussion, the Program Committee selected 17 papers (33%) for presentation at the conference. In addition to the 17 contributed papers, the symposium included talks by two invited speakers: Guy Steele (Sun Microsystems Laboratories) and Peter Van Roy (Université Catholique de Louvain).

On behalf of the Program Committee, we would like to thank the invited speakers who agreed to give talks and contribute papers, and all those who submitted papers to FLOPS 2006. As Program Chairs, we would like to sincerely thank all the members of the FLOPS 2006 Program Committee for their excellent job, and all the external reviewers for their invaluable contribution. The support of our sponsors is gratefully acknowledged. We are indebted to the Japan Society for Software Science and Technology (JSSST), the Association of Logic Programming (ALP), and the Asian Association for Foundation of Software (AAFS). Finally we would like to thank members of the Local Arrangements Committee, in particular Yoshihiko Kakutani, for their invaluable support throughout the preparation and organization of the symposium.

February 2006

Masami Hagiya
Philip Wadler
Program Co-chairs
FLOPS 2006

Symposium Organization

Program Chairs

Philip Wadler   Edinburgh, UK
Masami Hagiya   Tokyo, Japan

Program Committee

Vincent Danos   Paris, France
Jacques Garrigue   Nagoya, Japan
Manuel Hermenegildo   New Mexico, USA & Madrid, Spain
Gabrielle Keller   UNSW, Sydney, Australia
Michael Rusinowitch   INRIA Lorraine, France
Konstantinos Sagonas   Uppsala, Sweden
Ken Satoh   NII, Tokyo, Japan
Peter Selinger   Dalhousie, Canada
Eijiro Sumii   Tohoku, Japan
Naoyuki Tamura   Kobe, Japan
Peter Thiemann   Freiburg, Germany
David Warren   Stony Brook, USA

Local Arrangements Chair

Masami Hagiya   Tokyo, Japan

Referees

Tatsuya Abe
Amal Ahmed
Kenichi Asai
Demis Ballis
Maria Garcia de la Banda
Bruno Blanchet
Daniel Cabeza
Venanzio Capretta
Olga Caprotti
Francois Charoy
Ezra Cooper
Markus Degen
Rachid Echahed
Carl Christian Frederiksen
Naoki Fukuta
Martin Gasbichler
Samir Genaim
Michael Hanus
Ralf Hinze
Hiroshi Hosobe
Haruo Hosoya
Zhenjiang Hu
Atsushi Igarashi
Koji Kagawa
Yoshihiko Kakutani
Dominique Larchey
Pedro López
Ugo Dal Lago
Toshiyuki Maeda
Julio Mariño
Yasuhiko Minamide

Jean-Yves Moyen
Susana Muñoz
Keiko Nakata
Jorge Navas
Matthias Neubauer
Tobias Nipkow
Susumu Nishimura
Shin-ya Nishizaki
Martin Odersky
Yoshihiro Oyama
Mikael Pettersson
David Pichardie
Benjamin Pierce
Paola Quaglia
Christophe Ringeissen
Don Sannella
Ganesh Sittampalam
Yasuyuki Tahara
Yoshiaki Takata
Yasuyuki Tsukada
Satoshi Tojo
Akihiko Tozawa
Rafael del Vado
German Vidal
Dimitrios Vytiniotis
Hironori Washizaki
Stefan Wehr
Stephanie Weirich
Jeremy Yallop
Akihiro Yamamoto
Mitsuharu Yamamoto

Table of Contents

LP Extensions

Analysis

Contracts

Web and GUI

Parallel Programming and Parallel Abstractions in Fortress

Guy L. Steele

Sun Microsystems Laboratories

Abstract. The Programming Language Research Group at Sun Microsystems Laboratories seeks to apply lessons learned from the Java (TM) Programming Language to the next generation of programming languages. The Java language supports platform-independent parallel programming with explicit multithreading and explicit locks. As part of the DARPA program for High Productivity Computing Systems, we are developing Fortress, a language intended to support large-scale scientific computation. One of the design principles is that parallelism be encouraged everywhere (for example, it is intentionally just a little bit harder to write a sequential loop than a parallel loop). Another is to have rich mechanisms for encapsulation and abstraction; the idea is to have a fairly complicated language for library writers that enables them to write libraries that present a relatively simple set of interfaces to the application programmer. We will discuss ideas for using a rich polymorphic type system to organize multithreading and data distribution on large parallel machines. The net result is similar in some ways to data distribution facilities in other languages such as HPF and Chapel, but more open-ended, because in Fortress the facilities are defined by user-replaceable libraries rather than wired into the compiler.

M. Hagiya and P. Wadler (Eds.): FLOPS 2006, LNCS 3945, p. 1, 2006.

Convergence in Language Design:
A Case of Lightning Striking
Four Times in the Same Place

Peter Van Roy

Université catholique de Louvain,
B-1348 Louvain-la-Neuve, Belgium
pvr@info.ucl.ac.be
http://www.info.ucl.ac.be/people/cvvanroy.html

Abstract. What will a definitive programming language look like? By *definitive language* I mean a programming language that gives good solutions at its level of abstraction, allowing computer science researchers to move on and work at higher levels. Given the evolution of computer science as a field with a rising level of abstraction, it is my belief that a small set of definitive languages will eventually exist. But how can we learn something about this set, considering that many basic questions about languages have not yet been settled? In this paper, I give some tentative conclusions about one definitive language. I present four case studies of substantial research projects that tackle important problems in four quite different areas: fault-tolerant programming, secure distributed programming, network-transparent distributed programming, and teaching programming as a unified discipline. All four projects had to think about language design. In this paper, I summarize the reasons why each project designed the language it did. It turns out that all four languages have a common structure. They can be seen as layered, with the following four layers in this order: a strict functional core, then deterministic concurrency, then message-passing concurrency, and finally shared-state concurrency (usually with transactions). This confirms the importance of functional programming and message passing as important defaults; however, global mutable state is also seen as an essential ingredient.

1   Introduction

This paper presents a surprising example of convergence in language design.[1] I will present four different research projects that were undertaken to solve four very different problems. The solutions achieved by all four projects are significant contributions to each of their respective areas. The four projects are interesting to us because they all considered language design as a key factor to achieve success. The surprise is that the four projects ended up using languages that have very similar structures.

---

[1] This paper was written to accompany an invited talk at FLOPS 2006 and is intended to stimulate discussion.

M. Hagiya and P. Wadler (Eds.): FLOPS 2006, LNCS 3945, pp. 2–12, 2006.

This paper is structured as follows. Section 1.1 briefly presents each of the four projects and Section 1.2 sketches their common solution. Then Sections 2 to 5 present each of the four projects in more detail to motivate why the common solution is a good solution for it. Finally, Section 6 concludes the paper by recapitulating the common solution and making some conclusions on why it is important for functional and logic programming.

Given the similar structure of the four languages, I consider that their common structure deserves to be carefully examined. The common structure may turn out to be the heart of one possible *definitive* programming language, i.e., a programming language that gives good solutions at its level of abstraction, so that computer science researchers can move on and work at higher levels. My view is that the evolution of programming languages will follow a similar course as the evolution of parsing algorithms. In the 1970s, compiler courses were often built around a study of parsing algorithms. Today, parsing is well understood for most practical purposes and when designing a new compiler it is straightforward to pick a parsing algorithm from a set of "good enough" or "definitive" algorithms. Today's compiler courses are built around higher level topics such as dataflow analysis, type systems, and language design. For programming languages the evolution toward a definitive set may be slower than for parsing algorithms because languages are harder to judge objectively than algorithms.

1.1   The Four Projects

The four projects are the following:[2]

- Programming highly available embedded systems for telecommunications (Section 2). This project was undertaken by Joe Armstrong and his colleagues at the Ericsson Computer Science Laboratory. This work started in 1986. The Erlang language was designed and a first efficient and stable implementation was completed in 1991. Erlang and its current environment, the OTP (Open Telecom Platform) system, are being used successfully in commercial systems by Ericsson and other companies.
- Programming secure distributed systems with multiple users and multiple security domains (Section 3). This project was undertaken over many years by different institutions. It started with Carl Hewitt's Actor model and led via concurrent logic programming to the E language designed by Doug Barnes, Mark Miller, and their colleagues. Predecessors of E have been used to implement various multiuser virtual environments.
- Making network-transparent distributed programming practical (Section 4). This project started in 1995 with the realization that the well-factored design of the Oz language, first developed by Gert Smolka and his students in 1991 as an outgrowth of the ACCLAIM project, was a good starting point for making network transparent distribution practical. This resulted in the Mozart Programming System, whose first release was in 1999.

---

[2] Many people were involved in each project; because of space limitations only a few are mentioned here.

– Teaching programming as a unified discipline covering all popular programming paradigms (Section 5). This project started in 1999 with the realization by the author and Seif Haridi that Oz is well-suited to teaching programming because it covers many programming concepts, it has a simple semantics, and it has an efficient implementation. A textbook published in 2004 "reconstructs" the Oz design according to a principled approach. This book is the basis of programming courses now being taught at more than a dozen universities worldwide.

1.2   The Layered Language Structure

In all four research projects, the programming language has a layered structure. In its most general form, the language has four layers. This section briefly presents the four layers and mentions how they are realized in the four projects. The rest of the paper motivates the layered structure for each project in more detail. The layers are the following:

– The inner layer is a strict functional language. All four projects start with this layer.
– The second layer adds deterministic concurrency. Deterministic concurrency is sometimes called declarative or dataflow concurrency. It has the property that it cannot have race conditions. This form of concurrency is as simple to reason in as functional programming. In Oz it is realized with single-assignment variables and dataflow synchronization. Because Oz implements these variables as logic variables, this layer in Oz is also a logic language. In E it is realized by a form of concurrent programming called *event-loop concurrency*: inside a process all objects share a single thread. This means that execution inside a process is deterministic. The Erlang project skips this layer.
– The third layer adds asynchronous message passing. This leads to a simple message-passing model in which concurrent entities send messages asynchronously. All four projects have this layer. In E, this layer is used for communication between processes (deterministic concurrency is used for communication inside a single process).
– The fourth layer adds global mutable state.[3] Three of the four projects have global mutable state as a final layer, provided for different reasons, but always with the understanding that it is not used as often as the other layers. In the Erlang project, the mutable state is provided as a persistent database with a transactional interface. In the network transparency project, the mutable state is provided as an object store with a transactional interface and as a family of distributed protocols that is used to guarantee coherence of state across the distributed system. These protocols are expensive but they are sometimes necessary. In the teaching programming project, mutable state is used to make programs modular. The E project skips this layer.

---

[3] By *global*, I mean that the mutable state has a scope that is as large as necessary, not that it necessarily covers the whole program.

This layered structure has an influence on program design. In all four projects, the starting point is the functional inner layer, complemented by the message-passing layer which is just as important. In three of the four projects, the final layer (global mutable state) is less used than the others, but it provides a critical functionality that cannot be eliminated.

Note that the network-transparent distribution project and the teaching programming project were undertaken by many of the same people and started with the same programming language. Both projects were undertaken because we had reasons to believe Oz would be an adequate starting point. Each project had to adapt the Oz language to get a good solution. In the final analysis, both projects give good reasons why their solutions are appropriate, as explained in Sections 4 and 5.

2   Fault-Tolerant Programming

The Erlang programming language and system is designed for building high availability telecommunications systems. Erlang was designed at the Ericsson Computer Science Laboratory [5, 4]. Erlang is designed explicitly to support programs that tolerate both software and hardware faults. Note that software faults are unavoidable: studies have shown that even with extensive testing, software still has bugs. Any system with high availability must therefore have a way to tolerate faults due to software bugs. Erlang has been used to build commercial systems of very high availability [8]. The most successful of these systems is the AXD 301 ATM switch, which contains around 1 million lines of Erlang, a similar amount of C/C++ code, and a small amount of Java [29].

An Erlang program consists of a (possibly very large) number of processes. An Erlang process is a lightweight entity with its own memory space. A process is programmed with a strict functional language. Each process has a unique identity, which is a constant that can be stored in data structures and in messages. Processes communicate by sending asynchronous messages to other processes. A process receives messages in its mailbox, and it can extract messages from the mailbox with pattern matching. Note that a process can do dynamic code change by receiving a new function in a message and installing it as the new process definition. We conclude that this structure gives the Erlang language two layers: a functional layer for programming processes, and a message-passing layer for allowing them to communicate.

To support fault tolerance, two processes can be linked together. When one process fails, for example because of a software error, then the other fails as well. Each process has a supervisor bit. If a process is set to supervisor mode, then it does not fail when a linked process fails, but it receives a message generated by the run-time system. This allows the application to recover from the failure. Erlang is well-suited to implement software fault tolerance because of process isolation and process linking.

Erlang also has a database called Mnesia. The database stores consistent snapshots of critical program data. When processes fail, their supervisors can use the database to recover and continue execution. The database provides a transactional interface to shared data. The database is an essential part of Erlang programs. It can therefore be considered as a third layer of the Erlang language. This third layer, mutable state with a transactional interface, implements a form of shared-state concurrency [26].

Because Erlang processes do not share data, they can be implemented over a distributed system without any changes in the program. This makes distributed programming in Erlang straightforward. Using process linking and supervisors, Erlang programs can also recover from hardware failures, i.e., partial failures of the distributed system.

3   Secure Distributed Programming

The E programming language and system is designed for building secure distributed systems [21, 19]. The E language consists of objects (functions that share an encapsulated state) hosted in secure processes called *vats* that communicate through a secure message-passing protocol based on encryption. Within the language, security is provided by implementing all language references (including object references) as capabilities. A *capability* is an unforgeable reference that combines two properties that cannot be separated: it designates a language entity and it provides permission to perform a well-defined set of operations on the entity. The only way to perform an operation is to have a capability for that operation.

Capabilities are passed between language entities according to well-defined rules. The primary rule is that the only way to get a capability is that an entity to which you already have a capability passes you the capability ("connectivity begets connectivity"). A system based on capabilities can support the Principle of Least Authority (POLA): give each entity just enough authority to carry out its work. In systems based on POLA the destructive abilities of malicious programs such as viruses largely go away. Unfortunately, current programming languages and operating systems only have weak support for POLA. This is why projects such as E and KeyKOS (see below) are so important [25].

Inside a vat, there is a single thread of execution and all objects take turns executing in this thread. Objects send other objects asynchronous messages that are queued for execution. Objects execute a method when they receive a message. This is a form of deterministic concurrency that is called *event-loop concurrency*. Single threading within a vat is done to ensure that concurrency introduces no security problems due to the nondeterminism of interleaving execution. Event-loop concurrency works well for secure programs; a model based on shared-state concurrency is much harder to program with [20]. Between two or more vats, execution is done according to a general message-passing model.

In a system such as E that is based on capabilities, there is no *ambient authority*, i.e., a program does not have the ability to perform an operation just because it is executing in a certain context. This is very different from most other systems. For example, in Unix a program has all the authority of the user that executes it. The lack of ambient authority does not mean that E necessarily does not have global mutable state. For example, there could be a capability that is given by default to all new objects. However, the current design of E does not have global mutable state. If information needs to be shared globally, the sharing is programmed explicitly by using message-passing concurrency.

The history of E starts with Carl Hewitt's Actor model in the 1970s [13, 14] and continues with Norm Hardy's KeyKOS system [10], which is a pure capability operating system that provides orthogonal persistence. It continues with the Concurrent Prolog family of languages [23]. The Joule language, designed at Agorics [1], is E's most direct ancestor. E was originally designed at Electric Communities as an infrastructure for building a secure distributed collaborative computing environment, secure enough that you could spend real money and sign real contracts within it. Virtual environments now exist with currencies that are exchangeable with real currencies; they are called *virtual economies* [30].

4   Network-Transparent Distributed Programming

This project was motivated by the desire to simplify distributed programming by making a practical system that is both network transparent and network aware. This approach was first expressed clearly by Cardelli in his work on Obliq [6]. The idea is to make a distributed implementation of a language by implementing the basic language operations with distributed algorithms. By choosing the algorithms carefully, the implementation can be made efficient and can handle partial failure inside the language [12]. A program then consists of two separate parts: the functionality, in which distribution is ignored, and the choice of distributed algorithms, which is used to tune network performance and to handle partial failure. We are extending this approach to handle security [24].

Some researchers have maintained that this cannot work; that network transparency cannot be made practical, see, e.g., Waldo *et al* [28]. They cite four reasons: pointer arithmetic, partial failure, latency, and concurrency. The first reason (pointer arithmetic) disappears if the language has an abstract store. The second reason (partial failure) requires a reflective fault model, which we designed for the Distributed Oz language. The final two reasons (latency and concurrency) lead to a layered language design. Let us examine each of these reasons. Latency is a problem if the language relies primarily on synchronized operations. In the terminology of Cardelli, latency is a network awareness issue. The solution is that the language must make asynchronous programming both simple and efficient.

Concurrency is a problem if the language relies heavily on mutable state. To achieve network transparency, the mutable state has to be made coherent across all the machines of the system. It is well known that this is costly to achieve for a distributed system. The solution is to avoid the use of mutable state as much as possible, and to use it only when it is absolutely necessary. As a result, most of the program is concurrent and functional. Global state is necessary only in a few places, e.g., to implement servers and caches, and in general it can be avoided (note that local state, which is limited to a single machine, is fine).

Our distributed programming language therefore has a layered structure. The core has no state and is therefore a functional language. Extending the functional language with concurrency and a simple communications channel gives multi-agent programming or actor programming: concurrent entities that send each other asynchronous messages. The final step is to add mutable state, with a choice of protocols for its implementation. For example, stationary state corresponds to a standard server architecture. Mobile or cached state can be used to increase performance by moving the state to where it is currently being used [27]. Other protocols are possible too. We find that a good way to add mutable state is as part of a transactional protocol [3]. Transactions are a good way to hide both network latency and partial failure.

The final language is organized into four layers, in this order: a strict functional core, dataflow concurrency, communication channels, and mutable state. For language entities in each layer, distributed algorithms implement the distributed behavior. Inner layers have more efficient distributed behaviors. We implement dataflow concurrency with single-assignment variables, which are intermediate between no assignment (functional language) and any number of assignments (mutable state). Single-assignment variables are implemented with a distributed unification algorithm, which is more efficient than a state coherence protocol [11]. To write an efficient distributed program, one uses the lower layers preferentially and one chooses the appropriate distributed algorithm for each language entity that is distributed. Partial failure is handled at the language level by asynchronous notifications similar to the process linking provided by Erlang.

5   Teaching Programming as a Unified Discipline

A good way to organize a programming course is to start with a simple language and then to extend this language gradually. This organization was pioneered in the 1970s by Holt *et al*, who used carefully defined subsets of PL/I [15]. The most successful application of this organization was done by Abelson & Sussman in 1985, who use subsets of Scheme and start with a simple functional language [2]. A simple functional language is a good start for teaching programming, for many reasons. It is easy to explain because of its simple semantics and syntax, and yet it contains a key language concept, the lexically scoped closure, which is the basis for many other powerful concepts.

Abelson & Sussman made the important decision to organize the subsets according to the programming concepts they contain, and not the language features they use as Holt did. This makes the course less dependent on the details of one language and gives students a broader and more in-depth understanding. The second concept introduced by Abelson & Sussman is mutable state. With mutable state it is possible to express the object-oriented programming style, with an object as a collection of functions accessing a common mutable state that is hidden through lexical scoping. Unfortunately, by introducing mutable state early on, programs in the new language are no longer mathematical functions. This makes reasoning about programs harder.

In 1999, the author and Seif Haridi realized that they understood programming concepts well enough to teach programming in a more unified way than had been done before. We chose the Oz language because of its well-factored design. We set about writing a programming textbook and organizing courses [26]. During this work, we "reconstructed" the design of a large subset of Oz according to an organizing principle that states that a new concept is needed when programs start getting complicated for reasons unrelated to the problem being solved. More precisely, a new concept is needed in the language when programs require nonlocal transformations to encode the concept in the language. If the new concept is added to the language, then only local transformations are needed. We call this the *creative extension principle*. It was first defined by Felleisen [9].

We found that it is possible to add concurrency as the second concept instead of mutable state. The resulting language lets us write purely functional programs as collections of independent entities ("agents") that communicate through deterministic streams. This form of concurrency is called *declarative concurrency*. The streams are deterministic because the writer and readers of each stream element are known deterministically. The difference with a sequential functional language is that the output of a function can be calculated incrementally instead of all at once. Race conditions are not possible, i.e., there is no observable nondeterminism in the language.

Declarative concurrency is a deterministic form of concurrency that is much simpler to program with than the shared-state concurrency used in mainstream languages such as Java [18]. It is already widely used, e.g., Unix pipes and Google's MapReduce [7] are just two of many examples, but it is not well-known as a programming model. Because of its simplicity we consider that it deserves to become more popular. For example, Morrison shows how to use it for business software [22]. We have taught declarative concurrency as a first introduction to concurrent programming in second-year university courses at several large universities.

After introducing concurrency, the next concept we introduce is a simple communication channel. This extends the previous model by adding nondeterminism: the writer of the next stream element is chosen nondeterministically among the potential writers. The resulting language is both practical and easy to program in [16].

Finally, we introduce global mutable state. This is important for program modularity, i.e., the ability to change part of a program without having to change the rest. Without true mutable state, modularity is not possible [26]. State-threading techniques such as monads are not expressive enough [17].

6   Conclusions

This paper presents four successful research projects that were undertaken to solve quite different problems, namely fault-tolerant programming, secure distributed programming, network-transparent distributed programming, and teaching programming as a unified discipline. Each project had to consider language design to solve its problem. A surprising result is that the four resulting languages have a common structure. In the general case they are layered, with a strict functional inner layer, a deterministic concurrency layer, a message-passing concurrency layer, and a shared-state concurrency layer, in that order. I postulate that this common structure will be part of one possible definitive programming language, i.e., a programming language that gives good enough solutions at its level of abstraction so that computer scientists and developers can move on to higher levels.

Given this postulate one can deduce several important consequences for functional and logic programming. First, that the notion of declarative programming, i.e., functional and logic programming, is at the very core of programming languages. This is already well-known; our study reinforces this conclusion. Second, that declarative programming will stay at the core for the foreseeable future, because distributed, secure, and fault-tolerant programming are essential topics that need support from the programming language. A third conclusion is that it is important for declarative programmers to study how declarative programming fits in the larger scheme. A final conclusion is that message-passing concurrency seems to be the correct default for general-purpose concurrent programming instead of shared-state concurrency.

Acknowledgments

We would like to thank Kevin Glynn and Boris Mejias for their comments on a draft of this article. We would like to thank the members of the Programming Languages and Distributed Computing group at UCL for creating the environment in which the speculations of this article could arise. This work was partly funded by the EVERGROW project in the sixth Framework Programme of the European Union under contract number 001935 and by the MILOS project of the Wallonia Region of Belgium under convention 114856.

References

1. Agorics, Inc., 2004. www.agorics.com.
2. Harold Abelson, Gerald Jay Sussman, and Julie Sussman. *Structure and Interpretation of Computer Programs*. MIT Press, Cambridge, MA, 1985. Second edition 1996.
3. Mostafa Al-Metwally. *Design and Implementation of a Fault-Tolerant Transactional Object Store*. PhD thesis, Al-Azhar University, Cairo, Egypt, December 2003.
4. Joe Armstrong. *Making reliable distributed systems in the presence of software errors*. PhD thesis, Royal Institute of Technology (KTH), Kista, Sweden, November 2003.
5. Joe Armstrong, Mike Williams, Claes Wikström, and Robert Virding. *Concurrent Programming in Erlang*. Prentice-Hall, Englewood Cliffs, NJ, 1996.
6. Luca Cardelli. A language with distributed scope. In *Principles of Programming Languages (POPL)*, pages 286–297, San Francisco, CA, January 1995. ACM Press.
7. Jeffrey Dean and Sanjay Ghemawat. MapReduce: Simplified data processing on large clusters. In *6th Symposium on Operating Systems Design and Implementation (OSDI'04)*, pages 137–150, December 2004.

8. Ericsson. *Open Telecom Platform—User's Guide, Reference Manual, Installation Guide, OS Specific Parts.* Telefonaktiebolaget LM Ericsson, Stockholm, Sweden, 1996.

9. Matthias Felleisen. On the expressive power of programming languages. In *3rd European Symposium on Programming (ESOP 1990)*, pages 134–151, May 1990.

10. Norman Hardy. KeyKOS architecture. In *ACM SIGOPS Operating Systems Review*, volume 19, pages 8–25, October 1985.

11. Seif Haridi, Peter Van Roy, Per Brand, Michael Mehl, Ralf Scheidhauer, and Gert Smolka. Efficient logic variables for distributed computing. *ACM Transactions on Programming Languages and Systems*, 21(3):569–626, May 1999.

12. Seif Haridi, Peter Van Roy, Per Brand, and Christian Schulte. Programming languages for distributed applications. *New Generation Computing*, 16(3):223–261, May 1998.

13. Carl Hewitt. Viewing control structures as patterns of passing messages. *Journal of Artificial Intelligence*, 8(3):323–364, June 1977.

14. Carl Hewitt, Peter Bishop, and Richard Steiger. A universal modular ACTOR formalism for artificial intelligence. In *3rd International Joint Conference on Artificial Intelligence (IJCAI)*, pages 235–245, August 1973.

15. R.C. Holt, D.B. Wortman, D.T. Barnard, and J.R. Cordy. SP/k: A system for teaching computer programming. *Communications of the ACM*, 20(5):301–309, May 1977.

16. Sverker Janson, Johan Montelius, and Seif Haridi. Ports for Objects in Concurrent Logic Programs. In G. Agha, P. Wegner, and A. Yonezawa, editors, *Trends in Object-Based Concurrent Computing*, pages 211–231. MIT Press, Cambridge, MA, 1993.

17. Lambda the Ultimate discussion. State and modularity, October 2003. Available at `lambda-the-ultimate.org/classic/message9361.html`.

18. Doug Lea. *Concurrent Programming in Java,* 2nd edition. Addison-Wesley, 2000.

19. Mark S. Miller, Chip Morningstar, and Bill Frantz. Capability-based financial instruments. In *Proceedings of the 4th International Conference on Financial Cryptography*, volume 1962 of *Lecture Notes in Computer Science*, pages 349–378. Springer-Verlag, 2000.

20. Mark S. Miller and Jonathan Shapiro. Concurrency among strangers. In *Proceedings of the Symposium on Trustworthy Global Computing (TGC 2005)*, volume 3705 of *Lecture Notes in Computer Science*, pages 195–229. Springer-Verlag, April 2005.

21. Mark S. Miller, Marc Stiegler, Tyler Close, Bill Frantz, Ka-Ping Yee, Chip Morningstar, Jonathan Shapiro, Norm Hardy, E. Dean Tribble, Doug Barnes, Dan Bornstien, Bryce Wilcox-O'Hearn, Terry Stanley, Kevin Reid, and Darius Bacon. E: Open source distributed capabilities, 2001. Available at `www.erights.org`.

22. J. Paul Morrison. *Flow-Based Programming: A New Approach to Application Development.* Van Nostrand Reinhold, New York, 1994.

23. Ehud Shapiro. The family of concurrent logic programming languages. *ACM Computing Surveys*, 21(3):413–510, September 1989.

24. Fred Spiessens and Peter Van Roy. The Oz-E project: Design guidelines for a secure multiparadigm programming language. In *Multiparadigm Programming in Mozart/Oz, Second International Conference, MOZ 2004*, volume 3389 of *Lecture Notes in Computer Science*, pages 21–40. Springer-Verlag, 2005.

25. Marc Stiegler. The SkyNet virus: Why it is unstoppable; How to stop it. Talk available at `www.erights.org/talks/skynet/`.

26. Peter Van Roy and Seif Haridi. *Concepts, Techniques, and Models of Computer Programming*. MIT Press, Cambridge, MA, 2004.
27. Peter Van Roy, Seif Haridi, Per Brand, Gert Smolka, Michael Mehl, and Ralf Scheidhauer. Mobile objects in Distributed Oz. *ACM Transactions on Programming Languages and Systems*, 19(5):804–851, September 1997.
28. Jim Waldo, Geoff Wyant, Ann Wollrath, and Samuel C. Kendall. A note on distributed computing. In *Second International Workshop on Mobile Object Systems– Towards the Programmable Internet*, pages 49–64, July 1996. Originally published at Sun Microsystems Laboratories in 1994.
29. Ulf Wiger. Four-fold increase in productivity and quality – industrial-strength functional programming in telecom-class products. In *Proceedings of the 2001 Workshop on Formal Design of Safety Critical Embedded Systems*, 2001.
30. Wikipedia, the free encyclopedia. Entry "virtual economy", January 2006. Available at en.wikipedia.org/wiki/Virtual_economy.

"Scrap Your Boilerplate" Reloaded

Ralf Hinze[1], Andres Löh[1], and Bruno C.d.S. Oliveira[2]

[1] Institut für Informatik III, Universität Bonn,
Römerstraße 164, 53117 Bonn, Germany
{ralf, loeh}@informatik.uni-bonn.de
[2] Oxford University Computing Laboratory,
Wolfson Building, Parks Road, Oxford OX1 3QD, UK
bruno@comlab.ox.ac.uk

Abstract. The paper "Scrap your boilerplate" (SYB) introduces a combinator library for generic programming that offers generic traversals and queries. Classically, support for generic programming consists of two essential ingredients: a way to write (type-)overloaded functions, and independently, a way to access the structure of data types. SYB seems to lack the second. As a consequence, it is difficult to compare with other approaches such as PolyP or Generic Haskell. In this paper we reveal the structural view that SYB builds upon. This allows us to define the combinators as generic functions in the classical sense. We explain the SYB approach in this changed setting from ground up, and use the understanding gained to relate it to other generic programming approaches. Furthermore, we show that the SYB view is applicable to a very large class of data types, including generalized algebraic data types.

1 Introduction

The paper "Scrap your boilerplate" (SYB) [1] introduces a combinator library for generic programming that offers generic traversals and queries. Classically, support for generic programming consists of two essential ingredients: a way to write (type-)overloaded functions, and independently, a way to access the structure of data types. SYB seems to lacks the second, because it is entirely based on combinators.

In this paper, we make the following contributions:

– We explain the SYB approach from ground up using an explicit representation of data types, the *spine view*. Many of the SYB library functions are more easily defined in the spine view than using the combinators underlying the original SYB library.
– We compare the expressive power and applicability of the spine view to the original SYB paper, to PolyP [2] and to Generic Haskell [3, 4].
– Furthermore, we show that the SYB view is applicable to a very large class of data types, including generalized algebraic data types (GADTs) [5, 6].

We use Haskell [7] for all our examples. The source code of this paper [8] constitutes a Haskell program that can be compiled by GHC [9] in order to test and experiment with our implementation. While our implementation is not

M. Hagiya and P. Wadler (Eds.): FLOPS 2006, LNCS 3945, pp. 13–29, 2006.
© Springer-Verlag Berlin Heidelberg 2006

directly usable as a separate library, because it is not extensible (new data types cannot be added in a compositional way), this deficiency is not tied to the idea of the *Spine* view: the technical report version of this paper [8] contains a slightly less elegant implementation that is extensible.

In this introduction, we explain the ingredients of a system for generic programming, and argue that the original SYB presentation does not clearly qualify as such a system. In order to better understand the concept of generic programming, let us first look at plain functional programming.

1.1 Functional Programming and Views

As functional programmers in a statically typed language, we are used to define functions by case analysis on a data type. In fact, it is standard practice to define a function on a data type by performing case analysis on the input. The shape of the data type guides our function definitions, and affects how easy it is to define certain functions.

As an example, assume we want to implement a priority queue supporting among others the operation

$$splitMinimum :: PriorityQueue \rightarrow Maybe\ (Int, PriorityQueue)$$

to separate the minimum from the remaining queue if the queue is not empty. We can choose a heap-structured tree to implement the priority queue, and define

> **data** *Tree a*   = *Empty* | *Node* (*Tree a*) *a* (*Tree a*)
> **type** *PriorityQueue* = *Tree Int* .

The choice of a heap as the underlying data stucture makes the implementation of *splitMinimum* slightly tricky, requiring an auxiliary operation to merge two heaps.

If, on the other hand, we choose a sorted list to represent the priority queue

> **data** *PriorityQueue* = *Void* | *Min Int PriorityQueue* ,

we make our life much easier, because *splitMinimum* is now trivial to define. The price we pay is that the implementation on lists is likely to be less efficient than the one using the tree. Such different *views* on a data structure need not be mutually exclusive. Wadler and others have proposed language support for views [10, 11].

Many functions on a single data type follow common traversal and recursion patterns. Instead of defining each function by case analysis, it is possible to define combinators that capture these patterns. For instance, given functions

> *foldTree* :: $r \rightarrow (r \rightarrow a \rightarrow r \rightarrow r) \rightarrow$ *Tree a* $\rightarrow r$
> *mapTree* :: $(a \rightarrow b) \rightarrow$ *Tree a* $\rightarrow$ *Tree b* ,

we can write functions to perform an inorder traversal of the tree or to increase every label in a tree by one very concisely:

> *inorder* = *foldTree* [] $(\lambda l\ x\ r \rightarrow l + [x] + r)$
> *incTree* = *mapTree* $(+1)$.

1.2   Generic Programming

A *generic function* is a function that is defined once, but works for many data types. It can adapt itself to the structure of data types. Generic functions are also called *polytypic* or *structurally polymorphic*.

Genericity is different from *parametric polymorphism*, where the same code works for multiple types, and the structure of a data type is not available for analysis. It is also more specific than *ad-hoc polymorphism*, which allows a function to be defined for different data types, by providing one implementation for each type.

Typical examples of generic functions are equality or comparison, parsing and unparsing, serialization, traversals over large data structures and many others.

Support for generic programming consists of two essential ingredients. Firstly, support for ad-hoc polymorphism is required. This allows the programmer to write *overloaded functions*, i.e., functions that dispatch on a type argument. Secondly, we need a *generic view* on the structure of data types. In a nominal type system, types with similar structure are considered to be completely distinct. To employ generic programming, we need to lower this barrier and make the structure transparent if desired.

The two ingredients are orthogonal, and for both, there is a choice. Overloaded functions can be expressed in Haskell using the class system, using a type-safe cast operation, by reflecting the type system on the value level, or by a combination of the above. Any of these approaches has certain advantages and disadvantages, but they are mostly interchangeable and do not dramatically affect the expressivity of the generic programming system.

The structural view, on the other hand, dictates the flavour of the whole system: it affects the set of data types we can represent in the view, the class of functions we can write using case analysis on the structure, and potentially the efficiency of these functions. The structural view is used to make an overloaded function truly generic, working for a data type even if it has no ad-hoc case for that type.

For instance, PolyP views data types as fixed points of regular functors. Therefore its approach is limited to regular data types, but the view allows access to the points of recursion and allows the definition of recursion combinators such as catamorphisms. Generic Haskell uses a sum-of-products view which is more widely applicable, but limits the class of functions we can write. The concept of generic views is explained further in a recent paper [12], and is related to *universes* in dependently-typed programming [13].

In summary, it turns out that there is a close analogy between plain functional and generic programming: the concepts of views, function definition by case analysis, and combinators occur in both settings.

1.3   Scrap Your Boilerplate

In analogy with the situation on plain functions, not all generic functions are defined by case analysis. Just as there are powerful combinators for ordinary functions, such combinators also exist for generic programming. In fact, the very combinators we have used above, *foldTree* and *mapTree*, are typical candidates for generalization.

The paper "Scrap your boilerplate" (SYB) describes a library for *strategic programming* [14], i.e., it offers combinators for generic traversals and queries on terms. Two central combinators of the SYB library are *everywhere* to traverse a data structure and modify it in certain places, and *everything* to traverse a data structure and collect information in the process.

The SYB approach builds completely on combinators, and some fundamental combinators are assumed to be provided by the implementation. While this is fine in practice, it makes it difficult to compare SYB with other approaches such as PolyP or Generic Haskell. The reason is that the concept of a generic view seems to be missing. Functions are never defined by case analysis on the structure of types.

However, the generic view is only hidden in the original presentation. In this paper we reveal the structure that SYB uses behind the scenes and that allows us to define the SYB combinators as generic functions by case analysis on that structure.

We will explain the SYB approach in this changed setting from ground up. The focus of the presentation is on conceptual conciseness. We do not strive to replace the original implementation, but to complement it by an alternative implementation which may be easier to understand and relate to other approaches.

1.4 Organization of This Paper

The rest of this paper is organized as follows: We first describe the two orthogonal ingredients required for generic programming in our presentation of the SYB approach: overloaded functions (Section 2) and the *spine view*, the structure that is the hidden foundation of SYB (Section 3). We then review the central combinators of SYB in Section 4. Section 5 shows how we can access names of constructors.

In Section 6, we take a step back and relate SYB to other generic programming approaches. Inspired by our analysis on the expressiveness of the SYB approach, we demonstrate how to extend the spine view to generalized algebraic data types (Section 7). Section 8 discusses related work and concludes.

2   Overloaded Functions

The standard way in Haskell to express an overloaded function is to use a type class. In fact, this is the way taken by the original SYB papers: in the first SYB paper, type classes are used in conjunction with a type-safe cast operation, and in the third paper, overloaded functions are expressed solely based on type classes. However, type classes leave it to the compiler to find the correct instance, and thus hide a non-trivial aspect of the program. In this paper, we prefer to be more explicit and emphasize the idea that an overloaded function dispatches on a type argument. Haskell excels at embedded languages, so it seems a good idea to try to embed the type language in Haskell. The following way to encode overloaded functions is not new: it is based on Hinze's "Fun of Programming" chapter [15] and has been used widely elsewhere [16].

The whole point of static types is that they can be used at compile time to distinguish programs, hence we certainly do not want to use an unparameterized data type *Type* to represent types. Instead, we add a parameter so that *Type t* comprises only type representations for the type *t*. We now need ways to construct values of type *Type t*. For instance, *Int* can be a representation of the type *Int*, so that we have *Int* :: *Type Int*. Similarly, if we have a representation *r* of type *a*, we can make *List r* a representation of type [*a*], or formally *List* :: *Type a* → *Type* [*a*].

The notation we use suggests that *Int* and *List* are data constructors of type *Type*, but this impossible in Haskell 98, because the result type of a constructor must always be unrestricted, i.e., *Type a* for some type variable *a*. Fortunately, GHC now supports *generalized algebraic data types* (GADTs) [5, 6], which lift exactly this restriction. Therefore, we can indeed define *Type* in Haskell using the following GADT:

> **data** *Type* :: * → * **where**
>   *Int*   :: *Type Int*
>   *Char* :: *Type Char*
>   *List* :: *Type a* → *Type* [*a*]
>   *Pair* :: *Type a* → *Type b* → *Type* (*a, b*)
>   *Tree* :: *Type a* → *Type* (*Tree a*) .

This type allows us to represent integers, characters, lists, pairs, and trees – enough to give an example of a simple overloaded function that sums up all integers in a value:

> *sum* :: *Type a* → *a* → *Int*
> *sum Int*   *n*   = *n*
> *sum Char*   _   = 0
> *sum* (*List a*)   *xs*   = *foldr* (+) 0 (*map* (*sum a*) *xs*)
> *sum* (*Pair a b*) (*x, y*) = *sum a x* + *sum b y*
> *sum* (*Tree a*)   *t*   = *sum* (*List a*) (*inorder t*) .

The function *sum* works on all types that can be constructed from *Int*, *Char*, [], (,), and *Tree*, for instance, on a complex type such as [(*Char, Int*)]: the expression

> *sum* (*List* (*Pair Char Int*)) [('k', 6), ('s', 9), (' ', 27)]

evaluates to 42.

The function *sum* is an example of an ad-hoc-polymorphic function. There are a limited number of cases for different types, defining potentially unrelated behavior of *sum* for these types. The function will not work on types such as *Bool* or *Maybe* or even on a type

> **newtype** *MyPair a b* = *MyPair* (*a, b*) ,

because Haskell has a nominal type system, hence *MyPair a b* is isomorphic to, yet distinct from (*a, b*).

3   The Spine View

In this section, we learn how to define a truly generic *sum*, which works on *Bool* and *Maybe* and *MyType*, among others.

Take a look at any Haskell value. If it is not of some abstract type, it can always be written as a data constructor applied to other values. For example, *Node Empty* 2 *Empty* is the *Node* data constructor, applied to the three values *Empty*, 2, and *Empty*. Even built-in types such as *Int* or *Char* are not fundamentally different: every literal can be seen as a nullary constructor.

Let us make the structure of constructed values visible and mark each constructor using *Constr*, and each function application using ◇. The example from above becomes *Constr Node* ◇ *Empty* ◇ 2 ◇ *Empty*. The functions *Constr* and (◇)[1] are themselves constructors of a new data type *Spine*:[2]

> **data** *Spine* :: ∗ → ∗ **where**
> $\quad$ *Constr* :: a → *Spine a*
> $\quad$ (◇)$\quad$ :: *Spine* (a → b) → a → *Spine b* .

Given a value of type *Spine a*, we can recover the original value of type a by undoing the conversion step made before:

> *fromSpine* :: *Spine a* → a
> *fromSpine* (*Constr c*) = c
> *fromSpine* (f ◇ a)$\quad$ = (*fromSpine f*) a .

The function *fromSpine* is parametrically polymorphic, i.e., it works independently of the type in question: it just replaces *Constr* with the original constructor and (◇) with function application.

Unfortunately, *fromSpine* is the only interesting function we can write on a *Spine*. Reconsider the type of the (◇) constructor:

> (◇) :: *Spine* (a → b) → a → *Spine b* .

The type a is not visible in the final result (it is existentially quantified in the data type), so the only thing we can do with the component of type a is to combine it somehow with the component of type *Spine* (a → b).

Since we intend to call overloaded functions on the value of type a, we require a representation of the type of a. Our solution is thus that together with the value of type a, we store a representation of its type. To this end, we introduce a data type for typed values[3]

---

[1] We use (◇) as a symbol for an infix data constructor. For our presentation, we ignore the Haskell rule that names of infix data constructors must start with a colon.

[2] Note that in contrast to *Type*, the data type *Spine* is not necessarily a *generalized* algebraic data type. The result types of the constructors are not restricted, *Spine* could therefore be defined in GHC as a normal data type with existentials. However, we prefer the GADT syntax.

[3] We use (:) as data constructor for the type *Typed* in this paper. The *cons*-operator for lists, written (:) in Haskell, does not occur in this paper.

data *Typed a = a : Type a* ,

and then adapt ($\diamond$) to use *Typed a* instead of *a*:

data *Spine* :: $* \rightarrow *$ **where**
   Constr :: $a \rightarrow$ *Spine a*
   ($\diamond$)   :: *Spine* $(a \rightarrow b) \rightarrow$ *Typed a* $\rightarrow$ *Spine b* .

Of course, we have to adapt *fromSpine* to ignore the new type annotations:

fromSpine :: *Spine a* $\rightarrow$ *a*
fromSpine (*Constr c*) = *c*
fromSpine ($f \diamond (a : \_)$) = (*fromSpine f*) *a* .

We can define a right inverse to *fromSpine*, as an overloaded function. For each data type, the definition follows a trivial pattern. Here are the cases for the *Int* and *Tree* types:

toSpine :: *Type a* $\rightarrow$ *a* $\rightarrow$ *Spine a*
toSpine Int   *n*   = *Constr n*
toSpine (*Tree a*) *Empty*   = *Constr Empty*
toSpine (*Tree a*) (*Node l x r*) = *Constr Node*
                    $\diamond$ (*l* : *Tree a*) $\diamond$ (*x* : *a*) $\diamond$ (*r* : *Tree a*) .

With all the machinery in place, we can now write the truly generic *sum*:

sum :: *Type a* $\rightarrow$ *a* $\rightarrow$ *Int*
sum Int n = n
sum t   *x* = *sum'* (*toSpine t x*)

sum' :: *Spine a* $\rightarrow$ *Int*
sum' (*Constr c*) = 0
sum' ($f \diamond (x : t)$) = *sum' f* + *sum t x* .

This function requires only a single type-specific case, namely the one for *Int*. The reason is that we want to do something specific for integers, which does not follow the general pattern, whereas the formerly explicit behavior for the types *Char*, [], (,), and *Tree* is now completely subsumed by the function *sum'*. Note also that in the last line of *sum'*, the type information *t* for *x* is indispensable, as we call the generic function *sum* recursively.

   Why are we in a better situation than before? If we encounter a new data type such as *Maybe*, we still have to extend the representation type with a constructor *Maybe* :: *Type a* $\rightarrow$ *Type* (*Maybe a*) and provide a case for the constructor *Maybe* in the *toSpine* function. However, this has to be done only once per data type, and it is so simple that it could easily be done automatically. The code for the generic functions (of which there can be many) is completely unaffected by the addition of a new data type.

4   Generic Queries and Traversals

In this section, we implement the two central SYB combinators *everything* and *everywhere* that are used to construct generic queries and traversals.

4.1   Generic Queries

A query is an overloaded function that returns a result of a specific type:

type $Query\ r = \forall a.\ Type\ a \rightarrow a \rightarrow r$.

We have already seen an example of a query, namely the *sum* function from Section 3. There are many more applications of queries: computation of the size of a structure, collection of names, collection of free variables, building a finite map, finding a specific element etc.

If we look back at the generic *sum* function, we see that it performs several tasks at once, leading to a relatively complex definition: integers are preserved, while in general, constructors are replaced by 0; the subresults are added; finally, a recursive traversal is performed over the entire data structure.

In the following, we describe how to separate these different activities into different functions, and at the same time abstract from the specific problem of summing up values.

If we already have a query, we can define a derived query that applies the original query to all immediate children of a given constructor:

$$mapQ :: Query\ r \rightarrow Query\ [r]$$
$$mapQ\ q\ t = mapQ'\ q \circ toSpine\ t$$
$$mapQ' :: Query\ r \rightarrow (\forall a.Spine\ a \rightarrow [r])$$
$$mapQ'\ q\ (Constr\ c)\ = [\,]$$
$$mapQ'\ q\ (f \diamond (x : t)) = mapQ'\ q\ f \mathbin{+\!\!+} [q\ t\ x]\ .$$

The results of the original query q are collected in a list. The combinator $mapQ$ does not traverse the input data structure. The traversal is the job of *everything'*, which is defined in terms of $mapQ$:

$$everything' :: Query\ r \rightarrow Query\ [r]$$
$$everything'\ q\ t\ x = [q\ t\ x] \mathbin{+\!\!+} concat\ (mapQ\ (everything'\ q)\ t\ x)\ .$$

Here, we apply the given query q to the entire argument x, and then recurse for the immediate children. The SYB version of *everything* fuses *everything'* with an application of *foldl1*, using a binary operator to combine all the elements of the nonempty list returned by *everything'*:

$$everything :: (r \rightarrow r \rightarrow r) \rightarrow Query\ r \rightarrow Query\ r$$
$$everything\ op\ q\ t\ x = foldl1\ op\ ([q\ t\ x] \mathbin{+\!\!+} mapQ\ (everything\ op\ q)\ t\ x)\ .$$

In order to express the query *sum* in terms of *everything*, we need a simple query *sumQ* expressing that we want to count integers:

$sumQ :: Query\ Int$
$sumQ\ Int\ n = n$
$sumQ\ t\quad x = 0$

$sum :: Query\ Int$
$sum = everything\ (+)\ sumQ$.

4.2   Generic Traversals

While a query computes an answer of a fixed type from an input, a traversal is an overloaded function that preserves the type of its input:

type $Traversal = \forall a.\, Type\ a \to a \to a$.

The counterpart of $mapQ$ is $mapT$. It applies a given traversal to the immediate children of a constructor, then rebuilds a value of the same constructor from the results:

$mapT :: Traversal \to Traversal$
$mapT\ h\ t = fromSpine \circ mapT'\ h \circ toSpine\ t$

$mapT' :: Traversal \to (\forall a.\, Spine\ a \to Spine\ a)$
$mapT'\ h\ (Constr\ c)\ = Constr\ c$
$mapT'\ h\ (f \Diamond (x : t)) = mapT'\ h\ f \Diamond (h\ t\ x : t)$.

The function $mapT$ not only consumes a value of the type argument, but also produces one. Therefore we call not only $toSpine$ on the input value, but also $fromSpine$ before returning the result. The calls to $fromSpine$ and $toSpine$ are determined by the type of the generic function that is defined. The general principle is described elsewhere [3, Chapter 11].

Using $mapT$, we can build bottom-up or top-down variants of $everywhere$, which apply the given traversal recursively:

$everywhere_{BU} :: Traversal \to Traversal$
$everywhere_{BU}\ f\ t = f\ t \circ mapT\ (everywhere_{BU}\ f)\ t$

$everywhere_{TD} :: Traversal \to Traversal$
$everywhere_{TD}\ f\ t = mapT\ (everywhere_{TD}\ f)\ t \circ f\ t$.

There are many applications of traversals, such as renaming variables in an abstract syntax tree, annotating a structure with additional information, optimizing or simplifying a structure etc. Here is a simplified example of a transformation performed by the Haskell refactorer HaRe [17], which rewrites a Haskell **if** construct into an equivalent **case** expression according to the rule

if e **then** e_1 **else** e_2 $\rightsquigarrow$ **case** e **of** $True \to e_1;\ False \to e_2$.

We assume a suitable abstract syntax for Haskell. The rewrite rule is captured by the traversal

$ifToCaseT :: Traversal$
$ifToCaseT \; HsExp \; (HsIf \; e \; e_1 \; e_2) =$
    $HsCase \; e \; [HsAlt \; (HsPLit \; (HsBool \; True)) \; e_1,$
                $HsAlt \; (HsPLit \; (HsBool \; False)) \; e_2]$
$ifToCaseT \; \_ \qquad e \qquad\qquad = e \; .$

The traversal can be applied to a complete Haskell program using

$ifToCase = everywhere_{\mathrm{BU}} \; ifToCaseT \; .$

5   Generically Showing Values

We have seen that we can traverse data types in several ways, performing potentially complex calculations in the process. However, we cannot reimplement Haskell's *show* function, even though it looks like a *Query String*. The reason is that there is no way to access the name of a constructor. We have a case for constructors, *Constr*, in our *Spine* data type, but there is really not much we can do at this point. So far, we have either invented a constant value ($[\,]$ in the case of *mapQ*), or applied the constructor itself again (in the case of *mapT*).

But it is easy to provide additional information for each constructor. When we define *toSpine* for a specific data type, whether manually or automatically, we have information about the constructors of the data type available, so why not use it? Let us therefore modify *Spine* once more:

data $Spine :: * \rightarrow *$ **where**
    $As :: a \rightarrow ConDescr \rightarrow Spine \; a$
    $(\Diamond) :: Spine \; (a \rightarrow b) \rightarrow Typed \; a \rightarrow Spine \; b \; .$

We have renamed *Constr* to *As*, as we intend to use it as a binary operator which takes a constructor function and information about the constructor. In this paper, we use only the name to describe a constructor,

type $ConDescr = String \; ,$

but we could include additional information such as its arity, the name of the type, the "house number" of the constructor and so on. Adapting *Spine* means that the generation of *toSpine* has to be modified as well. We show as an example how to do this for the type *Tree*:

$toSpine \; (Tree \; a) \; Empty \qquad = Empty \; \text{`}As\text{`} \; \texttt{"Empty"}$
$toSpine \; (Tree \; a) \; (Node \; l \; x \; r) = Node \; \text{`}As\text{`} \; \texttt{"Node"}$
$\qquad\qquad\qquad\qquad\qquad \Diamond \; (l : Tree \; a) \Diamond (x : a) \Diamond (r : Tree \; a) \; .$

With the new version of *Spine*, the function *show* is straightforward to write:

$show :: Type \; a \rightarrow a \rightarrow String$
$show \; t \; x = show' \; (toSpine \; t \; x)$

$$show' :: Spine\ a \to String$$
$$show'\ (\_\ \text{`As`}\ c)\quad = c$$
$$show'\ (f \diamond (a : t)) = \text{"("} +\!\!+ show'\ f +\!\!+ \text{" "} +\!\!+ show\ t\ a +\!\!+ \text{")"}\ .$$

The result of the call

$$show\ (Tree\ Int)\ (Node\ (Node\ Empty\ 1\ Empty)\ 2\ (Node\ Empty\ 3\ Empty))$$

is "$(((Node\ (((Node\ Empty)\ 1)\ Empty))\ 2)\ (((Node\ Empty)\ 3)\ Empty))$".

Even though we have information about constructors, we cannot define a generic *read* without further extensions. In the next section, we will discuss this and other questions regarding the expressivity of the SYB approach.

6   SYB in Context

In the previous sections, we have introduced the SYB approach on the basis of the *Spine* data type. Generic functions are overloaded functions that make use of the *Spine* view by calling *toSpine* on their type argument.

We have seen that we can define useful and widely applicable combinators such as *everything* and *everywhere* using some basic generic functions. As long as we stay within the expressivity of these combinators, it is possible to perform generic programming avoiding explicit case analysis on types.

In this section, we want to answer how expressive the *Spine* view is in comparison to both the original presentation of SYB, which uses only a given set of combinators, and in relation to other views, as they are employed by other approaches to generic programming such as PolyP and Generic Haskell.

6.1   The Original Presentation

As described in the section of implementing SYB in the original paper, it turns out that *mapT* and *mapQ* are both instances of a function that is called *gfoldl*. We can define *gfoldl*, too. To do this, let us define the ordinary fold (or catamorphism, if you like) of the *Spine* type:

$$foldSpine :: (\forall a.a \to r\ a) \to (\forall a\ b.r\ (a \to b) \to Typed\ a \to r\ b) \to$$
$$\qquad\qquad Spine\ a \to r\ a$$
$$foldSpine\ constr\ (\blacklozenge)\ (c\ \text{`As`}\ \_)\quad = constr\ c$$
$$foldSpine\ constr\ (\blacklozenge)\ (f \diamond (x : t)) = (foldSpine\ constr\ (\blacklozenge)\ f) \blacklozenge (x : t)\ .$$

The definition follows the catamorphic principle of replacing data constructors with functions. The SYB *gfoldl* is just *foldSpine* composed with *toSpine*:

$$gfoldl :: Type\ a \to (\forall a.a \to r\ a) \to (\forall a\ b.r\ (a \to b) \to Typed\ a \to r\ b) \to$$
$$\qquad\qquad a \to r\ a$$
$$gfoldl\ t\ constr\ app = foldSpine\ constr\ app \circ toSpine\ t\ .$$

It is therefore clear that our approach via the *Spine* type and the original SYB approach via *gfoldl* are in principle equally expressive, because the *Spine* type can be recovered from *gfoldl*.

However, we believe that the presence of the explicit data type *Spine* makes the definitions of some generic functions easier, especially if they do not directly fall in the range of any of the simpler combinators.

The original SYB paper describes only generic functions that either consume a value based on its type (queries, consumers), or that consume a value based on its type and build up a similar value at the same time (traversals). There are also generic functions that construct values based on a type (producers). Such functions include the already mentioned generic *read*, used to parse a string into a value of a data type, or *some*, a function that produces some non-bottom value of a given data type. We cannot define such functions without further help: The definition of *some* would presumably follow the general pattern of overloaded functions on spines, the shape of the final case dictated by the type of *some* (cf. Section 4.2):

$$some :: Type\ a \rightarrow a$$
$$some\ \ldots = \ldots$$
$$some\ t\ \ = fromSpine\ some'$$

But we cannot define $some' :: Spine\ a$, because that would yield *fromSpine some'* $:: \forall a.a$, which has to be $\perp$ according to the parametricity theorem [18]. Due to the well-definedness of *fromSpine*, *some'* would have to be $\perp$, too.

It is nevertheless possible to define *some* :: *Type a* $\rightarrow$ *a*, but only if *Type* is augmented with more information about the type it represents and its constructors. Due to space limitations, the implementation is deferred to the technical report [8], where we give an equivalent of *gunfold* from the second SYB paper [19].

We *can*, however, define functions on multiple type arguments without further additions. The definition of generic equality is very straightforward using the spine view:

$$eq :: Type\ a \rightarrow Type\ b \rightarrow a \rightarrow b \rightarrow Bool$$
$$eq\ t_1\ t_2\ x\ y = eq'\ (toSpine\ t_1\ x)\ (toSpine\ t_2\ y)$$
$$eq' :: Spine\ a \rightarrow Spine\ b \rightarrow Bool$$
$$eq'\ (\_\ `As`\ c_1)\ \ \ \ (\_\ `As`\ c_2)\ \ \ \ \ = c_1 == c_2$$
$$eq'\ (f_1 \Diamond (a_1 : t_1))\ (f_2 \Diamond (a_2 : t_2)) = eq'\ f_1\ f_2 \wedge eq\ t_1\ t_2\ a_1\ a_2$$
$$eq'\ \_\ - \ = False\ .$$

The generalized type of *eq* avoids the necessity of a type-level equality test. In the second SYB paper, *eq* is defined in terms of a combinator called *zipWithQ*. Although we can mirror the definition of *zipWithQ*, we believe that the direct definition is much clearer.

6.2   Other Views and Their Strengths and Weaknesses

Let us now look at two other approaches to generic programming, PolyP and Generic Haskell. They are also based on overloaded functions, but they do not represent values using *Spine*. A different choice of view affects the class of generic functions that can be written, how easily they can be expressed, and the data types that can be represented.

PolyP. In PolyP [2], data types of kind $* \to *$ are viewed as fixed points of regular pattern functors. The regular functors in turn are of kind $* \to * \to *$ and represented as lifted sums of products. The view makes use of the following type definitions:

$$
\begin{aligned}
\textbf{data } Fix\ f & = In\ (f\ (Fix\ f)) \\
\textbf{type } LSum\ f\ g\ a\ r & = Either\ (f\ a\ r)\ (g\ a\ r) \\
\textbf{type } LProd\ f\ g\ a\ r & = (f\ a\ r, g\ a\ r) \\
\textbf{type } LUnit\ a\ r & = () \\
\textbf{type } Par\ a\ r & = a \\
\textbf{type } Rec\ a\ r & = r \ .
\end{aligned}
$$

Here, Fix is a fixed-point computation on the type level. The type constructors $LSum$, $LProd$, and $LUnit$ are lifted variants of the binary sum type $Either$, the binary product type $(,)$, and the unit type $()$. Finally we have Par to select the parameter, and Rec to select the recursive call.

As an example, our type $Tree$ has pattern functor $TreeF$:

$$\textbf{data } TreeF\ a\ r = EmptyF\ |\ NodeF\ r\ a\ r\ .$$

We have (modulo $\bot$) that $Tree\ a \cong Fix\ (TreeF\ a)$. Furthermore, we can view $TreeF$ as a binary sum (it has two constructors), where the right component is a nested binary product ($NodeF$ has three fields). The recursive argument r is represented by Rec, the parameter to $Tree$ by Par:

$$\textbf{type } TreeFS\ a\ r = LSum\ LUnit\ (LProd\ Rec\ (LProd\ Par\ Rec))\ a\ r\ .$$

Again, we have (modulo $\bot$) an isomorphism $TreeF\ a\ r \cong TreeFS\ a\ r$.

The view of PolyP has two obvious disadvantages: first, due to its two-level nature, it is relatively complicated; second, it is quite limited in its applicability. Only data types of kind $* \to *$ that are regular can be represented.

On the other hand, many generic functions on data types of kind $* \to *$ are definable. PolyP can express functions to parse, compare, unify, or print values generically. Its particular strength is that recursion patterns such as cata- or anamorphisms can be expressed generically, because each data type is viewed as a fixed point, and the points of recursion are visible.

Generic Haskell. In contrast to PolyP, Generic Haskell [3, 4] uses a view that is much more widely applicable and is slightly easier to handle: all data types are (unlifted) sums of products. The data type $Tree$ is viewed as the isomorphic

$$\textbf{type } TreeS\ a = Either\ ()\ (Tree\ a, (a,\ Tree\ a))\ .$$

The original type $Tree$ appears in $TreeS$, there is no special mechanism to treat recursion differently. This has a clear advantage, namely that the view is applicable to nested and mutually recursive data types of arbitrary kinds. In fact, in Generic Haskell all Haskell 98 data types can be represented. The price is that recursion patterns such as cata- or anamorphisms cannot be defined directly.

On the other hand, generic functions in Generic Haskell can be defined such that they work on types of all kinds. It is therefore significantly more powerful than PolyP. In Generic Haskell we can, for instance, define a generic *map* that works for generalized rose trees, a data type of kind $(* \to *) \to * \to *$:

data *Rose f a = Fork a (f (Rose f a))* .

Scrap your boilerplate. The *Spine* view is not so much based on the structure of types, but on the structure of values. It emphasizes the structure of a constructor application. We have already noticed that this limits the generic functions that can be written. Pure producers such as *read* or *some* require additional information. Furthermore, all generic functions work on types of kind $*$. It is not possible to define a generic version of *map* for type constructors, or to define a recursion pattern such as a catamorphism generically.

But the *Spine* view also has two noticeable advantages over the other views discussed. Firstly, the view is simple, and the relation between a value and its spine representation is very direct. As a consequence, the transformation functions *fromSpine* and *toSpine* are quite efficient, and it is easy to deforest the *Spine* data structure.

Secondly, as every (non-abstract) Haskell value is a constructor application, the view is very widely applicable. Not only all Haskell 98 data types of all kinds can be represented, the *Spine* view is general enough to represent data types containing existentials and even GADTs without any further modifications. This is particularly remarkable, because at the moment, GHC does not support automatic derivation of classes for GADTs. The methods of the classes *Eq*, *Ord*, and *Show* can easily be defined using the SYB approach. Thus, there is no theoretical problem to allow derivation of these classes also for GADTs. We discuss this newly found expressive power further in the next section.

7   Scrap Your Boilerplate for "Scrap Your Boilerplate"

There are almost no limits to the data types we can represent using *Spine*. One very interesting example is the GADT of types itself, namely *Type*. This allows us to instantiate generic functions on type *Type*. Consequently, we can show types by invoking the generic *show* function, or compute type equality using the generic equality *eq*! Both are useful in the context of dynamically typed values:

data *Dynamic* **where**
  Dyn :: t → Type t → Dynamic .

The difference between the types *Dynamic* and *Typed* is that *Dynamic* contains an existential quantification.

Before we can actually use generic functions on *Dynamic*, we require that *Type* has a constructor for types and dynamic values:

data *Type :: * → *$ **where**
  . . .

$$Type \quad :: Type\ a \to Type\ (Type\ a)$$
$$Dynamic :: Type\ Dynamic\ .$$

The function *toSpine* also requires cases for *Type* and *Dynamic*, but converting types or dynamics into the *Spine* view is entirely straightforward, as the following example cases demonstrate:

$$toSpine\ (Type\ a')\ (Type\ a) \ = Type\ 'As'\ \texttt{"Type"}\ \Diamond\ (a : Type\ a)$$
$$toSpine\ Dynamic\ (Dyn\ x\ t) = Dyn\ 'As'\ \texttt{"Dyn"}\ \Diamond\ (x : t)\ \Diamond\ (t : Type\ t)\ .$$

In the first line above, a' is always equal to a, but the Haskell type system does not know that, so we do not enforce it in the program. The output of *show Dynamic (Dyn (Node Empty 2 Empty) (Tree Int))* is now the string "((*Dyn* (((*Node Empty*) 2) *Empty*)) (*Tree Int*))", and comparing the dynamic value to itself using *eq Dynamic Dynamic* yields indeed *True*, incorporating a run-time type equality test.

8   Conclusions

The SYB approach has been developed by Peyton Jones and Lämmel in a series of papers [1, 19, 20]. Originally, it was an implementation of *strategic programming* [14] in Haskell, intended for traversing and querying complex, compound data such as abstract syntax trees.

The ideas underlying the generic programming extension PolyP [2] go back to the categorical notions of functors and catamorphisms, which are independent of the data type in question [21]. Generic Haskell [22] was motivated by the desire to overcome the restrictions of PolyP.

Due to the different backgrounds, it is not surprising that SYB and generic programming have remained difficult to compare for a long time. The recent work on *generic views* [12, 23] has been an attempt to unify different approaches. We believe that we bridged the gap in this paper for the first time, by presenting the *Spine* data type which encodes the SYB approach faithfully.

Our implementation handles the two central ingredients of generic programming differently from the original SYB paper: we use overloaded functions with explicit type arguments instead of overloaded functions based on a type-safe cast [1] or a class-based extensible scheme [20]; and we use the explicit spine view rather than a combinator-based approach. Both changes are independent of each other, and have been made with clarity in mind: we think that the structure of the SYB approach is more visible in our setting, and that the relations to PolyP and Generic Haskell become clearer. We have revealed that while the spine view is limited in the class of generic functions that can be written, it is applicable to a very large class of data types, including GADTs.

Our approach cannot be used easily as a library, because the encoding of overloaded functions using explicit type arguments requires the extensibility of the *Type* data type and of functions such as *toSpine*. One can, however, incorporate *Spine* into the SYB library while still using the techniques of the SYB papers to encode overloaded functions (see the technical report [8] for more details).

In this paper, we do not use classes at all, and we therefore expect that it is easier to prove algebraic properties about SYB (such as $mapT\ copy = copy$ where $copy\ \_ = id$ is the identity traversal) in this setting. For example, we believe that the work of Reig [24] could be recast using our approach, leading to shorter and more concise proofs.

Acknowledgements. We thank Jeremy Gibbons, Ralf Lämmel, Pablo Nogueira, Simon Peyton Jones, Fermin Reig, and the four anonymous referees for several helpful remarks.

References

1. Lämmel, R., Peyton Jones, S.: Scrap your boilerplate: a practical design pattern for generic programming. In: Types in Language Design and Implementation. (2003)
2. Jansson, P., Jeuring, J.: PolyP – a polytypic programming language extension. In: Conference Record 24th ACM SIGPLAN-SIGACT Symposium on Principles of Programming Languages, Paris, France, ACM Press (1997) 470–482
3. Löh, A.: Exploring Generic Haskell. PhD thesis, Utrecht University (2004)
4. Löh, A., Jeuring, J., Clarke, D., Hinze, R., Rodriguez, A., de Wit, J.: The Generic Haskell user's guide, version 1.42 (Coral). Technical Report UU-CS-2005-004, Institute of Information and Computing Sciences, Utrecht University (2005)
5. Xi, H., Chen, C., Chen, G.: Guarded recursive datatype constructors. In: Proceedings of the ACM SIGPLAN-SIGACT symposium on Principles of Programming Languages (POPL 2003), ACM Press (2003) 224–235
6. Peyton Jones, S., Washburn, G., Weirich, S.: Wobbly types: Type inference for generalised algebraic data types. Technical Report MS-CIS-05-26, University of Pennsylvania (2004)
7. Peyton Jones, S., ed.: Haskell 98 Language and Libraries: The Revised Report. Cambridge University Press (2003)
8. Hinze, R., Löh, A., Oliveira, B.: "Scrap Your Boilerplate" reloaded. Technical report, Universität Bonn (2006) Available from `http://www.informatik.uni-bonn.de/~loeh/SYB0.html`.
9. GHC Team: The Glasgow Haskell Compiler User's Guide. (2005) Available from `http://haskell.org/ghc/docs/latest/users_guide.ps.gz`.
10. Wadler, P.: Views: a way for pattern matching to cohabit with data abstraction. In: Principles of Programming Languages, ACM Press (1987) 307–313
11. Burton, F.W., Meijer, E., Sansom, P., Thompson, S., Wadler, P.: Views: an extension to Haskell pattern matching. Available from `http://www.haskell.org/development/views.html` (1996)
12. Holdermans, S., Jeuring, J., Löh, A.: Generic views on data types. Technical Report UU-CS-2005-012, Utrecht University (2005)
13. Benke, M., Dybjer, P., Jansson, P.: Universes for generic programs and proofs in dependent type theory. Nordic Journal of Computing **10** (2003) 265–289
14. Visser, E.: Language independent traversals for program transformation. In Jeuring, J., ed.: Workshop on Generic Programming (WGP'00), Ponte de Lima, Portugal, Technical Report UU-CS-2000-19, Department of Information and Computing Sciences, Universiteit Utrecht (2000)
15. Hinze, R.: Fun with phantom types. In Gibbons, J., de Moor, O., eds.: The Fun of Programming. Palgrave (2003) 245–262

16. Oliveira, B., Gibbons, J.: Typecase: A design pattern for type-indexed functions. In: Haskell Workshop. (2005) 98–109
17. Li, H., Reinke, C., Thompson, S.: Tool support for refactoring functional programs. In Jeuring, J., ed.: Haskell Workshop, Association for Computing Machinery (2003) 27–38
18. Wadler, P.: Theorems for free! In: Functional Programming and Computer Architecture. (1989)
19. Lämmel, R., Peyton Jones, S.: Scrap more boilerplate: reflection, zips, and generalised casts. In: Proceedings of the ACM SIGPLAN International Conference on Functional Programming (ICFP 2004), ACM Press (2004) 244–255
20. Lämmel, R., Peyton Jones, S.: Scrap your boilerplate with class: extensible generic functions. In: Proceedings of the ACM SIGPLAN International Conference on Functional Programming (ICFP 2005), ACM Press (2005) 204–215
21. Backhouse, R., Jansson, P., Jeuring, J., Meertens, L.: Generic programming: An introduction. In Swierstra, S.D., Henriques, P.R., Oliveira, J.N., eds.: Advanced Functional Programming. Volume 1608 of Lecture Notes in Computer Science., Springer-Verlag (1999) 28–115
22. Hinze, R.: Polytypic values possess polykinded types. In Backhouse, R., Oliveira, J.N., eds.: Proceedings of the Fifth International Conference on Mathematics of Program Construction, July 3–5, 2000. Volume 1837 of Lecture Notes in Computer Science., Springer-Verlag (2000) 2–27
23. Holdermans, S.: Generic views. Master's thesis, Utrecht University (2005)
24. Reig, F.: Generic proofs for combinator-based generic programs. In Loidl, H.W., ed.: Trends in Functional Programming. Volume 5. Intellect (2006)

Ruler: Programming Type Rules

Atze Dijkstra and S. Doaitse Swierstra

Department of Information and Computing Sciences,
Universiteit Utrecht,
P.O.Box 80.089,
Padualaan 14, Utrecht, Netherlands
{atze, doaitse}@cs.uu.nl
http://www.cs.uu.nl

Abstract. Some type systems are first described formally, to be sometimes followed by an implementation. Other type systems are first implemented as language extensions, to be sometimes retrofitted with a formal description. In neither case it is an easy task to keep both artefacts consistent. In this paper we introduce *Ruler*, a domain specific language for describing type rules. Type rules can be incrementally described, thus providing a means for building complex type systems on top of simpler ones. Besides checking well-formedness of *Ruler* programs we use them to generate (1) a visual LaTeX rendering, suitable for use in the presentation of formal aspects, and (2) an attribute grammar based implementation. Combining these two aspects in *Ruler* contributes to bridging the gap between theory and practice: mutually consistent representations can be generated for use in both theoretical and practical settings.

1 Introduction

Theory and practice of type systems often seem to be miles apart. For example, for the programming language Haskell there exists a language definition [20], a formal description of most of the static semantics [11], a Haskell description of type inferencing [17], several implementations [19, 2], and, on top of this, experimental language features like the class system [16, 21, 10]. However, the relationship between these artefacts is unclear with respect to their mutual consistency and the mutual effect of a change or extension.

1.1 The Problem

For example, if we were to extend Haskell with a new feature, we may start by exploring the feature in isolation from its context by creating a minimal type system for the feature, or an algorithmic variant of such a type system, or a proof of the usual properties (soundness, completeness), or perhaps a prototype. Upto this point the extension process is fairly standard; however, when we start to integrate the feature into a working implementation this process and the preservation of proven properties becomes less clear. Whatever route we take, that is, either retrofitting an implementation with a description or the other way around, there is little help in guaranteeing that the formal

M. Hagiya and P. Wadler (Eds.): FLOPS 2006, LNCS 3945, pp. 30–46, 2006.

description and the implementation are mutually consistent. Even worse, we cannot be sure that an extension preserves the possibility to prove desirable properties.

Based on these observations we can identify the following problems:

Problem 1. It is difficult, if not impossible, to keep separate (formal) descriptions and implementations of a complex modern programming language consistent.

Our approach to this problem is to maintain a single description of the static semantics of a programming language. from which we generate both the material which can be used as a starting point for a formal treatment as well as the implementation.

Problem 2. The extension of a language with a new feature means that the interaction between new and old features needs to be examined with respect to the preservation of desirable properties, where a property may be formal (e.g. soundness) or practical (e.g. sound implementation).

The *Ruler* language that we introduce in this paper makes it easy to describe language features in relative isolation. The separate descriptions for these features, however, can be combined into a description of the complete language. Note that traditional programming language solutions, like the use of modules and abstract data types to factor code, are not sufficient: a language extension often requires changes in the data types representing the abstract syntax and the required implementation may require changes across multiple modules. Usually, an additional language feature requires textual changes to numerous parts of the language description and implementation.

The feature interactions seem to be inescapable, no matter how much we try to keep language definitions orthogonal. Unfortunately we cannot give simple descriptions of complicated languages, but at least we can try to describe the various aspects in relative isolation. We do this by providing tools that help in building incremental, modular and stratified language descriptions.

The need for the *Ruler* system arose in the context of the Essential Haskell (EH) project [6, 7]. The design goal of EH is to construct a compiler for an extended version of Haskell, and to (simultaneously) build an explanation of its implementation, while keeping both versions consistent by generating corresponding parts from a single source. This approach resembles the one taken by Pierce [22, 18] who explains both non-algorithmic and algorithmic variants of type systems. The EH project starts with the description and implementation of a very simple language, and extends it in a sequence of steps by adding features like higher ranked polymorphism, mechanisms for explicitly passing implicit parameters [9], and higher order kinds. Each step corresponds to a working compiler. In this context, *Ruler* allows the description of a type system to be partitioned as a sequence of steps. In this paper we demonstrate our approach on a very small example, stepping from the declarative view on a type system towards its implementation view. Of these steps, the final one corresponds to a working implementation.

1.2 Running Example

We explore the above problems and our solution by looking at the final products that are generated by the *Ruler* system, in figures 1 through 3. We emphasize at this point that a

$$\boxed{\Gamma \vdash^e e : \tau}$$

$$\frac{}{\Gamma \vdash^e int : Int} \; \text{E.INT}_E \qquad \frac{\substack{i \mapsto \sigma \in \Gamma \\ \tau = inst\,(\sigma)}}{\Gamma \vdash^e i : \tau} \; \text{E.VAR}_E \qquad \frac{\substack{\Gamma \vdash^e a : \tau_a \\ \Gamma \vdash^e f : \tau_a \to \tau}}{\Gamma \vdash^e f\,a : \tau} \; \text{E.APP}_E$$

$$\frac{(i \mapsto \tau_i), \Gamma \vdash^e b : \tau_b}{\Gamma \vdash^e \lambda i \to b : \tau_i \to \tau_b} \; \text{E.LAM}_E \qquad \frac{\substack{(i \mapsto \sigma_e), \Gamma \vdash^e b : \tau_b \\ \Gamma \vdash^e e : \tau_e \\ \sigma_e = \forall \bar{v}.\tau_e, \quad \bar{v} \notin ftv\,(\Gamma)}}{\Gamma \vdash^e \mathbf{let}\, i = e\, \mathbf{in}\, b : \tau_b} \; \text{E.LET}_E$$

Fig. 1. Expression type rules (E)

$$\boxed{C^k; \Gamma \vdash^e e : \tau \leadsto C}$$

$$\frac{}{C^k; \Gamma \vdash^e int : Int \leadsto C^k} \; \text{E.INT}_A \qquad \frac{\substack{i \mapsto \sigma \in \Gamma \\ \tau = inst\,(\sigma)}}{C^k; \Gamma \vdash^e i : \tau \leadsto C^k} \; \text{E.VAR}_A$$

$$\frac{\substack{C^k; \Gamma \vdash^e f : \tau_f \leadsto C_f \\ C_f; \Gamma \vdash^e a : \tau_a \leadsto C_a \\ v \; fresh \\ \tau_a \to v \cong C_a \tau_f \leadsto C}}{C^k; \Gamma \vdash^e f\,a : C\,C_a v \leadsto C\,C_a} \; \text{E.APP}_A \qquad \frac{\substack{v \; fresh \\ C^k; (i \mapsto v), \Gamma \vdash^e b : \tau_b \leadsto C_b}}{C^k; \Gamma \vdash^e \lambda i \to b : C_b v \to \tau_b \leadsto C_b} \; \text{E.LAM}_A$$

$$\frac{\substack{v \; fresh \\ C^k; (i \mapsto v), \Gamma \vdash^e e : \tau_e \leadsto C_e \\ \sigma_e = \forall\, (ftv\,(\tau_e) \backslash ftv\,(C_e \Gamma)).\tau_e \\ C_e; (i \mapsto \sigma_e), \Gamma \vdash^e b : \tau_b \leadsto C_b}}{C^k; \Gamma \vdash^e \mathbf{let}\, i = e\, \mathbf{in}\, b : \tau_b \leadsto C_b} \; \text{E.LET}_A$$

Fig. 2. Expression type rules (A)

full understanding of these figures is not required nor intended. The focus of this paper is on the construction of the figures, not on their meaning: *Ruler* only tackles the problem of *consistency* between such figures and the corresponding implementation. Our aim is to look at these figures from a metalevel and to see how type rules can be specified and how their content can be generated using our *Ruler* system. Nevertheless, we have chosen a small, well known, and realistic example: the Hindley-Milner (HM) type system. Fig. 1 gives the well-known equational rules, Fig. 2 the algorithmic variant and

---

data *Expr*
  | *App f* : *Expr*
       a : *Expr*
attr *Expr* [*g* : *Gam* | *c* : *C* | *ty* : *Ty*]
sem *Expr*
  | *App* (*f*.*uniq*, **loc**.*uniq1*)
                = *rulerMk1Uniq* @**lhs**.*uniq*
      loc.*tv_* = *Ty_Var* @*uniq1*
      (**loc**.*c_*, **loc**.*mtErrs*)
                = (@*a*.*ty* '*Ty_Arr*' @*tv_*) ≅ (@*a*.*c* ⊕ @*f*.*ty*)
      lhs.*c* = @*c_* ⊕ @*a*.*c*
        .*ty* = @*c_* ⊕ @*a*.*c* ⊕ @*tv_*

Fig. 3. Part of the generated implementation for rule E.APP

Fig. 3 part of the generated implementation. In this section these figures demonstrate the general idea of *Ruler* and the artefacts generated by *Ruler*; later sections discuss the involved technicalities.

Both type rules and their implementation can be used to explain a type system. This is what we have done within the context of the EH project. For example, rules similar to rule E.APP from Fig. 2 and the corresponding attribute grammar (AG) implementation from Fig. 3 are jointly explained, each strengthening the understanding of the other. However, when features are combined, this inevitably leads to the following problems:

– Type rules and AG source code both become quite complex and increasingly difficult to understand.
– A proper understanding may require explanation of a feature both in isolation as well as in its context. These are contradictory requirements.
– With increasing complexity comes increasing likeliness of inconsistencies between type rules and AG source code.

Part of our solution to these problems is the use of the concept of *views* on both the type rules and AG source code. Views are ordered in the sense that later views are built on top of earlier views. Each view is defined in terms of its differences and extensions to its ancestor view; the resulting view on the artefact is the accumulation of all these incremental definitions.

This, of course, is not a new idea: version managment systems use similar mechanisms, and object-oriented systems use the notion of inheritance. However, the difference lies in our focus on a whole sequence of versions as well as the changes between versions: in the context of version management only the latest version is of interest, whereas for a class hierarchy we aim for encapsulation of changes. We need simultaneous access to all versions, which we call views, in order to build both the explanation and the sequence of compilers. A version management systems uses versions as a mechanism for evolution, whereas we use views as a mechanism for explaining and maintaining EH's sequence of compilers. We may e.g. change the very first view, and have these changes automatically included in all subsequent views.

For example, Fig. 1 displays view E (equational), and Fig. 2 displays view A (algorithmic) on the set of type rules, where each rule consists of judgements (premises and a single conclusion). View A is built on top of view E by specifying the differences with respect to view E. In the electronic version of this paper, the incremental definition of these views is exploited by using a color scheme to visualise the differences. The part which has been changed with respect to a previous view is displayed in blue, the unchanged part is displayed in grey (however, in the printed version all is black). In this way we address "Problem 2".

Independently from the view concept we exploit the similarity between type rules and AG based implementations. To our knowledge this similarity has never been crystallized into a working system. We use this similarity by specifying type rules using a single notation, which contains enough information to generate both the sets of type rules (in Fig. 1 and Fig. 2) as well as part of the AG implementation (in Fig. 3). Fig. 3 shows the generated implementation for rule E.APP. In this way we address "Problem 1".

The main goal of our *Ruler* system is to have one integrated definition of type rules, views on those rules, and the specification of information directing the generation of a partial implementation. As an additional benefit, *Ruler* allows one to describe the "type of the judgements" and checks whether the rules are "well-typed".

In the course of the EH project the Ruler system has become indispensable for us:

- *Ruler* is a useful tool for describing type rules and keeping type rules consistent with their implementation. In subsequent sections we will see how this is accomplished.
- It is relatively easy to extend the system to generate output to be used as input for other targets (besides LaTeX and AG). This makes *Ruler* suitable for other goals while at the same time maintaining a single source for type rules.
- We also feel that it may be a starting point for a discussion about how to deal with the complexities of modern programming languages: both their formal and practical aspects. In this light, this paper also is an invitation to the readers to improve on these aspects. In our conclusion (Section 7) we will discuss some developments we foresee and directions of further research.

We summarize *Ruler*'s strong points, such that we can refer to these points from the technical part of this paper:

Single source. Type rules are described by a single notation; all required type rule related artefacts are generated from this.

Consistency. Consistency between the various type rule related artefacts is automatically guaranteed as a consequence of being generated from a single source.

Incrementality. It is (relatively) easy to incrementally describe type rules.

Well-formedness checks. Judgements are checked against the 'type' of a judgement.

The remainder of this paper is organised as follows: in Section 2 we present an overview of the *Ruler* system. This overview gives the reader an intuition of what *Ruler* can do and how it interacts with other tools. Preliminaries for the example language and type systems are given in Section 3. In Section 4 we specify the contents of Fig. 1. In

Section 5 we continue with the extension towards an algorithmic version from which attribute grammar (AG) code can be generated. Finally, we discuss related work in Section 6, and experiences and future work in Section 7.

2 *Ruler* Overview

The design of *Ruler* is driven by the need to check the following *properties* of type rules:

- All judgements match an explicitly specified structure for the judgement. For example, in Fig. 1 all judgements for an expression should match the structure of the expression judgement in the box at the top of the same figure.
- If an identifier is used for the generation of an implementation, it must be defined before it can be used.

In the remainder of this section we give a high-level overview of the concepts manipulated by *Ruler*. Fig. 4 gives a schematic *Ruler* specification, showing how the concepts relate syntactically.

A *Ruler* specification consists of rules organized into rulesets. Each rule consists of judgements which must comply with a scheme which describes the structure of a judgement. We make this more precise in the remainder of this section.

The structure of a judgement is described by a (judgement) *scheme*. A scheme is the signature of a judgement. For each scheme we specify multiple *views*. A view on a scheme consists of named *holes* and judgeshapes, which come in the following varieties:

- One *judgespec*, used to specify the template for judgements.
- For each output target a *judgeuse*, used to specify how to map a judgement to an output format.

Holes are the parameters of a scheme and are given concrete values when instantiated as a judgement by means of a judgespec template.

Rules are grouped into *rulesets*. From a ruleset a figure like Fig. 1 is generated, so it specifies of a set of rules, the scheme for which the rules specify a conclusion, and additional information like the text for the caption of the figure.

A *rule* consists of a set of judgement instances (syntactically denoted by keyword **judge**) for the premises, and a judgement for the conclusion. Just as we specify views for schemes, we specify views for rules. For each view, each of the judgements of a rule should comply with the corresponding view of the scheme of the judgement. A judgement is defined by binding hole names to *Ruler* expressions.

Views are ordered by a *view hierarchy*. A view hierarchy specifies which view inherits from which other (ancestor) view. Both schemes and rules contain a collection of views. A view on a scheme inherits the holes and judgeshapes. A view on a rule inherits the hole bindings to *Ruler* expressions. Only new holes have to be given a binding to a *Ruler* expression; existing holes may be updated. This is how *Ruler* supports the incremental definition of views.

```
scheme X =
  view A =
    holes ...
    judgespec ...
    judgeuse ...
      ...
  view B =
    holes ...
    judgespec ...
    judgeuse ...
      ...
ruleset x scheme X =
  rule r =
    view A =
      judge ...    -- premises
        ...
        –
      judge ...    -- conclusion
    view B = ...
  rule s =
    view A = ...
    view B = ...
```

Fig. 4. High level structure of Ruler source

The incremental definition of views on a rule is supported by two different variants of specifying a judgement:

– A judgement in a (view on a) rule can be specified by using a judgespec as a macro where the values of the holes are defined by filling in the corresponding positions in the judgespec. This variant is useful for the first view in a view hierarchy, because all holes need to be bound to a *Ruler* expression.
– A judgement in a (view on a) rule can be specified by individually specifying *Ruler* expressions for each hole. This variant is useful for views which are built on top of other views, because only holes for which the value differs relative to the ancestor view need to be given a new value.

The *Ruler* system is open-ended in the sense that some judgements can be expressed in a less structured form, for which an implementation is defined externally. For example, the premises of rule E.VAR consist of conditions specified elsewhere. These arbitrary (i.e. as far as *Ruler* is concerned unstructured) conditions are treated like regular judgements, but their implementation has to be specified explicitly. We call the scheme of such a judgement variant a *relation*.

3   Our Example Language

In this section we explain notation in our example, that is, the set of type rules to be specified with *Ruler*. There should be no surprises here as we use a standard term language based on the λ-calculus (see Fig. 5). Our example language contains the following program:

> **let** $id = \lambda x \rightarrow x$
> **in** **let** $v_1 = id\ 3$
>   **in** **let** $v_2 = id\ id$
>   **in** $v_2\ v_1$

The type language for our example term language is given in Fig. 5. Types are either monomorphic types τ, called *monotypes*, or universally quantified types σ, called *polymorphic types* or *polytypes*. A monotype either is a type constant *Int*, a function type $\tau \rightarrow \tau$, or an unknown type represented by a type variable v. We discuss the use of these types when we introduce the type rules for our term language in the following sections.

The type rules use an environment Γ, holding bindings for program identifiers with their typings:

$$\Gamma ::= \overline{i \mapsto \sigma}$$

Value expressions:		Types:	
$e ::= int$	literals	$\tau ::= Int$	literals
$\mid i$	program variable	$\mid v$	variable
$\mid e\ e$	application	$\mid \tau \rightarrow \tau$	abstraction
$\mid \lambda i \rightarrow e$	abstraction	$\sigma ::= \forall \overline{v}.\tau$	universally quantified type, $\overline{v}$ possibly empty
$\mid$ **let** $i = e$ **in** e	local definitions		

Fig. 5. Terms and types

4   Describing Type Rules Using *Ruler* Notation

In this section we make the use of *Ruler* more precise. We describe *Ruler* notation, and explain how to specify the content of Fig. 1. The transition (instantiation) from polytypes to monotypes is performed by *inst*, whereas the transition (generalisation) from monotypes to polytypes is described in rule E.LET.

The use of an equational version of type rules usually serves to explain a type system and to prove properties about the type system. An algorithmic version is introduced subsequently to specify an implementation for such a type system. In this paper we follow the same pattern, but use it to show how *Ruler* can be used to describe the equational version in such a way that its type rule representation can be included in the documentation (read here: this paper). In the extended version of this paper [7] we also describe how to extend the equational version to an algorithmic one, and a version from which a partial implementation can be generated.

The basics: judgement schemes. A typing rule consists of judgements describing the conclusion and premises of the rule. A judgement has a structure of its own, described by a *scheme*. A scheme plays the same role in rules as a type does for an expression in our example term language. In our example, we want to specify a judgement for terms (expressions). We introduce such a judgement by a **scheme** declaration, which is immediately followed by the views on this scheme[1]:

> **scheme** *expr* =
>   **view** *E* =
>   **holes** [| *e* : *Expr*, *gam* : *Gam*, *ty* : *Ty* |]
>   **judgespec** *gam* ⊢ *e* : *ty*
>   **judgeuse tex** *gam* ⊢ .."e" *e* : *ty*
>
> **ruleset** *expr.base* **scheme** *expr* "Expression type rules" =
>   **rule** *e.int* =
>   **view** *E* =   -- no premises
>   ―
>   **judge** *R* : *expr* = *gam* ⊢ *int* : *Ty_Int*

We first examine the **scheme** definition in detail, and then the **ruleset** definition for the type rules themselves. The operator ⊢ .."e" forms a single operator in which the dot notation expresses subscripting and superscripting when pretty printed; the part after the first dot is used as a subscript, the part after the second dot as a superscript. Here the turnstyle symbol is superscripted with *e*. We refer to the extended version of this paper [7] for further explanation about the dot notation.

Here we have only a single, equational, view *E*, which defines three holes: *e*, *gam*, and *ty*. This scheme is instantiated in the conclusion of rule E.INT by using the judgespec of the scheme. In later views, we will (re)define individual holes. Each hole has an associated hole type, for instance *e* has type *Expr*; we will not discuss this further.

Judgeshapes are introduced by the keyword **judgespec** or **judgeuse**. A **judgespec** introduces a distfix operator template (here: ... ⊢ ... : ...) used for specifying instances of this judgement in a **rule**. A **judgeuse** judgement shape introduces the expression to be used for the generation for a *target*. The target **tex** indicates that the shape is to be used to generate LaTeX; the **ag** target is meant for attribute grammar generation. We will refer to these three shapes as the **spec**, **tex** and **ag** judgement shapes. The **spec** shape is used as the input template, the **tex** and **ag** shapes are used as output templates.

The identifiers in *Ruler* expressions should refer to the introduced hole names or externally defined identifiers. The **spec** shape of the scheme of a judgement is used to extract *Ruler* expressions from a judgement instance (defined by **judge**) and bind these to the corresponding hole identifiers.

Since the judgespec and an associated **judgeuse tex** are usually quite similar, we have decided to make the latter default to the first. For this reason we allow the dot notatation to be used in the judgespec too, although it only will play a role in its defaulted uses.

---

[1] The text for *Ruler* program fragments already appears in pretty printed form throughout this paper, but in the original source code the **judgespec** appears as: "judgespec gam :- e : ty".

The basics: rulesets. Rules are grouped in rulesets to be displayed together in a figure: the description of Fig. 1 starts with the **ruleset**. A ruleset specifies the name *expr.base* of the ruleset, the scheme *expr* for the conclusion of its contained rules, and text to be displayed as part of the caption of the figure. The judgespec of (a view on) the scheme is used to provide the boxed scheme representation in Fig. 1. The ruleset name *expr.base* is used to uniquely identify this figure, so it can be included in text such as this paper. We do not discuss this further; we only note that part of the LaTeX formatting is delegated to external LaTeX commands.

Before discussing its components, we repeat the LaTeX rendering of rule E.INT together with its *Ruler* definition to emphasize the similarities between the rule specification and its visual appearance:

> **rule** *e.int* =
>   **view** *E* =   -- no premises
>   −
>   **judge** *R* : *expr* = *gam* ⊢ *int* : *Ty_Int*

$$\frac{}{\Gamma \vdash^e int : Int}\ \text{E.INT}_E$$

All views of a rule are jointly defined, although we present the various views separately throughout this paper. For an individual figure and a particular view, the *Ruler* system extracts the relevant view of the rules present in a ruleset. We will come back to this in our discussion.

Each view for a rule specifies premises and a conclusion, separated by a '-'. The rule E.INT for integer constants only has a single judgement for the conclusion. The judgement is named *R*, follows scheme *expr*, and is specified using the **spec** judgement shape for view *E*. The name of the judgement is used to refer to the judgement from later views, either to overwrite it completely or to redefine the values of the individual holes.

The rule for integer constants refers to *Ty_Int*. This is an identifier which is not introduced as part of the rule, and its occurrence generates an error message unless we specify it to be external (we do not discuss this nor its proper LaTeX formatting further).

The rule E.APP for the application of a function to an argument is defined similar to rule E.INT. Premises now relate the type of the function and its argument:

> **rule** *e.app* =
>   **view** *E* =
>   **judge** *A* : *expr* = *gam* ⊢ *a* : *ty.a*
>   **judge** *F* : *expr* = *gam* ⊢ *f* : (*ty.a* → *ty*)
>   −
>   **judge** *R* : *expr* = *gam* ⊢ (*f a*) : *ty*

$$\frac{\Gamma \vdash^e a : \tau_a \quad \Gamma \vdash^e f : \tau_a \to \tau}{\Gamma \vdash^e f\, a : \tau}\ \text{E.APP}_E$$

5   Extending the Initial Version

The above demonstrates the basic features of *Ruler*. We continue with highlighting *Ruler* features. We construct an algorithmic view *A*, which is built upon the equational view *E*. The final attribute grammar view *AG* adds further implementation details required for the attribute grammar translation. We assume familiarity with the terminology of attribute grammar systems.

Algorithmic version. The following extends the scheme definition:

> **view** $A =$
> > **holes** $[e : Expr, gam : Gam \mid$ **thread** $cnstr : C \mid ty : Ty]$
> > **judgespec** $cnstr.inh; gam \vdash ..\text{"e"} \ e : ty \rightsquigarrow cnstr.syn$

The algorithmic view introduces computation order. *Ruler* assumes that a derivation tree corresponds to an abstract syntax tree (AST): rule conclusions correspond to parent (tree) nodes, rule premises to children nodes. An attribute grammar for such an AST specifies attributes traveling down the tree, called *inherited attributes*, and attributes traveling upwards, called *synthesized attributes*. Inherited attributes correspond to the assumptions of the conclusion of a type rule, and are usually propagated from the conclusion towards the premises of a rule. Synthesized attributes correspond to results. The **holes** declaration specifies its holes as inherited, inherited + synthesized, and synthesized, indicated by their respective positions between vertical bars '|'.

For example, *gam* is inherited because it provides the assumptions under which a type rule is satisfied. In our example we treat *gam* as given, not as something to be computed. In terms of a computation, *gam* provides an argument which may be used to compute synthesized values such as the type *ty* of the type rule. In addition to these attributes, a new hole *cnstr* is declared as inherited + synthesized, and is threaded through the type rule as indicated by the optional keyword **thread**. The inherited *cnstr* (referred to by *cnstr.inh*) represents already known assumptions about types, in particular about type variables; the synthesized *cnstr* (referred to by *cnstr.syn*) represents the combination of newfound and known information about type variables. These holes generate the *attr* declarations in Fig. 3.

For rule E.INT we extend its definition with values for *cnstr.inh* and *cnstr.syn*:

> **view** $A =$
> > $-$
> >
> > **judge** $R : expr$
> > $\mid cnstr.syn = cnstr..k$
> > $\mid cnstr.inh = cnstr..k$

$$\frac{}{C^k; \Gamma \vdash^e int : Int \rightsquigarrow C^k} \ \text{E.INT}_A$$

The difference between holes and the values bound to holes lies in the computation order assigned to the holes and its use in the mapping onto an attribute grammar. Both *cnstr.inh* and *cnstr.syn* are bound to *cnstr..k*, which appears as C^k in rule E.INT. However, within the context of a type rule the values bound to inherited holes of the conclusion and synthesized holes of the premises correspond to input values, that is, values which may be used further to define the synthesized holes of the conclusion and the inherited holes of the premises. For example, *cnstr..k* is the value bound to the inherited hole *cnstr.inh* and the synthesized hole *cnstr.syn* of the conclusion. In terms of the type rule this means that both must be equal; in terms of the computation *cnstr.inh* is passed to *cnstr.syn* via *cnstr..k*. The identifier *cnstr..k* is an argument to the judgements of the type rule, whereas for the computation it is the name (or pattern when more complicated) to which the value of the attribute associated with *cnstr.inh* is bound. It is subsequently used for the computation of *cnstr.syn*. This leads to the following AG code for rule E.INT[2]:

sem *Expr*
  | *Int* **lhs**.*c* = @**lhs**.*c*
          .*ty* = *Ty_Int*

Ruler supports a renaming mechanism which is used to rename identifiers when generating output. Strictly, this is not necessary, but in practice it is convenient to have such a mechanism to glue *Ruler* generated code non-*Ruler* implementation fragments more easily. For instance, in the full *Ruler* specification for the example *cnstr* is renamed to *c*; this shows in the attribute declaration in Fig. 3. The keyword **lhs** refers to the parent node of a AST fragment, @**lhs**.*c* to its inherited *c* attribute; the parent corresponds to the conclusion of a rule. The translation also assumes an infrastructure of AG and Haskell definitions, for example for the constant *Ty_Int* representing the *Int* type. We will not discuss such details further, and assume the reader is familiar enough with attribute grammars and Haskell to guess the semantics of the provided translation. A more detailed treatment of these features can be found elsewhere [7, 6].

More complex *Ruler* expressions can be bound to holes, as shown by the following extension to view *A* for rule E.APP:

view *A* =
  judge *V* : *tvFresh* = *tv*
  judge *M* : *match* = (*ty.a* → *tv*) ≅ (*cnstr.a ty.f*)
                        ⤳ *cnstr*
  judge *F* : *expr*
    | *ty*   = *ty.f*
    | *cnstr.syn* = *cnstr.f*
  judge *A* : *expr*
    | *cnstr.inh* = *cnstr.f*
    | *cnstr.syn* = *cnstr.a*
    −
  judge *R* : *expr*
    | *ty*   = *cnstr cnstr.a tv*
    | *cnstr.syn* = *cnstr cnstr.a*

$$\frac{\begin{array}{c} C^k; \Gamma \vdash^e f : \tau_f \rightsquigarrow C_f \\ C_f; \Gamma \vdash^e a : \tau_a \rightsquigarrow C_a \\ v \text{ fresh} \\ \tau_a \rightarrow v \cong C_a \tau_f \rightsquigarrow C \end{array}}{C^k; \Gamma \vdash^e f \, a : C \, C_a v \rightsquigarrow C \, C_a} \text{ E.APP}_A$$

The hole *cnstr.syn* for the conclusion (judgement *R*) is defined in terms of *cnstr* and *cnstr.a*. In the type rule this shows as a juxtaposition, which one may read as the first constraint *cnstr* applied to the second *cnstr.a*. However, for the AG code additional rewriting (specified by means of rewrite rules) is required to a form which is more explicit in how the juxtaposition is to be computed. Again, we omit further discussion of this feature, and show the translation to AG code instead:

---

[2] The actual AG code is optimized w.r.t. the elimination of straightforward copies like **lhs**.*c* = @**lhs**.*c*: the AG system provides a copy rule mechanism which automatically inserts copy rules for attributes when explicit attribute rules are absent.

```
sem Expr
  | App (f.uniq, loc.uniq1)
                = rulerMk1Uniq @lhs.uniq
    f  .c  = @lhs.c
       .g  = @lhs.g
    a  .c  = @f.c
       .g  = @lhs.g
    loc.tv_ = Ty_Var @uniq1
    (loc.c_, loc.mtErrs)
                = (@a.ty 'Ty_Arr' @tv_) ≅ (@a.c ⊕ @f.ty)
    lhs.c  = @c_ ⊕ @a.c
       .ty = @c_ ⊕ @a.c ⊕ @tv_
```

This translation is not yet optimized in order to show the correspondence with the type rule. Fig. 3 shows the optimized version. The overloaded operator ⊕ applies a constraint by substituting type variables with types in the usual way. The dataconstructors, of which the name starts with *Ty* represent the various type encodings.

Of the remaining judgements *V* and *M* we discuss jugement *M* in the next paragraph. Both judgements use the same mechanism for specifying arbitrary judgements.

External schemes: relations. Rule E.APP also demonstrates the use of judgements which are not directly related to the structure of the AST. For example, the freshness of a type variable (judgement *V*) and type unification (judgement *M*) are expressed in terms of attribute values, not children nodes of a parent node in an AST. *Ruler* automatically derives an implementation for judgements related to children nodes, but for the remaining judgements the *Ruler* programmer has to provide an implementation.

For example, type unification (or matching), is declared as a *relation*, which is a judgement scheme for which we have to define the AG implementation ourselves. Such an implementation is defined using **judgeuse** for target **ag**:

```
relation match =
  view A =
    holes [ty.l : Ty, ty.r : Ty || cnstr : C]
    judgespec ty.l ≅ ty.r ⤳ cnstr
    judgeuse ag (cnstr, mtErrs) '='(ty.l) ≅ (ty.r)
```

The scheme of *match* specifies how the judgement is to be translated to attribute grammar code by means of a **judgeuse ag**. It is the responsibility of the programmer to provide the correct form (an attribute rule) and translation, so the attribute grammar translation of *match* is expressed in terms of the Haskell function ≅, returning both additional constraints as well as (possibly zero) errors. It is the responsibility of the surrounding infrastructure to do something useful with reported errors as these are not part of the result of the relation. As such, a relation in *Ruler* has the same role as a foreign function in Haskell.

The rest. The expanded version of this paper [7] describes view *A* and the following additional aspects:

- The third (AG) view, which extends the specification of view A on rule E.INT and rule E.APP with information binding the type rules to the abstract syntax.
- Additional datastructures (e.g. substitutions/constraints C) required for an algorithmic version of the type rules, further surrounding infrastructure (error handling, parsing, commandline invocation)
- The creation and handling of fresh (or unique) values, as required by judgement V of scheme *tvFresh*.
- The use of rewrite rules and identifier formatting.

6   Related Work

Literate programming. Literate programming [4] is a style of programming where the program source text and its documentation are combined into a single document. So called *tangling* and *weaving* tools extract the program source and documentation. Our *Ruler* system is different:

- Within a literate programming document program source and documentation are recognizable and identifiable artefacts. In *Ruler* there is no such distinction.
- *Ruler* does not generate documentation; instead it generates fragments for use in documentation.

TinkerType. TinkerType [18], used for Pierce's book [22], comes closest to *Ruler*. Type system features can be combined into type systems. The system provides checks for valid combinations, and allows the specification of code fragments. The structure of judgements is not checked.

Twelf. The theorem proving environment Twelf [23] is used to describe and prove properties for programming languages [13], thus answering the POPLmark challenge [5]. Although we intend to generate descriptions for use in such theorem proving tools, we emphasize that *Ruler* is meant as a lightweight tool for the construction of well-documented compilers.

AST based tools. Various abstract syntax tree (AST) based compiler construction tools exist [1, 3, 24, 12], among which our AG system. Such tools have in common that they only allow programming on the level of AST's, whereas *Ruler* allows a higher form of programming. Furthermore, in our experience, stepwise AG descriptions [8] became too complex (which inspired us to design *Ruler* in the first place), and we expect this to be the case for similar formalisms as well.

Finally, we also mention the Programmatica project, which provides mechanisms and tools for proving properties of Haskell programs.

7   Discussion and Future Work

Experiences with Ruler. *Ruler* solves the problem of maintaining consistency and managing type rules. Within the context of constructing a documented Haskell compiler (EH project, [6, 7]) this was an acute problem. It is a relief not to have to write LaTeX for type rules by hand, to know that the formatted rules correspond directly to their implementation, and to know several checks have been performed.

Lightweight solution. *Ruler* is a lightweight solution to the general problem of maintaining consistency, tailored towards the needs of the EH project. This is reflected in the following:

- *Ruler* uses a few operator symbols for its own purposes, leaving available as much as possible to the user of *Ruler*. Similarly, judgements have minimal structure, using combinations of operator symbols as distfix operators. Both design choices give maximum typographical freedom and avoid a fixed meaning of judgements.
- The structure provided by holes and judgement schemes allows exactly the translation to AG. Although not formally defined, the correspondence between type rules and AG is relatively self-evident and often observed in literature.

These design decisions ensure that *Ruler* is what it is meant to be: a relatively simple solution for keeping type rules and their implementation consistent. However, the desire to check and generate more from a single description surely will motivate further evolution of the *Ruler* formalism (e.g.) to be more restrictive (thus allowing more checks) and more expressive (thus allowing more aspects to be specified). A more restrictive syntax for *Ruler* expressions would also enable a more concise, but implicit, notation, avoiding the need for keywords like *judge*.

Views as organizational structure. Rules are organized as groups of views; *Ruler* enforces all views on a type rule to be specified together. This is a consequence of our design paradigm in which we both isolate parts of the type rules specification (by using views), and need to know the context of these isolated parts (by rendering parts together with their context). In practice it works well to devlop all views together, to allow for a understandable partitioning into different views, while at the same time keeping an overview.

Emphasizing differences. We use colors in the electronic version of this paper to emphasize differences in type rules. For black-and-white print this is hardly a good way to convey information to the reader. However, we believe that to understand more complex material, more technical means (like colors, hypertext, collapsable/expandable text) must be used to manage the complexity of descriptions.

Future research. We foresee the following directions of further research and development of *Ruler*:

- The additional specification required to shift from equational to algorithmic type rules is currently done by hand. However, our algorithmic version of the type rules uses a heuristic for dealing with yet unknown information and finding this unknown information. We expect that this (and other) heuristics can be applied to similar problems as an automated strategy.
- In this paper, equational type rules are implemented by algorithmic ones, which easily map to AG rules. The transition from equation to algorithm involves a certain

strategy. In this paper we use HM inference, a greedy resolution of constraints. Alternate strategies exist [15, 14]; *Ruler* (or similar tools) can provide abstractions of such strategies.

- *Ruler* exploits the syntax-directed nature of type rules. This implies that the structure of an AST determines which rule has to be used. The choice of the right rule may also depend on other conditions (than the structure of the AST), or a choice may be non-deterministic. The consequence of this observation is that *Ruler* has to deal with multiple levels of rules, transformed into eachother, with the lowest level corresponding to an AST based target language.

- *Ruler* compiles to target languages (AG, TEX), but does not prove anything about the described rules. A plugin architecture would allow the translation to different targets, and in particular, into a description suitable for further use by theorem provers etc..

- Views are built on top of each other by introducing new holes and adapting rules. Currently we do not deal with possible conflicts between views. However, we expect that a combination with the more aspect oriented approach taken by Tinker-Type [18] eventually will lead to a more modular approach where type system aspects together with implementation fragments can be combined and checked for inconsistencies.

References

1. Projet CROAP. Design and Implementaiton of Programming Tools. http://www-sop. inria.fr/croap/, 1999.
2. Hugs 98. http://www.haskell.org/hugs/, 2003.
3. ASF+SDF. http://www.cwi.nl/htbin/sen1/twiki/bin/view/SEN1/ASF+SDF, 2005.
4. Literate Programming. http://www.literateprogramming.com/, 2005.
5. Brian E. Aydemir, Aaron Bohannon, Matthew Fairbairn, J. Nathan Foster, and Benjamin C. Pierce. Mechanized metatheory for the masses: The POPLmark challenge. In *The 18th International Conference on Theorem Proving in Higher Order Logics*, 2005.
6. Atze Dijkstra. EHC Web. http://www.cs.uu.nl/groups/ST/Ehc/WebHome, 2004.
7. Atze Dijkstra. *Stepping through Haskell*. PhD thesis, Utrecht University, Department of Information and Computing Sciences, 2005.
8. Atze Dijkstra and S. Doaitse Swierstra. Typing Haskell with an Attribute Grammar. In *Advanced Functional Programming Summerschool*, number 3622 in LNCS. Springer-Verlag, 2004.
9. Atze Dijkstra and S. Doaitse Swierstra. Making Implicit Parameters Explicit. Technical report, Utrecht University, 2005.
10. Dominic Duggan and John Ophel. Type-Checking Multi-Parameter Type Classes. *Journal of Functional Programming*, 2002.
11. Karl-Filip Faxen. A Static Semantics for Haskell. *Journal of Functional Programming*, 12(4):295, 2002.
12. GrammaTech. Synthesizer Generator. http://www.grammatech.com/products/sg/overview.html, 2005.

13. Robert Harper. Mechanizing Language Definitions (invited lecture at ICFP05). http://www.cs.cmu.edu/~rwh/, 2005.
14. Bastiaan Heeren and Jurriaan Hage. Type Class Directives. In *Seventh International Symposium on Practical Aspects of Declarative Languages*, pages 253 – 267. Springer-Verlag, 2005.
15. Bastiaan Heeren, Jurriaan Hage, and S. Doaitse Swierstra. Generalizing Hindley-Milner Type Inference Algorithms. Technical Report UU-CS-2002-031, Institute of Information and Computing Science, University Utrecht, Netherlands, 2002.
16. Mark P. Jones. *Qualified Types, Theory and Practice*. Cambridge Univ. Press, 1994.
17. Mark P. Jones. Typing Haskell in Haskell. http://www.cse.ogi.edu/~mpj/thih/, 2000.
18. Michael Y. Levin and Benjamin C. Pierce. TinkerType: A Language for Playing with Formal Systems. http://www.cis.upenn.edu/~milevin/tt.html, 1999.
19. Simon Marlow. The Glasgow Haskell Compiler. http://www.haskell.org/ghc/, 2004.
20. Simon Peyton Jones. Haskell 98, *Language and Libraries, The Revised Report*. Cambridge Univ. Press, 2003.
21. Simon Peyton Jones, Mark Jones, and Erik Meijer. Type classes: an exploration of the design space. In *Haskell Workshop*, 1997.
22. Benjamin C. Pierce. *Types and Programming Languages*. MIT Press, 2002.
23. Rob Simmons. The Twelf Project (Wiki Home). http://fp.logosphere.cs.cmu.edu/twelf/, 2005.
24. Eelco Visser. Stratego Home Page. http://www.program-transformation.org/Stratego/WebHome, 2005.

A Framework for Extended Algebraic Data Types

Martin Sulzmann[1], Jeremy Wazny[3], and Peter J. Stuckey[2,3]

[1] School of Computing,
National University of Singapore,
S16 Level 5, 3 Science Drive 2, Singapore 117543
`sulzmann@comp.nus.edu.sg`
[2] NICTA Victoria Laboratory
[3] Department of Computer Science and Software Engineering,
The University of Melbourne,
Vic. 3010, Australia
{`jermyrw, pjs`}`@cs.mu.oz.au`

Abstract. There are a number of extended forms of algebraic data types such as type classes with existential types and generalized algebraic data types. Such extensions are highly useful but their interaction has not been studied formally so far. Here, we present a unifying framework for these extensions. We show that the combination of type classes and generalized algebraic data types allows us to express a number of interesting properties which are desired by programmers. We support type checking based on a novel constraint solver. Our results show that our system is practical and greatly extends the expressive power of languages such as Haskell and ML.

1 Introduction

Algebraic data types enable the programmer to write functions which pattern match over user-definable types. There exist several extensions of algebraic data types which increase the expressiveness of the language significantly. Läufer and Odersky [LO94] consider the addition of (boxed) existential types whereas Läufer [Läu96] was the first to introduce a combination of single-parameter type classes and existential types [LO94]. Xi, Chen and Chen [XCC03] introduced yet another extension of algebraic data types known as guarded recursive data types (GRDTs). GRDTs are largely equivalent to Cheney's and Hinze's first-class phantom types [CH03] and Peyton Jones's, Washburns' and Weirich's generalized algebraic data types (GADTs) [PDWW05].[1] All these extensions are very interesting but have largely been studied independently.

Here, we present a system which unifies these seemingly unrelated extensions, something which has not been studied formally before.

---

[1] For the purposes of this paper, we will use the term GADTs which appears to be gaining popularity.

M. Hagiya and P. Wadler (Eds.): FLOPS 2006, LNCS 3945, pp. 47–64, 2006.

Specifically, our contributions are:

- We formalize an extension of Hindley/Milner where the types of constructors of algebraic data types may be constrained by type equations *and* type classes (Section 4). Such a system of *extended* algebraic data types subsumes GADTs and type classes with extensions [JJM97, Jon00].
- An important point of our system is that GADTs and type classes can interact freely with each other. Thus, we can express some interesting properties which are desired by programmers (Section 4.1).
- We support type checking based on a novel checking method for implication constraints (Section 5).
- We have implemented the type checker as part of the Chameleon system [SW] (experimental version of Haskell).

We continue in Section 2 where we introduce some basic notations and assumptions used throughout the paper. In Section 3 we review type classes with existential types and GADTs and summarize their differences and commonalities. Related work is discussed in Section 6. We conclude in Section 7. Note that we use Haskell-style syntax in example programs throughout the paper.

Additional details including a description of the semantic meaning of programs and its type soundness proof can be found in an accompanying technical report [SWP06].

2   Preliminaries

We write $\bar{o}$ to denote a sequence of objects $o_1,...,o_n$. As it is common, we write Γ to denote an environment consisting of a sequence of type assignments $x_1 : \sigma_1, ..., x_n : \sigma_n$. Types σ will be defined later. We commonly treat Γ as a set. We write "−" to denote set subtraction. We write $fv(o)$ to denote the set of free variables in some object o with the exception that $fv(\{x_1 : \sigma_1, ..., x_n : \sigma_n\})$ denotes $fv(\sigma_1, ..., \sigma_n)$. In case objects have binders, e.g. $\forall a$, we assume that $fv(\forall a.o) = fv([b/a]o) - \{b\}$ where b is a fresh variable and $[b/a]$ a renaming.

We generally assume that the reader is familiar with the concepts of substitutions, unifiers, most general unifiers (m.g.u.) etc [LMM87] and first-order logic [Sho67]. We write $[\bar{t}/\bar{a}]$ to denote the simultaneous substitution of variables a_i by types t_i for $i = 1, .., n$. Sometimes, we write $o_1 \equiv o_2$ to denote syntactic equivalence between two objects o_1 and o_2 in order to avoid confusion with $=$. We use common notation for Boolean conjunction ($\wedge$), implication ($\supset$) and universal ($\forall$) and existential quantifiers ($\exists$). Often, we abbreviate $\wedge$ by "," and use set notation for conjunction of formulae. We sometimes use $\bar{\exists}_V.Fml$ as a shorthand for $\exists fv(Fml) - V.Fml$ where Fml is some first-order formula and V a set of variables, that is existential quantification of all variables in Fml apart from V. We write $\models$ to denote the model-theoretic entailment relation. When writing logical statements we often leave (outermost) quantifiers implicit. E.g., let Fml_1 and Fml_2 be two formulae where Fml_1 is closed (contains no free variables). Then, $Fml_1 \models Fml_2$ is a short-hand for $Fml_1 \models \forall fv(Fml_2).Fml_2$ stating that in any (first-order) model for Fml_1 formula $\forall fv(Fml_2).Fml_2$ is satisfied.

3   Background: Type Classes with Existential Types and GADTs

In our first example program, we make use of existential types as introduced by Läufer and Odersky [LO94].

```
data KEY = forall a. Mk a (a->Int)
g (Mk x f) = f x
```

The algebraic data type KEY has one constructor Mk of type $\forall a.a \to (a \to Int) \to KEY$. Note that variable a does not appear in the result type. In the Haskell syntax we indicate this explicitly via **forall a**. When constructing a value of type KEY we are able to hide the actual values involved. Effectively, a refers to an existentially bound variable. [2] Thus, when pattern matching over KEY values we should not make any assumptions about the actual values involved. This is the case for the above program text. We find that the type of g is $KEY \to Int$.

The situation is different in case of

```
g1 (Mk x f) = (f x, x)
```

The type of x escapes as part of the result type. However, we have no knowledge about the actual type of x. Hence, function g1 should be rejected.

In some subsequent work, Läufer [Läu96] considers a combination of single-parameter type classes [WB89] and existential types. Consider

```
class Key a where getKey::a->Int
data KEY2 = forall a. Key a => Mk2 a
g2 (Mk2 x) = getKey x
```

where the class declaration introduces a single-parameter type class Key with method declaration getKey : $\forall a.Key\ a \Rightarrow a \to Int$. We use Key to constrain the argument type of constructor Mk2, i.e. Mk2 : $\forall a.Key\ a \Rightarrow a \to KEY2$. The pattern Mk2 x gives rise to $Key\ a$ and assigns the type a to x. In the function body of g2, expression getKey x has type Int and gives rise to $Key\ a$ which can be satisfied by the type class arising out of the pattern. Hence, function g2 is of type $KEY2 \to Int$.

GADTs are one of the latest extensions of the concept of algebraic data types. They have attracted a lot of attention recently [SP04, PG04, Nil05]. The novelty of GADTs is that the (result) types of constructor may differ. Thus, we may make use of additional type equality assumptions while typing the body of a pattern clause.

Here, we give excerpts of a standard program which defines a strongly-typed evaluator for a simple term language. We use the GADT notation as implemented in GHC 6.4 [GHC].

---

[2] It may helpful to point out that $\forall a.a \to (a \to Int) \to KEY$ is equivalent to $(\exists a.a \to (a \to Int)) \to KEY$. Hence, "existential" variables are introduced with the "universal" **forall** keyword.

```
data Term a where
     Zero : Term Int
     Pair : Term b->Term c->Term (b,c)
eval :: Term a -> a
eval Zero = 0
eval (Pair t1 t2) = (eval t1, eval t2)
```

The constructors of the above GADT `Term a` do *not* share the same (result) type (which is usually required by "standard" algebraic data types). In case of `Zero` the variable a in the GADT `Term a` is equal to `Int` whereas in case of `Pair` the variable a is equal to `(b,c)` for some b and c. Effectively, the constructors mimic the typing rules of a simply-typed language. That is, we can guarantee that all constructed terms are well-typed. The actual novelty of GADTs is that when pattern matching over GADT constructors, i.e. deconstructing terms, we can make use of the type equality assumptions implied by constructors to type the body of pattern clauses. E.g. in case of the second function clause we find that `Pair t1 t2` has type $Term\ a$. Hence, t1 has type $Term\ b$ and t2 has type $Term\ c$ where $a = (b,c)$. Hence, `(eval t1, eval t2)` has type (b,c) which is equivalent to a under the constraint $a = (b,c)$. The constraint $a = (b,c)$ is only available while typing the body of this particular function clause. That is, this constraint does not float out and therefore does not interact with the rest of the program. Hence, the type annotation `eval::Term a->a` is correct.

The short summary of what we have seen so far is as follows. Typing-wise the differences between GADTs and type classes with existential types are marginal. Both systems are extensions of existential types and both make temporary use of primitive constraints (either type equalities or type class constraints) arising out of patterns while typing the body of a function clause. E.g, in function g2 we temporarily make use of $Key\ a$ arising out of pattern `Mk2 x` whereas in the second clause of function `eval` we temporarily make use of $a = (b,c)$ arising out of pattern `Pair t1 t2`. A subtle difference is that the GADT type system has an additional typing rule to change the type of expressions under type equation assumptions (see upcoming rule (Eq) in Figure 2). Such a rule is lacking in the theory of qualified types [Jon92] which provides the basis for type classes with extensions. The consequence is that we cannot fully mimic GADTs via the combination of multi-parameter type classes [JJM97] with existential types and functional dependencies [Jon00]. We elaborate on this issue in more detail.

The following program is accepted in GHC.

```
class IsInt a b | ->a
instance IsInt Int b
class IsPair a b c | b c->a
instance IsPair (b,c) b c
data Term2 a = forall b. IsInt a b => Zero b
             | forall b c. IsPair a b c => Pair (Term b) (Term c)
```

The declaration `IsInt a b |->a` introduces a multi-parameter type class `IsInt`. The functional dependency `|->a` in combination with the instance declaration enforces that if we see `IsInt a b` the variable `a` will be improved by `Int`. The second parameter is somewhat redundant but necessary due to a GHC condition which demands that at least one type class parameter in a data definition must refer to an existential variable. Similarly, the declarations for type class `IsPair` enforce that in `IsPair a b c` the variable `a` will be improved by `(b,c)`. The up-shot of this encoding of type equations in terms of functional dependencies is that we can use the `Term2 a` type (and its constructors) instead of the GADT `Term a` to ensure that only well-typed terms will ever be constructed.

However, we cannot use the `Term2 a` type to deconstruct values. The following definition does not type check in GHC.

```
eval2 :: Term2 a -> a
eval2 (Zero _) = 0
eval2 (Pair t1 t2) = (eval t1, eval t2)
```

The pattern match in the first clause gives rise to the constraint `IsZero a b` which enforces that `a` is equal to `Int`. In the GHC implementation, the effect functional dependencies have on types in a program is "irreversible". Hence, the GHC type checker complains that variable `a` in the type annotation is unified with `Int`. In case of the GADT system, we can "undo" this effect by an extra (Eq) typing rule.

The immediate question is what kind of (type) behavior we can expect in a system which supports GADTs and type classes with extensions. The current GHC implementation treats both concepts separately and therefore function `eval` type checks but function `eval2` fails to type check. Given that types `Term a` and `Term2 a` effectively describe the same data structure, this may lead to confusion among programmers.

In the next section, we introduce a framework for extended algebraic types which unifies the concepts of type classes with existential types and GADTs. GADT and type class programs show a uniform behavior, e.g. functions `eval` and `eval2` are both accepted in our system.

4   Extended Algebraic Data Types

We start off by considering a few examples to show the benefit of extended algebraic data types (Section 4.1). Then, we describe the formal syntax of programs (Section 4.2) before we define the set of well-typed programs (Section 4.3).

4.1   Overview

Extended algebraic data types (EADTs) are introduced by declarations

```
data T a1 ... am = forall b1,...,bn. D => K t1 ... tl | ...
```

where constraint `D` may consist of type class and type equality constraints. As we will see next, GHC-style GADTs are represented via EADTs where `D` contains type equations.

Here is a re-formulation of the `eval` example from the previous section in terms of our syntax. Additionally, we add a new case that deals with division among terms motivated by a similar example suggested on the GHC-users mailing list [Mor05].

```
data Term a = (a=Int) => Zero
            | forall b c.(a=(b,c)) => Pair (Term b) (Term c)
            | Fractional a => Div (Term a) (Term a)
eval :: Term a -> a
eval Zero = 0
eval (Pair t1 t2) = (eval t1, eval t2)
eval (Div t u) = (eval t) / (eval u)
```

Type equations `(a=Int)` and `(a=(b,c))` exactly correspond to the type equality assumption "implied" by GHC-style GADT constructors. The additional case makes use of the method `(/)` which is part of the `Fractional` type class. Hence, the program text `(eval t) / (eval u)` gives rise to `Fractional a`. This constraint is satisfied by `Fractional a` which arises out of the pattern `Div t u`. We conclude that the program type checks.

The above shows that we can specify EADTs which combine GADTs and type classes with existential types. In our next example, we require the combination of GADTs with type classes with extensions. Our goal is to refine the type of the `append` function to state that appending two lists yields a lists whose length is the sum of the two input lists.

First, we introduce a EADT where the extra parameter keeps track of the length of the list. Type constructors `Zero` and `Succ` are used to represent numbers on the level of types.

```
data Zero
data Succ n
data List a n = (n=Zero) => Nil
              | forall m. (n=Succ m) => Cons a (List a m)
```

Then, we define a type class and instances to define addition among our (type) number representation.

```
class Add l m n | l m -> n
instance Add Zero m m                              -- (1)
instance Add l m n => Add (Succ l) m (Succ n)
```

Note that the functional dependency [Jon00] `l m->n` states that the first two parameters uniquely determine the third parameter. Hence, the `Add` type class behaves like a function. E.g., in case we encounter `Add Zero m n` the type `n` will be improved [Jon95] to `m`. We make use of the `Add` type class to refine the type of the `append` function. Thus, we can state the desired property that the length of the output list equals the sum of the length of the two input lists.

```
append ::  Add l m n => List a l -> List a m -> List a n
append Nil ys = ys
append (Cons x xs) ys = Cons x (append xs ys)
```

The above program type checks in our system. E.g, consider the first clause. When pattern matching over `Nil` and `ys` we encounter the constraint `l=Zero` and find that `ys` has type `List a m`. From the annotation, we obtain `Add l m n`. In combination with the functional dependency imposed on `Add` and instance (1) both constraints imply that `m=n`. Hence, the function body `ys` satisfies the annotation. A similar observation applies to the second clause.

The above examples show that EADTs are a natural generalization of GADTs and types classes with extensions. By employing some type programming we can even mimic type properties which previously required special-purpose systems [Zen99]. Next, we take a look at the formal underpinnings of EADTs.

4.2   Expressions, Types and Constraints

The syntax of programs can be found in Figure 1. We assume that K refers to constructors of user-defined data types. As usual patterns are assumed to be linear, i.e., each variable occurs at most once. In examples we will use pattern matching notation for convenience.

For simplicity, we assume that type annotations are *closed*, i.e. in `f::C=>t` we will quantify over all variables in $fv(C, t)$ when building `f`'s type. Though, the straightforward extension to lexically scoped annotations may be necessary to sufficiently annotate programs [SW05]. We also omit un-annotated recursive function definitions, another straightforward extension.

Expressions	e	$::= K \mid x \mid \lambda x.e \mid e\ e \mid \mathsf{let}\ g = e\ \mathsf{in}\ e \mid$
		$\mathsf{let}\ \begin{matrix} g :: C \Rightarrow t \\ g = e \end{matrix}\ \mathsf{in}\ e \mid \begin{matrix} \mathsf{case}\ e\ \mathsf{of} \\ [p_i \to e_i]_{i \in I} \end{matrix}$
Patterns	p	$::= x \mid K\ p...p$
Types	t	$::= a \mid t \to t \mid T\ \bar{t}$
Primitive Constraints	at	$::= t = t \mid TC\ \bar{t}$
Constraints	C	$::= at \mid C \wedge C$
Type Schemes	σ	$::= t \mid \forall \bar{a}.C \Rightarrow t$
Data Decls	$ddec$	$::= \mathsf{data}\ T\ a_1...a_m = \mathsf{forall}\ b_1, ..., b_n.D \Rightarrow K\ t_1...t_l$
Type Class Decls	$tcdec$	$::= \mathsf{class}\ TC\ \bar{a}\ \mathsf{where}\ m :: C \Rightarrow t \mid \mathsf{instance}\ C \Rightarrow TC\ \bar{t}$
CHRs	R	$::= \mathsf{rule}\ TC_1\ \bar{t_1}, ..., TC_n\ \bar{t_n} \Longleftrightarrow C \mid$
		$\mathsf{rule}\ TC_1\ \bar{t_1}, ..., TC_n\ \bar{t_n} \Longrightarrow C$

Fig. 1. Syntax of Programs

Our type language is standard. We assume that $T\ \bar{t}$ refer to user-definable data types. We use common Haskell notation for writing function, pair, list types etc. We assume that constructor and destructor functions are recorded in some initial environment Γ_{init}, e.g. $(\cdot, \cdot) : \forall a, b.a \to b \to (a, b)$, $fst : \forall a, b.(a, b) \to a$, $snd : \forall a, b.(a, b) \to b \in \Gamma_{init}$ etc.

A *primitive* constraint (a.k.a. *atom*) is either an equation $t = t'$ (a.k.a. type equality) or an n-ary *type class* constraint $TC\ \bar{t}$. We assume a special (always satisfiable) constraint $True$ representing the empty conjunction of constraints, and a special (never satisfiable) constraint $False$. Often, we treat conjunctions of constraints as sets and abbreviate Boolean conjunction $\wedge$ by ",". We generally use symbols C and D to refer to sets of constraints.

Type schemes have an additional constraint component which allows us to restrict the set of type instances. We often refer to a type scheme as a type for short. Note that we consider $\forall \bar{a}.t$ as a short-hand for $\forall \bar{a}.True \Rightarrow t$. The presence of equations makes our system slightly more general compared to standard Hindley/Milner. E.g., types $\forall a, b.a = b \Rightarrow a \rightarrow b$ and $\forall a.a \rightarrow a$ are equivalent. Equations will become interesting once we allow them to appear in type assumptions of constructors.

We assume that data type declarations

```
data T a1 ... am = forall b1,...,bn. D => K t1 ... tl | ...
```

are preprocessed and the types of constructors $K : \forall \bar{a}, \bar{b}.D \Rightarrow t_1 \rightarrow ... \rightarrow t_l \rightarrow T \bar{a}$ are recorded in the initial environment Γ_{init}. We assume that $\bar{a} \cap \bar{b} = \emptyset$. Note that $\bar{a}$ and $\bar{b}$ can be empty.

Similarly, for each class declaration class TC $\bar{a}$ where $m :: C \Rightarrow t$ we find $m : \forall fv(C, t, \bar{a}).(TC$ $\bar{a}, C) \Rightarrow t \in \Gamma_{init}$. Super-classes do not impose any challenges for typing and translation programs. Hence, we ignore them for brevity.

We also ignore the bodies of instance declarations. Details of how to type and translate instance bodies can be found elsewhere [SWP05].

In our source syntax, there is no explicit support for type improvement mechanisms such as functional dependencies [Jon00] or associated types [CKJ05]. Improvement conditions are encoded via CHRs as we will see shortly. Though, we may make use of the functional dependency notation in example programs.

Following our earlier work [SS05, DJSS04] we employ Constraint Handling Rules (CHRs) [Frü95] as the internal formalism to describe the valid type class relations. E.g., each declaration instance $C' \Rightarrow TC$ $\bar{t}$ is described by the *simplification* rule TC $\bar{t} \Longleftrightarrow C'$ whereas type improvement conditions are specified by the second kind of CHRs which are referred to as *propagation* rules.

Here are the CHRs describing the instance and functional dependency relations of the Add type class from the previous section.

```
rule Add Zero m m <==> True                     (A1)
rule Add (Succ l) m (Succ n) <==> Add l m n     (A2)
rule Add l m n1, Add l m n2 ==> n1=n2           (A3)
rule Add Zero m n ==> m=n                        (A4)
rule Add (Succ l) m n' ==> n'=Succ n            (A5)
```

How to systematically derive such CHRs from source programs can be found here [SS05, DJSS04]. For a given program we assume a fixed set P of CHRs to which we refer to as the *program logic*.

For the description of the set of well-typed expressions in the next section we apply the logic interpretation of CHRs which is as follows: Symbol ==> denotes Boolean implication and <==> denotes Boolean equivalence. Variables in the rule *head* (left-hand side) are universally quantified whereas all remaining variables on the right-hand side are existentially quantified. E.g., the CHR (A5) is interpreted as the formula $\forall l, m, n'.(Add$ $(Succ$ $l)$ m $n' \supset \exists n.n' = Succ$ $n)$.

4.3   Type System

To describe well-typing of expressions we make use of judgments of the form
$C, \Gamma \vdash e : t$ where C is a constraint, Γ refers to the set of lambda-bound
variables, predefined and user-defined functions, e is an expression and t is a
type. Note that we leave the program logic P implicit. None of the typing rules
affect P, hence, we can assume that P is fixed for a given expression. We say a
judgment is *valid* iff there is a derivation w.r.t. the rules found in Figure 2. Each
valid judgment implies that the expression is well-typed.

   Let us take a look at the typing rules in detail. In rule (Var-$\forall$E), we build a
type instance if we can verify that the instantiated constraint is logically contained by the given constraint under the given program logic. This is formally
expressed by the side condition $P \models C \supset \overline{[t/a]}D$.

   In rule (Eq) we can change the type of expressions.[3] Note that the set C of constraints may not necessarily be the same in all parts of the program (see upcoming rule (Pat)). Therefore, this rule plays a crucial role. Recall function append
from Section 4.1 where in case of the second clause we find $Add\ l\ m\ n, l = Zero$
in the constraint component and variable ys has type $List\ a\ m$. Here, P consists
of rules (A1-5) from the previous section. We find that $P \models Add\ l\ m\ n, l =$
$Zero \supset m = n$. Hence, we can change the type of ys to $List\ a\ n$. Thus, we can
verify that append's annotation is correct.

   Rules (Abs) and (App) are straightforward. In rule (Let), we include the
rule for quantifier introduction. Note that we could be more efficient by only
quantifying over the "affected" constraints. Further note that satisfiability of
the "final" constraint C_2 does not imply that C_1 is satisfiable. E.g., consider the
situation where g is not used. Hence, our formulation is more "lazy" compared to
other schemes. We refer to [OSW99, Sul00] for a detailed discussion of different
formulations of quantifier introduction.

   Rule (LetA) deals with a closed annotation. Variables in $C_1 \Rightarrow t_1$ are assumed
to be universally quantified. Note that via this rule we can support polymorphic
recursive functions (for simplicity, we omit the rule to deal with monomorphic
recursive functions).

   Rules (Case) and (Pat) deal with pattern matching. Rule (Pat) is in particular
interesting. For convenience, we consider $p \rightarrow e$ as a (special purpose) expression
only appearing in intermediate steps. We make use of an auxiliary judgment
$p : t \vdash \forall \overline{b}.(D \mid \Gamma_p)$ to establish a relation among pattern p of type t and the
binding Γ_p of variables in p. Constraint D arises from constructor uses in p.
Variables $\overline{b}$ are not allowed to escape which is captured by the side condition
$fv(C, \Gamma, t_2) \cap \overline{b} = \emptyset$. Note that we type the body of the pattern clause under the
"temporary" type assumption D and environment Γ_p arising out of p. Consider

---

[3] Some formulations allow us to change the type of (sub)patterns [SP05]. This may
matter if patterns are nested. For brevity, we neglect such an extension. Note that in
case patterns are evaluated in a certain order, say from left-to-right, we can simply
translate a nested pattern into a sequence of shallow patterns. This is done in GHC
and our Chameleon implementation.

$$(\text{Var-}\forall\text{E}) \quad \frac{\begin{array}{c} (x : \forall\bar{a}.D \Rightarrow t') \in \Gamma \\ P \models C \supset [\overline{t/a}]D \end{array}}{C,\Gamma \vdash x : [\overline{t/a}]t'} \qquad (\text{Eq}) \quad \frac{\begin{array}{c} C,\Gamma \vdash e : t_1 \\ P \models C \supset t_1 = t_2 \end{array}}{C,\Gamma \vdash e : t_2}$$

$$(\text{Abs}) \quad \frac{C,\Gamma \cup \{x : t_1\} \vdash e : t_2}{C,\Gamma \vdash \lambda x.e : t_1 \to t_2} \qquad (\text{App}) \quad \frac{\begin{array}{c} C,\Gamma \vdash e_1 : t_1 \to t_2 \\ C,\Gamma \vdash e_2 : t_1 \end{array}}{C,\Gamma \vdash e_1 e_2 : t_2}$$

$$(\text{Let}) \quad \frac{\begin{array}{c} C_1,\Gamma \vdash e_1 : t_1 \quad \bar{a} = fv(C_1, t_1) - fv(C_2, \Gamma) \\ C_2,\Gamma \cup \{g : \forall\bar{a}.C_1 \Rightarrow t_1\} \vdash e_2 : t_2 \end{array}}{C_2,\Gamma \vdash \text{let } g = e_1 \text{ in } e_2 : t_2}$$

$$(\text{LetA}) \quad \frac{\begin{array}{c} \bar{a} = fv(C_1, t_1) \quad C_2 \wedge C_1, \Gamma \cup \{g : \forall\bar{a}.C_1 \Rightarrow t_1\} \vdash e_1 : t_1 \\ C_2,\Gamma \cup \{g : \forall\bar{a}.C_1 \Rightarrow t_1\} \vdash e_2 : t_2 \end{array}}{C_2,\Gamma \vdash \text{let } \begin{array}{c} g :: C_1 \Rightarrow t_1 \\ g = e_1 \end{array} \text{ in } e_2 : t_2}$$

$$(\text{Case}) \quad \frac{\begin{array}{c} C,\Gamma \vdash e : t_1 \\ C,\Gamma \vdash p_i \to e_i : t_1 \to t_2 \quad \text{for } i \in I \end{array}}{C,\Gamma \vdash \text{case } e \text{ of } [p_i \to e_i]_{i \in I} : t_2} \qquad (\text{Pat}) \quad \frac{\begin{array}{c} p : t_1 \vdash \forall\bar{b}.(D \,\mathbf{I}\, \Gamma_p) \\ fv(C,\Gamma,t_2) \cap \bar{b} = \emptyset \\ C \wedge D, \Gamma \cup \Gamma_p \vdash e : t_2 \end{array}}{C,\Gamma \vdash p \to e : t_1 \to t_2}$$

$$(\text{Pat-Var}) \quad x : t \vdash (True \,\mathbf{I}\, \{x : t\})$$

$$(\text{Pat-K}) \quad \frac{\begin{array}{c} K : \forall\bar{a},\bar{b}.D \Rightarrow t_1' \to ... \to t_l' \to T\,\bar{a} \quad \bar{b} \cap \bar{a} = \emptyset \\ p_k : [\overline{t/a}]t_k' \vdash \forall\bar{b_k'}.(D_k' \,\mathbf{I}\, \Gamma_{p_k}) \quad \text{for } k = 1, ..., l \end{array}}{K\, p_1...p_l : T\,\bar{t} \vdash \forall\bar{b_1'}, ..., \bar{b_l'}, \bar{b}.(D_1' \wedge ...D_l' \wedge [\overline{t/a}]D \,\mathbf{I}\, \Gamma_{p_1} \cup ...\Gamma_{p_l})}$$

Fig. 2. Typing Rules

again function `append` from Section 4.1 where we temporarily make use of $l = Zero$ in the first clause and $l = Succ\ l'$ in the second clause.

The rules for the auxiliary judgment are as follows. In rule (Pat-K) we assume that variables $\bar{a}$ and $\bar{b}$ are fresh. Hence, w.l.o.g. there are no name clashes between variables $\bar{b_1'}, ..., \bar{b_l'}$. Rule (Pat-Var) is standard.

The description of the semantic meaning of programs and its type soundness proof had to be sacrificed due to space restrictions. Details can be found in an accompanying technical report [SWP06]. Here, we only consider type checking which we discuss next.

5   Type Checking

The problem we face is as follows. Given a constraint C, an environment Γ, a type t and an expression e where all let-defined functions are type annotated, we want to verify that $C,\Gamma \vdash e : t$ holds. This is known as type checking as opposed to inference where we compute C and t given Γ and e.

It is folklore knowledge that type checking can be turned into a entailment test among constraints. The path we choose is to translate in an intermediate step the type checking problem to a set of implication constraints [SP05]. A program type checks if the implication constraint holds. We then show how to reduce the decision problem for checking implication constraints to standard CHR solving. Thus, we obtain a computationally tractable type checking method.

5.1 Type Checking Via Implication Constraints

The syntax of implication constraints is as follows.

$$\text{Constraints} \quad C ::= t = t \mid TC\ \bar{t} \mid C \wedge C$$
$$\text{ImpConstraints}\ F ::= C \mid \forall \bar{b}.(C \supset \exists \bar{a}.F) \mid F \wedge F$$

The actual translation to implication constraints follows the description of [SP05]. We employ a deduction system in style of algorithm $\mathcal{W}$ where we use judgments of the form $\Gamma, e \vdash_W (F \mathbin{\mathbf{I}} t)$ to denote that under input environment Γ and expression e we obtain the output implication constraint F and type t. The rules can be found in Figure 3. Recall that let-defined functions are type annotated.

$$
\text{(LetA)}\ \frac{
\begin{array}{c}
\bar{a} = fv(C_1, t_1) \quad b_1, b_1' \text{ fresh} \\
\Gamma \cup \{g : \forall \bar{a}.C_1 \Rightarrow t_1\}, e_1 \vdash_W (F_1 \mathbin{\mathbf{I}} t_1') \quad \Gamma \cup \{g : \forall \bar{a}.C_1 \Rightarrow t_1\}, e_2 \vdash_W (F_2 \mathbin{\mathbf{I}} t_2) \\
F \equiv F_2 \wedge \forall \bar{a}.((C_1 \wedge t_1 = b_1 \wedge b_1 = b_1') \supset \exists_{fv(\Gamma, b_1')}.F_1 \wedge b_1 = t_1')
\end{array}
}{
\Gamma, \text{let}\ \begin{array}{l} g :: C_1 \Rightarrow t_1 \\ g = e_1 \end{array}\ \text{in}\ e_2 \vdash_W (F \mathbin{\mathbf{I}} t_2)
}
$$

$$
\text{(App)}\ \frac{
\begin{array}{c}
\Gamma, e_1 \vdash_W (F_1 \mathbin{\mathbf{I}} t_1) \\
tenv, e_2 \vdash_W (F_2 \mathbin{\mathbf{I}} t_2) \\
t \text{ fresh} \\
F \equiv F_1 \wedge F_2 \wedge t_1 = t_2 \to t
\end{array}
}{
\Gamma, e_1\ e_2 \vdash_W (F \mathbin{\mathbf{I}} t)
}
\qquad
\text{(Var)}\ \frac{(x : \forall \bar{a}.C \Rightarrow t) \in \Gamma}{\Gamma, x \vdash_W (C \mathbin{\mathbf{I}} t)}
$$

$$
\text{(Abs)}\ \frac{a \text{ fresh} \quad \Gamma \cup \{x : a\}, e \vdash_W (F \mathbin{\mathbf{I}} t)}{\Gamma, \lambda x.e \vdash_W (F \mathbin{\mathbf{I}} a \to t)}
$$

$$
\text{(Case)}\ \frac{
\begin{array}{c}
\Gamma, p_i \to e_i \vdash_W (F_i \mathbin{\mathbf{I}} t_i') \quad \text{for}\ i \in I \quad \Gamma, e \vdash_W (F_e \mathbin{\mathbf{I}} t_e) \quad t_1, t_2 \text{ fresh} \\
F \equiv F_e \wedge t_1 = t_e \to t_2 \wedge \bigwedge_{i \in I}(F_i \wedge t_1 = t_i')
\end{array}
}{
\Gamma, \text{case}\ e\ \text{of}\ [p_i \to e_i]_{i \in I} \vdash_W (F \mathbin{\mathbf{I}} t_2)
}
$$

$$
\text{(Pat)}\ \frac{
\begin{array}{c}
p \vdash \forall \bar{b}.(D \mathbin{\mathbf{I}} \Gamma_p \mathbin{\mathbf{I}} t_1) \quad \Gamma \cup \Gamma_p, e \vdash_W (F_e \mathbin{\mathbf{I}} t_e) \quad t \text{ fresh} \\
F \equiv \forall \bar{b}.(D \supset \exists_{fv(\Gamma, \bar{b}, t_e)}.F_e) \wedge t = t_1 \to t_e
\end{array}
}{
\Gamma, p \to e \vdash_W (F \mathbin{\mathbf{I}} t)
}
$$

$$
\text{(Pat-Var)}\ \frac{t \text{ fresh}}{x \vdash (True \mathbin{\mathbf{I}} \{x : t\} \mathbin{\mathbf{I}} t)}
$$

$$
\text{(Pat-K)}\ \frac{
\begin{array}{c}
K : \forall \bar{a}, \bar{b}.D \Rightarrow t_1 \to \dots \to t_l \to T\ \bar{a} \quad \bar{b} \cap \bar{a} = \emptyset \\
p_k \vdash \forall \bar{b}_k'.(D_k' \mathbin{\mathbf{I}} \Gamma_{p_k} \mathbin{\mathbf{I}} t_{p_k}) \quad \phi \text{ m.g.u. of } t_{p_k} = t_k \quad \text{for } k = 1, \dots, l \quad dom(\phi) \cap \bar{b} = \emptyset
\end{array}
}{
K\ p_1 \dots p_l \vdash \forall \bar{b}_1', \dots, \bar{b}_l', \bar{b}.(\phi(D_1') \wedge \dots \phi(D_l') \wedge \phi(D) \mathbin{\mathbf{I}} \phi(\Gamma_{p_1}) \cup \dots \cup \phi(\Gamma_{p_l}) \mathbin{\mathbf{I}} T\ \phi(\bar{a}))
}
$$

Fig. 3. Translation to Implication Constraints

We briefly review the individual rules. We write $\equiv$ to denote syntactic equality. In rules (Var) and (Pat-K) we assume that the bound variables $\bar{a}$ and $\bar{b}$ are fresh.

We assume that $dom(\phi)$ computes the variables in the domain of ϕ. In rule (Pat) we make use of the implication constraint $\forall \bar{b}.(D \supset \bar{\exists}_{fv(\Gamma,\bar{b},t_e)}.F_e)$ which states that under the temporary assumptions D arising out of the pattern p we can satisfy the implication constraint F_e arising out of e. The $\forall$ quantifier ensures that no existential variables $\bar{b}$ escape. Formula $\bar{\exists}_{fv(\Gamma,\bar{b},t_e)}.F_e$ is a short-hand for $\exists \bar{a}.F_e$ where $\bar{a} = fv(F_e) - fv(\Gamma,\bar{b},t_e)$. That is, we existentially quantify over all variables which are strictly local in F_e. In the special case of (existential) algebraic data types the constraint D equals $True$ and F_e is a constraint. In rule (LetA), we generate a formula to check that the type of the body e_1 subsumes the annotated type of function f. In logical terms, the subsumption condition is expressed by the formula $\forall \bar{a}(C_1 \supset \bar{\exists}_{fv(\Gamma,t_1)}.F_1 \wedge t_1 = t'_1)$. However, this form is not suitable for the upcoming checking procedure because we would need to guess the possible assignments under which $t_1 = t'_1$ holds. Therefore, we push the constraint $t_1 = t'_1$ into the assumption part (left-hand side of $\supset$). For technical reasons, we need to ensure that type schemes $\forall \bar{a}.C \Rightarrow t$ are in the (equivalent) normalized form $\forall \bar{a}, b.C \wedge b = t \Rightarrow b$ where b is fresh. Details are in [SS05]. Note that there is no (Let) rule because we assume that all let-defined functions must be annotated with a type.

The type checking problem says that for a given constraint C, environment Γ, expression e and type t we need to verify that $C, \Gamma \vdash e : t$ holds. We can reduce this problem to testing whether constraint C implies the implication constraint generated from Γ and e.

Theorem 1 (Type Checking via Implication Checking). *Let P be a program logic. Let Γ be an environment, e an expression, C a constraint and t a type. Let $\Gamma, e \vdash_W (F \mid t')$ such that $P \models (C, t = t') \supset \bar{\exists}_{fv(\Gamma,t')}.F$ holds where w.l.o.g. t and t' are variables. Then, $C, \Gamma \vdash e : t$.*

Note that $(C, t = t') \supset \bar{\exists}_{fv(\Gamma,t')}.F$ is itself again a implication constraint (we leave the outermost universal quantifier implicit). Hence, the type checking problem boils down to testing whether a implication constraint holds w.r.t. the program logic P. We neglect here the "opposite" task of finding C which corresponds to type inference.

5.2   Checking Implication Constraints

First, we review some background material on CHR solving. The operational reading of constraint rules (CHRs) is simple. In case of propagation rules we add the right-hand side if we find a matching copy of the lhs in the constraint store. In case of simplifications rules we remove the matching copy and replace it by the right-hand side. The formal definition is as follows [Frü95].

Definition 1 (CHR Semantics). *Let P be a set of CHRs.*

Propagation: *Let (R) $c_1, ..., c_n \Longrightarrow d_1, ..., d_m \in P$ and C be a constraint. Let ϕ be the m.g.u. of all equations in C. Let $c'_1, ..., c'_n \in C$ such that there exists a substitution θ on variables in rule (R) such that $\theta(c_i) = \phi(c'_i)$ for $i = 1...n$,* *that is user-defined constraints $c'_1,...,c'_n$ match the left-hand side of rule (R). Then, $C \rightarrowtail_R C, \theta(d_1), ..., \theta(d_m)$.*

Simplification: *Let (R) $c_1, ..., c_n \Longleftrightarrow d_1, ..., d_m \in P$ and C be a constraint. Let ϕ be the m.g.u. of all equations in C. Let $c'_1, ..., c'_n \in C$ such that there exists a substitution θ on variables in rule (R) such that $\theta(c_i) = \phi(c'_i)$ for $i = 1, ..., n.$, Then, $C \rightarrowtail_R C - \{c'_1, ..., c'_n\}, \theta(d_1), ..., \theta(d_m)$.*

Often, we perform some equivalence transformations (e.g. normalize equations by building the m.g.u. etc) which are either implicit or explicitly denoted by $\longleftrightarrow$. A *derivation*, denoted $C \rightarrowtail_P^* C'$ is a sequence of derivation steps using rules in P such that no further derivation step is applicable to C'. CHRs are applied exhaustively, being careful not to apply propagation rules twice on the same constraints (to avoid infinite propagation). For more details on avoiding re-propagation see e.g. [Abd97]. We say a set P of CHRs is *terminating* if for each C there exists C' such that $C \rightarrowtail_P^* C'$.

We repeat the CHR soundness result [Frü95] which states that CHR rule applications perform equivalence transformations.

Lemma 1 (CHR Soundness [Frü95]). *Let $C \rightarrowtail_P^* C'$. Then $P \models C \leftrightarrow \exists_{fv(C)}.C'$.*

Recall the CHRs for the Add type class.

```
rule Add Zero m m <==>                      (A1)
rule Add (Succ l) m (Succ n) <==> Add l m n (A2)
rule Add l m n1, Add l m n2 ==> n1=n2       (A3)
rule Add Zero m n ==> m=n                    (A4)
rule Add (Succ l) m n' ==> n'=Succ n         (A5)
```

We have that

$$Add\ (Succ\ Zero)\ m\ n, Add\ (Succ\ Zero)\ m\ n', m = Zero$$
$$\rightarrowtail_{A3} Add\ (Succ\ Zero)\ m\ n, m = Zero, n = n'$$
$$\longleftrightarrow Add\ (Succ\ Zero)\ Zero\ n, m = Zero, n = n'$$
$$\rightarrowtail_{A5} Add\ (Succ\ Zero)\ Zero\ (Succ\ n''), n = Succ\ n'', m = Zero, n = n'$$
$$\rightarrowtail_{A1} Add\ Zero\ Zero\ n'', n = Succ\ n'', m = Zero, n = n'$$
$$\rightarrowtail_{A4} Add\ Zero\ Zero\ Zero, n = Succ\ Zero, n'' = Zero, m = Zero, n = n'$$
$$\rightarrowtail_{A2} n = Succ\ Zero, n'' = Zero, m = Zero, n = n'$$

We show how to lift the (primitive) constraint solver $\rightarrowtail_P^*$ to the domain of implication constraints. We write $F \gg_P^* C$ to denote that checking of implication constraint F yields (after some n number of steps) solution C. Our idea is to turn the implication checking problem into an equivalence checking problem by making use of the fact that $C_1 \supset C_2$ iff $C_1 \leftrightarrow C_1, C_2$. Then, we can use the primitive constraint solver and execute $C_1 \rightarrowtail_P^* D_1$ and $C_1, C_2 \rightarrowtail_P^* D_2$. Next, we check for logical equivalence by testing whether D_1 and D_2 share the same m.g.u. and their user-defined constraints are renamings of each other. If equivalence holds, then $C_1 \supset C_2$ is solved and *True* is the solution. The exact checking details are as follows.

Definition 2 (CHR-Based Implication Checker). *Let P be a set of CHRs and F an implication constraint.*

Primitive: *We define $F \gg_P C'$ where $C \rightarrowtail^*_P C'$ if $F \equiv \exists \bar{a}.C$.*

General: *Otherwise $F \equiv C_0, (\forall \bar{a}.D \supset \exists \bar{b}.F_1), F_2$ where C_0 is a conjunction of primitive constraints, D is a set of assumptions and F_1 and F_2 are implication constraints.*

> *We compute (1) $C_0, D \rightarrowtail^*_P D'$ and (2) $C_0, D, F_1 \gg^*_P C'$ for some D' and C'. We distinguish among the following cases.*
> **Solved:** *We define $F \gg_P C_0, F_2$ if $\models (\bar{\exists}_V.D') \leftrightarrow (\bar{\exists}_V.C')$ where $V = fv(C_0, D, \bar{a})$.*
> **Failure:** *We define $F \gg_P$ False in all other cases.*

We assume that $\gg^*_P$ denotes the exhaustive application of CHR implication solving steps.

In the **Primitive** step we apply standard CHR solving. No surprises here. In the **General** step, we split the constraint store into C_0 containing sets of primitive constraints, a single implication constraint $(\forall \bar{a}.D \supset \exists \bar{b}.F_1)$ and F_2 containing the remaining implication constraints. Strictly speaking, F_2 itself could be a set of primitive constraints. Silently, we assume that all sets of primitive constraints are collected in C_0. Also note that we inductively solve nested implication constraints, see (2).

The **Solved** step applies if the equivalence check succeeds. Hence, the constraint $(\forall \bar{a}.D \supset \exists \bar{b}.F_1)$ is removed from the store. Note that w.l.o.g. we assume that $\bar{b} = fv(F_2) - fv(\bar{a}, C_0)$. Any variable not bound by a universal quantifier is (implicitly) existentially bound. The CHR Soundness result immediately yields that this step is sound, hence, the overall procedure is correct (see upcoming Lemma 2).

For example, the `append` function from Section 4.1 gives rise to the following (simplified) implication constraint.

$$\forall a, l, m, n. \; (Add \; l \; m \; n, t = List \; a \; l \to List \; a \; m \to List \; a \; n) \supset$$
$$\begin{pmatrix} (l = Zero \supset t = List \; a \; l \to List \; a \; m \to List \; a \; m), & (1) \\ \exists l'.(l = Succ \; l' \supset (Add \; l' \; m \; n', t = List \; a \; l \to List \; a \; m \to List \; a \; (Succ \; n'))) \end{pmatrix}$$

Based on our implication checking procedure, we can verify that the above formula F holds, i.e. $F \gg^*_P$ True. E.g., in an intermediate step, we find that

$$Add \; l \; m \; n, t = List \; a \; l \to List \; a \; m \to List \; a \; n, l = Zero$$
$$\rightarrowtail^* t = List \; a \; Zero \to List \; a \; m \to List \; a \; n, l = Zero, m = n$$

and thus we can verify the inner implication (1). A similar reasoning applies to the remaining part. Hence, from Theorem 1 and Lemma 2 we can conclude that the `append` function type checks.

Lemma 2 (Implication Checking Soundness). *Let P be a set of CHRs, F be an implication constraint and C be a set of primitive constraints such that $F \gg^*_P C$. Then, $P \models C \leftrightarrow F$.*

Our implication checking procedure is terminating if the underlying primitive constraint solver is terminating. Thus, we obtain decidable type checking. There are plenty of criteria (imposed on source EADT programs) such as the Haskell type class [Pey03] and Jones's functional dependency restrictions [Jon00] which ensure termination of the resulting CHRs. We refer to [DJSS04] for more details.

Though, termination does not ensure that type checking is complete. The problem is that type constraints arising out of the program text may be "ambiguous" which requires us to guess types. The solution is to reject such programs or demand further user assistance in form of type annotations.

Yet another source of incompleteness is our primitive constraint solver which we use for equivalence checking. We will elaborate on such issues and how to obtain complete type checking in an extended version of this paper.

6   Discussion and Related Work

Peyton Jones, Washburn and Weirich [PDWW05] have added GADTs to GHC. However, GADTs and type classes do not seem to interact well in GHC. E.g., the examples from Section 4.1 are not typable.

```
data Exp = ...                          -- resource automaton --
-- resource EADT                        data S0 -- states
data Cmd p q =                          data S1
  forall r. Seq (Cmd p r) (Cmd r q)     data Open -- alphabet
  | ITE Exp (Cmd p q) (Cmd p q)         data Close
  | (p=q) => While Exp (Cmd p q)        data Write
  -- while state is invariant           -- valid transition
  | Delta p Open q => OpenF             rule Delta S0 Open x <==> x=S1
  | Delta p Close q => CloseF           rule Delta S1 Close x <==> x=S0
  | Delta p Write q => WriteF           rule Delta S1 Write x <==> x=S1

-- improvement
rule Delta a b c, Delta a b d ==> c=d
rule Delta x Open y ==> x=S0, y=S1
rule Delta x Close y ==> x=S1, y=S0 -- (Imp)
rule Delta S1 Open x ==> False
-- failure
rule Delta S0 Close x ==> False
rule Delta S0 Write x ==> False -- (Fail)
```

Fig. 4. Resource EADT

Sheard [She05] and Chen/Xi [CX05] have extended GADTs to allow users to specify their own program properties which previously required external proof systems such as [PS99, BBC+96]. An interesting question is to what extent "extended GADTs" can be expressed in terms of EADTs. E.g., consider the **append** function from Section 4.1 which appears in very similar form in [CX05]. One difference is that the works in [She05, CX05] use type functions to specify type properties whereas we use CHRs. We claim that CHRs allow us to specify more complex type properties than specifiable via type functions as shown by the EADT in Figure 4.

We introduce a EADT to represent a while language which satisfies a resource usage analysis specified in terms of a DFA. The DFA relations are specified via CHRs. Type parameters p and q represent the input and output state, before and after execution of the command. Notice how we constrain states p and q by the constraint Delta which represents the DFA state transition function delta (see the last three cases).

The CHRs encode a specific automaton for a resource usage policy where we may open a file, write an arbitrary number of times to the file and close the file. The improvement and failure rules are particularly interesting here. They allow us to aggressively enforce the resource automaton. E.g., after closing a file we must return to the start state S0 (see (Imp)). We are not allowed to write if we are in the start state (see (Fail)) etc. We cannot see how to model this behavior via type functions in the systems described in [She05, CX05].

Simonet and Pottier [SP05] have also employed implication constraints for type inference in an extension of Hindley/Milner with GADTs but did not give any checking method in the general form as stated here. In some subsequent work, Pottier and Régis-Gianas [PRG06] showed how to perform complete type checking for GADTs without implication constraints on the expense of demanding an excessive amount of type annotations. These annotations are inferred by an elaboration phase. E.g., they show how to successfully elaborate the following program based on a heuristic algorithm Ibis.

```
data T = (a=Int) => I
double::T a->[a]->[a]
double t l = map (\x-> case t of I -> x+x) l
```

We also successfully accept the above program based on our type checking method. We consider this as an indication that implication constraints are an interesting approach to describe the elaboration of programs to achieve complete type checking.

7   Conclusion

We have formalized the concept of extended algebraic data types which unifies type classes with extensions and GADTs. We could provide evidence that the extension is useful and extends the expressiveness of languages such as Haskell significantly. We have introduced a novel method to support type checking for all instances of our framework.

For practical reasons, we also want to look into type inference to relieve the user from the burden of providing annotations. In this context, it is also important to consider how to give feedback in case of type errors. We have already started work in this direction which we plan to report in the near future.

Acknowledgments

We thank the reviewers for their constructive comments.

References

[Abd97]   S. Abdennadher. Operational semantics and confluence of constraint
           propagation rules. In *Proc. of CP'97*, LNCS, pages 252–266. Springer-
           Verlag, 1997.
[BBC⁺96]   B. Barras, S. Boutin, C. Cornes, J. Courant, J.-C. Filliâtre, H. Herbe-
           lin, G. Huet, P. Manoury, C. Muñoz, C. Murthy, C. Parent, C. Paulin-
           Mohring, A. Saïbi, and B. Werner. *The Coq Proof Assistant Reference
           Manual Version 6.1*. INRIA-Rocquencourt-CNRS-ENS Lyon, December
           1996.
[CH03]   J. Cheney and R. Hinze. First-class phantom types. Technical Report
           CUCIS TR2003-1901, Cornell University, 2003.
[CKJ05]   M. Chakravarty, G. Keller, and S. Peyton Jones. Associated types syn-
           onyms. In *Proc. of ICFP'05*, pages 241–253. ACM Press, 2005.
[CX05]   C. Chen and H. Xi. Combining programming with theorem proving. In
           Proc. of ICFP'05, pages 66–77. ACM Press, 2005.
[DJSS04]   G. J. Duck, S. Peyton Jones, P. J. Stuckey, and M. Sulzmann. Sound
           and decidable type inference for functional dependencies. In *Proc. of
           ESOP'04*, volume 2986 of *LNCS*, pages 49–63. Springer-Verlag, 2004.
[Frü95]   T. Frühwirth. Constraint handling rules. In *Constraint Programming:
           Basics and Trends*, LNCS. Springer-Verlag, 1995.
[GHC]   Glasgow haskell compiler home page. http://www.haskell.org/ghc/.
[JJM97]   S. Peyton Jones, M. P. Jones, and E. Meijer. Type classes: an exploration
           of the design space. In *Haskell Workshop*, June 1997.
[Jon92]   M. P. Jones. *Qualified Types: Theory and Practice*. D.phil. thesis, Oxford
           University, September 1992.
[Jon95]   M. P. Jones. Simplifying and improving qualified types. In *FPCA '95:
           Conference on Functional Programming Languages and Computer Archi-
           tecture*. ACM Press, 1995.
[Jon00]   M. P. Jones. Type classes with functional dependencies. In *Proc. of
           ESOP'00*, volume 1782 of *LNCS*. Springer-Verlag, 2000.
[Läu96]   K. Läufer. Type classes with existential types. *Journal of Functional
           Programming*, 6(3):485–517, 1996.
[LMM87]   J. Lassez, M. Maher, and K. Marriott. Unification revisited. In *Founda-
           tions of Deductive Databases and Logic Programming*. Morgan Kauffman,
           1987.
[LO94]   K. Läufer and M. Odersky. Polymorphic type inference and abstract data
           types. *ACM Trans. Program. Lang. Syst.*, 16(5):1411–1430, 1994.
[Mor05]   J. Garrett Morris. GADT question. http://www.haskell.org//
           pipermail/glasgow-haskell-users/2005-October/009076.html, 2005.
[Nil05]   H. Nilsson. Dynamic optimization for functional reactive programming
           using generalized algebraic data types. In *Proc. of ICFP'05*, pages 54–65.
           ACM Press, 2005.
[OSW99]   M. Odersky, M. Sulzmann, and M Wehr. Type inference with constrained
           types. *Theory and Practice of Object Systems*, 5(1):35–55, 1999.

[PDWW05] S. Peyton Jones, D.Vytiniotis, G. Washburn, and S. Weirich. Simple unification-based type inference for GADTs, 2005. Submitted to PLDI'06.

[Pey03]   S. Peyton Jones, editor. *Haskell 98 Language and Libraries: The Revised Report*. Cambridge University Press, 2003.

[PG04]   F. Pottier and N. Gauthier. Polymorphic typed defunctionalization. In *Proc. of POPL'04*, pages 89–98. ACM Press, January 2004.

[PRG06]   F. Pottier and Y. Régis-Gianas. Stratified type inference for generalized algebraic data types. In *Proc. of POPL'06*, pages 232–244. ACM Press, 2006.

[PS99]   F. Pfenning and C. Schürmann. System description: Twelf - a metalogical framework for deductive systems. In *CADE*, volume 1632 of *LNCS*, pages 202–206. Springer-Verlag, 1999.

[She05]   T. Sheard. Putting curry-howard to work. In *Proc. of Haskell'05*, pages 74–85. ACM Press, 2005.

[Sho67]   J.R. Shoenfield. *Mathematical Logic*. Addison-Wesley, 1967.

[SP04]   T. Sheard and E. Pasalic. Meta-programming with built-in type equality. In *Fourth International Workshop on Logical Frameworks and Meta-Languages*, 2004.

[SP05]   V. Simonet and F. Pottier. Constraint-based type inference for guarded algebraic data types. Research Report 5462, INRIA, January 2005.

[SS05]   P.J. Stuckey and M. Sulzmann. A theory of overloading. *ACM Transactions on Programming Languages and Systems*, 2005. To appear.

[Sul00]   M. Sulzmann. *A General Framework for Hindley/Milner Type Systems with Constraints*. PhD thesis, Yale University, Department of Computer Science, May 2000.

[SW]   M. Sulzmann and J. Wazny. Chameleon. http://www.comp.nus.edu.sg/~sulzmann/chameleon.

[SW05]   M. Sulzmann and J. Wazny. Lexically scoped type annotations. http://www.comp.nus.edu.sg/~sulzmann, 2005.

[SWP05]   M. Sulzmann, J. Wazny, and P.J.Stuckey. Co-induction and type improvement in type class proofs. http://www.comp.nus.edu.sg/~sulzmann, 2005.

[SWP06]   M. Sulzmann, J. Wazny, and P.J. Stuckey. A framework for extended algebraic data types. Technical report, The National University of Singapore, 2006.

[WB89]   P. Wadler and S. Blott. How to make *ad-hoc* polymorphism less *ad-hoc*. In *Proc. of POPL'89*, pages 60–76. ACM Press, 1989.

[XCC03]   H. Xi, C. Chen, and G. Chen. Guarded recursive datatype constructors. In *Proc. of POPL'03*, pages 224–235. ACM Press, 2003.

[Zen99]   C. Zenger. *Indizierte Typen*. PhD thesis, Universität Karlsruhe, 1999.

Lock Free Data Structures Using STM in Haskell

Anthony Discolo[1], Tim Harris[2], Simon Marlow[2],
Simon Peyton Jones[2], and Satnam Singh[1]

[1] Microsoft, One Microsoft Way,
Redmond, WA 98052, USA
{adiscolo, satnams}@microsoft.com
http://www.research.microsoft.com/~satnams
[2] Microsoft Research, 7 JJ Thomson Avenue,
Cambridge, CB3 0FB, United Kingdom
{tharris, simonmar, simonpj}@microsoft.com

Abstract. This paper explores the feasibility of re-expressing concurrent algorithms with explicit locks in terms of lock free code written using Haskell's implementation of software transactional memory. Experimental results are presented which show that for multi-processor systems the simpler lock free implementations offer superior performance when compared to their corresponding lock based implementations.

1 Introduction

This paper explores the feasibility of re-expressing lock based data structures and their associated operations in a functional language using a lock free methodology based on Haskell's implementation of composable *software transactional memory* (STM) [1]. Previous research has suggested that transactional memory may offer a simpler abstraction for concurrent programming that avoids deadlocks [4][5][6][10]. Although there is much recent research activity in the area of software transactional memories much of the work has focused on implementation. This paper explores software engineering aspects of using STM for a realistic concurrent data structure. Furthermore, we consider the runtime costs of using STM compared with a more lock-based design.

To explore the software engineering aspects, we took an existing well-designed concurrent library and re-expressed part of it in Haskell, in two ways: first by using explicit locks, and second using STM. The comparison between these two implementations is illuminating.

To explore performance, we instrumented both implementations. In particular, we instrument the implementations using a varying number of processors in order to discover how much parallelism can be exploited by each approach. Our results should be considered as highly preliminary, because our STM implementation is immature.

Finally, we draw a conclusion about the feasibility of lock free data structures in Haskell with STM from both a coding effort perspective and from a performance perspective. Although previous work has reported micro-benchmarks [3] and application level benchmarks [1] for various STM implementation schemes we focus here on benchmarks which compare explicitly locked and lock free implementations based on STM.

M. Hagiya and P. Wadler (Eds.): FLOPS 2006, LNCS 3945, pp. 65–80, 2006.

2 Background: STM in Concurrent Haskell

Software Transactional Memory (STM) is a mechanism for coordinating concurrent threads. We believe that STM offers a much higher level of abstraction than the traditional combination of locks and condition variables, a claim that this paper should substantiate. In this section we briefly review the STM idea, and especially its realization in concurrent Haskell; the interested reader should consult [2] for much more background and details.

Concurrent Haskell [8] is an extension to Haskell 98, a pure, lazy, functional programming language. It provides explicitly-forked threads, and abstractions for communicating between them. These constructs naturally involve side effects and so, given the lazy evaluation strategy, it is necessary to be able to control exactly when they occur. The big breakthrough came from using a mechanism called *monads* [9]. Here is the key idea: a value of type **IO a** is an "I/O action" that, when performed may do some input/output before yielding a value of type **a**. For example, the functions **putChar** and **getChar** have types:

```
putChar :: Char -> IO ()
getChar :: IO Char
```

That is, **putChar** takes a **Char** and delivers an I/O action that, when performed, prints the string on the standard output; while **getChar** is an action that, when performed, reads a character from the console and delivers it as the result of the action. A complete program must define an I/O action called **main**; executing the program means performing that action. For example:

```
main :: IO ()
main = putChar 'x'
```

I/O actions can be glued together by a *monadic bind* combinator. This is normally used through some syntactic sugar, allowing a C-like syntax. Here, for example, is a complete program that reads a character and then prints it twice:

```
main = do { c <- getChar; putChar c; putChar c }
```

Threads in Haskell communicate by reading and writing *transactional variables*, or **TVars**. The operations on **TVars** are as follows:

```
data TVar a
newTVar   :: a -> STM (TVar a)
readTVar  :: TVar a -> STM a
writeTVar :: TVar a -> a -> STM ()
```

All these operations all make use of the *STM monad*, which supports a carefully-designed set of transactional operations, including allocating, reading and writing transactional variables. The **readTVar** and **writeTVar** operations both return STM actions, but Haskell allows us to use the same **do {...}** syntax to compose STM actions as we did for I/O actions. These STM actions remain tentative during their execution: in order to expose an STM action to the rest of the system, it can be passed to a new function **atomically**, with type

```
atomically :: STM a -> IO a
```

It takes a memory transaction, of type **STM a**, and delivers an I/O action that, when performed, runs the transaction atomically with respect to all other memory transactions. For example, one might say:

```
main = do { ...; atomically (getR r 3); ... }
```

Operationally, **atomically** takes the tentative updates and actually applies them to the **TVar**s involved, thereby making these effects visible to other transactions. The **atomically** function and all of the **STM**-typed operations are built over the software transactional memory. This deals with maintaining a per-thread transaction log that records the tentative accesses made to **TVar**s. When **atomically** is invoked the STM checks that the logged accesses are *valid* − i.e. no concurrent transaction has committed conflicting updates. If the log is valid then the STM *commits* it atomically to the heap. Otherwise the memory transaction is re-executed with a fresh log.

Splitting the world into STM actions and I/O actions provides two valuable guarantees: (i) only STM actions and pure computation can be performed inside a memory transaction; in particular I/O actions cannot; (ii) no STM actions can be performed outside a transaction, so the programmer cannot accidentally read or write a **TVar** without the protection of **atomically**. Of course, one can always write **atomically (readTVar v)** to read a **TVar** in a trivial transaction, but the call to **atomically** cannot be omitted. As an example, here is a procedure that atomically increments a **TVar**:

```
incT :: TVar Int -> IO ()
incT v = atomically (do x <- readTVar v
                        writeTVar v (x+1))
```

The implementation guarantees that the body of a call to **atomically** runs atomically with respect to every other thread; for example, there is no possibility that another thread can read **v** between the **readTVar** and **writeTVar** of **incT**.

A transaction can block using **retry**:

```
retry :: STM a
```

The semantics of **retry** is to abort the current atomic transaction, and re-run it after one of the transactional variables has been updated. For example, here is a procedure that decrements a **TVar**, but blocks if the variable is already zero:

```
decT :: TVar Int -> IO ()
decT v = atomically (do x <- readTVar v
                        if x == 0
                           then retry
                           else return ()
                        writeTVar v (x-1))
```

Finally, the **orElse** function allows two transactions to be tried in sequence: (**s1** `orElse` **s2**) is a transaction that first attempts **s1**; if it calls **retry**, then **s2** is tried instead; if that retries as well, then the entire call to **orElse** retries. For example, this procedure will decrement **v1** unless **v1** is already zero, in which case it will decrement **v2**. If both are zero, the thread will block:

```
decPair v1 v1 :: TVar Int -> TVar Int -> IO ()
decPair v1 v2 = atomically (decT v1 `orElse` decT v2)
```

In addition, the STM code needs no modifications at all to be robust to exceptions. The semantics of **atomically** is that if an exception is raised inside the transaction, then no globally visible state change whatsoever is made.

3 Programming ArrayBlockingQueue Using STM

We selected the **ArrayBlockingQueue** class from JSR-166 [7] as the basis for our experiment. We use this class solely as an example from an existing library, rather than intending to make comparisons between the Haskell versions and those in Java. The name **ArrayBlockingQueue** is a bit of a misnomer, since this class represents a fixed length queue but contains blocking, non-blocking, and timeout interfaces to remove an element from the head of the queue and insert an element into the tail of the queue. The combination of these interfaces in one class complicates the implementation.

We built two implementations of (part of) the **ArrayBlockingQueue** data type in Haskell. The first, **ArrayBlockingQueueIO**, is described in Section 3.1, and uses a conventional lock-based approach. The second, **ArrayBlock- ingQueueSTM,** is described in Section 3.2, and uses transactional memory. Our goal is to contrast these two synchronization mechanisms, so we have tried to maintain as much shared code as possible, aside from synchronization.

We did not implement all interfaces of the Java ArrayBlockingQueue class. Instead, we selected representative methods from each of the three interfaces, as well as a few methods from other utility interfaces:

- **take:** Removes an element from the head of the queue, blocking if the queue is empty
- **put:** Inserts an element at the tail of the queue, blocking until space is available if the queue is full
- **peek:** Removes an element from the head of the queue if one is immediately available, otherwise return Nothing
- **offer:** Inserts an element at the tail of the queue only if space is available
- **poll:** Retrieves and removes the head of this queue, or returns null if this queue is empty
- **pollTimeout:** Retrieves and removes the head of this queue, waiting up to the specified wait time if necessary for an element to become available
- **clear:** Atomically removes all elements from the queue.
- **contains:** Returns true if this queue contains the specified element.
- **remainingCapacity:** Returns the number of additional elements that this queue can ideally (in the absence of memory or resource constraints) accept without blocking
- **size:** Returns the number of elements in this queue
- **toArray:** Returns an array containing all of the elements in this queue, in proper sequence.

3.1 The Conventional Locking Implementation

Here is the Haskell data structure definition for the locking implementation:

```
data ArrayBlockingQueueIO e = ArrayBlockingQueueIO {
  iempty :: QSem,
  ifull :: QSem,
  ilock :: MVar (),
  ihead :: IORef Int,
  itail :: IORef Int,
  iused :: IORef Int,
  ilen :: Int,
  ia :: IOArray Int e
  }
```

A bit of explanation is necessary for readers not familiar with Haskell. The data block defines a data structure with named fields. The *e* in the definition is a *type variable* enabling an arbitrary type to be used over the fields. The format of each field is <field name> :: <type>. The following lists the types used in the structure:

- **QSem**: a traditional counting semaphore
- **MVar ()**: a mutex
- **IORef Int** : a pointer to an integer
- **IOArray Int e**: a pointer to an array of objects of type *e* indexed over integers

Let's now take a look at the implementation of some of the methods. Here is the top-level implementation of **takeIO**, which removes an element from the queue:

```
takeIO :: ArrayBlockingQueueIO e -> IO e
takeIO abq
  = do b <- waitQSem (iempty abq)
       e <- withMVar
              (ilock abq)
              (\dummy -> readHeadElementIO abq True)
       return e
```

The **takeIO** method must first wait for the **iempty** semaphore using **waitQSem** and then lock the queue mutex with **withMVar**. The mutex is necessary because the **iempty** and **ifull** semaphores simply signal the availability of a queue element or an empty slot in the queue, and they do not guarantee mutual exclusion over any of the fields of the **ArrayBlockingQueueIO** structure. Given this structure may be accessed concurrently by multiple threads, the mutex is necessary. Therefore, after acquiring the **iempty** semaphore, the queue lock must also be acquired before calling **readHeadElementIO** to read a queue element. The complexity of managing the semaphores and the lock over all the methods is considerable, as we will see in the remainder of this section.

Here is the top-level implementation of **peekIO**, which looks at the first element of the queue, without removing it:

```
peekIO :: ArrayBlockingQueueIO e -> IO (Maybe e)
peekIO abq
  = do b <- tryWaitQSem (iempty abq)
       if b
         then do
           me <- withMVar
                   (ilock abq)
                   (\dummy -> do
                       u <- readIORef (iused abq)
                       if u == 0
                           then return Nothing
                           else do
                             e <- readHeadElementIO
                                     abq
                                     False
                             return (Just e))
           signalQSem (iempty abq)
           return me
         else return Nothing
```

Because **peek** is a non-blocking method, the acquisition of the **iempty** semaphore is attempted with **tryWaitQSem**, which returns true if the semaphore was acquired. The remainder of the peek logic is executed only if the semaphore is acquired. In addition, the **iempty** semaphore must be signaled since the queue element value was copied and not actually removed from the queue. Care has to be taken to prevent bugs such as returning without releasing the mutex or acquiring multiple mutexes in the correct order, for example. This shows how fragile the synchronization code is in the locking version.

In order to get a complete picture of the take/peek code path, we must look at the implementation of **readHeadElementIO**:

```
readHeadElementIO :: ArrayBlockingQueueIO e -> Bool
                     -> IO e
readHeadElementIO abq remove
  = do h <- readIORef (ihead abq)
       e <- readArray (ia abq) h
       if remove
         then do let len = ilen abq
                     newh = h `mod` len
                 u <- readIORef (iused abq)
                 writeIORef (ihead abq) newh
                 writeIORef (iused abq) (u-1)
                 signalQSem (ifull abq)
         else return ()
       return e
```

Here, the different types of synchronization require different logic from the implementation. The locking version **readHeadElementIO** requires that the initial acquisition of the **iempty** semaphore and the queue mutex occur outside the method invocation. If **readHeadElementIO** were only used by **takeIO** and **peekIO**, then this would not be the case, but we invite the curious reader to look at the implementation of **pollTimeoutIO** and **pollReaderIO** below for yet another synchronization requirement imposed by that code path. The **readHeadElementIO** method takes a remove parameter that specifies whether the head element is copied or removed from the queue. If the element is removed, then the **ifull** semaphore must be signaled to signify that the queue has shrunk by one element.

Finally, let us look at the implementation of the most complex method in the **ArrayBlockingQueue** implementation: **pollTimeoutIO**. This method issues a blocking read from the head of the queue with a timeout.

```
data TimeoutContext e = TimeoutContext {
  done :: MVar Bool,
  val :: Chan (Maybe e)
  }

newTimeoutContextIO :: IO (TimeoutContext e)
newTimeoutContextIO
  = do d <- newMVar False
       c <- newChan
       return (TimeoutContext d c)

pollTimeoutIO :: ArrayBlockingQueueIO e
                 -> TimeDiff -> IO (Maybe e)
pollTimeoutIO abq timeout
  = do ctx <- newTimeoutContextIO
       forkIO (pollReaderIO abq ctx)
       forkIO (pollTimerIO timeout ctx)
       me <- readChan (val ctx)
       return me
```

In order to achieve a temporarily blocking read, the implementation of **pollTimeoutIO** forks two new threads, one responsible for the read (**pollReaderIO**) and one responsible for the timeout (**pollTimerIO**). A data structure (**TimeoutContext**) is shared between them to synchronize which thread finishes first and to hold the return value, if any.

```
pollReaderIO :: ArrayBlockingQueueIO e
                -> TimeoutContext e -> IO ()
pollReaderIO abq ctx
  = do waitQSem (iempty abq)
       modifyMVar
         (done ctx)
         (\d -> do
            if not d
              then do
                e <- withMVar
                       (ilock abq)
```

```
        (\dummy ->
            readHeadElementIO abq True)
    writeChan (val ctx) (Just e)
    else signalQSem (iempty abq)
return True)
```

The **pollReaderIO** method requires a bit of explanation. It first must wait for the queue's **iempty** semaphore to become available, signifiying an element is able to be read. It then atomically reads the **TimeoutContext's** done flag to see if the timeout thread has already completed. If the timeout has not occurred, then it reads the element from the queue, placing it in the **TimeoutContext's** result channel. If the timeout has occurred, then the thread signals the **iempty** semaphore, effectively making the element readable by another thread. After the checks have been made, then the done flag is released.

```
startTimerIO :: TimeDiff -> IO (Chan ())
startTimerIO timeout
  = do c <- newChan
       forkIO (timerIO c timeout)
       return c

timerIO :: Chan () -> TimeDiff -> IO ()
timerIO c timeout
  = do let td = normalizeTimeDiff timeout
       let ps = (tdSec td) * 1000000
       threadDelay ps
       writeChan c ()
       return ()

pollTimerIO :: TimeDiff -> TimeoutContext e -> IO ()
pollTimerIO timeout ctx
  = do c <- startTimerIO timeout
       readChan c
       modifyMVar
         (done ctx)
         (\d -> do
            if not d
              then writeChan (val ctx) Nothing
              else return ()
            return True)
```

The **pollTimerIO** method implements a timer with respect to the read being performed by the **pollReaderIO** thread, It uses the **startTimerIO** method that simply writes **Nothing** into a channel after the timeout has occurred[1]. The **poll-TimerIO** method simply issues a blocking read on the timer channel to wait for the

---

[1] While threadDelay could be used directly instead of calling startTimerIO in the locking version, the additional thread is required by the STM implementation. See the next section for more detail.

timeout, and then writes **Nothing** into the **TimeoutContext**'s result channel signifying a timeout has occurred only if it is the first thread to access the **Timeout-Context** structure.

3.2 The STM Implementation

Here is the Haskell data structure definition for the STM version:

```
data ArrayBlockingQueueSTM e = ArrayBlockingQueueSTM {
  shead :: TVar Int,
  stail :: TVar Int,
  sused :: TVar Int,
  slen :: Int,
  sa :: Array Int (TVar e)
}
```

The following lists the types used in the structure above:

- **TVar Int**: a transacted integer
- **Array Int (TVar e)**: a array of transacted objects of type *e* indexed over integers

Note that the **ArrayBlockingQueueSTM** data structure definition is considerably simpler because it lacks the two semaphores and one mutex that are present in the **ArrayBlockingQueueIO** implementation. As we will see, this simplicity translates in to simpler implementations for all methods as well. For example, here is **takeSTM**:

```
takeSTM :: ArrayBlockingQueueSTM e -> IO e
takeSTM abq
  = do me <- atomically
               (readHeadElementSTM abq True True)
       case me of
         Just e -> return e
```

The atomic block in **takeSTM** provides the only synchronization necessary in order to call **readHeadElementSTM** in the STM version. The implementation of peek is equally simple:

```
peekSTM :: ArrayBlockingQueueSTM e -> IO (Maybe e)
peekSTM abq
  = atomically (readHeadElementSTM abq False False)
```

Again, in comparison with the locking version, there is considerably less complexity in the STM version, because the **readHeadElementSTM** method is simply called within an atomic block. Here is the implementation of **readHeadElementSTM**:

```
readHeadElementSTM :: ArrayBlockingQueueSTM e
                      -> Bool -> Bool -> STM (Maybe e)
readHeadElementSTM abq remove block
```

```
        = do u <- readTVar (sused abq)
             if u == 0
                then if block
                         then retry
                         else return Nothing
                else do h <- readTVar (ihead abq)
                         let tv = sa abq ! h
                         e <- readTVar tv
                         if remove
                             then do
                                 let len = slen abq
                                 let newh = h `mod` len
                                 writeTVar (shead abq) $! newh
                                 writeTVar (sused abq) $! (u-1)
                             else return ()
                         return (Just e)
```

The STM version **readHeadElementSTM** takes a **remove** parameter and a **block** parameter. In contrast to **readHeadElementIO**, the **readHeadElementSTM** method contains all the synchronization logic for the take/peek path. Note how the blocking read path is implemented with a **retry** statement. This effectively restarts the entire atomic block from the beginning and is much easier for the programmer to utilize correctly than the combination of semaphores and mutexes. The entire implementation of **readHeadElementSTM** is more concise and clear than the implementation of **readHeadElementIO**.

Finally, here is **pollTimeoutSTM**:

```
pollTimeoutSTM :: ArrayBlockingQueueSTM e
                         -> TimeDiff -> IO (Maybe e)
pollTimeoutSTM abq timeout
    = do c <- startTimerIO timeout
         atomically ((do readTChan c
                          return Nothing)
                     `orElse`
                     (do me <- readHeadElementSTM
                                   abq True True
                         return me))
```

Compared to **pollTimeoutIO**, notice how concise and natural the implementation of **pollTimeoutSTM** is with the use of the **orElse** statement within the atomic block. Fundamentally, there are three steps: (1) start the timer, (2) try to read from the timer channel signifying timeout period has elapsed, and if successful return **Nothing**, and (3) try to read an element from the head of the queue, and if successful return the element. If neither (2) nor (3) are satisfied, then the atomic block is restarted until one of these branches is successful.

The **retry** and **orElse** methods are very powerful features of the Haskell STM implementation and deserve more discussion. The **retry** method can be invoked anywhere inside the STM monad and restarts the atomic block from the beginning.

The Haskell STM runtime manages transacted variables in an intelligent way and transparently blocks the transaction until one of the transacted variables has been modified. (Note there *cannot* be non-transacted variables within the STM monad.) In this way, the atomic block does not execute unless there is some chance that it can make progress.

Conditional atomic blocks or join patterns can be implemented with the **orElse** method. Note how the locking version forks two worker threads with a custom synchronization data structure, and how the custom synchronization logic between the two worker threads affects the synchronization logic throughout the rest of the program. In the STM version, the worker threads and custom synchronization logic are replaced by *one* **orElse** statement. This one statement more accurately reflects the programmer's intent in that allows the runtime to more efficiently and intelligently manage the execution of the atomic block. For example, if additional processors are available, each branch of the **orElse** statement may be executed on different processors and synchronized within the runtime, or each branch may be run sequentially.

3.3 Summary

It should have become clear by now that it is much easier to write thread-safe code using STM than using locks and condition variables. Not only that, but the STM code is far more robust to exceptions. Suppose that some exception happened in the middle of **takeIO**. For example, a null-pointer dereference or divide by zero. If such a thing could happen, extra exception handlers would be required to restore invariants and release locks, otherwise the data structure might be left in an inconsistent state. This error recovery code is very hard to write, even harder to test, and in some implementations may have a performance cost as well.

In contrast, the STM code needs no modification at all to be robust to exceptions, since **atomically** prevents any globally visible state changes from occurring if an exception is raised inside the atomic block.

4 Performance Measurements

Once we completed the locking and lock-free implementations of ArrayBlockingQueue, we measured their performance under various test loads.

4.1 Test Setup

The test harness includes the following command line parameters:

- test implementation (locking or STM)
- number of reader and writer threads
- number of iterations per thread
- length of the ArrayBlockingQueue

For this paper, we chose to investigate the performance of the blocking ArrayBlockingQueue methods. Specifically, we wanted to determine whether the respective implementations ran faster as additional threads are created and/or additional processors are added, keeping all other parameters the same.

The test creates an ArrayBlockingQueue of type integer is created, and an equal number of reader and writer threads are created that simply loop for the specified number of iterations performing take or put operations on the queue. The test completes when all threads have terminated.

For each processor configuration (1-8 processors), we varied only the number of threads in each test, so that the parameters of each test were {2, 4, 6, 8, 10, 12, 14} reader/writer threads, 100000 iterations, and queue length 100.

All of our measurements were made on our prototype implementation of STM in Haskell. This implementation is immature and has received little performance tuning. In particular, memory is reclaimed by a basic single-threaded stop-the-world generational collector. This degrades the performance of the STM results because the current STM implementation makes frequent memory allocations. In ongoing work we are developing a parallel collector and also removing the need for dynamic memory allocation during transactions. Nevertheless the measurements are useful to give a very preliminary idea of whether or not the two approaches have roughly comparable performance.

While the GHC runtime has a wide variety of debugging flags that can be used to monitor specific runtime events, this paper only focuses on the elapsed time of the tests. We ran each test on a Dell Optiplex 260 Pentium 4 3GHz CPU with 1GB RAM running Windows XP Professional SP2 and with successive processors enabled on a 4-way dual core Opteron HP DL585 multiprocessor with 1MB L2 cache per processor and 32GB RAM running Windows XP Server 2003 64-bit SP1 resulting in nine runs total per test. Our main interest was not the actual elapsed time values, but how the performance changed as additional processors were enabled.

4.2 Performance Results

The performance results are shown in the following figures.

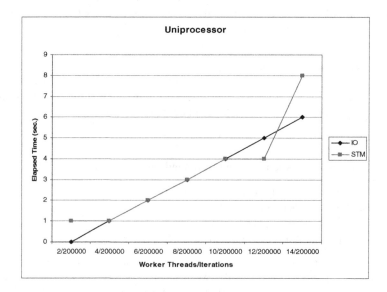

Fig. 1. Uniprocessor Performance

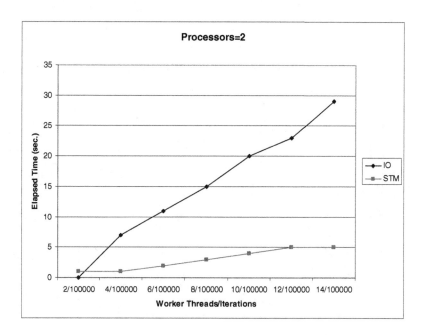

Fig. 2. Two Processor Performance

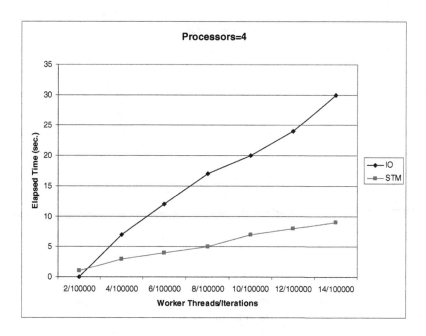

Fig. 3. Four Processor Performance

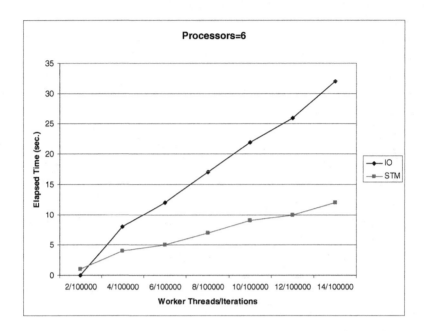

Fig. 4. Six Processor Performance

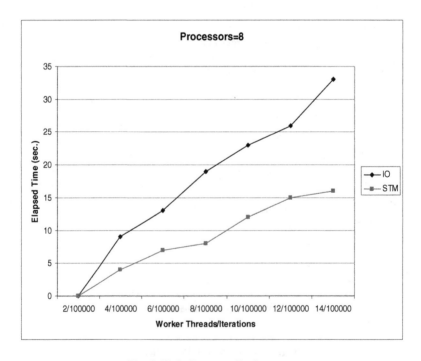

Fig. 5. Eight Processor Performance

The results are very encouraging. On a uniprocessor, the performance of the locking version and the STM version were virtually identical. Once two or more processors were enabled, the STM version was consistently faster than the locking version running on the same number of processors. In fact, the fastest times on two or more processors were achieved by the STM version.

The STM and locking implementations are not exactly identical in their behavior. An important difference is the way in which each implementation deals with exceptions. The STM implementation has, in effect, a built in default exception handler which will cause the transaction to be rolled back. The locking version does not have this robust behavior, so that unexpected exceptions could leave the queue in an inconsistent state. It could be modified to handle exceptions and restore invariants, but that would make the code more complicates still, and would degrade performance. Consequently we should expect the performance of the STM implementation to improve even further over the locking version once error handling code has been added.

5 Related Work

Related work by Carlstrom et. al. [1] has shown that the conversion of lock based Java programs to versions that use transactions is often straightforward and sometimes leads to performance improvements. Hammond et. al. [3] used the TestHistrogram micro-benchmark which counts random numbers between 0 and 100 in bins. They also observed scaling for a transactional version up to 8 CPUs. Many benchmarks compare a single processor lock version of an algorithm against a transactional version that can scale up with the number of processors. In our experimental work we designed both the lock version and transactional versions to have the potential for exploiting extra processors.

6 Future Work

We are now investigating to what extent our observations apply to STM implementations in an imperative language. We are taking the same **ArrayBlockingQueue** example and coding it in C# with explicit locks and then again using an STM library called SXM [5]. The SXM library has user configurable conflict managers which will give us greater experimental control to help understand what kind of polices work best under different kinds of loads. We believe the best way to understand the characteristics of various STM implementation schemes is to build libraries and applications that place representative stresses on the underlying implementation.

7 Conclusions

It has been claimed that lock free concurrent programming with STM is easier than programming explicitly with locks. Our initial investigation into the re-implementation of a concurrent data structure and its operations from the JSR-166 suite in a functional language suggests that it is indeed the case that STM based code is easier to write and far less likely to be subject to deadlocks. Furthermore, the optimistic concurrency features of the STM implementation that we used offer considerable performance advantages on SMP multi-processor and multi-core systems compared to pessimistic lock based implementations.

The STM programming methodology is much easier to understand, concise, and less error-prone than traditional locking methodology using mutexes and semaphores. A key feature of the Haskell STM implementation is the **orElse** combinator which we used to *compose* small transactions into composite transactions. Haskell's type system also helped to statically constrain our programs to avoid stateful operations in transactions which can not be rolled back by prohibiting expressions in the IO monad in transactions.

Even with a very early implementation of the STM multiprocessor runtime, the STM implementation consistently outperformed the locking version when two or more processors were available. We expect even better STM performance as the language runtime implementation matures.

The encouraging initial results with library level units of concurrent data structures and operations paves the path for us to now build and instrument entire applications built out of lock free data structures designed using the functional language based methodology presented in this paper. Although locks still have a role in certain kinds of low level applications we believe that application level concurrency may often be tackled more effectively with STM as demonstrated in this paper.

References

1. B. D. Carlstrom, J. Chung, H. Chafi, A. McDonald, C. Minh, L. Hammond, C. Kozyrakis, K. Olukotun. Transactional Execution of Java Programs. SCOOL 2005.
2. T. Harris, S. Marlow, S. Peyton Jones, M. Herlihy. Composable Memory Transactions. PPoPP 2005.
3. L. Hammond, B. D. Carlstrom, V. Wong, B. Hertzberg, M. Chen, C. Kozyrakis, and K. Olukotun. Programming with transactional coherence and consistency. In Proceedings of the 11th International Conference on Architecture Support for Programming Languages and Operating Systems, Oct. 2004.
4. T. Harris and K. Fraser. Language support for lightweight transactions. In OOPSLA '03: Proceedings of the 18th annual ACM SIGPLAN conference on Object-oriented programming, systems, languages, and applications, pages 388–402. ACM Press, 2003.
5. M. P. Herlihy, V. Luchangco, M. Moir, and W. M. Scherer. Software transactional memory for dynamic-sized data structures. In Proceedings of the 22nd Annual Symposium on Principles of Distributed Computing, July 2003.
6. M. Herlihy and J. E. B. Moss. Transactional memory: Architectural support for lock-free data structures. In Proceedings of the 20th International Symposium. on Computer Architecture 1993.
7. Itzstein, G. S, Kearney, D. Join Java: An alternative concurrency semantics for Java. Tech. Rep. ACRC-01-001, University of South Australia, 2001.
8. S. Peyton Jones, A. Gordon, and S. Finne. Concurrent Haskell. In 23rd ACM Symposium on Principles of Programming Languages (POPL'96), pp. 295–308.
9. S. Peyton Jones and P. Wadler. Imperative functional programming. In 20th ACM Symposium on Principles of Programming Languages (POPL'93), pp. 71–84.
10. N. Shavit and S. Touitou. Software transactional memory. In Proc. of the 14th Annual ACM Symposium on Principles of Distributed Computing, Ottawa, Canada, August 1995.

XML Type Checking Using High-Level Tree Transducer

Akihiko Tozawa

IBM Research,
Tokyo Research Laboratory, IBM Japan ltd., Japan
atozawa@jp.ibm.com

Abstract. XML type checking recently attracts interests of researchers. We discuss this problem for programs using higher order functions. In particular, we discuss programs modeled by the high-level tree transducer which was introduced by Engelfriet. We give one algorithm of XML type checking for this transducer.

1 Introduction

In this paper, we discuss *XML type checking*. XML type checking uses data types modeled by tree regular languages, which we call XML types. Such data types are very different from traditional data types. This is one reason why the XML type checking problem recently attracts much interests of researchers.

XDuce [HP03] and CDuce [FCB02] are examples of functional languages with XML type checking. They are general-purpose languages with full computational power. However the type checking for these languages is weak in some sense. In particular, they require programmers to figure out type annotations to make functions in the program pass the type check. To the contrary, it is also known in the literature, if we restrict the language, we achieve stronger properties in type-checking. Typically, we use tree transducers for this purpose. Two good properties of XML type checking for tree transducers are (1) exact type checking, and (2) type checking without redundant type annotation.

A number of tree transducers are studied in the literature as the model of XML programming. In this paper, we employ the *high-level tree transducer*, first introduced by Engelfriet [EV88]. As far as we know, this transducer is not yet discussed in the context of XML programming. Given an input tree, tree transducers output trees. The high-level tree transducer, similarly given an input tree, creates functional values. In other words, we can use higher order function – more precisely, simply-typed lambda calculus – in high-level tree transducers. This makes it even possible to translate certain higher-order (simply-typed) programs into high-level transducers.

The common technique in tree transducer approaches to XML type checking is the inverse type inference, i.e., from an *output* XML type and tree transducer, we create an *input* XML type. In this paper, to apply this technique to high-level tree transducers, we use the *abstract interpretation* of values emitted by transducers.

For the abstract interpretation, we start from the finite algebras called *binoids*. Any XML type can be captured by some binoid and homomorphism from XML values to this binoid. Such homomorphism can be extended to functional values. As far as type-checking is concerned, we always consider functional values under abstract interpretation by this homomorphism. Our inverse type inference is done by combining Maneth's

M. Hagiya and P. Wadler (Eds.): FLOPS 2006, LNCS 3945, pp. 81–96, 2006.

algorithm and such abstract interpretation. The correctness of the abstract interpretation is resulted from the property called *non-observability* of high-level tree transducers. Namely, functional values created by high-level tree transducers cannot inspect XML values given as their arguments.

Let us outline the rest of the paper. Section 2 discusses the problem we deal with in a ML-style functional language. Section 3 gives a formal discussion and high level tree transducers. Section 4 gives the type checking algorithm. Section 5 summarizes the related work. Section 6 discusses the future work.

2   The Language and Problem

An ML-like Language for XML Programming. We first introduce an ML-like yet simply-typed functional language with higher order functions. This language supports XML programming. In particular, this language manipulates two XML values, *input* XML values and *output* XML values. Input XML values are only processed. We however cannot create input XML values in the language, so that such values are always supplied from the outer world. On the other hand, output XML values, or we can say, *non-observable* XML values, are only constructed. We do not have any method to inspect their structures.

Let us explain the language step by step. As an example, we use the following program representing the identity tree transformation.

> letrec $id^{(i \to o)}$ $x :=$
> $*x[$if $x \models 1$ then $id\ x \cdot 1$ else $()]$, (if $x \models 2$ then $id\ x \cdot 2$ else $()$)
> in id

First, we have sorts. In the program, we see a superscript $i \to o$ appearing on id. This superscript indicates a sort, i.e., simple type, of the function variable id. Let $\mathcal{B} = \{i, o, \mathbb{B}, \mathbb{L}\}$. This $\mathcal{B}$ is the set of base sorts. Sort i corresponds to input XML values. Input XML values indicate some nodes in the input XML document. Sort o corresponds to output XML values. Output XML values are sequences of XML trees. Sorts $\mathbb{B}$ and $\mathbb{L}$ are sorts for boolean values and labels, respectively. We use b to range over base sorts. We extend base sorts $\mathcal{B}$ to sorts $\mathcal{S}(\mathcal{B})$ for functional values as

$$\mathcal{S}(\mathcal{B}) \ni s ::= b \mid s \to s$$

where $b \in \mathcal{B}$. We use s to range over sorts. Here $\to$ associates to the right as usual. Note that in sorts, their constructors $i, o, \mathbb{B}, \mathbb{L}$ and $\to$, are just syntactical objects.

In the rest of the paper, we often make sorts of function variables explicit for readability. In practice, sorts of variables as well as those of expressions can be, though not uniquely, inferred by known unification-based algorithms such as the one in a textbook [Mit96]. Note that sorts are not types in this paper – we will introduce types themselves later.

Next, this language has a set of constant primitives. They operate on input and output XML values of sorts i and o.

XML instances given as inputs, are seen as binary trees which are navigated by using the set of primitives. For input XML values of sort i, we define operators $\cdot 0$, $\cdot 1$, and $\cdot 2$ as follows.

This figure illustrates an XML instance a[b[]],c[] seen as a binary tree. Assume that a node $x^{(i)}$ is the root of the above XML instance. From x, we reach a node labeled by b using $x \cdot 1$, and a node labeled by c using $x \cdot 2$, and from these nodes we can move back to the root node by $x \cdot 1 \cdot 0$ or $x \cdot 2 \cdot 0$. Predicates $x \models 0$, $x \models 1$ and $x \models 2$ represent tests whether it is allowed to move to that direction. If there are no nodes in that direction the test fails. We can also obtain the label of the node by $*x$. For instance, we have $*x = $ a on the root node x.

For construction of output XML values, we have a constant $()^{(o)}$ which represents a null sequence, and two operators; $\_[\_]^{(\mathbb{L} \to o \to o)}$ and $(\_,\_)^{(o \to o \to o)}$. The operator $\_[\_]^{(\mathbb{L} \to o \to o)}$ creates a node $\ell[t]$ from the label ℓ and an output XML value t. The operator $(\_,\_)^{(o \to o \to o)}$ concatenates two output XML values.

Furthermore, the language has the if-construct and equality test on the finite set of labels. We also have letrec for defining mutually recursive functions.

Finally, we emphasize what this language does *not* have. Although we can convert an XML value x of sort i into the same value of sort o using $id^{(i \to o)} x$, the conversion in the reverse direction is not expressed in the language. Namely, the language does not have a primitive constant of sort $o \to i$ representing this reverse conversion. Neither we can define a program performing such a conversion. In general, our language can neither create input XML values, e.g., $x^{(i)} := $ a[], nor inspect the information of some output XML values, e.g., $*t$ for an output XML value t.

Using Higher-order Functions. In XML programming, the use of higher order functions have a number of advantages. Here we look through several use cases of higher order functions through examples. We later translate functional programs into transducers. We here only discuss functions for which such translation is possible.

A typical higher order function is the *map* function, which applies a function given as an argument to a set of elements at once. In XML programming, it is particularly useful to have map functions which apply argument functions to nodes selected by a certain criteria, e.g., children, following siblings, etc. The following functions *chilren* and *siblings* take argument functions of sort $i \to o$, and return the concatenation of the results of applications.

$children^{(i \to (i \to o) \to o)} \ x \ f := $ if $x \models 1$ then $siblings \ x \cdot 1 \ f$ else $()$
$siblings^{(i \to (i \to o) \to o)} \ x \ f := f \ x$, if $x \models 2$ then $siblings \ x \cdot 2 \ f$ else $()$

Example 1. For example, when applied to the root node x of an input tree a[b[],c[],d[]], *children* $x \ f$ returns $f \ (x \cdot 1), f \ (x \cdot 1 \cdot 2), f \ (x \cdot 1 \cdot 2 \cdot 2)$.

Functions such as *chilren* and *siblings* are usually supplied as library functions, rather than being a part of the user program. With such library functions, programmers do not have to deal with primitive navigation operators such as $x \cdot m$ ($x \cdot 0$, $x \cdot 1$ and $x \cdot 2$). Furthermore, by using these functions, we can implement the identity function simply as follows.

letrec $id^{(i \to o)} \ x := children \ x \ id$ in id

Not only map functions, but we can also provide library functions for testing the document structure. For example, a function which tests the existence of a child node of $x^{(i)}$ with a certain label $l^{(L)}$ i.e., corresponding to the XPath predicate $[x/l]$, can be written in a manner similar to the function *children*. More generally, we can even implement a deterministic (binary) tree automaton which tests the substructure of the input tree [Toz05].

Another interesting application of higher order functions is to use them for representing XML values containing holes. Such holes are also called *gap* in the language JWIG and XACT [CMS03, KMS04]. For instance, a value $p^{(o \to o)}$ represents a value (called *template*) with gaps whose gaps can be filled at once by a value $v^{(o)}$ by the application $(p\ v)^{(o)}$. E.g., $p^{(o \to o)}\ v := \text{dept}[v]$ is a template $\text{dept}[\square]$ where $\square$ is the position of a gap. This gap can be filled by $\text{emp}[]$ as $p\ \text{emp}[] = \text{dept}[\text{emp}[]]$.

We can implement a set of *gap operators* using higher order functions.

(i)	$(\square)^{(o \to o)}\ v$	$:= v$
(ii)	$(\text{`\_})^{(o \to o \to o)}\ v\ w$	$:= v$
(iii)	$conc^{((o \to o) \to (o \to o) \to o \to o)}\ p\ q\ v := p\ v, q\ v$	
(iv)	$node^{(L \to (o \to o) \to o \to o)}\ l\ p\ v := l[p\ v]$	
(v)	$plug^{((o \to o) \to (o \to o) \to o \to o)}\ p\ q\ v := p\ (q\ v)$	

The gap operators implement the following operations.

Example 2. Some examples on the use of the gap operators. (i) $\square$ is a template made of a single gap. (ii) `$\text{`dept}[]$ is a template $\text{dept}[]$ with no gaps. (iii) *conc* $\text{dept}[\square]\ \square =$ $\text{dept}[\square], \square$. (iv) *node* comp $\text{dept}[\square] = \text{comp}[\text{dept}[\square]]$. (v) *plug* $\text{dept}[\square]\ \text{emp}[\square] =$ $\text{dept}[\text{emp}[\square]]$.

Using gap operators, for example, we can implement the following function translating $\text{a}[\text{b}[]], \text{c}[]$ into $\text{a}[\text{b}[\square]], \text{c}[\square]$.

```
letrec gapid(i→o→o) x :=
   conc (node *x (if x ⊨ 1 then gapid x·1 else □)) (if x ⊨ 2 then gapid x·2 else `())
in gapid
```

As shown here, programs can create functions through partial application. Compared to other tree transducers, e.g., macro tree transducers, this creation of functional values adds an additional expressive power to the language. In general, by raising the order of sorts of functional values, i.e., $o, o \to o, (o \to o) \to o \to o$ and so on, we can arbitrarily increase the expressive power of the language.

Type-Checking Problem. Types for XML values, i.e., instances of sorts i or o, are described by tree regular expressions, such as $\tau = (\text{a}[\text{b}[]^*] \cup \text{c}[])^*$. For example, *id* transforms any XML value into itself, hence a value of type $(\text{a}[\text{b}[]^*] \cup \text{c}[])^*$ into the value of the same type. This observation is denoted by $id : (\text{a}[\text{b}[]^*] \cup \text{c}[])^* \to (\text{a}[\text{b}[]^*] \cup \text{c}[])^*$. For a function with sort $i \to o$, the type checking problem $f_I^{(i \to o)} : \upsilon_I \to \tau_I$ can be stated as follows.

Problem 1. (Type checking) Given a program $f_I^{(i \to o)}$, an input type υ_I and output type τ_I, the type checking problem $f_I^{(i \to o)} : \upsilon_I \to \tau_I$ is to test whether or not the transformation of any XML value of type υ_I produces an XML value of type τ_I.

In understanding Problem 1, we need to clarify the case when the transformation does not terminate. There is a choice whether or not we include the non-termination in type errors. In this paper, we chose to include it.

We say the type-checking is *decidable* for some class of transformations, if we have an algorithm exactly answering to Problem 1. The type checking for the language we are discussing, and satisfying the restrictions given in the next paragraph, is decidable.

Restrictions on the Functional Language. We can solve the type checking problem for the language introduced so far, when the program of interest can be translated into a high-level tree transducer. Unfortunately, not all programs can be translated into such tree transducers. Sufficient restrictions on programs which make this translation possible are as follows.

- Any function or variable $f^{(s)}$ declared in let or letrec as $f^{(s)}x := e$, either has their sort $s = b$ or $s = s_1 \rightarrow \cdots \rightarrow s_{n-1} \rightarrow b$, such that none of $s_2, ..., s_{n-1}, b$ are i. Namely, only the first argument can be of sort i. Note that we do not restrict sorts in the form $i \rightarrow s$ to appear other argument positions, e.g., $children^{(i\rightarrow(i\rightarrow o)\rightarrow o)}$.
- Any function of sort $i \rightarrow s$ must be declared in the top-level letrec of the program. In other words, they must not be defined in a letrec within another letrec.

These two restrictions correspond to the fact that the tree transducer only have a single input parameter (= first restriction) and a finite set of states (= first and second restrictions). Obviously, we cannot have a function definition of sort $i \rightarrow \underline{i} \rightarrow s$, because it means that this function has multiple input parameters (we underline the erroneous part). In the translation, functions of sort $i \rightarrow s$ are seen as the finite set of states. This is guaranteed only if there are finitely many possibilities for such functions. Assume that there is a function f with sort $(i \rightarrow s) \rightarrow \underline{i} \rightarrow s$ and g with sort $i \rightarrow s$. In our language, we can create fg, $f(fg) = f^2g$, $f(f(fg)) = f^3g$, and so on. In particular, we can enumerate such functional values up to $f^n g$, where, for example, n is the size of the input to the program. This makes the translation into tree transducers impossible, since the number of states should not be related to the size of any input. The use of nested let and letrec for functions of sort $i \rightarrow s$ also causes the same problem.

3   Values, Tree Automata and High-Level Tree Transducers

We introduce XML values, and then tree automata which are the model of XML types. We discuss the syntax and semantics of the high-level tree transducer in the latter half of this section.

Here are some notations used throughout. We consistently use bold font, e.g., $\boldsymbol{a}$, to emphasize meta-variables denoting words or tuples. We use $\epsilon \in A^*$ for an empty word, and an associative operator $(\cdot)$ for word concatenation. We let $\mathbb{B} = \{$true, false$\}$ be the set of boolean values. This $\mathbb{B}$ appears in the text, so that there should be no confusion with the symbol $\mathbb{B}$ appearing in sorts.

XML Values. An XML value is a sequence of unranked ordered trees over the finite set $\mathbb{L}$ of labels. We fix this set $\mathbb{L}$ throughout the paper. The set of XML values is defined as follows.

$$V \ni t ::= () \mid \ell[t] \mid t, t$$

where $\ell \in \mathbb{L}$. We omit () if it is directly enclosed in $\ell[\_]$. We assume that $\_,\_$ is associative and () is an identity. As explained earlier, an XML value can also be seen as a binary tree, since each t is represented either as $\ell[t_1]$, t_2 or (). For each t, its domain $dom(t) \subseteq \{1, 2\}^*$ is the set of locations, when seen as a binary tree, of that tree. We define the set of tree nodes U by

$$U = \bigcup_{t \in V} \Big(\{t\} \times dom(t) \Big).$$

That is, U is the set of all nodes in all trees. The label of a node $u \in U$ is denoted by $*u \in \mathbb{L}$. We can move inside XML trees by the operator $(\cdot m)$ $(m = 0, 1, 2)$. For $k \in dom(t)$

$$
\begin{array}{ll}
(t, k) \cdot m = (t, k \cdot m) & \text{if } m = 1, 2 \text{ and } k \cdot m \in dom(t) \\
(t, k \cdot k) \cdot m = (t, k) & \text{if } m = 0 \text{ and } k = 1, 2 \\
u \cdot m = \bot & \text{otherwise}
\end{array}
$$

The value $\bot$ here represents a non-existing node such that $\bot \notin U$. Finally, the set of root nodes $\Lambda(U) \subseteq U$ is a set $\{(t, \epsilon) \mid t \in V\}$.

XML Types and Tree Automata. We introduce XML types. Each XML type represents a certain set of XML values. We use metavariables τ, υ to range over XML types throughout the paper. As a candidate of models of XML types, we have tree regular expressions by Hosoya et al [HVP00]. For $\ell \in \mathbb{L}$, and α ranging over a set of type variables, tree regular expressions may use the syntax such as

$$T^{\mathbf{XML}} \ni \tau, \upsilon ::= () \mid \ell[\tau] \mid \tau, \tau \mid \tau \cup \tau \mid \tau^* \mid \mathtt{letrec}\ \alpha := \tau; \ldots \mathtt{in}\ \tau \mid \alpha.$$

Example 3. This is an example of XML type.

$$\mathtt{letrec}\ ds := \mathtt{dept}[es]^*;\ es := \mathtt{emp}[]^*\ \mathtt{in}\ \mathtt{comp}[ds]$$

It says that the root node is always comp and in which we have a sequence of dept nodes. Inside depts, we have emp nodes, and so on.

In this paper, we do not directly discuss the semantics $[\![\tau]\!] \subseteq V$ of the above syntax. Instead, we introduce tree automata which is well-known as a canonical model of XML types τ. Here we actually introduce three forms of them. The first one is the most standard.

Definition 1. *A (total) non-deterministic tree automaton $M = (Q, \Delta, F, \bullet)$ is a tuple where $\Delta \subseteq \mathbb{L} \times Q \times Q \times Q$ is a set of transitions, $F \subseteq Q$ is a set of final states and $\bullet \in Q$ is an initial state. A mapping $\mu \in U \rightarrow Q$ is called a run of M if $(*u, \mu(u), \mu(u \cdot 1), \mu(u \cdot 2)) \in \Delta$ for any $u \in U$, where we define $\mu(\bot) = \bullet$. An XML value with root node $u \in \Lambda(U)$ is accepted if there is a run μ such that $\mu(u) \in F$.*

We can assume for each XML type τ that we have a tree automaton $M(\tau)$ which defines the semantics $[\![\tau]\!] = \{t \in V \mid t \text{ accepted by } M(\tau)\}$. This is a standard assumption in the study of typed XML programming. See Hosoya et al. [HVP00], for this detail.

The second model of XML types has a form of algebra whose domain is finite. This algebra is called *binoid* [PQ68] in the literature, and is similar to *syntactic monoid* [Per90] for word languages. We employ this representation as a canonical model of output XML types in the type inference algorithm in Section 4. As we can see from the definition, this algebra classifies a set V of XML values into a certain set of finite equivalence classes. The equivalence classes are still diverse enough to check whether or not, an arbitrary XML construction creates the result inside $[\![\tau_I]\!]$. In other words, binoids provide the means of *abstract interpretation* of XML values.

Definition 2. *A binoid for* τ_I *is an algebra* $\mathcal{V}(\tau_I) = (V, \bullet, F, (\_[\_]), (\_ , \_))$ *such that (1)* V *is a finite set,* $\bullet \in V$ *and* $F \subseteq V$, *and (2)* $(V, (), [\![\tau^I]\!], (\_[\_]), (\_ , \_))$ *is homomorphic to* $\mathcal{V}(\tau_I)$. *That is, we have a mapping* $(\_^\circ) \in V \to \mathcal{V}$ *satisfying (i)* $()^\circ = \bullet$, *(ii)* $v \in [\![\tau^I]\!]$ *iff* $v^\circ \in F$, *(iii)* $(\ell[t])^\circ = \ell[t^\circ]$, *and (iv)* $(t , t')^\circ = t^\circ , t'^\circ$.

An algorithm, given a non-deterministic tree automaton representing τ_I, that constructs one binoid satisfying the above definition is known. For binoids $\mathcal{V}(\tau_I)$ with homomorphism $^\circ$, in what follows, we often use $()^\circ$ and $[\![\tau_I]\!]^\circ$ instead of $\bullet$ and F above, respectively.

Example 4. Consider the XML type comp[ds] in Example 3. Here, we give one binoid corresponding to this XML type. We here take a certain set of tree regular expressions as the domain of the binoid $\mathcal{V}(\text{comp}[ds])$. In the following, assume that τ_E represents a type for values that do not belong to other elements in the domain of $\mathcal{V}(\text{comp}[ds])$.

$$V = \{(), \text{dept}[es]^+, \text{emp}[]^+, \text{comp}[ds], \tau_E\}$$
$$()^\circ = ()$$
$$[\![\text{comp}[ds]]\!]^\circ = \{\text{comp}[ds]\}$$

$$\_[\_] = \begin{cases} \text{dept}, \text{emp}[]^+ \mapsto \text{dept}[es]^+ \\ \text{dept}, () \quad\quad \mapsto \text{dept}[es]^+ \\ \text{comp}, \text{emp}[]^+ \mapsto \tau_E \\ ... \end{cases}$$

$$\_,\_ = \begin{cases} (), \text{dept}[es]^+ \quad\quad\quad \mapsto \text{dept}[es]^+ \\ \text{dept}[es]^+, \text{dept}[es]^+ \mapsto \text{dept}[es]^+ \\ ... \end{cases}$$

We can confirm that this $\mathcal{V}(\text{comp}[ds])$ satisfies Definition 2 by using $(\_^\circ) \in V \to \mathcal{V}(\text{comp}[ds])$ such that $t \in [\![t^\circ]\!]$. For example, take $t = \text{dept}[], \text{dept}[]$. We have $(t,t)^\circ = \text{dept}[es]^+ = \text{dept}[es]^+ , \text{dept}[es]^+ = t^\circ , t^\circ$.

We lastly give yet another form of tree automata. This automaton provides a trick which will be used at the last step of the type inference algorithm, as the model of inferred input XML types. A short explanation of the automaton is that (1) it is a variant of deterministic 2-way tree automaton; (2) it allows cyclic runs; and (3) the transition function can look at a set of locations in the tree bounded by the finite set **Mov**.

We first explain the transition function δ of the look-around tree automaton. This δ takes as an argument, a set of information (the state-label pair) for each node $u \cdot m_i$ at the relative position m_i in $\textbf{Mov} = \{m_1, m_2, ...m_n\}$, and returns the state for the node u.

For each node u, this set of information is given as a *look-around function*, say $h \in \textbf{Mov} \to (\mathbb{L} \times Q)^{\perp} (= (\mathbb{L} \times Q) \uplus \{\perp\})$. This h takes an argument m representing a relative position, and returns the pair of the label of, and the state assigned to, the node $u \cdot m$. If there is no node at m i.e., $u \cdot m = \perp$, this h returns $\perp$.

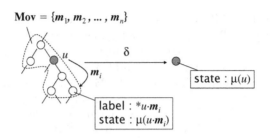

Definition 3. *A look-around tree automaton is* $M = (Q, \mathbf{Mov}, \delta, F)$ *such that* $\mathbf{Mov} \subset$ $\{0, 1, 2\}^*$ *is a finite set of moves,* $\delta \in (\mathbf{Mov} \to (\mathbb{L} \times Q)^{\perp}) \to Q$ *is a transition function. A mapping* $\mu \in U \to Q$ *is called a run of* M, *if* $\mu(u) = \delta(h)$ *for all* $u \in U$, *where the look-around function* $h \in \mathbf{Mov} \to (\mathbb{L} \times Q)^{\perp}$ *for this* u, *is defined from* μ *as*

$$h(\mathbf{m}) = (*u \cdot \mathbf{m}, \mu(u \cdot \mathbf{m})) \qquad \text{if } u \cdot \mathbf{m} \in U$$
$$h(\mathbf{m}) = \perp \qquad\qquad\qquad \text{otherwise}$$

The automaton accepts u *iff* $\mu(u) \in F$ *for some* μ.

Proposition 1. *[Toz05] Look-around tree automata accept exactly regular tree languages. And they can be efficiently converted into non-deterministic tree automata.*

High-level Tree Transducer. We introduce the high-level tree transducer as a model of XML transformation. Type checking for XML transformations in high-level tree transducers is decidable.

Tree transducers are tree automata with outputs. Recall that tree automata assign states to nodes. Another way to look at this is that tree automata associates state-node pairs with boolean values. On the other hand, tree transducers associate each such pair with an output value. For example, the identity function *id* given earlier, can be seen as a very simple tree transducer. This tree transducer has one state, say $\underline{id}$, and for each node u in the input tree, $\underline{id}$ is associated with an output tree identical to the subtree of u.

High-level tree transducers provide an extension of tree transducers. The distinction is that each evaluation step of the transducer creates a functional value rather than a tree value. In this sense, high-level tree transducers are closer to functional programs.

A rule of high-level tree transducer is of the form $f : y \triangleright e$ where f is a state, y is a sequence of parameter variables, and e is called a *term*. Here is an example of the rule, which corresponds to the function *children*.

$$\underline{children}^{(\mathbb{N} \to o)} : f \triangleright \mathtt{if}\ (\models 1)\langle \epsilon \rangle\ \mathtt{then}\ \underline{siblings}\langle 1 \rangle\ f\ \mathtt{else}\ ()$$

In this example, $\underline{children}$ is a state, f is a parameter variable, and $\mathtt{if} \cdots ()$ is a term. As we can see from above, a term is almost an expression of the functional language. Terms also should be well-sorted, cf., the definition of sorts $S(\mathcal{B})$ in Section 2. The only difference is that sorts for terms do not have any occurrence of i. Parameter variables y are also the same as those in $\mathtt{let}$ and $\mathtt{letrec}$. They just abbreviate λ-abstractions, i.e., $f : y \triangleright e$ is equivalent to $f : \triangleright \lambda y : e$ or $f : \triangleright \mathtt{let}\ g\ y := e\ \mathtt{in}\ g$.

The meaning of $\underline{siblings}\langle 1 \rangle$, $(\models 1)\langle \epsilon \rangle$, etc. in terms are supplied by looking into neighbor nodes. For example, the meaning of $\underline{siblings}\langle m \rangle$ is supplied by evaluating the state *siblings* at relative position m. Similarly, the meaning of $(*)\langle m \rangle$ is the label of the node at relative position m. And, the meaning of $(\models 1)\langle m \rangle$ is whether or not $\models 1$ holds at relative position m. Recall that the meaning of the tree transducer is given at each node $u \in U$. Therefore, when this node u is supplied, such relative positions 1 and ϵ are interpreted by $u \cdot 1$ and $u \cdot \epsilon = u$, respectively.

We call an arbitrary set X whose each element is associated with a sort, as *sorted set*.

- Figure 1 defines the sorted set **Term**(C, X) of terms over sorted sets C and X of constants and variables, respectively. We require that each term to be well-sorted in the usual sense for simple types.
- Figure 1 also defines a sorted set of basic constants **Con**.

Let N be a set of states, C be a set of constants which may include **Con**, and **Mov** $\subseteq$ $\{0, 1, 2\}^*$ be a set of moves. We call $(\models m)$ and $(*)$ *predicates*, whose set is denoted by P. We define $(N \uplus P)\langle \textbf{Mov} \rangle$ to be a set of pairs in the form $n\langle m \rangle$ such that $n \in N \uplus P$ and $m \in \textbf{Mov}$. Each term e appearing in the rule $f : y \triangleright e$, is an element of **Term**$(C, y \uplus (N \uplus P)\langle \textbf{Mov} \rangle)$.

Let us define the high-level tree transducer. Note that our high-level tree transducers are stronger than original versions by Engelfriet [EV88]. An essential difference is that our transducer allows the recursive inspection of the input tree. For example, the function *autom* in Section 2 cannot be captured by the Engelfriet's definition of the deterministic high-level tree transducer (which is a top-down tree transducer). This is comparable to the transducer with regular look-ahead [Eng77]. Also our tree transducer is a tree-walking transducer with upward moves inside the input tree using $(\_ \cdot 0)$-operator.

In the following, for each sorted set X, we denote by $X(s)$, a subpart of X whose elements are associated with sort s.

Definition 4. *A (look-around deterministic) high-level tree-transducer $\mathcal{H}$ over a finite set of labels $\mathbb{L}$ is a tuple $\mathcal{H} = (\mathcal{B}, N, C, P, \textbf{Var}, \textbf{Mov}, \underline{f}_I, R)$ where*

- *$\mathcal{B}$ is a set of base sorts. We have $o, \mathbb{L}, \mathbb{B} \in \mathcal{B}$, but not $i \in \mathcal{B}$. In the following, all elements of sorted sets have sorts in $\mathcal{S}(\mathcal{B})$.*
- *N is a sorted set of states.*
- *C is a sorted set of constants. We have $\textbf{Con} \subseteq C$.*
- *$P \subseteq \{(\models m) \mid m \in \{0, 1, 2\}\} \uplus \{(*)\}$ is a set of predicates. Predicates $(\models m)$ and $(*)$ are associated with sort $\mathbb{B}$ and $\mathbb{L}$ respectively.*
- *$\textbf{Var}$ is a sorted set of variables.*
- *$\textbf{Mov} \subseteq \{0, 1, 2\}^*$ is a finite set of moves.*
- *$\underline{f}_I \in N$ is an initial state.*
- *R is a finite set of rules in the form $f : y \triangleright e$.*
  - *For each $f \in N$, we have exactly one rule in R.*
  - *If $f \in \overline{N}(s_1 \to \cdots \to s_n)$ and $y = y_1, ..., y_{n-1}$, we have (i) $y_j \in \textbf{Var}(s_j)$ for $j \in \overline{1}..n-1$, (ii) $e \in \textbf{Term}(C, y \uplus (N \uplus P)\langle \textbf{Mov} \rangle)(s_n)$.*

We do not fix the set of base sorts $\mathcal{B}$, so that we can add a new sort. However we always require that such sorts are associated with finite domains. This will be used in defining the denotations of values of each sort. See Figure 2.

Term$(C, X) \ni e ::=$

| c | $(c \in C$, constants)
| x | $(x \in X$, variables)
| ee | (application)
| if e then e else e | (conditional)
| letrec $fx := e; \cdots$ in e | (recursive def.)

Con $\ni c ::=$

| $true^{(\mathbb{B})}$ | $false^{(\mathbb{B})}$ | (boolean constants)
| $\ell^{(\mathbb{L})}$ | $(\ell \in \mathbb{L}$, label constants)
| $(\_ = \_)^{(\mathbb{L} \to \mathbb{L} \to \mathbb{B})}$ | (label equality)
| $()^{(o)}$ | (empty tree)
| $(\_[\_])^{(o \to o \to o)}$ | (node constructor)
| $(\_, \_)^{(o \to o \to o)}$ | (tree concatenation)

Fig. 1. Definition of **Term**(C, X) and **Con**

Domains

$$\mathcal{D}[\![o]\!] = V^{\perp}$$
$$\mathcal{D}[\![b]\!] = b^{\perp} \quad \text{where } b \neq o$$
$$\mathcal{D}[\![s' \to s]\!] = [\mathcal{D}[\![s']\!] \to_{\perp} \mathcal{D}[\![s]\!]]^{\perp}$$

$\mathcal{D}[\![\text{if } e \text{ then } e' \text{ else } e'']\!]\rho =$

$$\begin{cases} \mathcal{D}[\![e']\!]\rho & \text{if } \mathcal{D}[\![e]\!]\rho = true \\ \mathcal{D}[\![e'']\!]\rho & \text{if } \mathcal{D}[\![e]\!]\rho = false \\ \perp & \text{otherwise} \end{cases}$$

$$\mathcal{D}[\![\text{letrec } \theta \text{ in } e]\!]\rho = \mathcal{D}[\![e]\!]lfp(\zeta_{\theta,\rho})$$

where

Semantic function

$$\mathcal{D}[\![x]\!]\rho = \rho(x)$$
$$\mathcal{D}[\![c]\!]\rho = c$$
$$\mathcal{D}[\![ee']\!]\rho = \mathcal{D}[\![e]\!]\rho(\mathcal{D}[\![e']\!]\rho)$$

$$\zeta_{\theta,\rho'} (\in (X(\cdot) \to \mathcal{D}[\![\cdot]\!]) \to (X(\cdot) \to \mathcal{D}[\![\cdot]\!])) =$$

$$\lambda\rho : \rho' \left[f \mapsto \begin{array}{l} \lambda v \in \mathcal{D}[\![s_1, ..., s_{n-1}]\!] : \\ \mathcal{D}[\![e]\!]\rho[x \mapsto v] \end{array} \right]_{(f^{(s_1 \to \cdots \to s_n)}x := e^{(s_n)}) \in \theta}$$

Fig. 2. Semantic function $\mathcal{D}[\![\_]\!]_\_ \in \textbf{Term}(C, X)(\cdot) \to (X(\cdot) \to \mathcal{D}[\![\cdot]\!]) \to \mathcal{D}[\![\cdot]\!]$

Functional programs introduced and satisfying the restriction in Section 2, can be translated into high-level tree transducers. Recall that those programs already have shapes similar to transducers, i.e., functions of sort $i \to s$ only occur at top-level letrec. Therefore, the translation is straightforward. We here just give ideas. See [Toz05] for the detailed steps.

Essentially, what we need is to remove the occurrence of expressions of sort $i, i \to i$, and $i \to s$. Functional variables of sorts $i \to s$ defined in the top-level letrec correspond to the finite set of states N. Their definitions are easily translated into rules of the tree transducer. However, variables of sort $i \to s$ may also occur as parameter variables, e.g., an argument of $children^{(i \to (i \to o) \to o)}$. In this case, we interpret such variables as variables of a new base sort $\mathbb{N}$. We then prepare a finite set of constants of sort $\mathbb{N}$, which has one-to-one correspondence to the state set N. We also prepare the equality operator $(\_ = \_)^{(\mathbb{N} \to \mathbb{N} \to \mathbb{B})}$ over $\mathbb{N}$.

Semantics of High-Level Tree Transducers. In the original definition by Engelfriet, the semantics of high-level tree transducers is given by means of rewrite systems, which correspond to the operational semantics. In this paper, we give a denotational semantics. This gives a clear meaning to functional values emitted by the high-level tree transducer.

In the denotational semantics, the meaning of a transducer $\mathcal{H}$ is defined on each node u in U. This meaning is an assignment $\rho \in (N \uplus P)(\cdot) \to \mathcal{D}[\![\cdot]\!]$, such that each element in subset $N(s)$ of states, as well as $P(s)$ of predicates, is associated with an element in $\mathcal{D}[\![s]\!]$. Here $\mathcal{D}[\![s]\!]$ is the cpo-based semantic domain given in Figure 2. In other words, $\mathcal{D}[\![s]\!]$ is the set of functional values of sort s (See the end of this paragraph). We give a meaning to each node by the following function $sem_{\mathcal{H}} : U \to (N \uplus P)(\cdot) \to \mathcal{D}[\![\cdot]\!]$.

Definition 5. *Given* $\mathcal{H} = (\mathcal{B}, N, C, P, \mathbf{Var}, \mathbf{Mov}, \underline{f}_{\mathbf{I}}, R)$. *The meaning function* $sem_{\mathcal{H}}$:
$U \rightarrow (N \uplus P)(\cdot) \rightarrow \mathcal{D}[\![\cdot]\!]$ *is defined as the least solution satisfying the following
equations. For any* $\underline{f} \in N$ *such that* $(\underline{f} : y \rhd e) \in R$, *and* $(*), (\models m) \in P$,

$$sem_{\mathcal{H}}(u)(*) = *u$$
$$sem_{\mathcal{H}}(u)(\models m) = (u \cdot m) \in U$$
$$sem_{\mathcal{H}}(u)(\underline{f}) = \mathcal{D}[\![\lambda y : e]\!][n\langle m\rangle \mapsto sem_{\mathcal{H}}(u \cdot m)(n)]_{n \in N \uplus P, m \in \mathbf{Mov}}$$

where $\mathcal{D}[\![e]\!]\rho$ *is a semantics of term* e *under* ρ *given in Figure 2, in which* $\lambda y : e$ *ab-
breviates* letrec $g\, y := e$ in g. *In particular, for the root node* $u \in \Lambda(U)$, $sem_{\mathcal{H}}(u)(f_{\mathbf{I}})$
defines the output of the transducer.

The definition of $\mathcal{D}[\![e]\!]\rho$ is the standard cpo semantics of simply-typed call-by-value
languages [Mit96]. Let us briefly recall this semantics. A cpo $(X, \sqsubseteq)$ is a poset whose any
directed subset has the lub. Starting from flat cpos $\mathcal{D}[\![b]\!]$ for base sorts, we can obtain cpo
for continuous function spaces $\mathcal{D}[\![s' \rightarrow s]\!]$. Partial orders for functions are defined as
$f \sqsubseteq g$ iff $\forall x : f(x) \sqsubseteq g(x)$. In the case of call-by-value, we use a strict continuous function
space $[A^{\perp} \rightarrow_{\perp} B^{\perp}](\simeq [A \rightarrow B^{\perp}])$ such that $f \in [A^{\perp} \rightarrow_{\perp} B^{\perp}]$ satisfies $f(\perp) = \perp$, i.e., the
application of a function to an error value results in an error value, i.e., non-termination.
In the cpo-based semantics, the meaning of recursive functions is the least fixpoint of
some equations. The above $sem_{\mathcal{H}}$ is indeed such a least fixpoint.

4   Type Checking

So far, we have introduced three tools, namely

- Binoids with homomorphism °,
- Look-around tree automata, and
- Tree-transducer and its semantics.

Here we connect these tools and derive our type inference algorithm. In particular,
the key idea is the extension of the homomorphism ° for binoids to functional spaces
$\mathcal{D}[\![s' \rightarrow s]\!]$.

A common technique to the tree transducer type checking is based on the inverse
type inference. In the case of tree transducers or macro tree transducers (mtts), the
inverse image $f_{\mathbf{I}}^{-1}(\tau_{\mathbf{I}})$ is regular. The expressiveness of high-level tree transducers is
the same as k-composition of mtts [EV88], where k is the height of sorts. Therefore the
inverse image $f_{\mathbf{I}}^{-1}(\tau_{\mathbf{I}})$ should be a regular language also for high-level tree transducers.
However, as far as we know, there is no direct construction algorithm of the inverse
image of high-level tree transducers. We give one such construction here.

Maneth [EM03] gave a simple algorithm inferring regular inverse images for deterministic mtts. His idea was to *run* the automaton, representing $\tau_{\mathbf{I}}$, on the term e of the
rule $\underline{f} : y \rhd e$. In his case, this term defines a tree value, while in our case, it defines
a functional value. To interpret e in our case, we extend the homomorphism ° between
the set of XML values V and the binoid $\mathcal{V}(\tau_{\mathbf{I}})$.

Extending Homomorphism ° to Functional Space. Given a type $\tau_{\mathbf{I}}$, we can obtain a
finite binoid $\mathcal{V}(\tau_{\mathbf{I}})$ with the homomorphism ° from V to $\mathcal{V}(\tau_{\mathbf{I}})$. This homomorphism is
seen as an abstraction function from infinite values to finite elements.

Here let us extend this definition of $^\circ$ to domains $\mathcal{D}[\![s]\!]$ where s is other than o. We define the domain of images of $^\circ$ as follows, so that for $v \in \mathcal{D}[\![s]\!]$ we have $v^\circ \in \mathcal{A}[\![s]\!]$.

$$\begin{aligned}
\mathcal{A}[\![o]\!] &= \mathcal{V}(\tau_I)^\perp \\
\mathcal{A}[\![b]\!] &= \mathcal{D}[\![b]\!] \quad \text{where } b \neq o \\
\mathcal{A}[\![s' \to s]\!] &= [\mathcal{A}[\![s']\!] \to_\perp \mathcal{A}[\![s]\!]]^\perp
\end{aligned}$$

Then, the idea is to define $^\circ \in \mathcal{D}[\![\cdot]\!] \to \mathcal{A}[\![\cdot]\!]$ so that it further satisfies

$$v^\circ(v'^\circ) = (v(v'))^\circ$$

for $v \in \mathcal{D}[\![s' \to s]\!]$ and $v' \in \mathcal{D}[\![s']\!]$. Intuitively, this means that the abstraction interpretation is equivalent to the abstraction of concrete evaluation. This property guarantees the correctness of abstract interpretation by $^\circ$.

Example 5. We assume the binoid $\mathcal{V}(\text{comp}[ds])$ in Example 4. Let us consider templates of sort $o \to o$. For example, $p = \text{comp}[\text{dept}[\Box]] \ (\in \mathcal{D}[\![o \to o]\!])$. What we need here is to define $p^\circ \in [\mathcal{V}(\text{comp}[ds])^\perp \to_\perp \mathcal{V}(\text{comp}[ds])]^\perp \ (= \mathcal{A}[\![o \to o]\!])$ as a function.

$$p^\circ(a) = \begin{cases} \text{comp}[ds] & \text{if } a = \text{emp}[]^+ \text{ or } a = () \\ \tau_E & \text{otherwise, } a \neq \perp \\ \perp & a = \perp \end{cases}$$

This function indeed satisfies $p^\circ(v'^\circ) = (p(v'))^\circ$ for $v' \in V$. For example, assume $v' = \text{dept}[]$. We have $p^\circ(v'^\circ) = p^\circ(\text{dept}[es]^+) = \tau_E$, and $(p(v'))^\circ = (\text{comp}[\text{dept}[\text{dept}[]]])^\circ = \tau_E$.

Note that the homomorphic images $\mathcal{A}[\![s]\!]$ of $\mathcal{D}[\![s]\!]$ are finite sets. The function $^\circ$ gives a way to interpret each value as an abstract value. Such abstract values are suitable for analysis, because they are finitely enumerable.

Definition 6. *The abstraction function* $^\circ \in \mathcal{D}[\![\cdot]\!] \to \mathcal{A}[\![\cdot]\!]$ *is a partial function defined as follows. We use the induction of the size of s in extending $^\circ$ to $\mathcal{D}[\![s]\!] \to \mathcal{A}[\![s]\!]$.*

- $v^\circ = v \ (\in \mathcal{A}[\![b]\!])$, *if* $v \in \mathcal{D}[\![b]\!]$ *for* $b \in \mathcal{B} \setminus \{o\}$.
- *A value* $v \in \mathcal{D}[\![s' \to s]\!]$ *is in the domain of* $^\circ$ *written* $v \in Dom(^\circ)$, *if for any* v' *and* $v'' \ (\in Dom(^\circ) \cap \mathcal{D}[\![s']\!])$ *such that* $v'^\circ = v''^\circ$, *this* v *satisfies* $(v(v'))^\circ = (v(v''))^\circ$.
- *For* $v \in Dom(^\circ) \cap \mathcal{D}[\![s' \to s]\!]$, *we define* $v^\circ \ (\in \mathcal{A}[\![s' \to s]\!])$ *to be the function defined as*

$$v^\circ(a) = \begin{cases} (v(v'))^\circ & \text{if } a = v'^\circ \text{ for some } v' \in \mathcal{D}[\![s']\!] \\ \perp & \text{otherwise} \end{cases}$$

The above definition, however, is not so interesting, since it just says that we ignore values $v \notin Dom(^\circ)$. That is, we ignore values do not satisfy the desired property. What is more interesting is the following result.

Lemma 1. *For any* $^\circ$, *all outputs* $v \ (\in \mathcal{D}[\![s]\!])$ *of transducers are in* $Dom(^\circ)$.

From this lemma, we can show that any output f of transducers of sort $o \to \mathbb{B}$ is a constant function. We take a singleton set $\mathcal{V} = \{\bullet\}$ as the homomorphic image of V. Then for any t, t', we have $t^\circ = t'^\circ = \bullet$, so that $f(t) = (f(t))^\circ = (f(t'))^\circ = f(t')$. This is the meaning of *non-observability* of values of sort o. We will discuss this again later.

Negative Inverse Type Inference. The remaining steps of the type inference algorithm are as follows.

- Interpreting the meaning function $sem_{\mathcal{H}}$ by $\circ$, and obtain $sem^{\circ}_{\mathcal{H}}$.
- Defining the look-around tree automaton $\mathcal{M}$ capturing $sem^{\circ}_{\mathcal{H}}$. This $\mathcal{M}$ gives the result of type inference.

Accurately speaking, what the above $\mathcal{M}$ represents, is a *negative* inverse image $f_{\mathbf{I}}^{-1}(V \setminus \tau_{\mathbf{I}})$. This is fortunate. After we inferred such an image, what we need is the emptiness check, which is known to be efficient.

$$[\![v_{\mathbf{I}}]\!] \cap [\![f_{\mathbf{I}}^{-1}(V \setminus \tau_{\mathbf{I}})]\!] = \emptyset$$

If this holds, the type checking succeeds. If $\mathcal{M}$ was $f_{\mathbf{I}}^{-1}(\tau_{\mathbf{I}})$, the above emptiness check turns to the containment test, which is not always efficient. We later explain why our construction creates an automaton for such a negative image.

First, we *interpret* the semantic function $sem_{\mathcal{H}}$ by means of $\circ$ just introduced. Indeed, this can be done. This gives a function $sem^{\circ}_{\mathcal{H}} (\in U \rightarrow (N \uplus P)(\cdot) \rightarrow \mathcal{A}[\![\cdot]\!])$ given as follows.

Definition 7. *The abstract meaning function* $sem^{\circ}_{\mathcal{H}} : U \rightarrow (N \uplus P)(\cdot) \rightarrow \mathcal{A}[\![\cdot]\!]$ *is the least solution of the following equations. For any* $\underline{f} \in N$ *such that* $(\underline{f} : y \triangleright e) \in R$, *and* $(*), (\models m) \in P$,

$$sem^{\circ}_{\mathcal{H}}(u)(*) = *u$$
$$sem^{\circ}_{\mathcal{H}}(u)(\models m) = (u \cdot m) \in U$$
$$sem^{\circ}_{\mathcal{H}}(u)(\underline{f}) = \mathcal{A}[\![\lambda y : e]\!][n\langle \boldsymbol{m}\rangle \mapsto sem^{\circ}_{\mathcal{H}}(u \cdot \boldsymbol{m})(n)]_{n \in N \uplus P, m \in \mathbf{Mov}}$$

where $\mathcal{A}[\![e]\!]\rho$ *is the abstract semantics of term* e *under* ρ *given similarly to Figure 2, except that it interprets* $()$, $\ell[\_]$ *and* $(\_,\_)$ *by the corresponding operators for* $\mathcal{V}(\tau_{\mathbf{I}})$.

This function satisfies the following property for all $u \in U$ and $n \in N \uplus P$, cf., Lemma 2(a).

$$(sem_{\mathcal{H}}(u)(n))^{\circ} = sem^{\circ}_{\mathcal{H}}(u)(n)$$

What remains is to define the look-around automaton that captures this $sem^{\circ}_{\mathcal{H}}$. The resulting automaton is given as follows.

Definition 8. *Given a transducer* $\mathcal{H}$, *and a binoid* $\mathcal{V}(\tau_{\mathbf{I}})$, *we define a look-around automaton* $\mathcal{M} = (Q, \mathbf{Mov}, \delta, F)$ *as follows.*

- **Mov** *is the same as* $\mathcal{H}$,
- $Q = (N \uplus P)(\cdot) \rightarrow \mathcal{A}[\![\cdot]\!]$,
- $\delta \in (\mathbf{Mov} \rightarrow (\mathbb{L} \times Q)^{\perp}) \rightarrow Q$ *is defined as follows where* $lab(\ell, q) = \ell$, $st(\ell, q) = q$ *and* $lab(\perp) = st(\perp) = \perp$.

$$\delta(h)(\models m) = (h(m) \neq \perp)$$
$$\delta(h)(*) = lab(h(\epsilon))$$
$$\delta(h)(\underline{f}) = \mathcal{A}[\![\lambda y : e]\!][n\langle \boldsymbol{m}\rangle \mapsto st(h(\boldsymbol{m}))(n)]_{n \in N \uplus P, m \in \mathbf{Mov}} \qquad \text{for all } \underline{f} : y \triangleright e \in R$$

- $F = \{\rho \in Q \mid \rho(f_{\mathbf{I}}) \notin [\![\tau_{\mathbf{I}}]\!]^{\circ}\}$.

This automaton has its state set $Q = (N \uplus P)(\cdot) \to \mathcal{A}[\![\cdot]\!]$. This set Q classifies the nodes of the input XML tree according to the (abstract) output value of the transducer at its each state. A run of $\mathcal{M}$ gives one such classification of nodes in the input XML tree. Now, recall that the same information was given by $sem^\circ_\mathcal{H}$, which defines the abstract semantics of the transducer for each state-node pair. Indeed, this automaton captures $sem^\circ_\mathcal{H}$ in the sense that $sem^\circ_\mathcal{H}$ is always a run of $\mathcal{M}$. Confirm that the run of automaton $\mu \in U \to Q$ and $sem^\circ_\mathcal{H}$ ($\in U \to (N \uplus P)(\cdot) \to \mathcal{A}[\![\cdot]\!]$) has the same signature. Also notice the similarity between the transition function δ of $\mathcal{M}$ and the definition of $sem^\circ_\mathcal{H}$. This δ is defined so that it simulates $sem^\circ_\mathcal{H}$.

As readers may expect, this $\mathcal{M}$ exactly defines the negative inverse image we want.

Lemma 2. *[Toz05] (a) For all $u \in U$ and $n \in N \uplus P$, we have $(sem_\mathcal{H}(u)(n))^\circ = sem^\circ_\mathcal{H}(u)(n)$. (b) $sem^\circ_\mathcal{H}$ is the least run of $\mathcal{M}$. (c) The automaton $\mathcal{M}$ in Definition 8 accepts u iff $sem_\mathcal{H}(u)(f_I) \notin [\![\tau_I]\!]$.*

We here note why we need to infer the *negative* inverse image. This is related to our treatment of *non-termination as error*, cf., Section 2.

In Definition 8, we define the final states F of $\mathcal{M}$ negatively, i.e., acceptance means type error. Note that if the program is correct, i.e., $sem_\mathcal{H}(u)(f_I) \in [\![\tau_I]\!]$, then $sem^\circ_\mathcal{H}$ should also give the correct result in $[\![\tau_I]\!]^\circ$. From the above lemma (b), if $sem^\circ_\mathcal{H}$ gives the correct result, i.e., is a *non-accepting* run of $\mathcal{M}$, then "any run" is also non accepting. This shows the *only-if* direction of Lemma (c) (the other direction is easy).

Now, assume that we include $\bot$ (non-termination) to the correct result. In this case, we cannot say more than "some run is correct" from the fact that $sem^\circ_\mathcal{H}$ gives the correct result. In fact, in this case, we must have defined the set of final states of $\mathcal{M}$ *positively*.

Non-observability. Lemma 1 says that the outputs of tree transducers are always in $Dom(\circ)$. This leads us to define the new semantic domain defined as follows. Let Ξ be the set of homomorphisms $\circ$ from V to arbitrary algebras $\mathcal{V} = (\mathcal{V}, (), (\_, \_), (\_[\_]))$.

$$\mathcal{D}_{NO}[\![s]\!] = \{v \in \mathcal{D}[\![s]\!] \mid \text{for any } (\circ) \in \Xi, \text{ we have } v \in Dom(\circ)\}$$

where $Dom(\circ)$ is defined by Definition 6.

This domain $\mathcal{D}_{NO}[\![s]\!]$ satisfies several interesting properties.

Proposition 2. *[Toz05] (a) All $f \in \mathcal{D}_{NO}[\![o \to \mathbb{B}]\!]$ and $f \in \mathcal{D}_{NO}[\![o \to \mathbb{L}]\!]$ are constant functions. (b) All $f \in \mathcal{D}_{NO}[\![o \to o]\!]$ represent XML templates, cf. Section 2.*

The proposition (a) can be understood from the analogy to types such as $\forall \alpha : \alpha \to \mathbb{B}$ in parametric polymorphism. In languages with parametric polymorphism and without side-effects, values of this type are always constant functions. The proposition (b) intuitively says that only XML templates are functions from XML values to XML values which do not inspect information, e.g., labels, widths, depths, etc., of arguments.

By assuming this non-observability semantics, we can extend our type checking algorithm for the higher-order cases, i.e., the type checking for problems of sort other than $i \to o$. Refer to the full paper for the detail of this result.

5   Related Work

Milo et al. [MSV00] first proposed a solution, based on *inverse type inference*, to the type checking for XML programming modeled by tree transducers. Milo et al. solved this problem for *k*-pebble transducers (a generalization of attribute grammars, cf. [EM03]). The *k*-pebble transducers are in theory $k + 1$-fold composition of macro tree transducers [EM03], and it is comparable to high-level tree transducers, which is also represented by *k*-composition of macro tree transducers where *k* is the height of sorts [EV88]. Similar approaches were studied for different kinds of tree transducers [MN02, MBPS05].

XDuce [HVP00, HP03] is a pioneering work on typed functional XML programming, which employs type checking *with* type-annotation. XDuce is a first order language. Its approach has also been employed in a number of typed XML processing languages, including an industrial language such as XQuery. Frisch et al. [FCB02] extended tree regular expression types in XDuce to higher order functional types. Their language is called CDuce.

XDuce and CDuce require type annotations. In general, they cannot solve the type checking problem such as id : a[b[]] $\rightarrow$ a[b[]] as it is, by the following reasons.

- When using XDuce, we can annotate id only by trivial types, e.g., *Any* $\rightarrow$ *Any*. For example, when we type-check id against a[b[]] $\rightarrow$ a[b[]], we have to check id also against b[] $\rightarrow$ b[]. This is not possible in XDuce which associates a single arrow type with each recursive function.
- CDuce has intersection types. By giving a type annotation a[b[]] $\rightarrow$ a[b[]] $\cap$ b[] $\rightarrow$ b[], the function id passes the type check. It is even possible to *prove* that id : a[b[]] $\rightarrow$ a[b[]] holds. This is based on their subtyping algorithm.

  a[b[]] $\rightarrow$ a[b[]] $\cap$ b[] $\rightarrow$ b[] <: a[b[]] $\rightarrow$ a[b[]]

  However this process is still not automatic. Users need to figure out what type annotation is necessary in beforehand.

Among other approaches to XML type checking for general-purpose languages, one employed in JWIG and XACT [CMS03, KMS04] is interesting. Their algorithm is based on forward inference. Recently, they also combined their approach with flow-sensitive analysis. As a result, they can check id without redundant type annotations. This should be compared with the inverse type inference approach.

6   Future Work

As a concluding remark, we note several future directions of this work.

- *Practical use with XML programming.* We implemented a prototype type-checker, and tried several experiments. Unfortunately, for programs using functions of large sorts, the initial result was not promising. This reflects the time complexity of the algorithm, which is *k*-exponential to the program size and $k + 1$-exponential to the size of τ_I, where *k* is the height of sorts. However, in practical programming, it is not so usual to use functions whose order is more than second. So it is too early to conclude that the approach is infeasible. Our implementation essentially implements the enumeration of states of automata M in Section 4. We are currently seeking a different algorithm for the practical use.

- *Connection to type systems.* Type-checking is the central issue of functional programming. It is interesting to ask if our XML type checking can be captured *type systems*. We believe that CDuce's type system is a candidate [FCB02]. However this is a type-annotation system. Therefore the next question is whether or not we have type-inference or partially type-annotated systems comparable to our type checking.

Acknowledgment

I thank to anonymous referees for suggestive comments to the earlier draft of this paper. I also thank to Makoto Murata for proof-reading.

References

[CMS03]   Aske Simon Christensen, Anders Møller, and Michael I. Schwartzbach. Extending Java for high-level Web service construction. *ACM Transactions on Programming Languages and Systems*, 25(6):814–875, November 2003.

[EM03]   J. Engelfriet and Sebastian Maneth. A comparison of pebble tree transducers with macro tree transducers. *Acta Informatica*, 39:613–698, 2003.

[Eng77]   Joost Engelfriet. Top-down tree transducer with regular look-ahead. *Mathematical Systems Theory*, 9(3):289–303, 1977.

[EV88]   Joost Engelfriet and Heiko Vogler. High level tree transducers and iterated pushdown tree transducers. *Acta Informatica*, 26(2):131–192, 1988.

[FCB02]   Alain Frisch, Giuseppe Castagna, and Veronique Benzaken. Semantic Subtyping. In *Proceedings, Seventeenth Annual IEEE Symposium on Logic in Computer Science*, pages 137–146. IEEE Computer Society Press, 2002.

[HP03]   Haruo Hosoya and Benjamin C. Pierce. Regular expression pattern matching for XML. *J. Funct. Program.*, 13(6):961–1004, 2003.

[HVP00]   Haruo Hosoya, Jérôme Vouillon, and Benjamin C. Pierce. Regular expression types for XML. In *Proceedings of the International Conference on Functional Programming (ICFP)*, pages 11–22, Sep., 2000.

[KMS04]   Christian Kirkegaard, Anders Møller, and Michael I. Schwartzbach. Static analysis of XML transformations in Java. *IEEE Transactions on Software Engineering*, 30(3):181–192, March 2004.

[MBPS05]   Sebastian Maneth, Alexandru Berlea, Thomas Perst, and Helmut Seidl. Xml type checking with macro tree transducers. In *PODS 2005, to appear*, 2005.

[Mit96]   John C. Mitchell. *Foundations of programming languages*. MIT Press, 1996.

[MN02]   Wim Martens and Frank Neven. Typechecking top-down uniform unranked tree transducers. In *ICDT 2002*, pages 64–78, 2002.

[MSV00]   Tova Milo, Dan Suciu, and Victor Vianu. Type-checking for XML transformers. In *Proceedings of the 19th ACM SIGACT-SIGMOD-SIGART Symposium on Principles of Database Systems*, pages 11–22, 2000.

[Per90]   Dominique Perrin. Finite automata. In *Handbook of Theoretical Computer Science*, volume B, pages 1–57. 1990.

[PQ68]   C. Pair and A. Quere. Definition et etude des bilangages reguliers. *Information and Control*, (6):565–593, Dec 1968.

[Toz05]   Akihiko Tozawa. XML type checking using high-level tree transducer, 2005. full paper, in prepation, http://www.trl.ibm.com/people/akihiko/pub/curry-full.pdf.

A Computational Approach to Pocklington Certificates in Type Theory

Benjamin Grégoire[1], Laurent Théry[1], and Benjamin Werner[2]

[1] INRIA Sophia-Antipolis, France
{Benjamin.Gregoire, Laurent.Thery}@sophia.inria.fr
[2] INRIA Futurs, France
Benjamin.Werner@inria.fr

Abstract. Pocklington certificates are known to provide short proofs of primality. We show how to perform this in the framework of formal, mechanically checked, proofs. We present an encoding of certificates for the proof system Coq which yields radically improved performances by relying heavily on computations inside and outside of the system (two-level approach).

1 Formal Computational Proofs

1.1 Machines and the Quest for Correctness

It is generally considered that modern mathematical logic was born towards the end of 19th century, with the work of logicians like Frege, Peano, Russell or Zermelo, which lead to the precise definition of the notion of logical deduction and to formalisms like arithmetic, set theory or early type theory. From then on, a mathematical proof could be understood as a mathematical object itself, whose *correction* obeys some well-defined syntactical rules. In most formalisms, a formal proof is viewed as some tree-structure; in natural deduction for instance, given to formal proofs σ_A and σ_B respectively of propositions A and B, these can be combined in order to build a proof of $A \wedge B$:

$$\frac{\dfrac{\sigma_A}{\vdash A} \quad \dfrac{\sigma_B}{\vdash B}}{\vdash A \wedge B}$$

To sum things up, the logical point of view is that a mathematical statement holds in a given formalism if there exists a formal proof of this statement which follows the syntactical rules of the formalism. A traditional mathematical text can then be understood as an informal description of the formal proof. Things changed in the 1960-ties, when N.G. de Bruijn's team started to use computers to actually build formal proofs and verify their correctness. Using the fact that data-structures like formal proofs are very naturally represented in a computer's memory, they delegated the proof-verification work to the machine; their software Automath is considered as the first *proof-system* and is the common

M. Hagiya and P. Wadler (Eds.): FLOPS 2006, LNCS 3945, pp. 97–113, 2006.
© Springer-Verlag Berlin Heidelberg 2006

ancestor of today's systems, including Coq. The main motivation for all these systems, apart from the satisfaction of bringing mathematical objects "into life", is that the non-imaginative mechanical verification of a proof rules out the possibility of errors to a much higher degree than the relying on human understanding.

The arrival of proof systems triggered a new interest in the study of formalisms which were, from then on, judged by their facility of use. Indeed, when one tries to actually build a formal proof in practice, some issues become much more important than when one simply tries to persuade an intelligent reader of the existence of such a proof in principle. For example, an issue like the *size* of the formal proof can become crucial.

1.2   The Question of Computations

In this particular respect, the subject of computations inside proofs deserves particular attention. In traditional formalisms, *deduction steps* are the only valid way to build a proof. In some cases however, one wishes to also proceed by *calculation steps*. For instance when "proving" that $2 + 2$ is equal to 4.

Typically, addition will be characterized by axioms of lemmas stating that $0+n = n$ and $(n+1)+m = 1+(n+m)$. Even if we omit the steps corresponding to the properties of equality, the proof of $2 + 2 = 4$ will look like

$$\frac{\dfrac{\dfrac{\overline{4 = 4}}{0 + 4 = 4}}{1 + 3 = 4}}{2 + 2 = 4}$$

Of course, this approach leads to unreasonably large proofs if one deals with larger numbers.

This issue is particularly acute when dealing with concepts that are highly computational in nature like primality. Since 1951, the largest numbers established as being prime have been so with the use of computer calculations. Of course, this fact is widely accepted. The largest number having been proved prime "by hand" by Ferrier is $(2^{148} + 1)/17$. In other words, if one wants to prove, formally or not, the primality of a number which is not ridiculously small by today standards, one has to somehow incorporate computations into the proof.

Even if it seems clear that proof systems cannot reach the same performances as state-of-the-art dedicated software, one should hope that modern proof systems should be able to go further than what humans could do in 1951. The most natural way to go is to include computations into proofs. Fortunately, modern logical formalisms are often well-equipped for that purpose.

1.3   Conversion Rule

The logical formalisms underlying systems like NuPRL, Agda, Alf, Lego, PVS or Coq have an important feature in common. First, the language of objects of these formalisms includes a programming language. In general, this language can be described as the functional core of ML, with some restrictions to ensure termination. In Coq, as in most flavors of type theory, the fact that under assumptions Γ, the object p is a valid proof of proposition P is stated by the sequent $\Gamma \vdash p : P$. Programs, like the addition function, being part of the language, may appear in P, as they do in proposition $2 + 2 = 4$. These programs bear a notion of *evaluation* which corresponds to small-step operational semantics. One writes $=_c$ for the reflexive, symmetric and transitive closure of this relation, which extends to propositions by straightforward congruence.

The fact that programs have a first-class status in these formalisms appears in the logical conversion rule, which, in Coq, reads:

$$\frac{\Gamma \vdash p : A}{\Gamma \vdash p : B} \quad (\text{IF} \quad A =_c B)$$

which states that congruent propositions are identified up to the point that they enjoy the same proof-objects. A crucial point is that the calculation steps to go from A to B are not book-kept in the proof object p, as they would be in traditional proofs in, say, first-order logic. This means that lengthy or complex computations may result in proofs that take time to check but remain of manageable size. The idea of computational proofs is thus to exploit this feature by exchanging deduction against computation, aiming at proof objects as small as possible.

As an example, in the case of primality, a very simplified version of computational proofs would be to construct the function which tries to divide a natural number n by all numbers between 2 and $n - 1$. If nat is the type of natural numbers, we have

$$\text{test} : \text{nat} \rightarrow \text{bool}.$$

It is then easy to prove the following correctness "theorem":

$$\forall n : \text{nat}, \text{test}(n) = \text{true} \rightarrow \text{prime}(n).$$

Since $\text{test}(1789)$ evaluates to true, the proposition $\text{test}(1789) = \text{true}$ is proved using the conversion rule and the canonical proof that $\text{true} = \text{true}$. A simple combination with the theorem above yields the proof of $\text{prime}(1789)$.

We can see that through this theorem, we obtain very small primality proofs for any prime number. Of course, these small proofs are uncheckable for large numbers because of the naive algorithm: $\text{test}(n)$ needs too much time to evaluate if n is large. However, following the same idea, we can now build on the tremendous effort made to provide efficient primality checks and import this technology into type theory. Schematically, we only have to provide a cleverer (i.e. faster) version of test.

Safe Computations vs. Fast Computations

The programming language embedded in type theory bears some restrictions since it is primarily meant to be the base of a well-understood logical formalism. As such, it discards imperative features like mutable variables or arrays. Having to check primality of large numbers with a form of "toy programming language" may look like arbitrary self-restraint. On the other hand, there is a line to draw to decide what computations are safe enough to be considered part of the proof, and which ones lie outside the formal system.

Things are not too bad yet, since the recent versions of Coq benefit from a much faster execution mechanism which uses technology from the programming language world: programs are compiled on-the-fly to a state-of-the-art byte-code. This way to proceed can, we hope, be considered to be a reasonable trade-off between efficiency and safety. With respect to previous execution mechanism using interpreters, one can observe a gain in speed by a factor of 40 and when we write these lines, Coq can probably execute programs much faster than most other comparable proof-systems. Indeed, this work arose largely as an attempt to explore the new possibilities opened by this fast computations in proofs.

Autarkic Computation vs. Certificates

Once one accepts the dichotomy between fast but unsafe computations outside of the proof-checker and slower computations which are part of the proof-checking process, one has to choose between two possibilities. A first one is to perform all computations inside the system, in an *autarkic* way [3]; this is what happens with the trivial algorithm mentioned above. Another one, is to remark it is easier to find a way out of a labyrinth, when some outside source provides one with an Ariadne's thread (a red line) leading to the exit. In other words, a possibility is to perform some computations outside the system by some dedicated software and then pass-on a *trace* (the red line) of this computation to the proof-checker. This trace gives some information on how computations should be performed and is thus a part of the resulting proof-object. This approach is called *skeptical* computations by Barendregt and was pioneered by Harrison and Théry [8], although in a very different context.

This work is typical for the skeptical computational approach. The idea of building a proof using a *Pocklington certificate* computed by outside means was first used by Caprotti and Oostdijk [6] whose work was the starting base for our effort.

2   Pocklington Certificates

2.1   The Theorem

Pocklington's theorem [10] dates back to 1914 and provides a sufficient condition for primality of natural numbers:

Theorem 1. *Given a natural numbers $n > 1$ and a witness a and some pairs $(p_1, \alpha_1), \ldots, (p_k, \alpha_k)$, it is sufficient for n to be prime that the following conditions hold:*

$$p_1 \ldots p_k \text{ are prime numbers} \tag{0}$$

$$(p_1^{\alpha_1} \ldots p_k^{\alpha_k}) \mid (n-1) \tag{1}$$

$$a^{n-1} = 1 (\text{mod } n) \tag{2}$$

$$\forall i \in \{1, \ldots, k\} \; \gcd(a^{\frac{n-1}{p_i}} - 1, n) = 1 \tag{3}$$

$$p_1^{\alpha_1} \ldots p_k^{\alpha_k} > \sqrt{n}. \tag{4}$$

It is worth mentioning, that there is no precisely stated theorem in Pocklington's work. Therefore, the literature often mentions slightly less powerful variants of the previous statement under the same denomination. There are three simple but central observations to make:

- The first one is that, given n, it requires much more computation power to determine suitable numbers $a, p_1, \alpha_1, \ldots, q_k, \alpha_k$ than to check that these numbers verify the conditions 1-4 above. Thus, one says that $a, p_1, \alpha_1 \ldots, p_k, \alpha_k$ form a *Pocklington certificate*. Caprotti and Oostdijk rightly concluded that this was a typical case for the skeptical approach: the certificate is constructed by some outside software and only its verification is done inside the proof system.
- The second observation is that for a natural number n, provided we are given $p_1, \ldots, p_k$ and a, checking primality of n boils down to:
  1. verification of conditions 1-4 which are purely done by numerical computations,
  2. verification of condition 0 which can be done recursively.
- The last observation is that Theorem 1 is the only theorem that needs to be formalized in the prover to insure the correctness of the verification of the certificate, but we also use implicitly its converse: if a number n is prime it is always possible to find a certificate. Given a sufficiently large partial decomposition of $n - 1$, a generator of the multiplicative group $\mathbb{Z}/n\mathbb{Z}$ is a valid candidate for a. Such a generator exists because n is prime so $\mathbb{Z}/n\mathbb{Z}$ is cyclic.

Theorem 1 was the one used by Caprotti and Oostdijk in their experiment described in [6]. Condition 4 indicates that in order to generate a certificate one needs to be able to partially factorize $n - 1$ at least till its square root. For our experiment we are using an improved version proposed by Brillhart, Lehmer and Selfridge in [4]. With this new version, we only need to partially factorize till the cube root. As factorizing $n-1$ is the time-consuming part of finding a certificate, this is a considerable improvement. The theorem that we have formalized in Coq is the following:

Theorem 2. *Given a number n, a witness a and some pairs $(p_1, \alpha_1), \ldots, (p_k, \alpha_k)$ where all the p_i are prime numbers, let*

$$F_1 = p_1^{\alpha_1} \ldots p_k^{\alpha_k}$$
$$R_1 = (n - 1)/F_1$$
$$s = R_1/(2F_1)$$
$$r = R_1 \bmod (2F_1)$$

it is sufficient for n to be prime that the following conditions hold:

$$F_1 \text{ is even, } R_1 \text{ is odd, and } F_1 R_1 = n - 1 \tag{5}$$
$$(F_1 + 1)(2F_1^2 + (r - 1)F_1 + 1) > n \tag{6}$$
$$a^{n-1} = 1 (\bmod\ n) \tag{7}$$
$$\forall i \in \{1, \ldots, k\}\ \gcd(a^{\frac{n-1}{p_i}} - 1, n) = 1 \tag{8}$$
$$r^2 - 8s \text{ is not a square or } s = 0 \tag{9}$$

The remarks we made about Theorem 1 remain valid for Theorem 2. The existence of a certificate is not direct from Theorem 2 but derives from the exact theorem given in [4] which is a stronger statement:

If conditions 5-8 hold then n is prime iff condition 9 holds.

2.2   The Certificates

A certificate is not composed of the $a,p_1,\alpha_1,\ldots,p_k,\alpha_k$ alone. In order to be self-contained, it needs also to contain certificates for the p_i's and the factors occurring in these new certificates. This leads to a recursive notion of Pocklington certificate whose verification consists entirely of computations.

This straightforwardly translates to the following recursive definition. A certificate for a single number n is given by the tuple $c = \{n, a, [c_1^{\alpha_1};\ldots;c_k^{\alpha_k}]\}$ where $c_1,\ldots,c_k$ are certificates for the prime numbers $p_1,\ldots,p_k$. This means certificates can be understood as trees whose branches are themselves certificates corresponding to the prime divisors.

Such structures are easily handled in Coq as an inductive type. A certificate is either:

- such tuples: $c = \{n, a, [c_1^{\alpha_1};\ldots;c_k^{\alpha_k}]\}^1$
- a pair (n, ψ) composed by a number n and a proof ψ that this number is prime.

The second case is added in order to allow primality proofs which do not rely on Pocklington's theorem. This is useful for 2 (which cannot be proved prime using Pocklington's theorem) but also for using other methods which may be more efficient than Pocklington for some numbers.

Using this representation, a possible certificate[2] for 127 is:

$$\{127, 3, [\{7, 2, [\{3, 2, [(2, \mathsf{prime2})]\}; (2, \mathsf{prime2})]\};$$
$$\{3, 2, [(2, \mathsf{prime2})]\};$$
$$(2, \mathsf{prime2})]\}$$

where prime2 is a proof that 2 is prime. One can remark that this kind of representation duplicates some certificates (here 3 and 2). So, the verification routine will verify many times these certificates. It order to share certificates, we drop trees by flattening them to lists. In this case this yields:

$$[\{127, 3, [7; 3; 2]\}; \{7, 2, [3; 2]\}; \{3, 2, [2]\}; (2, \mathsf{prime2})].$$

We have replaced recursive certificates by their corresponding prime number in decompositions. These certificates appear in the tail of the list. Note that doing so, the certificates for 2 and 3 now appear only once.

---

[1]   In the following, to shorten certificate we write c_i instead of c_i^1.

[2]   This certificate is just an illustration for our purpose, the certificate we automatically generate for 127 is much more concise: $\{127, 3, [\{3, 2, [(2, \mathsf{prime2})]\}; (2, \mathsf{prime2})]\}$.

This translates straightforwardly into the following Coq definitions:

```
Definition dec_prime := list (positive*positive).
```

```
Inductive pre_certif : Set :=
 | Pock_certif : forall n a : positive, dec_prime -> pre_certif
 | Proof_certif : forall n : positive, prime n -> pre_certif.
```

```
Definition certificate := list pre_certif.
```

First, we introduce the notion of partial factorization which is a list of prime numbers and their exponent (dec_prime). Second, we define the notion of pre-certificates which are either a pair of a prime number n and its primality proof (Proof_certif), or a tuple of a prime number n, a witness a and a list of numbers representing a partial factorization of the predecessor of n (Pock_certif). This case is not self contained, since it does not contain the primality proofs of the numbers in the partial factorization. This is why we call it pre-certificate.

A complete certificate is a list of pre-certificates. The head of the list is generally a triple (Pock_certif n a d), the tail contains pre-certificates for numbers appearing in the factorization list d of the first one (and recursively).

3   Checking Certificates

Since this last definition is basically a free structure, the existence of an object of type certificate does not yet allow to state anything about primality. We focus on the function C which verifies the validity of a certificate and on the correctness proof of this function.

Our goal is to define C as a function from certificates to boolean, returning true if the list implies the primality of the numbers it contains. Remark that, for our purpose, the completeness of the function C is not required; the correctness lemma we want to prove is:

$$\text{Pock\_refl} : \forall c, l, \ C \ (c :: l) = true \Rightarrow \text{prime} \ (n \ c)$$

where $(n \ c)$ is the prime number contained in the pre-certificate c. In fact, we prove a more general lemma:

$$\forall l, \ C \ l = true \Rightarrow \forall c \in l, \ \text{prime} \ (n \ c)$$

The function C is defined recursively over the list l. If the list l is empty, the function returns true. If the list is not empty ($l = c :: l'$), the function performs a recursive call over l', this implies the validity of all the pre-certificates in l' and so the primality of their associated numbers. Then the function verifies the validity of the pre-certificate c, there are two cases:

- If c is given by its proof form $c = (n, \psi)$, in that case there is nothing to do (the type checking of Coq ensures that ψ is a valid primality proof for n).

– If c is a Pocklington pre-certificate $c = \{n, a, [p_1^{\alpha_1}; \ldots; p_k^{\alpha_k}]\}$. The function first verifies that all the divisors $p_1, \ldots, p_k$ have a corresponding pre-certificate in the list l' (this implies that all the divisors are prime). If this is the case, the function checks that the pre-certificate verifies conditions 5-9; this is done by another function C_c.

Checking the Computational Conditions

The function C_c starts by computing the numbers F_1, R_1, s, r as defined in theorem 2. Verifying conditions 5 and 6 is then straightforward. For conditions 7 and 8 the difficulty is to efficiently compute $a^{n-1} \bmod n$ and $\gcd(a^{\frac{n-1}{p_i}} - 1, n)$ for $i = 1 \ldots k$. It is important not to compute a^{n-1} and $a^{\frac{n-1}{p_i}}$, which can be huge. We do this by always working modulo n since $\gcd(b, n) = \gcd(b \bmod n, n)$. Furthermore, we can compute only one gcd using the fact that $\gcd(b_1 \ldots b_l, n) = 1$ iff for all $i = 1 \ldots l$, $\gcd(b_i, n) = 1$.

We define the following functions working modulo n:

– a predecessor function (Npred_mod);
– a multiplication function (times_mod);
– a power function (Npow_mod) (using the *repeated square-and-multiply algorithm*);
– a multi-power function (fold_pow_mod) that given a, $l = [q_1; \ldots; q_r]$ and n computes $a^{q_1 \cdots q_r} \bmod n$.

Another optimization is to share parts of the computations of

$$a^{\frac{n-1}{p_1}} \bmod n, \quad \ldots, \quad a^{\frac{n-1}{p_k}} \bmod n, \quad a^{n-1} \bmod n.$$

Let $m = (n-1)/(p_1 \ldots p_k)$, if we perform these computations separately, $a^m \bmod n$ is computed $k+1$ times, $(a^m \bmod n)^{p_1} \bmod n$ is computed k times, and so on.

To share computation we define the following function:

```
Fixpoint all_pow_mod (P A : N) (l:list positive) (n:positive)
                                           {struct l}: N*N :=
  match l with
  | nil => (P,A)
  | p :: l =>
    let m := Npred_mod (fold_pow_mod A l n) n in
    all_pow_mod (times_mod P m n) (Npow_mod A p n) l n
  end.
```

If P and A are positive numbers less than n and l the list $[q_1; \ldots; q_r]$, the function all_pow_mod returns the pair:

$$\left(P \prod_{1 \le i \le r} A^{\frac{q_1 \ldots q_r}{q_i}} \bmod n, A^{q_1 \ldots q_r} \bmod n\right)$$

Remark that the application of this function to $P = 1$, $A = a^m \bmod n$ and $l = [p_1; \ldots; p_k]$ leads to the numbers we need to compute. Note that the order of the list l is important for efficiency. A^{p_1} is computed only once, but power of elements in the tail of the list are computed more than once. So, the function is more efficient if l in sorted in decreasing order.

Finally, the function C_c checks the condition 9 ($s = 0 \lor r^2 - 8s$ is not a square). If $s \neq 0$ and $r^2 - 8s \geq 0$ it should check that $r^2 - 8s$ is not a square. To do so, we slightly adapt the definition of pre-certificates by adding the low integer square root[3] sqrt, and we only verify that

$$\mathsf{sqrt}^2 < r^2 - 8s < (\mathsf{sqrt} + 1)^2$$

To sum up the extended inductive type for pre-certificate is

```
Inductive pre_certif : Set :=
 | Pock_certif : forall n a sqrt: positive, dec_prime -> pre_certif
 | Proof_certif : forall n : positive, prime n -> pre_certif.
```

Defining Arithmetic Operations in Coq

The programming language of Coq is functional. Datatypes can be defined using inductive types. One can then write recursive functions over datatypes using structural recursion only. This restriction and the type system ensure the strong normalization of the language from which the logical soundness of the system is derived.

When doing computational proofs, each time we define a function we also need to prove formally its correctness. This means that most of the time we have to do a compromise between the efficiency of the function, the difficulty of writing it in a structural recursive functional language and the cost of proving its correctness.

For verifying Pocklington certificate, we need basic integer operations. Instead of starting from scratch, we have decided to use the standard library of Coq for integer arithmetic. In this library, positive numbers are represented by a list of bits as follows:

```
Inductive positive : Set :=
 | xH : positive
 | xO : positive -> positive
 | xI : positive -> positive.
```

xH represents 1, xO x represents $2x$, xI x represents $2x+1$. So 6 is represented by (xO (xI xH)). All the operations are purely functional (i.e. no machine arithmetic and no side effect). This means that every time an operation returns a number, this number has to be allocated. In our application, allocating and garbage collecting are particularly time consuming.

To minimize allocation we had to re-implement some operations. For example, in the standard library the remainder function is defined as the second component of the euclidean division. This means that computing a remainder also allocates for the quotient. We provide a more direct implementation. Also we have implemented a special function for squaring numbers.

---

[3] In the case where $r^2 - 8s < 0$ we put a dummy number 1, since $r^2 - 8s$ is trivially not a square.

4   Building Certificates

The goal of this section is to explain how to build certificates for large prime numbers. The main difficulty is to compute a partial factorization of the predecessor of the prime n we want to prove.

As said above, this factorization is naturally done relying on tools outside of the proof system. The software building the certificate thus plays the role of an oracle whose prediction is however carefully verified. We built this software as a C program based on the ECM library [1] and the GMP library [2]. Given a number n, the program generates Coq files whose lemmas have the following form:

```
Lemma prime_n : prime n.
Proof.
 apply (Pock_refl (Pock_certif n a d sqrt) l).
 exact_no_check (refl_equal true).
Qed.
```

where a is the witness of the Pocklington theorem, d a partial factorization of $n-1$, sqrt the square root of $r^2 - 8s$ (if $r^2 - 8s$ is positive otherwise 1) and l is the list of pre-certificates proving that all numbers in the factorization are prime. The proof starts by an application of the reflexive theorem Pock_refl. At proof-checking time, the system checks that $C((n, a, d, \mathsf{sqrt}) :: l) = \mathsf{true}$ or, to be more precise, that this proposition is convertible with the proposition $\mathsf{true} = \mathsf{true}$. Indeed, refl_equal true simply stands for the canonical proof of $\mathsf{true} = \mathsf{true}$.

This last step is really the reflexive part of the proof, where deduction is replaced by computation. As we can see, the computation step does not appear in the proof which allows to build very small proofs. In our case, the size of the proof is mainly the size of the certificate $(n, a, d, \mathsf{sqrt}) :: l$.

A technical detail for Coq users: during the construction of the proof, we ask the system not yet to check that $C((n, a, d, \mathsf{sqrt}) :: l) = \mathsf{true}$ is convertible with $\mathsf{true} = \mathsf{true}$. This is done only once at the validation step (Qed). The ability of the proof checker to compute $C((n, a, d, \mathsf{sqrt}) :: l)$ is crucial, for the verification time.

4.1   Generating Certificates for Arbitrary Numbers

The difficult task for the oracle is to obtain the partial factorization and to find the witness. The basic options of the oracle are the following:

$$\texttt{pocklington [-v] [-o } \textit{filename}\texttt{] [} \textit{prime} \texttt{ | -next } \textit{num} \texttt{]}$$

pocklington is the oracle that generates a certificate for the prime number *prime* or the next prime number following the number *num*. The -v option is for verbose mode, -o allows to chose the name of the output file, if none is given a default name is created depending of the prime number.

The oracle first checks that the number n has a large probability to be prime, and then tries to find a pseudo decomposition of its predecessor. To compute this decomposition it first tries to get all the small factors of n using trivial divisions by 2, 3, 5 and 7 and then by all the numbers greater than 7 that are not a multiples of 2, 3, 5 and 7. The division limit is the maximum of one million and $\log_2(n)^2$. Then, if the pseudo decomposition obtained so far is still less than the cubic root of n, the oracle tries to find larger factors using the ECM library.

The ECM library proposes three methods to find factors: (p-1, p+1 and ecm). We have developed a simple heuristic that successively calls the three methods to find, first, factors of less that 20 digits, then, less that 25 digits and so on up to factors less than 65 digits. This process is not deterministic and not exhaustive. The iteration terminates as soon as we get a sufficiently large partial decomposition. So, we can miss some factors and we are not sure that the process terminates in a reasonable time.

When a partial decomposition has been found, the oracle tries to find the witness a for the Pocklington criteria by testing 2, 3, 4 and so on. Finally it calls itself recursively on the numbers in the decomposition for which no certificate has yet been generated.

In order to share computations, the certificates for the first 5000 primes (form 2 to 48611) are provided at the start in a separated file `BasePrimes.v`. Thus certificates for prime numbers less than 48611 are not regenerated.

Using this technique, the oracle is able to generate certificates for most of the prime numbers containing less that 100 digits (in base 10), and for some larger primes.

4.2   Generating Certificates for Mersenne Numbers

Mersenne numbers are those of the form $2^n - 1$. Not all of them are prime. The first ones are for $n = 2, 3, 5, 7, 13, 17, 19, 31, 61, 89, 107, 127$. Until now only 43 are known to be prime and it is still open whether there are infinitely many or not. Currently, the last one has been found by Curtis Cooper and Steven R. Boone on December 15, 2005. $2^{30402457} - 1$ is the new largest known prime number and has 9152052 digits!

The first striking remark is that such a number is written $1111\ldots1111$ in base 2. The second is that the decomposition of its predecessor always contains 2, since $(2^n - 1) - 1 = 2(2^{n-1} - 1)$. So, finding a decomposition of its predecessor is equivalent to finding a decomposition of $2^{n-1} - 1$.

Here we can use some very simple arithmetical properties to start the decomposition:

- $2^{2p} - 1 = (2^p - 1)(2^p + 1)$
- $2^{3p} - 1 = (2^p - 1)(2^{2p} + 2^p + 1)$

The oracle uses those tricks recursively to start the decomposition of the predecessor of Mersenne number, this allows to considerably reduce the size of the numbers to factorize. Since $2^n - 1$ can be prime only if n is odd, we know $n - 1$ is even and the first remark always applies. When we reach the point where these two remarks do not apply any more, the oracle uses the method for arbitrary numbers to factorize the resulting numbers as described above.

The syntax to compute the certificate for the Mersenne number $2^n - 1$ is the following: `pocklington -mersenne` n. This technique allows to build certificates for the 15 firsts Mersenne numbers, the largest one is for $n = 1279$ and has 386 digits.

When n grows further the resulting numbers are too big for their factorizations to be computed. So we have added a new entry to the oracle that takes as argument a file containing a prime number and a partial decomposition of its predecessor. The syntax is the following: `pocklington -dec` *file*.

We can use the trick described below and the tables [5] to build the file. These tables contain most of the factorizations of $b^n \pm 1$ for $b = 2, 3, 5, 6, 7, 10, 11, 12$ and n a high power (for $b = 2$, n should be less than 1200). Those tables are available directly on the Web[4]. Using these techniques we have been able to compute a certificate for 16th ($n = 2203$) and the 17th ($n = 2281$) Mersenne numbers.

4.3   Going to the Limit

Some similar problems appears for the 18th Mersenne number ($n = 3217$): using the table we are able to compute the complete factorization of

$$2^{1608} - 1 = (2^{804} - 1)(2^{804} + 1)$$

but we are not able to find a certificate for one of the prime divisors, which is a number of only 90 digits.

To solve this, our idea is to find some prime divisors of $2^{1608} + 1$ big enough to replace the prime divisor of 90 digits in the pseudo decomposition. The problem is that $2^{1608} + 1$ is not in the table. To factorize $2^{1608} + 1$ we used a well known property of cyclotomic polynomial[5]:

$$x^n + 1 = (x^{2n} - 1)/(x^n - 1) = \prod_{d | 2n} \Phi_d(x) / \prod_{d | n} \Phi_d(x)$$

where $\Phi_d(x)$ is the cyclotomic polynomial, given by:

$$\Phi_d(x) = \prod_{\delta | d} (x^\delta - 1)^{\mu(d/\delta)}$$

where μ is the Möbius function [9].

Setting $2n = 2^t m$ with m odd, leads to:

$$x^n + 1 = \prod_{d | m} \Phi_{2^t d}(x)$$

where all the $\Phi_{2^t d}(x)$ are divisors of $x^n + 1$ that we can factorize.

Using this trick we have been able to compute enough prime divisors of $2^{1608} + 1$ to replace the 90 digits prime divisors of $2^{1608} - 1$, and to build certificates for

---

[4] http://homes.cerias.purdue.edu/~ssw/cun/prime.php
[5] A complete explanation can be found in [9].

all its prime divisors. Finally this allowed us to build a certificate for the 18th Mersenne number which yields 969 digits. This number was first proved prime by Riesel in 1957.

Note that Pocklington certificate is known not to be the most efficient way to verify the primality of Mersenne numbers. Lucas test gives a much simpler criterion since it does not require any factorization:

Theorem 3. *Let (S_n) be recursively defined by $S_0 = 4$ and $S_{n+1} = S_n^2 - 2$, for $n > 2$, $2^n - 1$ is prime if and only if $(2^n - 1)|S_{n-2}$.*

We have also formalized this theorem in our prover to compare the running time of this test with our generated Pocklington certificates for Mersenne numbers.

To do so we add a new entry `Lucas_certif` in our inductive type:

```
Inductive pre_certif : Set :=
 | Pock_certif : forall n a : positive, dec_prime -> pre_certif
 | Proof_certif : forall n : positive, prime n -> pre_certif
 | Lucas_certif : forall n p : positive, pre_certif.
```

where n should be $2^p - 1$.

To generate certificates for Mersenne numbers using Lucas test, we add a new entry to the oracle: `pocklington -lucas` p.

4.4 Generating Certificate for Proth Numbers

A more friendly set of prime numbers for Pocklington certificate are the Proth numbers. They are numbers of form $k2^p + 1$, where k is odd.

Providing that k is sufficiently small with respect to 2^p, the partial decomposition reduces to 2^p. So the generation of the corresponding certificate is trivial.

To generate Pocklington certificates for Proth number we add a new entry to the oracle: `pocklington -proth` k p.

5 Performances

All the certificates described in the section above have been checked in Coq. The software and formal material are available at the following location:

`http://www-sop.inria.fr/everest/Benjamin.Gregoire/primnumber.html`

Certificates are generated by the `pocklington` program that is composed of 1721 lines of C code. They are then checked in Coq using our library that consists of 6653 lines of proof script. We provide some performance figures for the cvs version 8.0 of Coq with processor Intel Pentium 4 (3.60 GHz) and a RAM of 1Gb. Of course, this version of Coq uses the compilation scheme described in [7].

Figure 1 gives the time to build the certificates for the 100000 first primes, the size of the certificate and the time for the Coq system to check them. On average, generating certificates for a small prime number takes about 3.10^{-5} seconds, their sizes are 215 bytes average, and it takes about 0.0144 seconds to verify.

from - to	build	size	verify
2 - 5000	0.15s	989K	35.85s
5001 - 10000	0.17s	1012K	42.59s
10001 - 20000	0.38s	2.1M	134.14s
20001 - 30000	0.38s	2.1M	138.30s
30001 - 40000	0.38s	2.1M	145.81s
40001 - 50000	0.38s	2.2M	153.65s
50001 - 60000	0.41s	2.2M	153.57s
60001 - 70000	0.43s	2.2M	158.13s
70001 - 80000	0.39s	2.2M	160.07s
80001 - 90000	0.40s	2.2M	162.58s
90001 - 100000	0.44s	2.2M	162.03s

Fig. 1. Time to verify the first 100000 prime numbers

prime	digits	size deduc.	size refl.	time deduc.	time refl.	refl. + VM
1234567891	10	94K	0.453K	3.98s	1.50s	0.50s
74747474747474747	17	145K	0.502K	9.87s	7.02s	0.56s
1111111111111111111	19	223K	0.664K	17.41s	16.67s	0.66s
$(2^{148} + 1)/17$	44	1.2M	0.798K	350.63s	338.12s	2.77s
P_{200}	200	_	2.014K	_	_	190.98s

Fig. 2. Comparison with the non recursive method

Figure 2 makes a comparison between the deductive approach (the one developed by Oostdijk and Caprotti) and our reflexive one, using curious primes. The 44 digits prime number $(2^{148} + 1)/17$ is the biggest one proved in Coq before our work.

As expected, the reflexive method considerably reduces the size of the proof, as showed by the size column of the table. For the prime number $(2^{148} + 1)/17$, the size is reduced by a factor 1500. The reduction of the proof size is natural since explicit deduction is replaced by implicit computation.

The three last columns compare the verification time for the different approaches. Without the use of the virtual machine, the reflexive approach is a little bit faster, but the times are comparable. If we verify the proof with the version of Coq using a virtual machine to perform the conversion test (here to compute the result of the C function), we can observe a gain of a factor 9 for small examples to more than 120 for the biggest ones. This means that the combination of computational reflexion with the virtual machine allows small proofs that are quickly verified.

Note that when verifying a reflexive proof the time consuming task is the reduction of decision procedure. It is precisely the reduction that the virtual machine improves. This explains why we get such a speed up. Using virtual machine for checking deductive proofs usually does not provide any speed up since these proofs do not use much reduction.

Using the reflexive approach, we have been able to prove a new random prime number of 200 digits:

$$P_{200} = \begin{aligned} &679484782202204247190000812427871295833546607696251\\ &708449749369500113085567719496425753736503543981434\\ &650243928089694516285823439004920100845398699127\\ &458434985921125470131158882933777700659260273705507 \end{aligned}$$

in 191 seconds and the proof size is 2K. In practice, it is difficult to find factors of more than 35 digits. Most numbers with less than 100 digits contain sufficient factors of less than 20 digits, so ECM finds them rapidly. For larger numbers, being able to generate a certificate for N is a question of luck, $N - 1$ must be smooth (i.e. it contains a lot of small factors). This is the case for P_{200}.

Figure 3 gives the time to verify the certificates of the 18th first Mersenne numbers (using a Pocklington certificate), except for the 7th first which are part of the first 100000 primes. The biggest one is a 969 digit number. We have not been able to generate certificates for numbers greater than the 18th. For the 19th Mersenne number, we have not been able to find a sufficiently large partial factorization of its predecessor. For the 20th, we have such a factorization (using the table of aurifeuillian polynomial from [5]), but we are not able to recursively generate the certificates for two of its factors.

For Mersenne numbers, we can do better than using a Pocklington certificate using Lucas test. The last column gives the time to verify in Coq the 20 first Mersenne number using this test. As far as we know, the 20th Mersenne number is the biggest prime number that has been formally proved in a proof assistant.

For all these benchmarks, we have to keep in mind that Coq uses its own arithmetic: numbers are encoding by a inductive type, i.e. a chained list of booleans. No native machine arithmetic is used. This means that the computations which are done to check certificates are more similar to symbolic computation than to numerical computation. For example, when dealing with the 20th Mersenne

#	n	digits	years	discoverer	certificate	time	time(Lucas)
8	31	10	1772	Euler	0.527K	0.51s	0.01s
9	61	19	1883	Pervushin	0.648K	0.66s	0.08s
10	89	27	1911	Powers	0.687K	0.94s	0.25s
11	107	33	1914	Powers	0.681K	1.14s	0.44s
12	127	39	1876	Lucas	0.775K	2.03s	0.73s
13	521	157	1952	Robinson	2.131K	178.00s	53.00s
14	607	183	1952	Robinson	1.818K	112.00s	84.00s
15	1279	386	1952	Robinson	3.427K	2204.00s	827.00s
16	2203	664	1952	Robinson	5.274K	11983.00s	4421.00s
17	2281	687	1952	Robinson	5.995K	44357.00s	4964.00s
18	3217	969	1957	Riesel	7.766K	94344.00s	14680.00s
19	4253	1281	1961	Hurwitz	-	-	35198.00s
20	4423	1332	1961	Hurwitz	-	-	39766.00s

Fig. 3. Time to verify Mersenne numbers

number, a 4422 digits number in base 2 (1332 in base 10), we manipulate list of 4423 elements. The fact that we are capable to perform such a symbolic computation clearly indicates that the introduction of the virtual machine in Coq is an effective gain in computing power.

6   Conclusion

Proofs are what ensures the correctness of computations, but many results of mathematics or computer science can only be established through computations. It does even seem likely that the proportion of computationally obtained results will grow in the future. But the more intricated computation and deduction become, the more difficult it is to have a global overview of the resulting construction; this raises a serious question regarding the reliability of the final statement. This issue is important, especially when considering that important mathematical results now rely, at least partly, on computations. Famous examples are the four color theorem or the Kepler conjecture.

The ultimate goal of works as the present one is to establish proof systems as the place where proofs and computations interleave in a fruitful and yet safe way. In the case of Coq, recent progress in the implementation of reduction was a significant step in reducing the overhead for doing computations inside the proof system rather than outside. Even if progress should still be made in that respect, it appears that what we have been able to prove, for typically computational statements, is not ridiculous and represents a step in the right direction.

In order to go further on the topic of formal primality proofs, two ways should obviously be explored. A first one is to formalize more modern primality proofs, as the ones relying on algebraic curves. This means translating to Coq an interesting body of mathematics. A second direction is to pursue the work on the system itself. Indeed, a current mechanical bottleneck is certainly the very inefficient representation of numbers in the proof system (basically as lists of bits). Integrating numbers into type theory with a more primitive status, allowing operations which could be implemented using more low-level features of the processor and doing this in a safe way is an interesting challenge and would be a further step in the quest of computationally efficient proof systems. Once this done, we can hope for a powerful system for combining deduction, symbolic computation and numerical computation in a safe and integrated way.

Acknowledgments. Thanks are due to Henk Barendregt who initially motivated this work, to Paul Zimmermann for answering all our arithmetic questions and for developing the wonderful ECM library. Finally, we want to thank our anonymous referees for their stimulating comments.

References

1. *Elliptic Curve Method Library.*   http://www.loria.fr/~zimmerma/records/ecmnet.html.
2. *GNU Multiple Precision Arithmetic Library.* http://www.swox.com/gmp/.

3. H. Barendregt and E. Barendsen. Autarkic computations in formal proofs. *J. Autom. Reasoning*, 28(3):321–336, 2002.

4. J. Brillhart, D. H. Lehmer, and J. L. Selfridge. New primality criteria and factorizations of $2^m \pm 1$. *Mathematics of Computation*, 29:620–647, 1975.

5. J. Brillhart, D. H. Lehmer, J. L. Selfridge, B. Tuckerman, and S. S. Wagstaff, Jr. *Factorizations of $b^n \pm 1$*, volume 22 of *Contemporary Mathematics*. American Mathematical Society, Providence, R.I., 1983. $b = 2, 3, 5, 6, 7, 10, 11, 12$ up to high powers.

6. O. Caprotti and M. Oostdijk. Formal and efficient primality proofs by use of computer algebra oracles. *Journal of Symbolic Computation*, 32(1/2):55–70, July 2001.

7. B. Grégoire and X. Leroy. A compiled implementation of strong reduction. In *International Conference on Functional Programming 2002*, pages 235–246. ACM Press, 2002.

8. J. Harrison and L. Théry. A skeptic's approach to combining HOL and Maple. *J. Autom. Reasoning*, 21(3):279–294, 1998.

9. S. Lang. *Algebra*, volume 211 of *Graduate Texts in Mathematics*. Springer-Verlag, New York, third edition, 2002.

10. H. C. Pocklington. The determination of the prime or composite nature of large numbers by Fermat's theorem. volume 18, pages 29–30, 1914.

Defining and Reasoning About Recursive Functions: A Practical Tool for the Coq Proof Assistant

Gilles Barthe[1], Julien Forest[1], David Pichardie[1], and Vlad Rusu[2]

[1] EVEREST Team, INRIA Sophia-Antipolis, France
{Gilles.Barthe, Julien.Forest, David.Pichardie}@sophia.inria.fr
[2] VERTECS Team, IRISA/INRIA Rennes, France
rusu@irisa.fr

Abstract. We present a practical tool for defining and proving properties of recursive functions in the Coq proof assistant. The tool generates
from pseudo-code the *graph* of the intended function as an inductive relation. Then it proves that the relation actually represents a function,
which is by construction the function that we are trying to define. Then,
we generate *induction and inversion principles*, and a *fixpoint equation*
for proving other properties of the function. Our tool builds upon state-
of-the-art techniques for defining recursive functions, and can also be
used to generate executable functions from inductive descriptions of their
graph. We illustrate the benefits of our tool on two case studies.

1 Introduction

Dependent type theory provides a powerful language in which programs can be
specified, proved and executed. Yet defining and reasoning about some simple
recursive functions is surprisingly hard, and may rapidly become overwhelming
for users, as too much effort is spent on dealing with difficult concepts not
related to their verification problems. We detail these difficulties below, with an
emphasis on the Coq proof assistant [13, 7], which is the focus of this article.

Difficulties with Defining Functions. In order to ensure decidability of type-
checking (and hence of proof-checking), proof assistants based on type
theory require that functions are provably terminating, total, and deterministic. Within Coq [13], totality and determinacy are enforced by requiring
definitions by pattern matching to be exhaustive and unambiguous, and termination is enforced through a guard criterion that checks that recursive calls are
performed on structurally smaller arguments. The guard predicate is designed
to enable a translation from definitions by pattern matching to definitions by
recursors, but it is difficult to use. As a result, users may be tempted to circum-
vent its use by adding a counter as an extra argument to recursive functions,
and by performing a "large enough" number of iterations. This pragmatic solution is acceptable for specific programs, see e.g. [18], but cannot be adopted
systematically.

M. Hagiya and P. Wadler (Eds.): FLOPS 2006, LNCS 3945, pp. 114–129, 2006.

A more general solution consists in defining functions by well-founded recursion. Two approaches prevail in the current state-of-the-art: the so-called *accessibility predicate* approach [21] (and its variant *converging iterations* [1]), and the so-called *ad-hoc predicate* approach [9] (which has been developed for a type theory different from Coq, and whose adaptation to Coq involves some subtleties); the two approaches make an advanced use of type theory, and are described in Section 2.

Both approaches help users in modeling functions. However, for lack of an appropriate and tool supported method, defining general recursive functions in Coq remains more difficult than defining those functions in proof assistants based on different logicals frameworks. For example, PVS [23], Isabelle [20] and HOL [15] allow users to provide a measure to prove termination, and generate proof obligations that must be discharged by the user in order for the system to accept the function as terminating. The possibility of relying on measures to guarantee termination makes the task of defining functions significantly easier. Yet the approach has never been implemented in proof assistants such as Coq.

Difficulties with reasoning about functions. Proof assistants based on type theory only offer limited support for reasoning about (structurally or generally recursive, total or partial) functions. There are three principles that can be used to reason about recursive functions: induction principles (which allow to prove properties about the function's output), inversion principles (which allow to deduce possible values of the function's input knowing the output), and fixpoint equations (which allow to unfold the function's definition in proofs). Unfortunately, users are not systematically provided with these results: for the Coq proof assistant, the tool of Balaa and Bertot [1] only generates the fixpoint equation for generally recursive functions, whereas the new tactic **functional induction**, which stems from the work of Barthe and Courtieu [2], only generates the induction principle for structurally recursive functions. The *ad-hoc predicate* approach of Bove and Capretta [9] provides an induction principle, but does not help in showing the totality of the function (and as stated above, cannot be adapted immediately to Coq).

Our objectives and contributions. The purpose of this article is to rectify this situation for the Coq proof assistant by proposing a tool that considerably simplifies the tasks of writing **and reasoning** about recursive functions. The tool takes as input the definition of a recursive function as pseudo-code (a language similar to type theory, but not subject to the restrictions imposed by the guard condition or by any criterion for totality), and generates Coq terms for its representation as a partial recursive function, its induction and inversion principles, and its fixpoint equation. Furthermore, the tool allows users to provide a well-founded order or a measure to prove termination, and generates from this information proof obligations that, if discharged, prove the termination of the function considered. Thus, if the pseudo-code describes a total function $f : A \to B$ that can be proved to be terminating, our tool will generate a Coq function $\bar{f}$ of the same type. The function $\bar{f}$ may not have exactly the same code as f, but this is of no concern to the user, because the tool has provided her with all the principles needed to reason about $\bar{f}$ (so she does not need to use the definition). Moreover, Coq will extract from $\bar{f}$ a Caml function which is (almost) the same program as f.

At the heart of our tool lies a simple observation: inductive relations provide a convenient tool to describe mathematical functions by their graph (in particular they do not impose any restriction w.r.t. termination and totality), and to reason about them (using automatically generated induction and inversion principles derived from inductive definitions). Thus, relating a recursive function to its graph gives us for free reasoning principles about the function. Despite its simplicity, the observation does not seem to have been exploited previously to help defining and reasoning about recursive functions. Technically, the observation can be exploited both following the general accessibility approach and the *ad-hoc* predicate approach, leading to two mechanisms whose relative merits are discussed in Section 3. In Section 4, we illustrate the benefits of the tool.

2   A Critical Review of Existing Methods

Programming a nontrivial application inside a proof assistant is typically a long and tedious process. To make such developments easier for the user, mechanisms to define recursive functions should comply with the requirements below. They are by no means sufficient (see the conclusion for further requirements), but they definitely appear to be necessary:

- **deferred termination (DT):** the system should allow the user to define her functions without imposing that this very definition includes a termination proof;
- **support for termination proofs (ST):** termination proofs, which are usually not the main concern of the user, should be automated as much as possible;
- **support for reasoning (SR):** the system should provide the user with reasoning principles for proving all other properties of her functions;
- **executability (X):** when applied to structurally recursive definitions, mechanisms should yield the same result as, e.g., the **Fixpoint** construction of Coq.

Unfortunately, the current version of the Coq proof assistant does not satisfy these requirements, neither for structurally recursive nor for general recursive functions.

In the sequel, we briefly review the state-of-the-art approaches for general recursive definitions, and other related works, assessing in each case its benefits and limitations. A summary is presented in Figure 1.

For the sake of concreteness, we center our discussion around the fast exponentiation function, which is informally defined by the clauses $2^n = 2 \cdot 2^{n-1}$ if n is odd and $(2^{n/2})^2$ if n is even. The natural definition of the function in Coq would be:

Approach	Deferred termination	Induction principle	Inversion principle	Fixpoint equation	Support for termination	Implemented in Coq
Balaa & Bertot	no	no	no	yes	no	prototype
Barthe & Courtieu	n.a.	yes*	no	no	n.a.	yes
Bove & Capretta	yes	yes	no	no	no	no
this paper	yes	yes	yes	yes	yes	prototype

* for structurally recursive functions

Fig. 1. Comparaison of state-of-the-art approaches

```
Fixpoint pow2 (n: nat) :  nat  :=
  match n with
  |0 ⇒ 1
  |S q ⇒ match (even_odd_dec (S q)) with
            |left _ ⇒ square (pow2 (div2 (S q)))
            |right _ ⇒ n * (pow2 q)
          end
  end.
```

where even_odd_dec is a function, returning either left and a proof of the fact that its argument is even, or right and a proof of the fact that its argument is odd. Proofs are irrelevant here and are replaced by the _ placeholder. However this definition is not structurally recursive, as the guard predicate does not see div2 (S q) as structurally smaller than q. As a consequence, the current Coq tool rejects this definition and we must use one of the approaches described later in this paper for defining the function pow2 : nat →nat.

Then, assuming the function pow2 : nat →nat is defined in Coq, we need the following tools in order to reason about it:

- a *fixpoint equation* which allows to unfold the definition of the pow2 in a proof:

```
Lemma pow2_fixpoint : ∀ n, pow2 n  =
  match n with
  |0 ⇒ 1
  |S q ⇒
    match (even_odd_dec (S q)) with
            |left _ ⇒  square (pow2 (div2 (S q)))
            |right _ ⇒ 2 * (pow2 q)
    end
  end.
```

- a *general induction principle* which only focuses on the domain of the function:

```
Lemma pow2_ind_gen : ∀ P : nat  →  Prop,
  P 0 →
  (∀ q, even_odd_dec (S q) = left _  →  P (div2 (S q))  →  P (S q) )  →
  (∀ q, even_odd_dec (S q) = right _  →  P q  →  P (S q))  →
  ∀ n, P n.
```

This principle was initially proposed by Slind [24] and is currently implemented in Coq by the command **functional induction** (only for structural recursive functions). It often needs to be combined with the fixpoint equation to simulate the inputs/outputs induction principle below.

- an *inputs/outputs induction principle* which allows to deduce a relation between inputs and outputs from the proof that the relation holds for all the pairs consisting of input and output to the recursive calls, for all situations in which these calls are performed:

```
Lemma pow2_ind : ∀ P : nat → nat → Prop,
 P 0 1 →
(∀ q, even_odd_dec (S q) = left _ →
          P (div2 (S q)) (pow2 (div2 (S q))) →
          P (S q) (square (pow2 (div2 (S q))))) →
(∀ q, even_odd_dec (S q) = right _ → P q (pow2 q) →
          P (S q) (2*pow2 q)) →
 ∀ n, P n (pow2 n).
```

This principle is less general than the previous induction principle. Nevertheless, it produces more instantiated proof obligations. As a consequence, it often facilitates proof automation.

- an *inversion principle* to deduce some information about the inputs of a function from the value of the result of the function on these inputs. Such inversion lemmas are of great help in reasoning about executable semantics (most clauses in such semantics yield to error states, see e.g. [3], and the inversion principle allows users to deal directly with states which do not go wrong). Due to space constraints, we do not discuss inversion principles further.

The inputs/outputs induction principles allow the user to reason about functions: consider a proof of a simple theorem stating that the fast exponentation is equivalent to the slow (structural) one, shown below together with a lemma:

```
Fixpoint pow2_slow (n: nat) :  nat  :=
  match  n  with
  |0 ⇒  1
  |S  q ⇒ 2 * (pow2_slow q)
  end
```

```
Lemma pow2_slow_div2: ∀ n, even n  →  square (pow2_slow (div2 n)) = pow2_slow n.
```

The theorem can be proved simply by applying the induction principle pow2_ind to the predicate **fun** n res ⇒res = pow2_slow n. This leaves us with one unproved subgoal, which is solved by applying the pow2_slow_div2 lemma:

```
Theorem pow2_prop: ∀ n, pow2 n = pow2_slow n.
Proof.
  apply pow2_ind with (P:=fun n res ⇒ res = pow2_slow n); intros;
     subst; try reflexivity.
  apply pow2_slow_div2; auto.
Qed.
```

On the other hand, simple induction principles such as that on natural numbers are too weak for proving properties about non-structural recursive functions such as pow2_prop. We may of course use a *well-founded* induction principle, but using it is as hard as building the function in the first place: indeed, the well-founded induction principle for *reasoning* about a function is almost identical to that for building the function (well_founded_induction discussed in Section 2.1 below).

2.1   General Accessibility

This approach is based on so-called *accessibility predicates* and consists in defining the function by induction on some well-founded relation for which recursive calls are decreasing (i.e. made on strictly smaller arguments). This approach originates from [21], and is embodied in Coq by the `well_founded_induction` principle from its library: using this principle, one can define a general recursive function f: A →B from a relation R:A → A → **Prop**, a proof P that R is well-founded, and an "induction step" I of type ∀ y:A, (∀z: A, R z y →B) →B. Formally, f is defined as (`well_founded_induction` A R P I).

It is possible, but cumbersome, to circumvent the lack of reasoning principles. For example, assume that we want to prove that some post-condition (Post x (f x)) holds, whenever the argument x satisfies a pre-condition (Pre x). Then, it is enough if we *define* f right from the start to have the dependent type ∀ x: A, (Pre x) →{y : B | (Post x y)}. In this way, the pre/post condition information about f is immediately available. However, this approach assumes that one *knows* already when defining f *all* the properties that one will ever need about it! This is not realistic, because any nontrivial development typically requires the user to state and prove many intermediate lemmas, *not known in advance*, between the definition of a function and the final theorem about the function. The above approach would then require to *re-define* f with *each* new lemma, and this definition requires to *prove* the new lemma *while* the function is defined, in addition to re-proving all lemmas previously proved.

Moreover, the approach does not easily scale up to mutually recursive functions such as those considered in Section 4.2. Hence, this approach is clearly not useable in any nontrivial development.

2.2 Ad-Hoc Predicate

The second approach has been described by Bove and Capretta [9] in the context of Martin-Löf's type theory.

The approach is based so-called on *ad-hoc predicates*, and consists in providing for each function an inductive predicate, called its *domain*, that characterizes its domain *and* the way recursive calls are performed. The domain is defined in such a way that if an element belongs to it, then all the arguments of the recursive calls needed to compute the result of the function on this argument also belong to it. For example, the domain Dpow2 of fast exponentiation is defined as follows:

```
Inductive Dpow2 : nat → Set :=
  DPow2_0 : Dpow2 0
| DPow2_S_even : ∀ (q : nat) (H : even (S q)),
                   even_odd_dec (S q) = left _ H →
                     Dpow2 (div2 (S q)) → Dpow2 (S q)
| DPow2_S_odd : ∀ (q : nat) (H : odd (S q)),
                  even_odd_dec (S q) = right _ H →
                    Dpow2 q → Dpow2 (S q)
```

Using the closure property of Dpow2, one can define an auxiliary (dependently typed) function Ppow2: ∀a:nat, Dpow2 a →nat that takes an additional argument a proof of membership in the domain; the function is defined by induction on its last argument. Finally, one can obtain a function in one argument by showing that Dpow2 a is inhabited for each natural number a.

The approach is elegant, allows users to defer the proof of totality of the function, and provides induction principles for free: thus it satisfies the criteria

(DT) and (SR). However, it does not satisfy the criteria (ST) and (X). More importantly, in the above we have departed from standard practice by defining Dpow2 as a dependent set, rather than as a proposition (observe that the type of Dpow2 is nat → **Set**). As a result, the extracted function is not that expected because it looks like:

```
let rec ppow2 x = function
  | DPow2_0 → S O
  | DPow2_S_odd (q, x0) →
      mult (ppow2 (div2 (S q)) x0) (ppow2 (div2 (S q)) x0)
  | DPow2_S_even (q, x0) → mult (S (S O)) (ppow2 q x0)
```

This phenomenon is due to the fact that, in Coq's type theory, the sorts **Set** and **Prop** are not equivalent: the sort **Set** is the sort of datatypes (which are relevant from a computational point of view and are therefore translated to Caml code by Coq's extraction mechanism), whereas **Prop** is the sort of logical properties (which are not translated to Caml).

Bertot and Castéran [7] point out a possible approach for adapting the *ad-hoc predicate* approach to the Calculus of Inductive Constructions—which amounts to defining Dpow2 with type nat → **Prop**, and still being able to define pow2 afterwards. Once more, the difficulty arises from the guard predicate which requires users to prove in a very specific manner so-called inversion theorems:

```
Lemma Dpow2_even_inv : ∀ n (p:Dpow2 n) (q : nat) (H_eq:n = S q )
    (H : even (S q)),even_odd_dec (S q) = left _ H → Dpow2 (div2 (S q)).

Lemma Dpow2_odd_inv :  ∀ n (p:Dpow2 n) (q : nat) (H_eq:n = S q )
    (H : odd (S q)), even_odd_dec (S q) = right _ H → Dpow2 q.
```

These lemmas show how to deduce from a proof of Dpow2 (S q), either a proof of Dpow2 (div2 (S q)) if (S q) is even or a proof of Dpow2 q if (S q) is odd. Whether or not we can define the recursive function pow2 depends on the way one proves these lemmas—a blatant violation of the principle of proof irrelevance—and the guard condition makes it impossible for users to apply existing tools to reason about relations or for dealing with equalities. If we prove them in the correct way, we can define Ppow2 by structural induction on an argument of type Dpow2 n. The corresponding extracted Caml program is the one we expected:

```
let rec ppow2 = function
  | O → S O
  | S q →
      (match even_odd_dec (S q) with
       | Left → let rec_res = ppow2 (div2 (S q)) in mult rec_res rec_res
       | Right → mult (S (S O)) (ppow2 q))
```

but using the *ad-hoc predicate* approach in Coq definitively requires a lot of expertise and pushes Coq (and users) to their limits.

2.3 Functional Induction

functional induction is a new Coq tactic that originates from work by Barthe and Courtieu [2]; it generates automatically induction principles which have proved very useful in reasoning about executable semantics [3], but its scope of application is limited to structurally recursive functions. In addition, the tactic builds the induction principle from the internal representation of the function instead of building it from the user definition of the function, which leads to unnecessarily verbose induction principles which in some circumstances are hard to use. For example, it was not possible to use this tactic in the work [18].

2.4   Other Approaches in Coq

The "converging iterations" approach In [1], a recursive function f is defined as the solution of a fixpoint equation involving a functional F. The definition involves proving that the fixpoint equation terminates in a finite number of iterations. The fixpoint equation of f is then obtained almost for free. Induction principles are not provided. The approach has been implemented in a prototype tool that automatically generates some of the definitions, proof obligations, and corresponding proofs.

The tool of Balaa and Bertot [1], which is currently the sole tool for Coq based on this approach, does not satisfy the criteria (DT) and (ST) and (X), and only partially satisfies the criterion (SR), as it only provides the fixpoint equation for the function.

Combining [9] and [1]. In [6], the "converging iterations" and "ad-hoc predicate" approaches are merged into a powerful technique for recursive function definition, allowing for partial functions with nested recursive calls. The method is implementable in Coq. It satisfies criteria (DT) and (SR) but it also adds up all the difficulties of the two combined approaches, which makes it quite hard to grasp and to use for practical verification purposes.

Using coinductive types. Capretta [12] uses co-inductive types to encode the tick monad, which associates to every type its type of partial elements, and shows how the monad can-be used to formalize all recursive functions between two given types.

2.5   Yet Another Approach: Extending Coq

Another approach is to increase the class of recursive functions that are accepted by Coq's termination criterion by introducing increasingly powerful syntactic schemes [8], or more semantical schemes based on size information [4] (the latter also bears some resemblance with work of Xi [25] on enforcing termination using restricted dependent types). In fact, the implementation of the *ad-hoc* predicate approach could be significantly simplified by abandoning the guard predicate in favor of type-based termination methods, especially for inversion lemmas. However, it is unavoidable to fall back on general recursion in the end.

The developers of Epigram are exploring a more radical approach and elaborate a powerful theory of pattern-matching that lends well to programming with dependent types [19]. They use views, which play a similar role to inductive domain predicates and enlarge the set of acceptable fixpoint definitions.

3   Overview of the Tool

Our tool[1] is based on the notion of graph associated with a function. In link with the previous section, the function pow2 will be used as a running example for describing our tool. The tool takes as input functions defined in a pseudo-code style (without guard conditions on recursive calls). The new command by the user is:

```
GenFixpoint pow2 (n: nat) {wf nat_measure}:  nat  :=
  match n with
  |0 ⇒ 1
  |S q ⇒ match (even_odd_dec (S q)) with
           |left _ ⇒ square (pow2 (div2 (S  q)))
           |right _ ⇒ n * (pow2 q)
          end
  end.
```

3.1   Proof Obligations Delegated to the User

By default, the definition of the function must be provided with a relation (named nat_measure in the current example) between function arguments to justify the termination (with the **wf** keyword). Our tool then generates two kinds of proof obligations to be interactively proved: the user must first prove that all recursive calls respect the given relation (*compatibility property*) and the relation must be proved well founded (*well-founded property*). For the pow2 function, three subgoals are generated. Subgoals 1 and 2 deal with compatibility properties, and subgoal 3 deals with the well-founded property.

```
3 subgoals

  ==============================
   ∀ (n q : nat) (h : even (S q)),
   n = S q  →  even_odd_dec (S q) = left h  →  nat_measure (div2 (S q)) n

subgoal 2 is:
  ∀ (n q : nat) (h : odd (S q)),
  n = S q  →  even_odd_dec (S q) = right h  →  nat_measure q n
subgoal 3 is:
  well_founded nat_measure
```

Our tool proposes other termination criteria, each of them with different kinds of proof obligations :

- {**measure** f}: the termination relies on a measure function f. The generated proof obligations require to prove that measures of recursive calls are smaller than measure of initial arguments. These kind of proof obligations are often easily discharged with arithmetic decision procedures.
- {**struct** arg}: the function is structurally recursive on argument arg (standard Coq criterion). No proof obligation is required.
- {**adhoc**}: the user doesn't want to prove termination. The generated function will be partial: pow2 : ∀n:nat, Dpow2 n →nat, where Dpow2 is the adhoc predicate associated with pow2.

---

[1] The current implementation of the tool is available at http://www-sop.inria.fr/everest/personnel/David.Pichardie/genfixpoint with several examples of generated coq files.

3.2   Automated Generation of the Function

The first task of the tool is to generate the graph relation of the function, as an inductive relation that completely "mimics" its definition. We use one constructor for each branch of the function pattern matching.

```
Inductive pow2_rel : nat → nat → Prop :=
|pow2_0 : pow2_rel 0 1
|pow2_1 : ∀ q res, (even_odd_dec (S q)) = left _ →
    pow2_rel (div2 (S q)) res → (pow2_rel (S q) (square res))
|pow2_2 : ∀ q res, (even_odd_dec (S q)) = right _ →
    pow2_rel q res → pow2_rel (S q) (2*res).
```

The next step is then to implement this relation : program a Coq function pow2:nat→nat which satisfies the relation pow2_rel: ∀ n, pow2_rel n (pow2 n). We have experimented (and implemented) two techniques to achieve this task.

– A first approach is to use a well founded induction principle for defining an auxiliary function pow2_rich with a rich dependent type. This type specifies that the function satisfies its graph relation:

```
Definition pow2_type (n:nat) := {pow2_n: nat | pow2_rel n pow2_n}.
```

We automatically generate a proof script for this definition[2]. During the proof, applications of the induction hypothesis are justified using compatibility properties previously discharged by the user. It is then straightforward to define pow2

```
Definition pow2 (n:nat) : nat := let (f,_) := pow2_rich n in f.
```

– The second technique is based on ad-hoc predicates. The predicate is extracted from the graph relation by projection. We hence exactly generate the predicate Dpow2 described in Section 2.2. Two approaches may then be used, depending on whether this predicate is in **Set** or **Prop**.
  - Dpow2:nat→**Set**: this is the simplest approach. A function pow2_adhoc of type ∀ n, Dpow2 n →nat is directly programmed by pattern matching on its argument of type Dpow2 n. This technique has a more general application: it allows to generate executable code from inductive relations (see Section 3.4).
  - Dpow2:nat→**Prop**: in this approach, we must first generate inversion lemmas to justify recursive calls, as explained in Section 2.2. These lemmas rely on a more general property which establishes that distinct branches of the graph are pairwise incompatible. All these lemmas (statements and proofs) are automatically generated by inspection of the graph relation. It is a particularly difficult part for the tool since statements must be proved in a very specific manner (they are proof-relevant, see Section 2.2).

  In both cases the totality of the function must still be proved. We hence generate an implementation of the ad-hoc domain by well-founded induction over the relation nat_measure.

---

[2] We use here the possibility of programming by proof.

Lemma compute_Dpow2 : ∀ n, Dpow2 n.

The definition of pow2 is then straightforward by combining compute_Dpow2 and pow2_ahdoc.

Definition pow2 (n:nat) : nat := pow2_ahdoc n (compute_Dpow2 n).

As a final result, we obtain a Coq function verifying the graph relation whose extracted code is exactly as expected (except for the technique using an ad-hoc predicate in **Set**).

In the next section, we only require to have an implementation pow2 of the graph relation pow2_rel: the actual technique used for defining pow2 is not relevant.

3.3   Automatic Generation of Reasoning Principles

We now turn to generate the reasoning principles presented at the beginning of Section 2. All steps are carried automatically. The first step is to characterize pow2_rel as the graph of pow2.

$$∀ x \; y, \; pow2\_rel \; x \; y \; →pow2 \; x = y$$

This is done by proving that the graph has the following "functional" property:

$$∀ x \; y1 \; y2, \; pow2\_rel \; x \; y1 \; →pow2\_rel \; x \; y2 \; →y1=y2$$

Using the now proved equivalence between pow2 and pow2_rel we generate:

- the inputs/outputs induction principle: starting from the induction principle of the relation pow2_rel (automatically generated by Coq, as for all inductive definitions) we remove all occurrences of pow2_rel using pow2.
- the general induction principle: the construction is similar to the previous principle, but using the induction principle of ad-hoc domain instead of the graph relation. This proof only relies on the fact that pow2 satisfies its associated graph.
- fixpoint equation: once again proving the fixpoint equation by reasoning on pow2_rel is easy. We only have to follow the definition of the pseudo code.
- inversion principle: an hypothesis of the form e' = pow2 e is first transformed into pow2_rel e e', then we use the Coq tactic inversion to discriminate some incompatible cases, and we replace all generated hypotheses dealing with pow2_rel with their equivalent form dealing with pow2.

Definitions by pattern matching are internally represented in Coq by case analysis. As a result, users wanting to prove a property about a function they have defined with a few cases may be faced with an artificially large number of cases [18]. Our tool avoids the explosion of cases in reasoning about functions by providing appropriate induction principles, with exactly the same number of cases as the definition of the function. An extension of our tool is currently planned to correctly handle the default case which could occurs in a pattern matching.

3.4   Applications to relations

The tools we developed for the *ad-hoc* approach can serve a much more general purpose than defining and reasoning about recursive functions presented using pseudo-code. In fact, our work can be used to generate executable code from inductive relations. Such a possibility is interesting, because many existing developments, especially those concerned with programming language semantics, favor an inductive style of formalization. As mentioned above, inductive formalizations are attractive, because they elude issues of partiality, termination, and determinacy, and also because they make reasoning principles immediately available to users. However, defining a semantics inductively does not yield an executable semantics. Several works have attempted to overcome this weakness of inductive relations by providing mechanisms that transform inductively defined relations in a proof assistant based on type theory into recursive programs in a typed functional language, see e.g. [5]. While such a translation allows users to specify and verify inductively defined functions, and to extract an executable program for computing the result of the functions, it forces computations to take place *outside* the proof assistant. In contrast, our tool provides a means to generate *within* the proof assistant executable functions that realize inductive relations. By doing so, our tool makes it possible to prove the correctness of the executable semantics w.r.t the inductive one. This brings higher guarantees in the context of safety or security critical applications (which will typically use extracted code), because only the extraction mechanism of Coq needs to be trusted. We are currently experimenting with the tool for generating executable semantics of virtual machines from inductive semantics.

Note that our tools do not require determinacy in order to transform inductive relations into functions. Indeed, for non-deterministic relations the *ad-hoc* domain will not only encode the stack of recursive calls, but also the evaluation strategy used to compute a result. Thus our tool opens interesting perspectives in the context of encoding arbitrary term rewriting systems as functions (with an additional argument, i.e. the strategy) *within* the proof assistant. Potential applications include the design of reflective tactics, which encode decision procedures in Coq, and allow to achieve smaller and faster proofs, see e.g. [16] for a reflective tactic based on rewriting. The encoding is also of interest for confluent term rewriting systems, because it allows to defer the proof of confluence, or equivalently of functionality of its graph; this allows for example to rely on termination to prove confluence.

4   Case Studies

4.1   Interval Sets

We have built a library for finite sets of natural numbers encoded using ordered lists of intervals, it was planned to be part of the development of a framework for certified static analyses [10]. It includes functions for union, intersection, inclusion, and membership tests.

Among all those operations, the union operation is the most involved. We describe in some detail its definition and some of the proofs that we have written around it using our method.

First, interval sets are defined using the following two inductive relations (: : is the Coq notation for *cons* on lists, and fst, snd return the first, resp. the second element of a pair):

```
Inductive  is_interval (i:Z*Z) : Prop :=
 |is_interval_cons :  fst i <= snd i  →  is_interval i.

Inductive is_interval_set : list (Z*Z)  →  Prop :=
  |Nil_set : is_interval_set nil
  |Single_set : ∀ i, is_interval i  →  is_interval_set (i::nil)
  |Cons_set : ∀ i j l,
     is_interval i  →  is_interval j  →   (1+ snd i) < fst j  →
     is_interval_set (j::l)  →  is_interval_set (i::j::l).
```

In particular, note that successive intervals in an interval set may not intersect each other, touch each other, or even be *adjacent*: $1 + snd\ i < fst\ j$, otherwise, they would form a single interval.

An inductive definition compare_intervals_dec a1 a2, not shown here, compares the relative positions of two intervals a1, a2. An implementation of the union operation linear in the size of its arguments cannot be structural, as it cannot predict in advance how the lists begin (more specifically, how many initial intervals of one list are included in the second one):

```
Fixpoint union (li1 li2: list (Z*Z)) : list (Z*Z) :=
match li1, li2 with
|nil, l' ⇒ l'
|l'', nil ⇒ l''
|a1::l1, a2::l2 ⇒
  match compare_intervals_dec a1 a2 with
   |snd_far_after _  ⇒ a1::(union l1 (a2::l2))
   |snd_close_after _ _ _⇒ union l1 ((fst a1,snd a2)::l2) (*not structural*)
   |snd_includes _ _ _  ⇒ union l1 (a2::l2)
   |snd_equal_fst _ _ ⇒ a1::(union l1 l2)
   |fst_includes _ _ _  ⇒  union (a1::l1) l2
   |fst_close_after _ _ _⇒ union ((fst a2,snd a1)::l1) l2 (*not structural*)
   |fst_far_after _ ⇒ a2::(union (a1::l1) l2)
      end
end.
```

One property that we need to prove about the union function is that, although its arguments are lists of pairs of integers, by applying it to two interval_sets one obtains an interval_set.

This turned out to be a nontrivial exercise. We have solved it as follows: we have defined a *weak interval set* structure, which is a list of intervals in which consecutive intervals may overlap, and a *weak union* operation, which is closed on weak interval sets (but not on proper interval sets). Then, a *grouping* operation transforms a weak interval set into a proper interval set. Weak union and grouping are also non-strucuturally recursive, but somewhat simpler that the proper union. We then show that the proper union is equal to the composition of the weak union and the grouping operations, and that the result of the composition is an interval set.

For this, we make a heavy use of the induction principles for proper union, union, and grouping functions. Several dozens of lemmas were proved using those principles; without them, we could not have completed the development.

4.2 Systems of Affine Recurrence Equations

Consider the following system:

```
W[n,i] =
    if  n<=N+D-1 then 0
    if  N+D<=n then W[n-1,i] +  (E[n-D] * x[n-i-D])
Y[n,i] =
    if i=-1 then 0
    if 0<=i then Y[n,i-1] + (W[n,i] * x[n-i])
E[n] = (d[n] - res[n]);
res[n] = Y[n,N-1];
```

which implements an auto adaptive filter [17] used in signal processing for noise cancellation or system identification. It takes an input signal x and a reference input d and updates its convolution coefficients so that the output signal res will converge towards the reference input.

The program can be rewritten in pseudo-code, yielding mutually recursive partial recursive functions. We now want to prove the following:

```
(∀ n, d n = 0)  →  (∀ n, res n = 0)
```

A basic analysis of the dependencies in the system of equations reveals a circularity in the proof: in order to prove the property, we must prove that Y is uniformly null, which requires to prove that x is uniformly, which requires to prove that res is uniformly null. Without appropriate induction principles on the structure of the function, the proof is intractable. In [11], Cachera and Pichardie report on a tool that generates induction principles for this specific class of systems. Our tool subsumes their work, as we dispose of a general tool which produces the same principles for the class of systems they consider. In particular, applying the induction principle generated by our tool allows us to conclude the proof with a few applications of the ring tactic of Coq.

5 Conclusion

We have presented a tool to define and reason about recursive functions in Coq, and shown on non-trivial examples that the tool significantly improves over earlier work by simplifying the definition of functions, and generating automatically all reasoning principles required to prove properties about the function. Our tool is very similar in spirit to the TFL tool developed by Slind [24] for Isabelle and HOL, but differently from TFL, our tool is based on the observation that the graph of a function is the most powerful property satisfied by the function, and exploits state-of-the-art techniques for defining recursive definitions in type theory.

Further work is required to enhance the applicability of the tool. In order to increase usability, we plan to allow in pseudo-code non-exhaustive and ordered pattern matching (a specific instance of ordered pattern matching being default cases). Such an extension would solve common problems encountered by Coq users:

- *partial functions:* the prevailing approach with partial functions is to use the lift monad, i.e. to encode partial functions from A to B as total functions from A to $B_\perp$. Yet, experience in the formalization of programming language semantics has demonstrated that the use of the lift monad clutters definitions, and hence later proofs [3]. The extended tool shall simplify the definition of partial functions by omitting cases of undefinedness in pseudo-code, and reasoning about partial functions by combining the induction and inversion principles into a principle to reason about the defined cases of the function.

- *increasing support for termination proofs:* proving termination is made easier by our tool, but still requires some work from the users. In the future, we intend to extend pseudo-code to accept not only well-founded orders and measures, but also reduction orders. The extended tool shall enable users to benefit immediately from ongoing efforts to develop libraries for certifying termination proofs in Coq [22], and to reduce even further the effort dedicated to termination proofs.

It could also be interesting to extend our tool to nested recursive functions. One well-known difficulty is that applying the *ad hoc* predicate approach to nested functions requires to use inductive-recursive definitions [14], which are not part of the Calculus of Inductive Constructions. In an unpublished note, Capretta has shown how induction-recursion can be given an impredicative encoding in the Calculus of Inductive Constructions; unfortunately, the use of impredicativity severely restricts the possibilities of exploiting the encoding, and solutions that cater for predicative universes must be sought.

References

1. A. Balaa and Y. Bertot. Fix-point equations for well-founded recursion in type theory. In M. Aagaard and J. Harrison, editors, *Proceedings of TPHOLs'00*, volume 1689 of *Lecture Notes in Computer Science*, pages 1–16. Springer-Verlag, 2000.
2. G. Barthe and P. Courtieu. Efficient Reasoning about Executable Specifications in Coq. In V. Carreño, C. Muñoz, and S. Tahar, editors, *Proceedings of TPHOLs'02*, volume 2410 of *Lecture Notes in Computer Science*, pages 31–46. Springer-Verlag, 2002.
3. G. Barthe, G. Dufay, L. Jakubiec, B. Serpette, and S. Melo de Sousa. A Formal Executable Semantics of the JavaCard Platform. In D. Sands, editor, *Proceedings of ESOP'01*, volume 2028 of *Lecture Notes in Computer Science*, pages 302–319. Springer-Verlag, 2001.
4. G. Barthe, M. J. Frade, E. Giménez, L. Pinto, and T. Uustalu. Type-based termination of recursive definitions. *Mathematical Structures in Computer Science*, 14:97–141, February 2004.

5. S. Berghofer and T. Nipkow. Executing higher order logic. In P. Callaghan, Z. Luo, J. McKinna, and R. Pollack, editors, *Proceedings of TYPES'00*, volume 2277 of *Lecture Notes in Computer Science*, pages 24–40. Springer-Verlag, 2002.

6. Y. Bertot, V. Capretta, and K. Das Barman. Type-theoretic functional semantics. In V. Carreño, C. Muñoz, and S. Tahar, editors, *Proceedings of TPHOLs'02*, volume 2410 of *Lecture Notes in Computer Science*, pages 83–98. Springer-Verlag, 2002.

7. Y. Bertot and P. Castéran. *Interactive Theorem Proving and Program Development— Coq'Art: The Calculus of Inductive Constructions*. Texts in Theoretical Computer Science. Springer-Verlag, 2004.

8. F. Blanqui. Definitions by rewriting in the calculus of constructions. *Mathematical Structures in Computer Science*, 15(1):37–92, February 2005.

9. A. Bove and V. Capretta. Modelling general recursion in type theory. *Mathematical Structures in Computer Science*, 15:671–708, February 2005.

10. D. Cachera, T. Jensen, D. Pichardie, and V. Rusu. Extracting a data flow analyser in constructive logic. *Theoretical Computer Science*, 342, 2005. To appear.

11. D. Cachera and D. Pichardie. Embedding of Systems of Affine Recurrence Equations in Coq. In *Proceedings of TPHOLs'03*, number 2758 in Lecture Notes in Computer Science, pages 155–170. Springer-Verlag, 2003.

12. Venanzio Capretta. General recursion via coinductive types. *Logical Methods in Computer Science*, 1(2):1–18, 2005.

13. Coq Development Team. *The Coq Proof Assistant User's Guide. Version 8.0*, January 2004.

14. P. Dybjer. A general formulation of simultaneous inductive-recursive definitions in type theory. *Journal of Symbolic Logic*, 65(2):525–549, June 2000.

15. M.J.C. Gordon and T.F. Melham, editors. *Introduction to HOL: A theorem proving environment for higher-order logic*. Cambridge University Press, 1993.

16. B. Grégoire and A. Mahboubi. Proving equalities in a commutative ring done right in coq. In J. Hurd and T. Melham, editors, *Proceedings of TPHOLs'05*, volume 3603 of *Lecture Notes in Computer Science*, pages 98–113. Springer-Verlag, 2005.

17. M. Katsushige, N. Kiyoshi, and K. Hitoshi. Pipelined LMS Adaptive Filter Using a New Look-Ahead Transformation. *IEEE Transactions on Circuits and Systems*, 46:51–55, January 1999.

18. X. Leroy. Formal certification of a compiler back-end, or: programming a compiler with a proof assistant. In *Proceedings of POPL'06*. ACM Press, 2006.

19. C. McBride and J. McKinna. The view from the left. *Journal of Functional Programming*, 14:69–111, 2004.

20. T. Nipkow, L. C. Paulson, and M. Wenzel. *Isabelle/HOL: A Proof Assistant for Higher-Order Logic*, volume 2283 of *Lecture Notes in Computer Science*. Springer-Verlag, 2002.

21. B. Nordström. Terminating general recursion. *BIT*, 28(3):605–619, 1988.

22. Color Project. http://color.inria.fr

23. N. Shankar, S. Owre, and J.M. Rushby. *The PVS Proof Checker: A Reference Manual*. Computer Science Laboratory, SRI International, February 1993. Supplemented with the PVS2 Quick Reference Manual, 1997.

24. K. Slind. *Reasoning about Terminating Functional Programs*. PhD thesis, TU München, 1999.

25. H. Xi. Dependent types for program termination verification. *Higher-Order and Symbolic Computation*, 15(1):91–131, March 2002.

Soutei, a Logic-Based Trust-Management System

System Description

Andrew Pimlott[1] and Oleg Kiselyov[2]

[1] Planning Systems, Inc., Slidell, LA
andrew@pimlott.net
[2] Fleet Numerical Meteorology and Oceanography Center, Monterey, CA
oleg@pobox.com

Abstract. We describe the design and implementation of a trust-management system Soutei, a dialect of Binder, for access control in distributed systems. Soutei policies and credentials are written in a declarative logic-based security language and thus constitute distributed logic programs. Soutei policies are modular, concise, and readable. They support policy verification, and, despite the simplicity of the language, express role- and attribute-based access control lists, and conditional delegation.

We describe the real-world deployment of Soutei into a publish-subscribe web service with distributed and compartmentalized administration, emphasizing the often overlooked aspect of authorizing the creation of resources and the corresponding policies.

Soutei brings Binder from a research prototype into the real world. Supporting large, truly distributed policies required non-trivial changes to Binder, in particular mode-restriction and goal-directed top-down evaluation. To improve the robustness of our evaluator, we describe a fair and terminating backtracking algorithm.

Keywords: Access control, Security Language, Logic Programming, Datalog, Non-determinism, Backtracking, Haskell.

1 Introduction

An authorization system is called upon to advise whether an access request, such as fetching a web page, should be permitted. To reach a decision, the system consults attributes of the request (such as the users and resources involved), information about the world, and policies. While simple data structures like access control lists suffice as policies in some cases, they fail to accommodate large and volatile sets of users and resources, complicated constraints, and distributed administration.

Blaze et al. [3] introduced the trust-management system as a standard interface for applications (web servers, etc.) to ask an authorization system whether a requested action should be allowed, and a standard language for writing distributed and interoperable policies. Trust management is characterized by the following design principles, which have proved to be both flexible and efficiently implementable:

- The application provides facts about the requested action (axioms);
- policies specify the derivation of other facts (inference rules);

M. Hagiya and P. Wadler (Eds.): FLOPS 2006, LNCS 3945, pp. 130–145, 2006.

- the authorization system is a policy compliance checker, which advises the application whether an application-defined action (formula) should be allowed (can be inferred from the axioms and inference rules);
- the compliance checker is a deduction engine.

These principles have been validated by KeyNote [2], the most well-known trust-management system with several real-world applications. The security language of KeyNote however has several notable drawbacks [15, 13]: It is impossible in general to analyze the effect of KeyNote assertions, for example to verify global policy constraints.

We argue that a trust-management system should be based upon a single, declarative language, with transparent semantics and a minimum of primitives. The language should be easy to read, write, and modify. It should express complicated policies without redundancy, and allow independent policies to be composed. It should be amenable to automated formal analysis and efficient, robust, high-assurance implementation.

Experience with a common class of policies, firewall configurations, illustrates the hazards when these requirements are not met. Firewall rules are numerous, and their overall effect is difficult to understand; a seemingly small change may lead to a cascade failure [19], which, absent policy verification, may go undetected. A study of firewall configuration errors [23] found flaws in every firewall examined: "Only one of the 37 firewalls exhibited just a single misconfiguration. All the others could have been easily penetrated by both unsophisticated attackers and mindless automatic worms."

DeTreville [7] introduced a logic-based security language Binder for expressing policies in distributed systems. Binder is an extension of the logic programming language Datalog, which, in turn, is a subset of pure Prolog. Despite having few primitive constructs (only one distinguished relation says), Binder is shown to be more expressive than most existing security languages. The ease of naming and referring to other policies via says is especially attractive. Despite its power, Binder is concise and comprehensible: A statement in Binder can be read as a declarative, stand-alone English sentence [7]. Binder has a clean design and sound logical foundations [1]. In our view, Binder meets the criteria for a trust-management language put forth above. Alas, it was just a research prototype with no implementation.

Soutei can be viewed as KeyNote whose security language is replaced with Binder—or as the first practical implementation of Binder. However in producing a working system, we had to specify many aspects left undefined in DeTreville's paper, and add several extensions. Many of the extensions, such as the interaction between an application and Soutei, are notably influenced by KeyNote.

Our contributions are:

- An extension of Binder to specify the interaction between the authorization system and the application. We introduce a dedicated application namespace for the application to supply attributes of the request and environment data, which can be used in policies.
- A re-interpretation of the distinguished Binder relation says, allowing us to use a goal-directed resolution-based strategy, which can cope with the large number of distributed policies.

- A mode system for assertions, with mode-restricted forms and static checking of the satisfaction of the restrictions.
- A general-purpose efficient backtracking algorithm with fairness and termination properties.
- Two implementations, designed to support various applications.[1]
- Deployment of Soutei into a publish-subscribe web service with distributed and compartmentalized administration. Administrative actions such as the creation of resources and the attachment of authorization policies are themselves subject to authorization.

The next section introduces Soutei by a series of examples. Section 3 presents a real-world use case, using Soutei with a publish-subscribe web service. In Section 4, we describe three aspects of Soutei implementation: its goal-directed resolution-based evaluation, modes, and backtracking algorithm. These aspects represent notable deviations from Binder, influenced by practical requirements, and can be re-used in other similar systems. We present performance measurements in Section 5. Section 6 examines related work; and Section 7 concludes. The formal semantics of Soutei is given in the Appendix.

2   Soutei by Example

We present the fundamentals of Soutei with a simple policy:

```
may(read)  :- application says ip-address(?IP),
              internal(?IP).
internal(#p10.10.1.1). ; trusted internal clients
internal(#p10.10.1.2).
```

The syntax of Soutei is taken mainly from Binder and Datalog; however, there are minor departures: A leading question mark rather than a capital letter identifies logical variables, to avoid confusion with proper names. Atomic constants include symbols (which may be enclosed in double quotes, to escape spaces and similar characters) and IP addresses. A semicolon begins a single-line comment.

The semantics of Soutei is likewise close to Binder and Datalog [7]. The above example consists of three clauses: an inference rule for the predicate may, and two axioms for the predicate internal. The may rule has a body consisting of two atoms, both of which must be satisfied to derive may(read). The internal predicate has two clauses, either of which may satisfy ip-address(?IP). Informally, the policy can be read, "read access is granted to clients with internal IP addresses, which are 10.10.1.1 and 10.10.1.2".

The interpretation of the predicate may is *not* built-in, but given by the application requesting advice, which presents the formula for Soutei to derive. In our example, an application would submit formulas such as may(read) and may(write). The application also sends additional axioms representing facts about the request; in this

---

[1] A simple web interface to Soutei is available at http://www.metnet.navy.mil/cgi-bin/mcsrvr/soutei-demonstration.

case, we expect it to send an `ip-address` axiom. Again, the application, not Soutei, chooses the predicates. These axioms, along with the formula to prove, are analogous to an action in KeyNote.

We have created an s-expression-based protocol for applications to request advice from Soutei. The application in this example might open a TCP connection to a Soutei server and send

```
(req-17 query (may read) (ip-address #p10.10.1.1) ...)
```

Soutei responds with a boolean result, indicating whether it could derive the formula: `(req-17 #t)`.[2] It is the responsibility of the application to ensure that Soutei's advice is followed. In RFC 3198 [22] terms, Soutei acts as a Policy Decision Point, and the application as a Policy Enforcement Point.

We have left to explain the primitive form `says`. As in Binder, the policy in Soutei is a set of (distributed) *assertions*, named collections of facts and rules. The distinguished assertion `system`, analogous to the `POLICY` principal in KeyNote, represents the top-level policy, and is loaded from a start-up configuration file. Derivation of the formula presented by the application is always attempted within the `system` assertion.[3] The distinguished assertion `application` contains the facts sent by the application (as well as some some built-in predicates that cannot be defined within Soutei; see Section 4.2). The form `says` indicates that a predicate should be resolved within another assertion, allowing assertions to refer to each other. In our example, the `ip-address` predicate is to be resolved within the `application` assertion. The semantics of `says` is discussed further in Section 4.1.

Assertions (other than `system` and `application`) may come from various sources, depending on the system architecture. In our current implementation, they are pushed to Soutei; however, they might instead be stored in a local, remote, or distributed database, pulled from a subscription service, or be delivered with a decision request as signed credentials. Because an assertion has no force unless referred to by `says`, we can allow every user to control his own assertion without worrying about compromising the policy.

Let us consider some more sophisticated examples. We can model access control lists, statements enumerating the users and roles who have access to given resources. The user and resource data are, like the IP address, passed as application facts.

```
may(?access) :- application says resource(?resource),
                application says public-key(?key),
                user-key(?user, ?key),
                role-member(?user, ?role),
                acl-may(?access, ?resource, ?role).
; users and their public keys
user-key(Peter, "rsa:Z2FuZ3N0YQ==").
user-key(Bill, "rsa:eWVhaCBoaQ==").
; roles
role-member(Peter, programmer).
```

---

[2] `req-17` is a request identifier chosen by the client; it is not interpreted Soutei.

[3] Our example policy was tacitly the `system` assertion.

```
role-member(Bill, manager).
; ACLs
acl-may(read, TPS-report-memo, programmer).
acl-may(read, TPS-report-memo, manager).
acl-may(write, TPS-report-memo, manager).
```

Following KeyNote, we identify users by their public keys, which may be delivered to the application in an SSL handshake. As public keys are unwieldy, we create convenient aliases with `user-key`. The predicate `role-member` expresses role membership, and `acl-may` lists the permissions of different roles on resources.

Storing role membership, ACLs and associations of user names with their keys in the top-level policy is generally inappropriate. The `system` policy is modifiable only by the Soutei administrator, but (hypothetically) the human resources (HR) department should maintain users' keys, the application owner should manage roles, and resource owners should control ACLs. We can divide authority in this way using `says`.

```
may(?access) :- application says resource(?resource),
                application says resource-owner(?owner),
                application says public-key(?key),
                hr says user-key(?user, ?key),
                app-owner says role-member(?user, ?role),
                ?owner says acl-may(?access, ?resource, ?role).
```

The assertions of HR, the application owner, and the resource owner are now all involved in the authorization decision, although each has a different and limited role. These assertions may use the full Soutei language; in particular, they may use `says` to further delegate their authority.

Another use of `says` is to reconcile policies, even policies using different vocabularies.

```
may(?access) :- authority1 says can(?access)
                application says resource(?resource),
                authority2 says ok(?access, ?resource).
may(read) :- authority1 says can(read).
```

In this example, `authority1` alone may grant read access, but other access requires the agreement of both authorities. Note it is not a problem that the authorities use different predicates.

The Soutei documentation [13] describes the use of Soutei for role-based and capability-based access control, discusses monotonicity, revocation, blacklisting, and introduces additional use cases (which we use as the regression test of our implementation).

3   A Real-Life Use Case

We have integrated Soutei with a general purpose publish-subscribe data distribution web service, Metcast Channels [12]. Clients of this service can publish data into a channel, monitor a channel for data, and request the list of all channels. Metcast Channels have been used in an operational environment for several years. Previously, Metcast Channels used simple access control lists, which were quite inflexible. Assistance of the administrator was required to install or modify access control lists of any channel. As the system became more widely used and the number of user communities and their channels increased, so did the load on the administrator. Ideally the administrator should set up the top-level policy and leave managing particular channels to their owners.

Now, Metcast Channels is a Soutei application. Upon receiving a request to read, write, create, or delete a channel, the server seeks the advice of Soutei. Users may also submit their own Soutei assertions, via a special channel. A submitted assertion is associated with the user's authenticated name and stored in a local database. Since they pass through a channel, policy changes are authorized by Soutei, though we currently allow any authenticated user to submit an assertion. The following scenario demonstrates how this system overcomes the previous difficulties, and provides additional benefits.

The `system` policy is quite minimal: it does not grant privileges itself, it only delegates them. Specifically, it delegates permission to administer channels to a system administrator; permission to read and write channels to the channel owner; and all permissions to a security officer, for use in emergencies. In order to emphasize the distinction between channel administration and channel access operations (and to guard against carelessness), Metcast Channels uses two predicates, `may-admin` and `may`.

```
; delegate channel administration to sam.sysadmin
may-admin(?access)  :- sam.sysadmin says may-admin(?access).
; delegate channel access to the channel owner
may(?access)  :- application says channel-owner(?owner),
                 ?owner says may(?access).
; delegate all access to the security officer
may-admin(?access) :- ed.emergency says may-admin(?access).
may(?access)       :- ed.emergency says may(?access).
```

The security officer's assertion will normally be empty, so access will only be granted by the first two rules; however when the security officer does submit an assertion, it may bypass the usual rules.

A user, `cam.create`, wishes to create a channel, in order to publish his blog. In some systems, create access is tricky because there is no existing resource on which to hang the permissions. Soutei does not have a rigid vocabulary, though, so we can express an action not involving a resource naturally. On `cam.create`'s request, `sam.sysadmin` submits the rule

```
may-admin(create) :- application says user(cam.create).
```

The user `cam.create` then creates the channel `CamsBlog`. Note that by the very creation of this channel (and without administrator intervention), `cam.create`'s assertion comes into force to control access. He submits the following policy, granting himself read and write permissions, and authorizing `don.delegate` to grant read permission—but only within the computer science department.

```
may(?access)  :- application says channel(CamsBlog),
                 application says user(cam.create),
                 known-access(?access).
```

```
known-access(read).
known-access(write).
may(read)  :- application says channel(CamsBlog),
               application says user-department(CS),
               don.delegate says may(read).
```

The ability to delegate, in a controlled way, represents a major advance over access control lists.

don.delegate is careless. His policy is:

```
may(read)  :- application says channel(CamsBlog).
```

This permissive rule appears to grant read access to everyone. Of course, it does not: the chain of proof stops in cam.create's policy if the user is outside the CS department; don.delegate's assertion is never considered.

The stipulation of cam.create can, however, be circumvented by ed.emergency, because his authority comes directly from the system assertion. In a situation where access to information is paramount, he submits the policy

```
may(read).
```

Anyone can now read all channels. In the defense community, this flexibility is called Risk Adaptable Access Control (RAdAC), and is considered a critical requirement for the Global Information Grid [5].

4   Implementation

We initially implemented Soutei in Scheme, using the logical programming system Kanren [11]. We then re-implemented Soutei in Haskell. Decisive factors in this decision were static typing, manifest distinction between pure and effectful code, closeness to the specification language, and QuickCheck property testing. These all help increase one's confidence in the code, which is of special importance to us since Soutei is intended for high-assurance applications.

In this section, we discuss three particular aspects: goal-directed resolution-based evaluation, mode analysis, and a fair and terminating backtracking algorithm. These aspects represent advances over Binder and illustrate how practical needs for scalability, robustness, and error reporting influence design decisions.

4.1   Goal-Directed Resolution-Based Evaluation

Binder implicitly assumed that all assertions are immediately available. The relation says was taken to qualify predicates with assertion names. The formal qualification rules are given in [7] and logically justified in [1]. Once all predicates become qualified, one may regard the qualifier as an extra argument to the predicate, and then treat the collection of all available assertions as an ordinary, non-distributed Datalog program, to be evaluated with the conventional bottom-up strategy.

We assume a potentially large number of assertions, which makes keeping them all in memory impractical. We further assume that not all assertions are locally known—the logical program of Soutei is truly distributed. Under these conditions, whole-program translation into Datalog is not feasible. Goal-directed resolution-based evaluation seems more suitable, as it consults only those assertions that may actually be needed for the goal at hand. In fact, Soutei needs only one proof to advise access, so it may consult fewer.

We therefore view each assertion as a set of clauses [17], and a says B as a judgement that there is a proof of formula B given the clauses in assertion a. When such a judgement is required—and only then—we load the assertion and proceed with resolution. We use the backchaining rule to prove a formula given the clauses in an assertion [17, 4]. Appendix A shows the formal semantics of Soutei in full.

Our Haskell implementation follows the established pattern [18, 6] of embedding a resolution-based logical programming system in Haskell. To apply the backchaining rule, we non-deterministically choose a clause for the target predicate (see Section 4.3), unify with the head to build up the substitution, then sequentially resolve the body.

4.2 Modes

The distributed nature of Soutei motivates another aspect of the design. In Binder, one may use says whose left argument, the assertion name, is a logical variable—even an uninstantiated variable. This would have the effect of enumerating all assertions, which is fine when all assertions are locally available, but impractical in a distributed system. Therefore, we disallow this situation: the first argument of says must be instantiated, that is, it must have the In mode [20]. The application namespace has several built-in predicates that are similarly mode-restricted, such as ip-of, for matching an IP address against a network range. It expects both arguments to be instantiated, so they have the In mode.

Mode enforcement can be performed as a run-time instantiatedness check, whose failure either triggers an error or suspends the evaluation of a goal. But debugging these cases—which could arise from the interaction of many assertions—would be painful, and one could never be sure they are all eliminated. We prefer to detect and report ill-moded assertions when they are submitted. Therefore, we have designed and implemented a static mode analysis, which ensures that logical variables are used with the correct modes.

The static mode analysis poses several challenges. For ease of use, we would like to avoid explicit mode declarations. On the other hand, the distributed nature of Soutei makes whole-program mode analysis all but impossible. Fortunately, we can impose a simplifying and yet not-too-limiting restriction. For any predicate defined in an assertion, we require that all of its arguments be instantiated when the predicate succeeds. This requirement is tantamount to an implicit Out mode declaration for all arguments. We reject an assertion at submission time if it is not well-moded with respect to the implicit mode declaration.

The application assertion, which consists of application facts and built-in predicates, is treated specially. Facts trivially satisfy the Out mode; however the built-in predicates may have other modes, which must be known to the mode checker.

The intuition for the mode checker is that after a logical variable is used with an Out mode, it is safe to use in mode-restricted contexts. More precisely, we first assume that all atoms in the body of a rule, except those with mode-restricted application predicates, instantiate their logical variable arguments when they succeed. We then attempt to demonstrate two safety conditions: that all mode-restricted arguments to application predicates and to says are instantiated by a previous body atom; and that all logical variables in the head of the rule are instantiated somewhere in the body, that is, they satisfy the implicit Out mode. If so, the rule is well-moded. We leave a full elaboration of the mode inference judgments, and a proof of soundness, for future work.

We can apply this procedure to the rule

```
may(?access) :- application says ip-address(?IP),
                application says ip-of(?IP, #n192.168.0.0/8),
                administrator(?admin),
                ?admin says may(?access).
```

The logical variable ?IP is instantiated by the non-mode-restricted application predicate ip-address before it is used in the mode-restricted ip-of. The logical variable ?admin is instantiated by the predicate administrator before it is used to the left of says. And the head variable ?access is instantiated by the body predicate may. So the rule passes the mode checker. If the last two body atoms were reversed, so that ?admin were used with says before being instantiated, the rule would be rejected with a mode error.[4]

The requirement that predicates have the Out mode has a practical impact on their design. To give full access to a super-user, we cannot write

```
may(?access) :- application says user(?user),
                super-user(?user).
```

If may were called with ?access uninstantiated, it would remain uninstantiated, violating the implicit Out mode declaration.

Rather, we write the assertion as[5]

```
may(?access) :- application says user(?user),
                super-user(?user),
                known-access(?access).
known-access(read).
known-access(write).
```

We find that this style, while more verbose, is clearer about what is being granted. It will also give more information to a future policy verifier.

For similar reasons, we model users and resources as application facts, rather than (following DeTreville) as arguments to the formula to prove. Consider the proposed super-user rule

---

[4] We are investigating allowing the mode checker to reorder atoms in order to satisfy mode restrictions, as in Mercury [20].

[5] This explains the use of known-access in Section 3.

```
may(?user, ?access, ?resource) :- super-user(?user),
                                   known-access(?access).
```

The mode checker rejects this rule, as the `?resource` argument does not satisfy the `Out` mode. To repair it, we would need a predicate enumerating all resources, which is often infeasible. Our style sidesteps the issue.

4.3   Fair and Terminating Backtracking Algorithm

The goal-directed evaluation of Section 4.1 relied upon backchaining, which involves non-deterministic selection of the clause to apply. In this section we describe a backtracking algorithm implementing that non-deterministic choice. Although expressed as a Haskell monad, it can be implemented in other languages (and has been, in OCaml and Scheme). We use Haskell as a typed, executable specification language.

Following Wadler [21], we realize non-deterministic computations in Haskell as computations in a particular monad, `MonadPlus`. Specifically, the type class `MonadPlus` defines the interface for the minimal set of operations to express non-deterministic computations: `mzero` creates a failing computation; `return a` creates a deterministic computation that yields a; `m >>= k` sequences two computations, passing the results of computation m to k; and `mplus m1 m2` represents choice between computations m1 and m2. There is also an operation to run the computation, obtaining its answer (if any).

Wadler also introduced the list monad, an implementation of the `MonadPlus` interface that amounts to depth-first search. Although the most common `MonadPlus` implementation, and part of Haskell98 standard, we cannot use it for Soutei if we intend to be robust against careless or malicious policies. Consider the assertion:

```
loop(?x) :- loop(?x).
may(read) :- loop(1).
may(read).
```

Attempting to prove `may(read)` with depth-first backchaining, and selecting clauses in the order given, will diverge trying to prove `loop(1)`. We will never get to the second may clause, so access will not be granted, and—worse—Soutei will enter an infinite loop. If `loop` were in a separate assertion, referred to by `says`, that assertion could effect a denial of service attack.

Seres and Spivey [18] suggest using breadth-first search instead, and give a monad implementing this strategy. Breadth-first search is complete: it always finds a solution, provided one exists. However, it has large memory requirements, to hold the entire frontier of the computation, and so is not practical.

Depth-first search with iterative deepening brings completeness to depth-first search, at the cost of repeating parts of the computation, including side-effects such as loading assertions. We prefer to avoid this duplicate work.

Kiselyov, Shan, Friedman, and Sabry [14] present a non-determinism monad with fair operations for combining computations that may make an infinite number of choices. Alas, these operations are of no help in dealing with computations, such as our proof of `loop(1)`, that never yield an answer.

```
import Control.Monad

data FStream a = Nil | One a | Choice a (FStream a)
               | Incomplete (FStream a)

instance Monad FStream where
    return = One

    Nil          >>= f = Nil
    One a        >>= f = f a
    Choice a r   >>= f = f a `mplus` (Incomplete (r >>= f))
    Incomplete i >>= f = Incomplete (i >>= f)

instance MonadPlus FStream where
    mzero = Nil

    mplus Nil r'              = Incomplete r'
    mplus (One a) r'          = Choice a r'
    mplus (Choice a r) r'     = Choice a (mplus r' r)   -- interleave
    mplus r@(Incomplete i) r' =
        case r' of                                      -- try alternative
                 Nil          -> r
                 One b        -> Choice b i
                 Choice b r'  -> Choice b (mplus i r')
                 Incomplete j -> Incomplete (mplus i j)

yield :: FStream a -> FStream a
yield = Incomplete

runFS :: Maybe Int -> FStream a -> [a]
runFS _ Nil = []
runFS _ (One a) = [a]
runFS n (Choice a r) = a : (runFS n r)
runFS (Just 0) (Incomplete r) = []                      -- exhausted cost
runFS n (Incomplete r) = runFS n' r
    where n' = liftM pred n
```

Fig. 1. Complete FStream implementation

To overcome non-termination in such cases, we introduce a search algorithm that enjoys fairness, termination, and efficiency properties not found in prior work. Figure 1 shows the *complete* implementation.[6] We represent non-deterministic computations by terms of the algebraic type FStream a. In addition to the conventional terms Nil and Choice (analogous to [] and (:) in the list monad) representing failure and a choice [10], we add a term One a for a deterministic computation, and a term Incomplete (FStream a) denoting a suspended computation. The function runFS runs the computation.

The introduction of Incomplete allows us to capture the continuation of a computation—even a divergent one. Denotationally, Incomplete is the identity on

---

[6] We have also implemented the algorithm as a monad transformer, which allows us to execute IO operations, such as fetching a remote assertion, during computation.

computations. Operationally, it is a hint to the evaluator to explore alternative computations, if any. The definition of `mplus` honors the hint by deferring a computation marked with `Incomplete`; it also adopts the interleaving technique from [14] to achieve fairness. The result is a balance between depth- and breadth-first search strategies that performs well in practice. We leave a complete analysis of `FStream` for future work.

The programmer must apply the `Incomplete` hint (using the exported function `yield`) to potentially divergent computations. In Soutei, we call `yield` every time we choose a clause in the backchaining rule. Therefore, even a tight recursion such as proving `loop(1)` can be interrupted to try the second `may` clause. We believe that our use of `FStream` makes Soutei's resolution algorithm complete.

A final problem remains, of a top-level computation that neither fails nor succeeds in any evaluation strategy, such as our example with the second `may` clause removed. We require a way of giving up a fruitless search. Here `Incomplete` provides a separate benefit, as a measurement of the cost of a query. We take advantage of this in the top-level `runFS`. When `runFS` eliminates an `Incomplete`, it decrements a counter, allowing the programmer to control how long the computation should run.

Soutei passes a number chosen by the Soutei administrator to `runFS`, and of course does not advise access if the cost is consumed before finding a proof. We emphasize that although Soutei may fail to find an existing proof in this case, our logic itself is decidable, as can be seen from the translation to Datalog in Section 4.1. Further, while Datalog is decidable in polynomial time with a bottom-up strategy, the large number of possible assertions would make running this algorithm to completion impractical for providing timely authorization advice; a timeout would still be needed. Thus, the effectiveness of Soutei is not fundamentally hampered by our choice of evaluation strategy.

As a demonstration of the power of `FStream`, Soutei is able to deal with left-recursive and divergent rules, such as this search for paths in a directed graph:

```
path(?x, ?y) :- path(?x, ?z), edge(?z, ?y).
path(?x, ?y) :- edge(?x, ?y).
edge(1, 2).
edge(2, 1).
edge(2, 3).
```

The graph contains a loop between points 1 and 2. Further, the `path` predicate is left-recursive, so a depth-first evaluation strategy would loop without even deriving `path(1, 2)`. However, Soutei avoids these pitfalls and can derive `path(1, 3)`.

5   Performance Measurements

We use the scenario in Section 3 as the primary benchmark of our implementations. When used with Metcast Channels, the overhead added by Soutei was within measurement error. Therefore, we extracted the Soutei requests performed by Metcast Channels during the scenario, five new assertions and 17 queries, into a script that calls Soutei directly.

We ran this script against the Haskell implementation of Soutei running as a TCP server. As an average over many repetitions, the scenario took 55 ms. (This and all other measurements were performed on a 1.8 GHz Pentium 4 PC with 1 GB RAM. Programs were compiled by the Glasgow Haskell Compiler, version 6.4.1, with the -O2 flag.)

This test included the overhead of network communication, protocol processing, and saving assertions to disk. To eliminate this, we added a mode to the script to call Soutei in-process. In this mode, the scenario took only 5.9 ms. We suspect that the overhead in the server version of Soutei could be trimmed; however since its performance is adequate, we have not attempted this.

Both tests placed a large weight on submission of assertions. A new assertion requires parsing, mode checking, and transformation into a form optimized for query execution. In real use, queries would likely be far more common than policy changes, so we modified the script to submit the assertions once and run the queries many times. This gave us a measurement of just the logic engine. The 17 queries in the scenario took 2.7 ms, or .16 ms per query.

The total virtual memory required by these tests was around 4-5 MB, as reported by the operating system; however, some of this can be accounted to the Haskell garbage collector.

6   Related Work

Because of its obvious importance, the area of access control has been the subject of much research and development. Unfortunately, many deployed access control systems (e.g., firewall access control lists and UNIX permissions) are ad hoc and inexpressive. Trust-management systems [3, 2] introduced a principled approach and a security language. Alas, the design of an expressive, tractable and logically sound security language turns out to be quite hard: Li and Mitchell [15] show that the language in KeyNote has features that impede analysis, and Abadi [1] points out other languages and their shortcomings. The same paper describes the logical justification for Binder. It seems to us that Binder offers the best balance of simplicity and expressivity.

Li and Mitchell [15] investigate constrained Datalog in trust-management systems, prove the tractability of important domains such as trees and ranges, and describe the application to a particular trust-management system RT. We believe Binder offers a better modularity, via `says`. However, adding constraints to Soutei would increase its expressiveness and remains an interesting research direction.

Garg and Pfenning [9] introduce a constructive logic for authorization, and prove non-interference theorems: for instance, only users mentioned directly or indirectly by the `system` assertion can affect decisions. Their logic appears quite similar to Soutei, and we are investigating whether their techniques can be adopted for off-line policy verification.

XACML (eXtensible Access Control Markup Language) 2.0 [24] is an OASIS standard for authorization policies. It is a large specification, and contains some of the same features, such as arithmetic functions, that reduce the tractability of KeyNote; yet XACML cannot express delegation. Fisler et al. [8] have verified XACML policies using decision diagrams, but their work is limited to a subset of the language, and faces scalability questions. They acknowledge that certain XACML constructs "fall outside the scope of static validation."

Backtracking transformers are derived in [10] and [14]. Only the second paper deals with fairness and neither can handle left-recursion.

7 Conclusions and Future Work

We have presented a trust-management system Soutei that combines the strengths of KeyNote and Binder and is a practical alternative to various ad hoc user-, role-, and attribute-based access control lists. We inherit from Binder distributed policies, simplicity, and independence of any application vocabulary. The system is implemented and can be used with any application.

We have validated the system by integrating it with a publish-subscription web service. With the current (quite small) number of assertions, the impact of Soutei on the performance of the system is negligible.

The practical requirements of scalability to many, possible remote assertions motivated goal-directed resolution-based evaluation. To implement this robustly, we have designed a novel fair and terminating backtracking algorithm. To ensure statically that all assertions will not have to be loaded to resolve a query, we have designed a mode analysis for assertions, which places only a light burden on policy authors.

We are currently developing policy administration user interfaces and off-line policy verification tools, and integrating Soutei into additional applications.

Acknowledgements. We thank Paul Steckler, Frank Pfenning, Christopher Thorpe, and the anonymous reviewers for many helpful suggestions.

References

1. ABADI, M. Logic in access control. In LICS [16], pp. 228–233.
2. BLAZE, M. Using the KeyNote Trust Management System. http://www. crypto.com/trustmgt/, Mar. 2001.
3. BLAZE, M., FEIGENBAUM, J., AND LACY, J. Decentralized trust management. In *IEEE Symposium on Security and Privacy* (May 1996).
4. BRUSCOLI, P., AND GUGLIELMI, A. A tutorial on proof theoretic foundations of logic programming. In *ICLP* (2003), C. Palamidessi, Ed., vol. 2916 of *Lecture Notes in Computer Science*, Springer, pp. 109–127.
5. CHISHOLM, P. IA roadmap. *Military Information Technology 9*, 5 (25 July 2005).
6. CLAESSEN, K., AND LJUNGLÖF, P. Typed logical variables in haskell. *Electr. Notes Theor. Comput. Sci. 41*, 1 (2000).
7. DETREVILLE, J. Binder, a logic-based security language. In *IEEE Symposium on Security and Privacy* (2002), pp. 105–113.
8. FISLER, K., KRISHNAMURTHI, S., MEYEROVICH, L. A., AND TSCHANTZ, M. C. Verification and change impact analysis of access-control policies. In *International Conference on Software Engineering* (May 2005).
9. GARG, D., AND PFENNING, F. Non-interference in constructive authorization logic. Submitted for publication, Oct. 2005.
10. HINZE, R. Deriving backtracking monad transformers. In *ICFP '00: Proceedings of the 5th ACM SIGPLAN International Conference on Functional Programming* (2000), ACM Press, pp. 186–197.

11. A declarative applicative logic programming system. http://kanren.sourceforge.net/, 2005.
12. KISELYOV, O. Metcast Channels. http://www.metnet.navy.mil/Metcast/Metcast-Channels.html, Feb. 2003. The working server with Soutei Authorization can be accessed via http://www.metnet.navy.mil/cgi-bin/oleg/server.
13. KISELYOV, O. Soutei: syntax, semantics, and use cases. http://www.metnet.navy.mil/Metcast/Auth-use-cases.html, 13 June 2005.
14. KISELYOV, O., SHAN, C., FRIEDMAN, D. P., AND SABRY, A. Backtracking, interleaving, and terminating monad transformers. In *ICFP '05: ACM SIGPLAN International Conference on Functional Programming* (2005), ACM Press.
15. LI, N., AND MITCHELL, J. C. Datalog with constraints: A foundation for trust management languages. In *PADL* (2003), V. Dahl and P. Wadler, Eds., vol. 2562 of *Lecture Notes in Computer Science*, Springer, pp. 58–73.
16. *18th IEEE Symposium on Logic in Computer Science (LICS 2003), 22-25 June 2003, Ottawa, Canada, Proceedings* (2003), IEEE Computer Society.
17. MILLER, D., AND TIU, A. F. A proof theory for generic judgments: An extended abstract. In LICS [16], pp. 118–127.
18. SERES, S., AND SPIVEY, J. M. Embedding Prolog in Haskell. In *Proceedings of the 1999 Haskell Workshop* (1999), E. Meier, Ed., Tech. Rep. UU-CS-1999-28, Department of Computer Science, Utrecht University.
19. SINGER, A. Life without firewalls. *USENIX ;login: 28*, 6 (Dec. 2003), 34–41.
20. SOMOGYI, Z., HENDERSON, F., AND CONWAY, T. The execution algorithm of Mercury, an efficient purely declarative logic programming language. *J. Log. Program. 29*, 1-3 (1996), 17–64.
21. WADLER, P. How to replace failure by a list of successes: A method for exception handling, backtracking, and pattern matching in lazy functional languages. In *FPCA* (1985), pp. 113–128.
22. WESTERINEN, A., SCHNIZLEIN, J., STRASSNER, J., SCHERLING, M., QUINN, B., HERZOG, S., HUYNH, A., CARLSON, M., PERRY, J., AND WALDBUSSER, S. Terminology for policy-based management. RFC 3198, Nov. 2001.
23. WOOL, A. A quantitative study of firewall configuration errors. *IEEE Computer 37*, 6 (2004), 62–67.
24. OASIS eXtensible Access Control Markup Language (XACML). Version 2.0. http://www.oasis-open.org/committees/tc_home.php?wg_abbrev=xacml, Feb. 2005.

A   The Formal Semantics of Soutei

Table 1 describes syntax and meta-variables used in this section. Predicate constants have the implied arity $n \geq 1$. Logic variables range over constants. A substitution is a finite map from logic variables to terms, mapping no variable to itself. An application of a substitution is written in postfix notation.

In an assertion clause, H is an unqualified formula, $\overline{B}$ is a set of zero or more general formulas, $\{y_1 \cdots y_m\}, m \geq 0$ is a set of variables free in $\overline{B}$ but not in H, $\{x_1 \cdots x_n\}, n \geq 0$ is a set of variables that are free in H (they are all free in $\overline{B}$, too); symbol $\stackrel{\triangle}{=}$ is just a separator.

Table 1. Syntax and meta-variables

$$
\begin{aligned}
\textit{Constants} \ &= \ a, b, \texttt{application}, \texttt{system} \\
\textit{Predicate constants} \ &= \ p, q \\
\textit{Logic variables} \ &= \ x, y, z \\
\textit{Terms} \quad t &::= a \mid x \\
\textit{Substitutions} \ &= \ \theta, \rho \\
\textit{Unqualified formulas} \quad A, H &::= p\, t_1 \ldots t_n \\
\textit{Qualified formulas} \quad Q &::= t \ \textsf{says} \ A \\
\textit{General formulas} \quad B &::= A \mid Q \\
\textit{Assertion clause} \quad c &::= \forall x_1 \cdots \forall x_n \, \exists y_1 \cdots \exists y_m \ H \triangleq \overline{B} \\
\textit{Assertion} \quad \Gamma &::= \{c, \ldots\}
\end{aligned}
$$

Table 2. Judgments

$a \vdash_n \Gamma$	a is the name of the assertion Γ
$\Gamma \vdash B$	Formula B holds in the assertion Γ
$a \vdash B$	Formula B holds in the assertion named a

Table 3. Semantics

$$\frac{b \vdash A}{\Gamma \vdash b \ \textsf{says} \ A} \ (says)$$

$$\frac{a \vdash_n \Gamma \quad \Gamma \vdash A}{a \vdash A} \ (lookup)$$

$$\frac{\{\Gamma \vdash B\theta \mid B \in \overline{B}\} \quad \forall x_1 \cdots \forall x_n \, \exists y_1 \cdots \exists y_m \ H \triangleq \overline{B} \in \Gamma \quad A = H\theta}{\Gamma \vdash A} \ (backchain)$$

$$\frac{}{\texttt{application} \vdash \textsf{neq} \ a \ b} \ (neq) \qquad \text{constants } a \text{ and } b \text{ are distinct}$$

$$\frac{}{\texttt{application} \vdash \textsf{ip-of} \ a \ b} \ (ip) \qquad a, b \text{ represent IP network addresses and } a \text{ is included in } b$$

Table 2 lists the judgements. Soutei accepts a formula A as input and replies whether there exists a substitution ρ such that the judgement $\texttt{system} \vdash A\rho$ can be deduced according to the rules in Table 3. The latter table omits the axioms for $a \vdash_n \Gamma$ judgements: These axioms specify the contents of $\texttt{system}$, $\texttt{application}$, and other assertions; the set of such axioms is specific to a particular invocation of Soutei.

The rule *(says)* is similar to the conventional modality law: if $b \vdash A$ holds, then $\Gamma \vdash b \ \textsf{says} \ A$ holds in any any *existing* assertion Γ [1]. In the rule *(backchain)* the set of premises of the rule is given explicitly as a set, which may be empty. The domain of the substitution θ includes both $\{x_1 \cdots x_n\}$ and $\{y_1 \cdots y_m\}$.

A Syntactic Approach to Combining Functional Notation, Lazy Evaluation, and Higher-Order in LP Systems[*]

Amadeo Casas[1], Daniel Cabeza[2], and Manuel V. Hermenegildo[1,2]

[1] Depts. of Comp. Science and Electr. and Comp. Eng., Univ. of New Mexico, USA
{amadeo, herme}@cs.unm.edu
[2] School of Computer Science, T.U. Madrid (UPM), Spain
{dcabeza, herme}@fi.upm.es

Abstract. Nondeterminism and partially instantiated data structures give logic programming expressive power beyond that of functional programming. However, functional programming often provides convenient syntactic features, such as having a designated implicit output argument, which allow function call nesting and sometimes results in more compact code. Functional programming also sometimes allows a more direct encoding of lazy evaluation, with its ability to deal with infinite data structures. We present a *syntactic* functional extension, used in the Ciao system, which can be implemented in ISO-standard Prolog systems and covers function application, predefined evaluable functors, functional definitions, quoting, and lazy evaluation. The extension is also composable with higher-order features and can be combined with other extensions to ISO-Prolog such as constraints. We also highlight the features of the Ciao system which help implementation and present some data on the overhead of using lazy evaluation with respect to eager evaluation.

Keywords: Declarative Languages; Logic, Functional, and Logic-Functional Programming; Lazy Evaluation; Higher Order.

1 Introduction

Logic Programming offers a number of features, such as nondeterminism and partially instantiated data structures, that give it expressive power beyond that of functional programming. However, certain aspects of functional programming provide in turn syntactic convenience. This includes for example having a syntactically designated output argument, which allows the usual form of function call nesting and sometimes results in more compact code. Also, lazy evaluation,

---

[*] M. Hermenegildo and A. Casas are supported in part by the Prince of Asturias Chair in Information Science and Technology at UNM. This work is also funded in part by projects EC FET IST-2001-38059 *ASAP*, and Spanish MEC TIC 2002-0055 *CUBICO*, TIN-2005-09207-C03-01 *MERIT*, and CAM S-0505/TIC/0407 *PROMESAS*. The authors also thank the anonymous referees for their useful comments.

M. Hagiya and P. Wadler (Eds.): FLOPS 2006, LNCS 3945, pp. 146–162, 2006.

which brings the ability to deal with infinite (non-recursive) data structures [1, 2], while subsumed operationally by logic programming features such as delay declarations, enjoys a more direct encoding in functional programming. Bringing this syntactic convenience to logic programming can result in a more compact program representation in certain cases and is therefore a desirable objective.

With this objective in mind, in this paper we present a design for an extensive functional syntactic layer for logic programing. While the idea of adding functional features to logic programming systems is clearly not new, and there are currently a good number of systems which integrate functions and higher-order programming into some form of logic programming, we feel that our proposal and its implementation offer a combination of features which make it interesting in itself (see Section 6 for a discussion of related work).

Our approach was inspired by some of the language extension capabilities of the Ciao system [3]: Ciao offers a complete ISO-Prolog system, but one of its most remarkable features is that, through a novel modular design [5], all ISO-Prolog features are library-based extensions to a simple declarative kernel. This allows on one hand not loading any (for example, impure) features from ISO-Prolog when not needed, and on the other hand adding many additional features at the source (Prolog) level, without modifying the compiler or the low-level machinery. The facilities that allow this (grouped under the Ciao *packages* concept [5]) are the same ones used for implementing the functional extensions proposed herein, and are also the mechanism by which other syntactic and semantic extensions are supported in the system. The latter include constraints, objects, feature terms/records, persistence, several control rules, etc., giving Ciao its multi-paradigm flavor.

However, while the Ciao extension mechanisms make implementation smoother and more orthogonal in our view,[1] a fundamental design objective and feature of our functional extensions is that they are to a very large extent directly applicable to (and also relatively straightforward to implement in) any modern (ISO-)Prolog system [6], and we hope to contribute in that way to their adoption in such systems. Thus, we will also discuss ISO-Prolog when describing the implementation of the proposed extensions.

The rest of the paper is organized as follows: first, we discuss in Section 2 our general approach to integrating functional notation. Section 3 presents how we implemented this approach in Ciao. Section 4 shows an example of the use of lazy evaluation, and how it is achieved by our implementation. Section 5 presents some experimental results. Finally, section 6 presents our conclusions and discusses related work.

2   Functional Notation in Ciao

Basic Concepts and Notation: Our notion of functional notation for logic programming departs in a number of ways from previous proposals. The fundamental one is that functional notation in principle simply provides *syntactic*

---

[1] As we will try to highlight with the upfront intention of motivating the adoption of the extension model by other logic programming systems.

sugar for defining and using predicates as if they were functions, but they can still retain the power of predicates. In this model, any function definition is in fact defining a predicate, and any predicate can be used as a function. The predicate associated with a function has the same name and one more argument, meant as the place holder for the result of the function. This argument is by default added to the right, i.e., it is the last argument, but this can be changed by using a declaration. The syntax extensions provided for functional notation are the following:

Function applications: Any term preceded by the ~ operator is a function application, as can be seen in the goal `write(~arg(1,T))`, which is strictly equivalent to the sequence `arg(1,T,A)`, `write(A)`. To use a predicate argument other than the last as the return argument, a declaration like:
`:- fun_return functor(~,_,_).`
can be used, so that `~functor(f,2)` is evaluated to `f(_,_)` (where `functor/3` is the standard ISO-Prolog builtin). This definition of the return argument can also be done on the fly in each invocation in the following way: `~functor(~,f,2)`. Functors can be declared as *evaluable* (i.e., being in calls in functional syntax) by using the declaration `fun_eval/1`. This allows avoiding the need to use the ~ operator. Thus, "`:- fun_eval arg/2.`" allows writing `write(arg(1,T))` instead of `write(~arg(1,T))` as above. This declaration can also be used to change the default output argument:
`:- fun_eval functor(~,_,_).`
Note that all these declarations, as is customary in Ciao, are local to the module where they are included.

Predefined evaluable functors: In addition to functors declared with the declaration `fun_eval/1`, several functors are evaluable, those being:
  − The functors used for disjunctive and conditional expressions, `(|)/2` and `(?)/2`. A disjunctive expression has the form `(V1|V2)`, and its value when first evaluated is `V1`, and on backtracking `V2`. A conditional expression has the form `(Cond ? V1)`, or, more commonly, `(Cond ? V1 | V2)`. If the execution of `Cond` as a goal succeeds the return value is `V1`. Otherwise in the first form it causes backtracking, and in the second form its value is `V2`. Due to operator precedences, a nested expression
  `(Cond1 ? V1 | Cond2 ? V2 | V3)`
  is evaluated as `(Cond1 ? V1 | (Cond2 ? V2 | V3))`.
  − If the declaration `:- fun_eval arith(true)` is used, all the functors understood by `is/2` are considered evaluable (they will be translated to a call to `is/2`). This is not active by default because several of those functors, like `(-)/2` or `(/)/2`, are traditionally used in Prolog for creating structures. Using `false` instead of `true` the declaration can be disabled.

Functional definitions: A functional definition is composed of one or more functional clauses. A functional clause is written using the binary operator `:=`, as in `opposite(red) := green.`
Functional clauses can also have a body, which is executed before the result value is computed. It can serve as a guard for the clause or to provide the equivalent of where-clauses in functional languages:

```
fact(0) := 1.
fact(N) := N * ~fact(--N) :- N > 0.
```

Note that guards can often be defined more compactly using conditional expressions:

```
fact(N) := N = 0 ? 1
         | N > 0 ? N * ~fact(--N).
```

If the declaration `:- fun_eval defined(true)` is active, the function defined in a functional clause does not need to be preceded by ~ (for example the `fact(--N)` calls above).

The translation of functional clauses has the following properties:

- The translation produces *steadfast* predicates [7], that is, output arguments are unified after possible cuts.
- Defining recursive predicates in functional style maintains the tail recursion of the original predicate, thus allowing the usual compiler optimizations.

Quoting functors: Functors (either in functional or predicate clauses) can be prevented from being evaluated by using the `(^)/1` prefix operator (read as "quote"), as in:

```
pair(A,B) := ^(A-B).
```

Note that this just prevents the evaluation of the principal functor of the enclosed term, not the possible occurrences of other evaluable functors inside.

Scoping: When using function applications inside the goal arguments of meta-predicates, there is an ambiguity as they could be evaluated either in the scope of the outer execution or in the scope of the inner execution. The default behavior is to evaluate function applications in the scope of the outer execution. If they should be evaluated in the inner scope the goal containing the function application needs to be escaped with the `(^^)/1` prefix operator, as in `findall(X, (d(Y), ^^(X = ~f(Y)+1)), L)` (which could also be written as `findall(X, ^^(d(Y), X = ~f(Y)+1), L)`), and whose expansion is `findall(X, (d(Y),f(Y,Z),T is Z+1,X=T), L)`. With no escaping the function application is evaluated in the scope of the outer execution, i.e., `f(Y,Z), T is Z+1, findall(X, (d(Y),X=T), L)`.

Laziness: Lazy evaluation is a program evaluation technique used particularly in functional languages. When using lazy evaluation, an expression is not evaluated as soon as it is assigned, but rather when the evaluator is forced to produce the value of the expression. The `when`, `freeze`, or `block` control primitives present in many modern logic programming systems are more powerful operationally than lazy evaluation. However, they lack the simplicity of use and cleaner semantics of functional lazy evaluation. In our design, a function (or predicate) can be declared as lazy via the declarations:

```
:- lazy fun_eval function_name/N.
```

(or, equivalently in predicate version, "`:- lazy pred_name/M.`", where $M = N + 1$). In order to achieve the intended behavior, the execution of each function declared as lazy is suspended until the return value of the function is needed. Thus, lazy evaluation allows dealing with infinite data structures and also evaluating function arguments only when needed.

Definition of real functions: In the previous scheme, functions are (at least by default) not forced to provide a single solution for their result, and, furthermore, they can be partial, producing a failure when no solution can be found. A predicate defined as a function can be declared to behave as a real function using the declaration ":- funct name/N.". Such predicates are then converted automatically to real functions by adding pruning operators and a number of Ciao assertions [8] which pose (and check) additional restrictions such as determinacy, modedness, etc., so that the semantics will be the same as in traditional functional programming.

We now illustrate with examples the use of the functionality introduced above.

Example 1. The following example defines a simple unary function der(X) which returns the derivative of a polynomial arithmetic expression:

```
der(x)      := 1.
der(C)      := 0                      :- number(C).
der(A + B)  := der(A) + der(B).
der(C * A)  := C * der(A)             :- number(C).
der(x ** N) := N * x ** ~(N - 1) :- integer(N), N > 0.
```

Note that if we include the directive mentioned before which makes arithmetic functors evaluable then we would have to write the program in the following (clearly, less pleasant and more obfuscated) way:

```
:- fun_eval(arith(true)).
der(x)        := 1.
der(C)        := 0                        :- number(C).
der(^(A + B)) := ^(der(A) + der(B)).
der(^(C * A)) := ^(C * der(A))            :- number(C).
der(^(x ** N)) := ^(N * ^(x ** (N - 1))) :- integer(N), N > 0.
```

Both of the previous code fragments translate to the following code:

```
der(x, 1).                      der(C * A, C * X) :-
der(C, 0) :-                            number(C),
        number(C).                      der(A, X).
der(A + B, X + Y) :-            der(x ** N, N * x ** N1) :-
        der(A, X),                      integer(N),
        der(B, Y).                      N > 0,
                                        N1 is N - 1.
```

Note that in all cases the programmer may use der/2 as a function or as a predicate indistinctly.

Example 2. Functional notation interacts well with other language extensions. For example, it provides compact and familiar notation for regular types and other properties (assume fun_eval declarations for them):

```
color      := red | blue | green.
list       := [] | [_ | list].
list_of(T) := [] | [~T | list_of(T)].
```

which are equivalent to (note the use of higher-order in the third example):

```
color(red). color(blue). color(green).
list([]).
list([_|T]) :- list(T).
list_of(_, []).
list_of(T, [X|Xs]) :- T(X), list_of(T, Xs).
```

Such types and properties are then admissible in Ciao-style assertions [8], such as the following, and which can be added to the corresponding definitions and checked by the preprocessor or turned into run-time tests [9]:

```
:- pred append/3 :: list * list * list.
:- pred color_value/2 :: list(color) * int.
```

Example 3. The combination of functional syntax and user-defined operators brings significant flexibility, as can be seen in the following definition of a list concatenation (append) operator:[2]

```
:- op(600, xfy, (.)).
:- op(650, xfy, (++)).
:- fun_eval (++)/2.
[]    ++ L := L.
X.Xs ++ L := X.(Xs ++ L).
```

This definition will be compiled exactly to the standard definition of append in Prolog (and, thus, will be reversible). The functional syntax and user-defined operators allow writing for example write("Hello" ++ Spc ++ "world!") instead of the equivalent forms write(append("Hello", append(Spc, "world!"))) (if append/2 is defined as evaluable) or append(Spc, "world!", T1), append("Hello", T1, T2), write(T2).

Example 4. As another example, we define an array indexing operator for multi-dimensional arrays. Assume that arrays are built using nested structures whose main functor is 'a' and whose arities are determined by the specified dimensions, i.e., a two-dimensional array A of dimensions $[N, M]$ will be represented by the nested structure a(a($A_{11}, \ldots, A_{1M}$), a($A_{21}, \ldots, A_{2M}$), ..., a($A_{N1}, \ldots, A_{NM}$)), where $A_{11}, \ldots A_{NM}$ may be arbitrary terms.[3] The following recursive definition defines the property array/2 and also the array access operator @:

---

[2] This operator, as well of other conveniences to be able to program in a more functional-flavored style, are defined in an additional Ciao package.

[3] We ignore for simplicity possible arity limitations, solved in any case typically by further nesting with logarithmic access time (as in Warren/Pereira's classical library).

```
array([N],A) :-
        functor(A,a,N).
array([N|Ms],A) :-
        functor(A,a,N),
        rows(N,Ms,A).

:- op(55, xfx, '@').
:- fun_eval (@)/2.
V@[I]    := ~arg(I,V).        %% Or: V@[] := V.
V@[I|Js] := ~arg(I,V)@Js.
```

```
rows(0,_,_).
rows(N,Ms,A) :-
        N > 0,
        arg(N,A,Arg),
        array(Ms,Arg),
        rows(N-1,Ms,A).
```

This allows writing, e.g., M = array([2,2]), M@[2,1] = 3 (which could also be expressed as array([2,2])@[2,1] = 3), where the call to the array property generates an empty 2×2 array M and M@[2,1] = 3 puts 3 in $M[2,1]$. Another example would be: A3@[N+1,M] = A1@[N-1,M] + A2@[N,M+2].

Example 5. As a simple example of the use of *lazy evaluation* consider the following definition of a function which returns the (potentially) infinite list of integers starting with a given one:

```
:- lazy fun_eval nums_from/1.
nums_from(X) := [ X | nums_from(X+1) ].
```

Ciao provides in its standard library the hiord package, which supports a form of higher-order untyped logic programming with predicate abstractions [10, 11, 12]. Predicate abstractions are Ciao's translation to logic programming of the lambda expressions of functional programming: they define unnamed predicates which will be ultimately executed by a higher-order call, unifying its arguments appropriately.[4] A function abstraction is provided as functional syntactic sugar for predicate abstractions:

Predicate abstraction $\Rightarrow$ Function abstraction
{''(X,Y) :- p(X,Z), q(Z,Y)} $\Rightarrow$ {''(X) := ~q(~p(X))}
and function application is syntactic sugar over predicate application:
Predicate application $\Rightarrow$ Function application
..., P(X,Y), ... $\Rightarrow$ ..., Y = ~P(X), ...

The combination of this hiord package with the fsyntax and lazy packages (and, optionally, the type inference and checking provided by the Ciao preprocessor [9]) basically provide the functionality present in modern functional languages,[5] as well as some of the functionality of higher-order logic programming.

Example 6. This map example illustrates the combination of functional syntax and higher-order logic programming:

---

[4] A similar concept has been developed independently for Mercury, but there higher-order predicate terms have to be moded.

[5] Currying is not syntactically implemented, but its results can be obtained by deriving higher-order data from any other higher-order data (see [11]).

```
:- fun_eval map/2.
map([], _)     := [].
map([X|Xs], P) := [P(X) | map(Xs, P)].
```

With this definition, after calling:

```
["helloworld", "byeworld"] = map(["hello", "bye"], ++(X)).
```

(where (++)/2 corresponds to the above definition of **append**) X will be bound to "world", which is the only solution to the equation. Also, when calling:

```
map(L, ++(X), ["hello.", "bye."]).
```

several values for L and X are returned through backtracking:

```
L = ["hello","bye"],   X = "." ? ;
L = ["hello.","bye."], X = [] ?
```

3 Implementation Details

As mentioned previously, certain Ciao features have simplified the proposed extension to handle functional notation. In the following we introduce the features of Ciao that were used and how they were applied in this particular application.

Code Translations in Ciao. Traditionally, Prolog systems have included the possibility of changing the syntax of the source code through the use of the op/3 builtin/directive. Furthermore, in many Prolog systems it is also possible to define *expansions* of the source code (essentially, a very rich form of "macros") by allowing the user to define (or extend) a predicate typically called term_expansion/2 [13, 14]. This is usually how, e.g., definite clause grammars (DCG's) are implemented.

However, these features, in their original form, pose many problems for modular compilation or even for creating sensible standalone executables. First, the definitions of the operators and, specially, expansions are often global, affecting a number of files. Furthermore, it is not possible to determine statically which files are affected, because these features are implemented as a side-effect, rather than a declaration: they become active immediately after being read by the code processor (top-level, compiler, etc.) and remain active from then on. As a result, it is impossible just by looking at a source code file to know if it will be affected by expansions or definitions of operators, which may completely change what the compiler really sees, since those may be activated by the load of other, possibly unrelated, files.

In order to solve these problems, the syntactic extension facilities were redesigned in Ciao, so that it is still possible to define source translations and operators, but such translations are local to the module or user file defining them [5]. Also, these features are implemented in a way that has a well-defined behavior in the context of a standalone compiler, separate compilation, and global analysis (and this behavior is implemented in the Ciao compiler, ciaoc [15]). In particular, the load_compilation_module/1 directive allows separating code that will be used at compilation time (e.g., the code used for program transformations) from code which will be used at run-time. It loads the module defined by its argument *into the compiler*.

In addition, in order to make the task of writing source translations easier, the effects usually achieved through `term_expansion/2` can be obtained in Ciao by means of four different, more specialized directives, which, again, *affect only the current module* and *are (by default) only active at compile-time*. The proposed functional syntax is implemented in Ciao using these source translations. In particular, we have used the `add_sentence_trans/1` and `add_goal_trans/1` directives. A sentence translation is a predicate which will be called by the compiler to possibly convert each *term* (clause, fact, directive, input, etc.) read by the compiler to a new term, which will be used in place of the original term. A goal translation is a predicate which will be called by the compiler to possibly convert each *goal* present in each clause of the current text to another goal which replaces the original one. The proposed model can be implemented in Prolog systems similarly using the traditional `term_expansion/2` and operator declarations, but having operators and syntactic transformation predicates local to modules is the key to making the approach scalable and amenable to combination with other packages and syntactic extensions in the same application.

Ciao Packages. Packages in Ciao are libraries which define extensions to the language, and have a well defined and repetitive structure. These libraries typically consist of a main source file which defines only some declarations (operator declarations, declarations loading other modules into the compiler or the module using the extension, etc.). This file is meant to be *included* as part of the file using the library, since, because of their local effect, such directives must be part of the code of the module which uses the library. Any auxiliary code needed at compile-time (e.g., translations) is included in a separate module which is to be loaded into the compiler via a `load_compilation_module/1` directive placed in the main file. Also, any auxiliary code to be used at run-time is placed in another module, and the corresponding `use_module` declaration is also placed in the include file.

In our implementation of functional notation in Ciao we have provided two packages: one for the bare function features without lazy evaluation, and an additional one to provide the lazy evaluation features. The reason for this is that in many cases the lazy evaluation features are not needed and thus the translation procedure is simplified.

The Ciao Implementation of Functional Extensions. To translate the functional definitions, we have used as mentioned above the `add_sentence_trans/1` directive to provide a translation procedure which transforms each functional clause to a predicate clause, adding to the function head the output argument, in order to convert it to the predicate head. This translation procedure also deals with functional applications in heads, as well as with `fun_eval` directives. Furthermore, all function applications are translated to an internal normal form.

On the other hand, we have used the `add_goal_trans/1` directive to provide a translation procedure for dealing with function applications in bodies (which were previously translated to a normal form). The rationale for using a goal translation is that each function application inside a goal will be replaced by a variable, and the goal will be preceded by a call to the predicate which implements the function in order to provide a value for that variable. A simple recursive application of this rule achieves the desired effect.

An additional sentence translation is provided to handle the `lazy` directives. The translation of a lazy function into a predicate is done in two steps. First, the function is converted into a predicate using the procedure sketched above. Then, the resulting predicate is transformed in order to suspend its execution until the value of the output variable is needed. We explain the transformation in terms of the `freeze/1` control primitive that many modern logic programming systems implement quite efficiently [16], since it is the most widespread (but obviously `when` [17] or, specially, the more efficient `block` [16] declarations can also be used). This transformation renames the original predicate to an internal name and add a *bridge predicate* with the original name which invokes the internal predicate through a call to `freeze/2`, with the last argument (the output of the function) as suspension variable. This will delay the execution of the internal predicate until its result is required, which will be detected as a binding (i.e., demand) of its output variable. The following section will provide a detailed example of the translation of a lazy function. The implementation with `block` is even simpler since no bridge predicate is needed.

We show below, for reference, the main files for the Ciao library packages `fsyntax`:

```
% fsyntax.pl
:- include(library('fsyntax/ops')).  %% Operator definitions
:- load_compilation_module(library('fsyntax/functionstr')).
:- add_sentence_trans(defunc/3).
:- add_goal_trans(defunc_goal/3).
```

and `lazy` (which will usually be used in conjunction with the first one):

```
% lazy.pl
:- include(library('lazy/ops')). %% Operator definitions
:- use_module(library(freeze)).
:- load_compilation_module(library('lazy/lazytr')).
:- add_sentence_trans(lazy_sentence_translation/3).
```

These files will be *included* in any file that uses the package. The Ciao system source provides the actual detailed code, which follows the our description.

4 Lazy Functions: An Example

In this section we show an example of the use of lazy evaluation, and how a lazy function is translated by our Ciao package. Figure 1 shows in the first row the definition of a lazy function which returns the infinite list of Fibonacci numbers, in the second row its translation into a lazy predicate[6] (by the `fsyntax` package)

---

[6] The `:- lazy fun_eval fiblist/0.` declaration is converted into a `:- lazy fiblist/1.` declaration.

```
:- lazy fun_eval fiblist/0.
fiblist := [0, 1 | ~zipWith(+, FibL, ~tail(FibL))]
         :- FibL = fiblist.
```

```
:- lazy fiblist/1.
fiblist([0, 1 | Rest]) :-
        fiblist(FibL),
        tail(FibL, T),
        zipWith(+, FibL, T, Rest).
```

```
fiblist(X) :-
        freeze(X, fiblist_lazy_$$$(X)).

fiblist_lazy_$$$([0, 1 | Rest]) :-
        fiblist(FibL),
        tail(FibL, T),
        zipWith(+, FibL, T, Rest).
```

Fig. 1. Code translation for a Fibonacci function, to be evaluated lazily

and in the third row the expansion of that predicate to emulate lazy evaluation (where `fiblist_lazy$$$` stands for a fresh predicate name).

In the `fiblist` function defined, any element in the resulting *infinite* list of Fibonacci numbers can be referenced, as, for example, `nth(X, ~fiblist, Value)`. The other functions used in the definition are `tail/2`, which is defined as lazy and returns the tail of a list; `zipWith/3`, which is also defined as lazy and returns a list whose elements are computed by a function having as arguments the successive elements in the lists provided as second and third argument;[7] and `(+)/2` which is defined as by the rule `+(X, Y) := Z :- Z is X + Y`.

Note that the `zipWith/3` function (respectively the `zipWith/4` predicate) is in fact a *higher-order* function (resp. predicate).

5   Some Performance Measurements

Since the functional extensions proposed simply provide a syntactic bridge between functions and predicates, there are only a limited number of performance issues worth discussing. For the case of *real* functions, it is well known that performance gains can be obtained from the knowledge that the corresponding predicate is moded (all input arguments are ground and the "designated output" will be ground on output), determinate, non-failing, etc. [18, 20]. In Ciao this information can in general (i.e., for any predicate or function) be inferred by the Ciao preprocessor or declared with Ciao assertions [9, 8]. As mentioned

---

[7] It has the same semantics as the `zipWith` function in Haskell.

```
:- fun_eval nat/1.                :- fun_eval nat/1.
nat(N) := ~take(N, nums_from(0)).  :- fun_eval nats/2.
                                  nat(X) := nats(0, X).
:- lazy fun_eval nums_from/1.     nats(X, Max) := X > Max ? []
nums_from(X) :=                               | [X | nats(X+1, Max)].
    [X | nums_from(X+1)].
```

Fig. 2. Lazy and eager versions of function nat(X)

before, for declared "real" (func) functions, the corresponding information is added automatically. Some (preliminary) results on current Ciao performance when this information is available are presented in [20].

In the case of lazy evaluation of functions, the main goal of the technique presented herein is not really any increase in performance, but achieving new functionality and convenience through the use of code translations and delay declarations. However, while there have also been some studies of the overhead introduced by delay declarations and their optimization (see, e.g., [21]), it is interesting to see how this overhead affects our implementation of lazy evaluation by observing its performance. Consider the nat/2 function in Figure 2, a simple function which returns a list with the first N numbers from an (infinite) list of natural numbers.

Function take/2 in turn returns the list of the first N elements in the input list. This nat(N) function cannot be directly executed eagerly due to the infinite list provided by the nums_from(X) function, so that, in order to compare time and memory results between lazy and eager evaluation, an equivalent version of that function is provided.

Table 1 reflects the time and memory overhead of the lazy evaluation version of nat(X) and that of the equivalent version executed eagerly. As a further example, Table 2 shows the results for a quicksort function executed lazily in comparison to the eager version of this algorithm. All the results were obtained by averaging ten runs on a medium-loaded Pentium IV Xeon 2.0Ghz, 4Gb of RAM memory, running Fedora Core 2.0, with the simple translation of Figure 1, and compiled to traditional bytecode (no global optimizations or native code).

We can observe in both tables that there is certainly an impact on the execution time when functions are evaluated lazily, but even with this version the results are quite acceptable if we take into account that the execution of the predicate does really suspend. Related to memory consumption we show heap sizes, without garbage collection (in order to observe the raw memory consumption rate). Lazy evaluation implies as expected some memory overhead due to the need to copy (freeze) program goals into the heap. Also, while comparing with standard lazy functional programming implementations is beyond the scope of this paper, some simple tests done for sanity check purposes (with HUGS) show that the results are comparable, our implementation being for example slower on nat but faster on qsort, presumably due to the different optimizations being performed by the compilers.

Table 1. Performance for `nat/2` (time in ms. and heap sizes in bytes)

List	Lazy Evaluation		Eager Evaluation	
	Time	Heap	Time	Heap
10 elements	0.030	1503.2	0.002	491.2
100 elements	0.276	10863.2	0.016	1211.2
1000 elements	3.584	104463.0	0.149	8411.2
2000 elements	6.105	208463.2	0.297	16411.2
5000 elements	17.836	520463.0	0.749	40411.2
10000 elements	33.698	1040463.0	1.277	80411.2

Table 2. Performance for `qsort/2` (time in ms. and heap sizes in bytes)

List	Lazy Evaluation		Eager Evaluation	
	Time	Heap	Time	Heap
10 elements	0.091	3680.0	0.032	1640.0
100 elements	0.946	37420.0	0.322	17090.0
1000 elements	13.303	459420.0	5.032	253330.0
5000 elements	58.369	2525990.0	31.291	1600530.0
15000 elements	229.756	8273340.0	107.193	5436780.0
20000 elements	311.833	11344800.0	146.160	7395100.0

An example when lazy evaluation can be a better option than eager evaluation in terms of performance (and not only convenience) can be found in a concurrent or distributed system environment (such as, e.g., [22]), and in the case of Ciao also within the active modules framework [3, 23]. The example in Figure 3 uses a function, defined in an active module, which returns a big amount of data. Function `test/0` in module `module1` needs to execute function `squares/1`, in (active, i.e., remote) module `module2`, which will return a very long list (which could be infinite for our purposes). If `squares/1` were executed eagerly then the entire list would be returned, to immediately execute the `takeWhile/2` function with the entire list. `takeWhile/2` returns the first elements of a (possibly infinite) list while the specified condition is true. But creating the entire initial list is very wasteful in terms of time and memory requirements. In order to solve this problem, the `squares/1` function could be moved to module `module1` and merged with `takeWhile/2` (or, also, they could exchange a size parameter). But rearranging the program is not always possible and it may also perhaps complicate other aspects of the overall design.

If on the other hand `squares/1` is evaluated lazily, it is possible to keep the definitions unchanged and in different modules, so that there will be a smaller time and memory penalty for generating and storing the intermediate result. As more values are needed by the `takeWhile/2` function, more values in the list returned by `squares/1` are built (in this example, only while the new generated value is less than 10000), considerably reducing the time and memory consumption that the eager evaluation would take.

```
:- module(module1, [test/1], [fsyntax, lazy, hiord, actmods]).
:- use_module(library('actmods/webbased_locate')).

:- use_active_module(module2, [squares/2]).

:- fun_eval takeWhile/2.
takeWhile(P, [H|T]) := P(H) ? [H | takeWhile(P, T)]
                             | [].
:- fun_eval test/0.
test := takeWhile(condition, squares).
condition(X) :- X < 10000.
```

```
\vspace*{6mm}
:- module(module2, [squares/1], [fsyntax, lazy, hiord]).

:- lazy fun_eval squares/0.
squares := map_lazy(take(1000000, nums_from(0)), square).

:- lazy fun_eval map_lazy/2.
map_lazy([], _)     := [].
map_lazy([X|Xs], P) := [~P(X) | map_lazy(Xs, P)].

:- fun_eval take/2.
take(0, _)     := [].
take(X, [H|T]) := [H | take(X-1, T)] :- X > 0.

:- lazy fun_eval nums_from/1.
nums_from(X) := [X | nums_from(X+1)].

:- fun_eval square/1.
square(X) := X * X.
```

Fig. 3. A distributed (active module) application using lazy evaluation

6   Conclusions and Related Work

As mentioned in the introduction, the idea of adding functional features to logic programming systems is clearly not new [24, 25, 17] and there are currently a good number of systems which integrate functions and higher-order programming into some form of logic programming. However, we feel that our proposal and its implementation offer a combination of features which make it interesting in itself. More concretely, the approach is completely syntactic, functions can be limited or retain the power of predicates, any predicate can be called through functional syntax, and lazy evaluation is supported both for functions and predicates. Furthermore, functional syntax can be combined with numerous (Ciao) syntactic and semantic extensions such as higher-order, assertions, records, constraints, objects, persistence, other control rules, etc., without any modification to the compiler or abstract machine. Finally, and perhaps most importantly, and again because of the syntactic nature of the extensions, they can be the target of analysis, optimization, static checking, and verification (of types, modes, determinacy, nonfailure, cost, etc.), as performed by, e.g., the Ciao preprocessor [9]. Finally, another important characteristic of our approach is that most of it can be applied directly (or with minor changes) to any ISO-standard Prolog system.

The original version of the functional extensions was first distributed in Ciao 0.2 [4] and later used as an example in [5]. The full description presented herein includes some minor changes with respect to the currently distributed version [3] which will be available in the next release. The performance of the package for lazy evaluation was tested in this system with several examples. As expected, lazy evaluation implies time and memory overhead, which justifies making lazy evaluation optional via a declaration.

Returning to the issue of related work, Lambda Prolog [26] offers a highly expressive language with extensive higher-order programming features and lambda-term (pattern) unification. On the other hand it pays in performance the price of being "higher order by default," and is not backwards compatible with traditional Prolog systems. It would be clearly interesting to support pattern unification, but we propose to do it as a further (and optional) extension, and some work is in progress along these lines. HiLog [27] is a very interesting logic programming system (extending XSB-Prolog) which allows using higher-order syntax, but it does not address the issue of supporting functional syntax or lazyness. Functional-logic systems such as Curry or Babel [31, 32] perform a full integration of functional and logic programming, with higher-order support. On the other hand, their design starts from a lazy functional syntax and semantics, and is strongly typed. However, it may also be interesting to explore supporting narrowing as another optional extension. Mercury [28] offers functional and higher-order extensions based on Prolog-like syntax, but they are an integral part of the language (as opposed to an optional extension) and, because of the need for type and mode declarations, the design is less appropriate for non strongly-typed, unmoded systems. As mentioned above, in our design type and mode declarations are optional and handled separately through the assertion mechanism. Also, Mercury's language design includes a number restrictions with respect to Prolog-like systems which bring a number of implementation simplifications. In particular, the modedness (no unification) of Mercury programs brings them much closer to the functional case. As a result of these restrictions, Mercury always performs the optimizations pointed out when discussing our funct declaration (or when that type of information is inferred by CiaoPP).[8] Oz [30] also allows functional and (a restricted form of) logic programming, and supports higher-order in an untyped setting, but its syntax and semantics are quite different from those of LP systems. BIM Prolog offered similar functionality to our ~/2 operator but, again, by default and as a builtin.

---

[8] However, recent extensions to support constraints [29] recover unification, including the related implementation overheads and mechanisms (such as the trail), and will require analysis for optimization, moving Mercury arguably closer to Ciao in design.

References

1. Narain, S.: Lazy evaluation in logic programming. In: Proc. 1990 Int. Conference on Computer Languages. (1990) 218–227
2. Antoy, S.: Lazy evaluation in logic. In: Symp. on Progr. Language Impl. and Logic Progr (PLILP'91), Springer Verlag (1991) 371–382 LNCS 528.
3. Bueno, F., Cabeza, D., Carro, M., Hermenegildo, M., López-García, P., (Eds.), G.P.: The Ciao System. Reference Manual (v1.10). The ciao system documentation series–TR, School of Computer Science, Technical University of Madrid (UPM) (2004) System and on-line version of the manual available at http://clip.dia.fi.upm.es/Software/Ciao/.
4. Bueno, F., Cabeza, D., Carro, M., Hermenegildo, M., López-García, P., Puebla, G.: The Ciao Prolog System. Reference Manual. The Ciao System Documentation Series–TR CLIP3/97.1, School of Computer Science, Technical University of Madrid (UPM) (1997) System and on-line version of the manual available at http://clip.dia.fi.upm.es/Software/Ciao/.
5. Cabeza, D., Hermenegildo, M.: A New Module System for Prolog. In: International Conference on Computational Logic, CL2000. Number 1861 in LNAI, Springer-Verlag (2000) 131–148
6. Deransart, P., Ed-Dbali, A., Cervoni, L.: Prolog: The Standard. Springer-Verlag (1996)
7. O'Keefe, R.: The Craft of Prolog. MIT Press (1990)
8. Puebla, G., Bueno, F., Hermenegildo, M.: An Assertion Language for Constraint Logic Programs. In Deransart, P., Hermenegildo, M., Maluszynski, J., eds.: Analysis and Visualization Tools for Constraint Programming. Number 1870 in LNCS. Springer-Verlag (2000) 23–61
9. Hermenegildo, M.V., Puebla, G., Bueno, F., López-García, P.: Integrated Program Debugging, Verification, and Optimization Using Abstract Interpretation (and The Ciao System Preprocessor). Science of Computer Programming **58** (2005) 115–140
10. Cabeza, D., Hermenegildo, M.: Higher-order Logic Programming in Ciao. Technical Report CLIP7/99.0, Facultad de Informática, UPM (1999)
11. Cabeza, D.: An Extensible, Global Analysis Friendly Logic Programming System. PhD thesis, Universidad Politécnica de Madrid (UPM), Facultad Informatica UPM, 28660-Boadilla del Monte, Madrid-Spain (2004)
12. Cabeza, D., Hermenegildo, M., Lipton, J.: Hiord: A Type-Free Higher-Order Logic Programming Language with Predicate Abstraction. In: Ninth Asian Computing Science Conference (ASIAN'04). Number 3321 in LNCS, Springer-Verlag (2004) 93–108
13. Quintus Computer Systems Inc. Mountain View CA 94041: Quintus Prolog User's Guide and Reference Manual—Version 6. (1986)
14. Carlsson, M., Widen, J.: Sicstus Prolog User's Manual, Po Box 1263, S-16313 Spanga, Sweden. (1994)
15. Cabeza, D., Hermenegildo, M.: The Ciao Modular Compiler and Its Generic Program Processing Library. In: ICLP'99 WS on Parallelism and Implementation of (C)LP Systems, N.M. State U. (1999) 147–164
16. Carlsson, M.: Freeze, Indexing, and Other Implementation Issues in the Wam. In: Fourth International Conference on Logic Programming, University of Melbourne, MIT Press (1987) 40–58

17. Naish, L.: Adding equations to NU-Prolog. In: Proceedings of The Third International Symposium on Programming Language Implementation and Logic Programming (PLILP'91). Number 528 in Lecture Notes in Computer Science, Passau, Germany, Springer-Verlag (1991) 15–26
18. Van Roy, P.: 1983-1993: The Wonder Years of Sequential Prolog Implementation. Journal of Logic Programming **19/20** (1994) 385–441
19. Henderson et al., F.: (The Mercury Language Reference Manual) URL: http://www.cs.mu.oz.au/research/mercury/information/doc/reference_manual_toc.html.
20. Morales, J., Carro, M., Hermenegildo, M.: Improving the Compilation of Prolog to C Using Moded Types and Determinism Information. In: Proceedings of the Sixth International Symposium on Practical Aspects of Declarative Languages. Number 3507 in LNCS, Heidelberg, Germany, Springer-Verlag (2004) 86–103
21. Marriott, K., de la Banda, M.G., Hermenegildo, M.: Analyzing Logic Programs with Dynamic Scheduling. In: 20th. Annual ACM Conf. on Principles of Programming Languages, ACM (1994) 240–254
22. Carro, M., Hermenegildo, M.: A simple approach to distributed objects in prolog. In: Colloquium on Implementation of Constraint and LOgic Programming Systems (ICLP associated workshop), Copenhagen (2002)
23. Cabeza, D., Hermenegildo, M.: Distributed Concurrent Constraint Execution in the CIAO System. In: Proc. of the 1995 COMPULOG-NET Workshop on Parallelism and Implementation Technologies, Utrecht, NL, U. Utrecht / T.U. Madrid (1995) Available from http://www.clip.dia.fi.upm.es/.
24. Barbuti, R., Bellia, M., Levi, G., Martelli, M.: On the integration of logic programming and functional programming. In: International Symposium on Logic Programming, Atlantic City, NJ, IEEE Computer Society (1984) 160–168
25. Bellia, M., Levi, G.: The relation between logic and functional languages. Journal of Logic Programming **3** (1986) 217–236
26. Nadathur, G., Miller, D.: An overview of λprolog. In: Proc. 5th Conference on Logic Programming & 5th Symposium on Logic Programming (Seattle), MIT Press (1988) 810–827
27. Chen, W., Kifer, M., Warren, D.: HiLog: A foundation for higher order logic programming. Journal of Logic Programming **15** (1993) 187–230
28. Somogyi, Z., Henderson, F., Conway, T.: The execution algorithm of Mercury: an efficient purely declarative logic programming language. JLP **29** (1996)
29. Becket, R., de la Banda, M.G., Marriott, K., Somogyi, Z., Stuckey, P.J., Wallace, M.: Adding constraint solving to mercury. In: Eight International Symposium on Practical Aspects of Declarative Languages. Number 2819 in LNCS, Springer-Verlag (2006) 118–133
30. Haridi, S., Franzén, N.: The Oz Tutorial. DFKI. (2000) Available from http://www.mozart-oz.org.
31. Hanus et al, M.: Curry: An Integrated Functional Logic Language. (http://www.informatik.uni-kiel.de/~mh/curry/report.html)
32. Moreno Navarro, J., Rodríguez-Artalejo, M.: BABEL: A functional and logic programming language based on constructor discipline and narrowing. In: Conf. on Algebraic and Logic Programming (ALP). LNCS 343 (1989) 223–232

Resource Analysis by Sup-interpretation

Jean-Yves Marion and Romain Péchoux

Loria, Calligramme project, B.P. 239,
54506 Vandœuvre-lès-Nancy Cedex, France
École Nationale Supérieure des Mines de Nancy, INPL, France
{Jean-Yves.Marion, Romain.Pechoux}@loria.fr

Abstract. We propose a new method to control memory resources by static analysis. For this, we introduce the notion of sup-interpretation which bounds from above the size of function outputs. We establish a criteria for which the stack frame size is polynomially bounded. The criteria analyses terminating as well as non-terminating programs. This method applies to first order functional programming with pattern matching. This work is related to quasi-interpretations but we are now able to determine resources of different algorithms and it is easier to perform an analysis with this new tools.

1 Introduction

This paper deals with general investigation on program complexity analysis. It introduces the notion of sup-interpretation, a new tool that provides an upper bound on the size of every stack frame if the program is non-terminating, and establishes an upper bound on the size of function outputs if the program is terminating.

A sup-interpretation of a program is a *partial* assignment of function symbols, which ranges over reals and which bounds the size of the computed values.

The practical issue is to provide program static analysis in order to guarantee space resources that a program consumes during an execution. There is no need to say that this is crucial for at least many critical applications, and have strong impact in computer security. There are several approaches which are trying to solve the same problem. The first protection mechanism is by monitoring computations. However, if the monitor is compiled with the program, it could crash unpredictably by memory leak. The second is the testing-based approach, which is complementary to static analysis. Indeed, testing provides a lower bound on the memory while static analysis gives an upper bound. The gap between both bounds is of some value in practical applications (See [22] for an interesting discussion). Lastly, the third approach is type checking done by a bytecode verifier. In an untrusted environment (like embedded systems), the type protection policy (Java or .Net) does not allow dynamic allocation. Our approach is an attempt to control resources, and provide a proof certificate, of a high-level language in such a way that the compiled code is safe wrt memory overflow. Thus, we capture and deal with memory allocation features.

M. Hagiya and P. Wadler (Eds.): FLOPS 2006, LNCS 3945, pp. 163–176, 2006.

Similar approaches are the one by Hofmann [15, 16] and the one by Aspinall and Compagnoni [5].

For that purpose we consider first order functional programming language with pattern matching but we firmly believe that such a method could be applied to other languages such as resource bytecode verifier by following the lines of [2], language with synchronous cooperative threads as in [3] or first order functional language including streams as in [14] .

The notion of sup-interpretation can be seen as a kind of annotation provided in the code by the programmer. Sup-interpretations strongly inherit from the notion of quasi-interpretation developed by Bonfante, Marion and Moyen in [10, 11, 21]. Consequently the notion of sup-interpretation comes from the notion of polynomial interpretation used to prove termination of programs in [13, 18] and more recently in [8, 20]. Quasi-interpretation, like sup-interpretation, provides a bound over function outputs by static analysis for first order functional programs and allows the programmer to find a bound on the size of every stack frame. Quasi-interpretation was developed with the aim to pay more attention to the algorithmic aspects of complexity than to the functional (or extensional) one and then it is part of study of the implicit complexity of programs.

However the notions of sup-interpretation and quasi-interpretation differ for two reasons. First, the sup-interpretations are partial assignments which do not satisfy the subterm property, and this allows to capture a larger class of algorithms. In fact, programs computing logarithm or division admits a sup-interpretation but have no quasi-interpretation. Second, the sup-interpretation is a partial assignment over the set of function symbols of a program, whereas the quasi-interpretation is a total assignment on function symbols. On the other hand, sup-interpretations come with a companion, which is a weight to measure argument size of recursive calls involved in a program run. In order to obtain a polynomial space bound, some constraints are developed over weights and sup-interpretations using the underlying notion of dependency pairs by Arts and Giesl [4]. The dependency pairs were initially introduced for proving termination of term rewriting systems automatically. Even if this paper no longer focuses on termination, the notion of dependency pair is used for forcing the program to compute in polynomial space. There is a very strong relation between termination and computational complexity. Indeed, in order to prove some complexity bounds and termination, we need to control the arguments occurring in a function recursive call. Since we try to control together the arguments of a recursive call, the sup-interpretation is closer to the dependency pairs method than to the size-change principle method of [19] which consider the arguments of a recursive call separately (See more rencently [17]). Section 2 introduces the first order functional language and its semantics. Section 3 defines the main notions of sup-interpretation and weight used to bound the size of a program outputs. Section 4 presents the notion of fraternity used to control the size of values added by recursive calls. In section 5, we define the notion of polynomial and additive assignments for sup-interpretations and weights. Finally, section 6 introduces the notion of friendly programs and the main theorems of this paper providing a polynomial bound on the values computed by friendly programs. The full paper with all proofs is available at http://www.loria.fr/~pechoux. The appendix of the full paper presents examples of friendly programs, an example of non-friendly program and some examples over streams.

2 First Order Functional Programming

2.1 Syntax of Programs

We define a generic first order functional programming language. The vocabulary $\Sigma = \langle Cns, Op, Fct \rangle$ is composed of three disjoint domains of symbols. The arity of a symbol is the number n of arguments that it takes. The set of programs are defined by the following grammar.

$$
\begin{array}{lll}
\textbf{Programs} \ni \mathbf{p} & ::= & def_1, \cdots, def_m \\
\textbf{Definitions} \ni def & ::= & \mathbf{f}(x_1, \cdots, x_n) = e^{\mathbf{f}} \\
\textbf{Expression} \ni e & ::= & x \mid \mathbf{c}(e_1, \cdots, e_n) \mid \mathbf{op}(e_1, \cdots, e_n) \mid \mathbf{f}(e_1, \cdots, e_n) \\
& & \mid \textbf{Case } e_1, \cdots, e_n \textbf{ of } \overline{p_1} \to e^1 \ldots \overline{p_\ell} \to e^\ell \\
\textbf{Patterns} \ni p & ::= & x \mid \mathbf{c}(p_1, \cdots, p_n)
\end{array}
$$

where $\mathbf{c} \in Cns$ is a constructor, $\mathbf{op} \in Op$ is an operator, $\mathbf{f} \in Fct$ is a function symbol, and $\overline{p_i}$ is a sequence of n patterns. Throughout, we generalize this notation to expressions and we write $\overline{e}$ to express a sequence of expressions, that is $\overline{e} = e_1, \ldots, e_n$, for some n clearly determined by the context.

The set of variables Var is disjoint from Σ and $x \in Var$. In a definition, $e^{\mathbf{f}}$ is called the body of $\mathbf{f}$. A variable of $e^{\mathbf{f}}$ is either a variable in the parameter list $x_1, \cdots, x_n$ of the definition of $\mathbf{f}$ or a variable which occurs in a pattern of a case definition. In a case expression, patterns are not overlapping. The program's main function symbol is the first function symbol in the program's list of definitions. We usually don't make the distinction between this main symbol and the program symbol $\mathbf{p}$.

Lastly, it is convenient, because it avoids tedious details, to restrict case definitions in such a way that an expression involved in a **Case** expression does not contain nested **Case** (In other words, an expression e^j does not contain an expression **Case**). This is not a severe restriction since a program involving nested **Case** can be transformed in linear time in its size into an equivalent program without the nested case construction.

2.2 Semantics

The set *Values* is the constructor algebra freely generated from *Cns*.

$$
Values \ni v ::= \mathbf{c} \mid \mathbf{c}(v_1, \cdots, v_n) \qquad \mathbf{c} \in Cns
$$

Put $Values^* = Values \cup \{\mathbf{Err}\}$ where $\mathbf{Err}$ is the value associated to an error. Each operator $\mathbf{op}$ of arity n is interpreted by a function $[\![\mathbf{op}]\!]$ from $Values^n$

to *Values**. Operators are essentially basic partial functions like destructors or characteristic functions of predicates like $=$. The destructor **tl** illustrates the purpose of **Err** when it satisfies $[\![\mathbf{tl(nil)}]\!] = \mathbf{Err}$.

The computational domain is *Values*$^{\#}$ $=$ *Values* $\cup \{\mathbf{Err}, \bot\}$ where $\bot$ means that a program is non-terminating. The language has a closure-based call-by-value semantics which is displayed in Figure 1. A few comments are necessary. A substitution σ is a finite function from variables to *Values*. The application of a substitution σ to an expression e is noted $e\sigma$.

$$\frac{t_1 \downarrow w_1 \ldots t_n \downarrow w_n}{\mathbf{c}(t_1, \cdots, t_n) \downarrow \mathbf{c}(w_1, \cdots, w_n)} \quad \mathbf{c} \in Cns \text{ and } \forall i, w_i \neq \mathbf{Err}$$

$$\frac{t_1 \downarrow w_1 \ldots t_n \downarrow w_n}{\mathbf{op}(t_1, \cdots, t_n) \downarrow [\![\mathbf{op}]\!](w_1, \cdots, w_n)} \quad \mathbf{op} \in Op \text{ and } \forall i, w_i \neq \mathbf{Err}$$

$$\frac{e \downarrow u \quad \exists \sigma, i : p_i\sigma = u \quad e_i\sigma \downarrow w}{\mathbf{Case} \ e \ \mathbf{of} \ p_1 \rightarrow e_1 \ldots p_\ell \rightarrow e_\ell \downarrow w} \quad \mathbf{Case} \text{ and } u \neq \mathbf{Err}$$

$$\frac{e_1 \downarrow w_1 \ldots e_n \downarrow w_n \quad \mathbf{f}(x_1, \cdots, x_n) = e^{\mathbf{f}} \quad e^{\mathbf{f}}\sigma \downarrow w}{\mathbf{f}(e_1, \cdots, e_n) \downarrow w} \quad \text{where } \sigma(x_i) = w_i \neq \mathbf{Err} \text{ and } w \neq \mathbf{Err}$$

Fig. 1. Call by value semantics of ground expressions wrt a program **p**

The meaning of $e \downarrow w$ is that e evaluates to the value w of *Values**. If no rule is applicable, then an error occurs, and $e \downarrow \mathbf{Err}$. So, a program **p** computes a partial function $[\![\mathbf{p}]\!]$: *Values*$^n \rightarrow$ *Values*$^{\#}$ defined as follows. For all $v_i \in$ *Values*, $[\![\mathbf{p}]\!](v_1, \cdots, v_n) = w$ iff $\mathbf{p}(v_1, \cdots, v_n) \downarrow w$. Otherwise $[\![\mathbf{p}]\!](v_1, \cdots, v_n) = \bot$. Throughout, we shall say that $[\![\mathbf{p}]\!](v_1, \cdots, v_n)$ is defined when $[\![\mathbf{p}]\!](v_1, \cdots, v_n)$ is a constructor term of *Values*.

3   Sup-interpretations

3.1   Partial Assignment

A partial assignment θ is a partial mapping from a vocabulary Σ such that for each symbol $\mathbf{f}$ of arity n, in the domain of θ, it yields a partial function $\theta(f) : (\mathbb{R})^n \longmapsto \mathbb{R}$. The domain of a partial assignment θ is noted $\mathrm{dom}(\theta)$. Because it is convenient, we shall always assume that partial assignments that we consider, are defined on constructors and operators. That is $Cns \cup Op \subseteq \mathrm{dom}(\theta)$.

An expression e is defined over $\text{dom}(\theta)$ if each symbol belongs to $\text{dom}(\theta)$ or is a variable of Var. Take a denumerable sequence $X_1, \ldots, X_n, \ldots$. Assume that an expression e is defined over $\text{dom}(\theta)$ and has n variables. The partial assignment of e wrt θ is the extension of the assignment θ to the expression e that we write $\theta^*(e)$. It denotes a function from $\mathbb{R}^n$ to $\mathbb{R}$ and is defined as follows:

1. If x_i is a variable of Var, let $\theta^*(x_i) = X_i$
2. If b is a 0-ary symbol of Σ, then $\theta^*(b) = \theta(b)$.
3. If $\bar{e}$ is a sequence of n expressions, then $\theta^*(\bar{e}) = \max(\theta^*(e_1), \ldots, \theta^*(e_n))$
4. If e is a **Case** expression of the shape **Case** $\bar{e}$ **of** $\overline{p_1} \rightarrow e^1 \ldots \overline{p_\ell} \rightarrow e^\ell$,

$$\theta^*(e) = \max(\theta^*(\bar{e}), \theta^*(e^1), \ldots, \theta^*(e^\ell))$$

5. If f is a symbol of arity $n > 0$ and $e_1, \cdots, e_n$ are expressions, then

$$\theta^*(f(e_1, \cdots, e_n)) = \theta(f)(\theta^*(e_1), \ldots, \theta^*(e_n))$$

3.2 Sup-interpretation

Definition 1 (Sup-interpretation). *A sup-interpretation is a partial assignment θ which verifies the three conditions below :*

1. *The assignment θ is weakly monotonic. That is, for each symbol $f \in \text{dom}(\theta)$, the function $\theta(f)$ satisfies*

$$\forall i = 1, \ldots, n \ \ X_i \geq Y_i \Rightarrow \theta(f)(X_1, \cdots, X_n) \geq \theta(f)(Y_1, \cdots, Y_n)$$

2. *For each $v \in Values$,*

$$\theta^*(v) \geq |v|$$

   The size of an expression e is noted $|e|$ and is defined by $|\mathbf{c}| = 0$ where $\mathbf{c}$ is a 0-ary symbol and $|\mathbf{b}(e_1, \ldots, e_n)| = 1 + \sum_i |e_i|$ where $\mathbf{b}$ is a n-ary symbol.
3. *For each symbol $f \in \text{dom}(\theta)$ of arity n and for each value $v_1, \ldots, v_n$ of Values, if $[\![f]\!](v_1, \ldots, v_n)$ is defined, that is $[\![f]\!](v_1, \ldots, v_n) \in Values$, then*

$$\theta^*(f(v_1, \ldots, v_n)) \geq \theta^*([\![f]\!](v_1, \ldots, v_n))$$

Now an expression e admits a sup-interpretation θ if e is defined over $\text{dom}(\theta)$. The sup-interpretation of e wrt θ is $\theta^*(e)$.

Intuitively, the sup-interpretation is a special program interpretation. Instead of yielding the program denotation, a sup-interpretation provides an approximation from above of the size of the outputs of the function denoted by the program. It is worth noticing that sup-interpretations are a complexity measure in the sense of Blum [7].

Lemma 1. *Let e be an expression with no variable and which admits a sup-interpretation θ. Assume that $[\![e]\!]$ is defined. We then have*

$$\theta^*([\![e]\!]) \leq \theta^*(e)$$

Proof. The proof is done by structural induction on expression. The base case is a consequence of Condition 2 of Definition 1.

Take an expression $e = f(e_1, \cdots, e_n)$ that has a sup-interpretation θ. By induction hypothesis (IH), we have $\theta^*(e_i) \geq \theta^*(\llbracket e_i \rrbracket)$. Now,

$$
\begin{aligned}
\theta^*(e) &= \theta(f)(\theta^*(e_1), ..., \theta^*(e_n)) && \text{by definition of } \theta^* \\
&\geq \theta(f)(\theta^*(\llbracket e_1 \rrbracket), ..., \theta^*(\llbracket e_n \rrbracket)) && \text{by 1 of Dfn 1 and (IH)} \\
&= \theta^*(f(\llbracket e_1 \rrbracket, ..., \llbracket e_n \rrbracket)) && \text{by definition of } \theta^* \\
&\geq \theta^*(\llbracket f \rrbracket(\llbracket e_1 \rrbracket, ..., \llbracket e_n \rrbracket)) && \text{by 3 of Dfn 1} \\
&= \theta^*(\llbracket e \rrbracket) && \square
\end{aligned}
$$

Given an expression e, we define $\|e\|$ thus:

$$
\|e\| = \begin{cases} |\llbracket e \rrbracket| & \text{if } \llbracket e \rrbracket \text{ is defined} \\ 0 & \text{otherwise} \end{cases}
$$

Corollary 1. *Let e be an expression with no variable and which admits a sup-interpretation θ. Assume that $\llbracket e \rrbracket$ is defined. We then have*

$$
\|e\| \leq \theta^*(e)
$$

Proof.

$$
\begin{aligned}
\theta^*(e) &\geq \theta^*(\llbracket e \rrbracket) && \text{by Lemma 1} \\
&\geq \|e\| && \text{by Condition 2 of Dfn 1} && \square
\end{aligned}
$$

Example 1.

$$
\begin{aligned}
\mathtt{half}(x) \; = \; &\textbf{Case } x \textbf{ of } 0 \to 0 \\
&\mathbf{S(0)} \to 0 \\
&\mathbf{S(S(}y\mathbf{))} \to \mathbf{S}(\mathtt{half}(y))
\end{aligned}
$$

In this example, the function $\mathtt{half}$ computes $\lfloor n/2 \rfloor$ on an entry of size n. So by taking $\theta(\mathbf{S})(X) = X + 1$ and $\theta(\mathtt{half})(X) = X/2$, we define a sup-interpretation of the function symbol $\mathtt{half}$. In fact, both functions are monotonic. For every unary value v of size n, $\theta^*(v) = n \geq n = |v|$ by definition of $\theta(\mathbf{S})$, so that condition 2 on sup-interpretation is satisfied. Finally, it remains to check that for every value v, $\theta^*(\mathtt{half}(v)) \geq \theta^*(\llbracket \mathtt{half}(v) \rrbracket)$. For a value v of size n, we have by definition of θ^* that $\theta^*(\mathtt{half}(v)) = \theta^*(v)/2 = n/2$ and $\theta^*(\llbracket \mathtt{half}(v) \rrbracket) = \|\mathtt{half}(v)\| = \lfloor n/2 \rfloor$. Since $n/2 \geq \lfloor n/2 \rfloor$, condition 3 of sup-interpretation is satisfied. Notice that such a sup-interpretation is not a quasi-interpretation (a fortiori not an interpretation for proof termination) since it does not have the subterm property (see below for a definition of this property).

3.3   Weight

The weight allows us to control the size of the arguments in recursive calls. A weight is an assignment having the subterm property but no longer giving a bound on the size of a value computed by a function. Intuitively, whereas the sup-interpretation controls the size of the computed values, the weight can be seen as a control point for the computation of recursive calls.

Definition 2 (Weight). *A weight ω is a partial assignment which ranges over Fct. To a given function symbol f of arity n it assigns a total function ω_f from $\mathbb{R}^n$ to $\mathbb{R}$ which satisfies:*

1. ω_f is weakly monotonic.

$$\forall i = 1, \ldots, n, \ X_i \geq Y_i \Rightarrow \omega_f(\ldots, X_i, \ldots) \geq \omega_f(\ldots, Y_i, \ldots)$$

2. ω_f has the subterm property

$$\forall i = 1, \ldots, n, \ \omega_f(\ldots, X_i, \ldots) \geq X_i$$

The weight of a function is often taken to be the maximum or the sum functions.

The monotonicity property combined with the fact that a weight ranges over function symbols ensures suitable properties on the number of occurrences of a loop in a program when we consider the constraints given in section 6. Moreover, the subterm property allows to control the size of each argument in a recursive call, in opposition to the size-change principle as mentioned in the introduction.

4 Fraternities

In this section we define fraternities which are an important notion based on dependency pairs, that Arts and Giesl [4] introduced to prove termination automatically. Fraternities allow to tame the size of arguments of recursive calls.

A *context* is an expression $\mathsf{C}[\diamond_1, \cdots, \diamond_r]$ containing one occurrence of each $\diamond_i$. Here, we suppose that the $\diamond_i$'s are new symbols which are not in Σ nor in *Var*. The substitution of each $\diamond_i$ by an expression d_i is noted $\mathsf{C}[d_1, \cdots, d_r]$.

Definition 3. *Assume that $f(x_1, \cdots, x_n) = e^f$ is a definition of a program. An expression d is activated by $f(p_1, \cdots, p_n)$ where the p_i's are patterns if there is a context with one hole $\mathsf{C}[\diamond]$ such that:*

- *If e^f is a compositional expression (that is with no case definition inside it), then $e^f = \mathsf{C}[d]$. In this case, $p_1 = x_1 \ldots p_n = x_n$.*
- *Otherwise, $e^f = \mathbf{Case} \ e_1, \cdots, e_n \ \mathbf{of} \ \overline{q_1} \to e^1 \ldots \overline{q_\ell} \to e^\ell$, then there is a position j such that $e^j = \mathsf{C}[d]$. In this case, $p_1 = q_{j,1} \ldots p_n = q_{j,n}$ where $\overline{q_j} = q_{j,1} \ldots q_{j,n}$.*

At first glance, this definition may look a bit tedious. However, it is convenient in order to predict the computational data flow involved. Indeed, an expression is activated by $f(p_1, \cdots, p_n)$ when $f(v_1, \cdots, v_n)$ is called and each v_i matches the corresponding pattern p_i.

The notion of activated expression provides a precedence $\geq_{Fct}$ on function symbols. Indeed, set $f \geq_{Fct} g$ if there are $\overline{e}$ and $\overline{p}$ such that $g(\overline{e})$ is activated by $f(\overline{p})$. Then, take the reflexive and transitive closure of $\geq_{Fct}$, that we also note $\geq_{Fct}$. It is not difficult to establish that $\geq_{Fct}$ is a preorder. Next, say that $f \approx_{Fct} g$ if $f \geq_{Fct} g$ and inversely $g \geq_{Fct} f$. Lastly, $f >_{Fct} g$ if $f \geq_{Fct} g$ and $g \geq_{Fct} f$ does not hold.

Intuitively, $f \geq_{Fct} g$ means that f calls g in some executions. And $f \approx_{Fct} g$ means that f and g call themselves recursively.

Say that an expression d activated by $f(p_1, \cdots, p_n)$ is maximal if there is no context $C[\diamond]$, distinct from the empty context, such that $C[d]$ is activated by $f(p_1, \cdots, p_n)$.

Definition 4. *In a program p, an expression $d = C[g_1(\overline{e_1}), \ldots, g_r(\overline{e_r})]$ activated by $f(p_1, \cdots, p_n)$ is a fraternity if*

1. *d is maximal*
2. *For each $i \in \{1, r\}$, $g_i \approx_{Fct} f$.*
3. *For every function symbol h that appears in the context $C[\diamond_1, \cdots, \diamond_r]$, we have $f >_{Fct} h$.*

All along, we suppose that there is no nested fraternities, which means that a fraternity d does not contain any fraternity inside it. This restriction prevents definitions of the shape $f(S(x)) = f(f(x))$. This restriction is not too strong since such functions are not that natural in a programming perspective and either they have to be really restricted or they rapidly generate complex functions like the Ackermann one. The following examples illustrate typical fraternity constructions.

Example 2. Consider the program $\log$ computing $\log_2(n) + 1$ on an entry of size n and using the program $\mathtt{half}$ of example 1.

$$\log(x) = \textbf{Case } x \textbf{ of } \mathbf{0} \to \mathbf{0}$$
$$\mathbf{S}(y) \to \mathbf{S}(\log(\mathtt{half}(\mathbf{S}(y))))$$
$$\mathtt{half}(x) = \textbf{Case } x \textbf{ of } \mathbf{0} \to \mathbf{0}$$
$$\mathbf{S}(\mathbf{0}) \to \mathbf{0}$$
$$\mathbf{S}(\mathbf{S}(y)) \to \mathbf{S}(\mathtt{half}(y))$$

This program admits two fraternities $\mathbf{S}(\log[\mathtt{half}(\mathbf{S}(y))])$ and $\mathbf{S}[\mathtt{half}(y)]$ since $\log >_{Fct} \mathtt{half}$. Take $\mathbf{S}(\log[\mathtt{half}(\mathbf{S}(y))])$, this fraternity is decomposed into a context $\mathbf{S}(\log[\diamond])$ and an expression $\mathtt{half}(\mathbf{S}(y))$.

Example 3 (division). Consider the following definitions that encode the division $\lceil n/m \rceil$ on two entries of sizes n and $m > 0$:

$$\mathtt{minus}(x, y) = \textbf{Case } x, y \textbf{ of } \mathbf{0}, z \to \mathbf{0}$$
$$\mathbf{S}(z), \mathbf{0} \to \mathbf{S}(z)$$
$$\mathbf{S}(u), \mathbf{S}(v) \to \mathtt{minus}(u, v)$$

$$q(x, y) = \textbf{Case } x, y \textbf{ of } 0, S(z) \rightarrow 0$$
$$S(z), S(u) \rightarrow S(q(\texttt{minus}(z, u), S(u)))$$

This program admits two fraternities $\texttt{minus}(u, v)$ and $S[q(\texttt{minus}(z, u), S(u))]$ since $q >_{Fct} \texttt{minus}$.

Definition 5. *A* state *is a tuple* $\langle f, u_1, \cdots, u_n \rangle$ *where* f *is a function symbol of arity* n *and* $u_1, \ldots, u_n$ *are values. Assume that* $\eta_1 = \langle f, u_1, \cdots, u_n \rangle$ *and* $\eta_2 = \langle g, v_1, \cdots, v_k \rangle$ *are two states. Assume also that* $C[g(e_1, \cdots, e_k)]$ *is activated by* $f(p_1, \cdots, p_n)$. *A* transition *is a triplet* $\eta_1 \overset{C[\diamond]}{\rightsquigarrow} \eta_2$ *such that:*

1. *There is a substitution* σ *such that* $p_i \sigma = u_i$ *for* $i = 1, \ldots, n$,
2. *and* $[\![e_j \sigma]\!] = v_j$ *for* $j = 1 \ldots k$.

   We call such a graph a call-tree *of* f *over values* $u_1, \ldots, u_n$ *if* $\langle f, u_1, \cdots, u_n \rangle$ *is its root. A state may be seen as a stack frame. A call-tree of root* $\langle f, u_1, \cdots, u_n \rangle$ *represents all the stack frames which will be pushed on the stack when we compute* $f(u_1, \ldots, u_n)$.

5   Polynomial Assignments

Definition 6. *A partial assignment* θ *is* polynomial *if for each symbol* f *of arity* n *of* $dom(\theta)$, $\theta(f)$ *is* **bounded** *by a polynomial of* $\mathbb{R}[X_1, \cdots, X_n]$. *A polynomial sup-interpretation is a polynomial assignment. A polynomial weight* ω *of arity* n *is a weight which is bounded by some polynomial of* $\mathbb{R}[X_1, \cdots, X_n]$.

An assignment of $\mathbf{c} \in dom(\theta)$ is *additive* if

$$\theta(\mathbf{c})(X_1, \cdots, X_n) = \sum_{i=1}^{n} X_i + \alpha_{\mathbf{c}} \qquad \qquad \alpha_{\mathbf{c}} \geq 1$$

If the polynomial assignment of each constructor is additive then the assignment is additive. Throughout the following paper we consider additive assignments. As a consequence we have the following lemma:

Lemma 2. *There is a constant* α *such that for each value* v *of Values, the inequality is satisfied :*

$$|v| \leq \theta^*(v) \leq \alpha |v|$$

6   Local Criteria to Control Space Resources

Definition 7 (Friendly). *A program* p *is* friendly *iff there is a polynomial sup-interpretation* θ *and a polynomial weight* ω *such that for each fraternity expression* $d = C[g_1(\overline{e_1}), \ldots, g_r(\overline{e_r})]$ *activated by* $f(p_1, \cdots, p_n)$ *we have,*

$$\theta^*(\mathsf{C}[\diamond_1,\ldots,\diamond_r]) = \max_{i=1..r}(\diamond_i + R_i(Y_1,\ldots,Y_m))$$

with R_i polynomials where each Y_i corresponds to a variable occurring in C. Moreover, for each $i \in \{1,r\}$, we have that for each substitution σ,

$$\omega_f(\theta^*(p_1\sigma),\ldots,\theta^*(p_n\sigma)) \geq \omega_{g_i}(\theta^*(e_{i,1}\sigma),\ldots,\theta^*(e_{i,m}\sigma))$$

Moreover, if

$$\exists\sigma \quad \omega_f(\theta^*(p_1\sigma),\ldots,\theta^*(p_n\sigma)) = \omega_{g_i}(\theta^*(e_{i,1}\sigma),\ldots,\theta^*(e_{i,m}\sigma))$$

Then $R_i(Y_1,\ldots,Y_m)$ is the null polynomial.

Example 4. The program of example 2 is friendly. We take $\theta(\mathbf{S})(X) = X + 1$ and $\theta(\mathtt{half})(X) = X/2$. The contexts of the two fraternities involved in this program are $\mathbf{S}[\diamond]$, thus having a sup-interpretation $\theta^*(\mathbf{S}[\diamond]) = \diamond + 1$. We have to find $\omega_{\mathtt{log}}$ and $\omega_{\mathtt{half}}$ such that for every σ:

$$\omega_{\mathtt{log}}(\theta^*(\mathbf{S}(y\sigma))) > \omega_{\mathtt{log}}(\theta^*(\mathtt{half}(\mathbf{S}(y\sigma))))$$
$$\omega_{\mathtt{half}}(\theta^*(\mathbf{S}(\mathbf{S}(y\sigma)))) > \omega_{\mathtt{half}}(\theta^*(y\sigma))$$

Both inequalities are satisfied by taking $\omega_{\mathtt{log}}(X) = \omega_{\mathtt{half}}(X) = X$. Thus the program is friendly.

Example 5. The program of example 3 is friendly by taking $\theta(\mathbf{S})(X) = X + 1$, $\theta(\mathtt{minus})(X,Y) = X$, $\omega_{\mathtt{minus}}(X,Y) = \max(X,Y)$ and $\omega_{\mathtt{q}}(X,Y) = X + Y$. An example of an unfriendly program is given in the full paper.

Theorem 1. *Assume that $\boldsymbol{p}$ is a friendly program. For each function symbol f of $\boldsymbol{p}$ there is a polynomial P such that for every value $v_1,\ldots,v_n$,*

$$\|f(v_1,\ldots,v_n)\| \leq P(\max(|v_1|,...,|v_n|))$$

Proof. The proof can be found in the full paper. It begins by assigning a polynomial P_f to every function symbol $\mathtt{f}$ of a friendly program. This polynomial is the sum of a bound on the size of values added by the contexts of recursive calls and of a bound on the size of values added by the calls which are no longer recursive. Then it checks both bounds thus showing that the values computed by the program are polynomially bounded. □

The programs presented in examples 2 and 3 are examples of friendly programs and thus computing polynomially bounded values. More examples of friendly programs can be found in the appendix of the full paper.

The next result strengthens Theorem above. Indeed it claims that even if a program is not terminating then the intermediate values are polynomially bounded. This is quite interesting because non-terminating process are common, and moreover it is not difficult to introduce streams with a slight modification of the above Theorem, which is essentially based on the semantics change.

Theorem 2. *Assume that p is a friendly program. For each function symbol f of p there is a polynomial R such that for every node $\langle g, u_1, \cdots, u_m \rangle$ of the call-tree of root $\langle f, v_1, \cdots, v_n \rangle$,*

$$\max_{j=1..m} (|u_j|) \leq R(\max(|v_1|, ..., |v_n|))$$

even if $f(v_1, \ldots, v_n)$ is not defined.

Proof. The proof is in the full paper and is a consequence of previous theorem since in every state of the call-tree, the values are computed and thus bounded polynomially. $\square$

Remark 1. As mentioned above, this theorem holds for non-terminating programs and particularly for a class of programs including streams. For that purpose we have to give a new definition of substitutions over streams. In fact, it would be meaningless to consider a substitution over stream variables. Thus stream variables are never substituted and the sup-interpretation of a stream l is taken to be a new variable L as in the definition of the sup-interpretations.

Example 6 (Streams). Let e::l be a stream with :: a stream constructor symbol, e an expression (the head of the stream) and l a stream variable (the tail of the stram) and suppose that we have already defined a semantics over streams in a classical way.

$$\texttt{addstream}(x, y) = \textbf{Case } x, y \text{ of } z :: l, u :: l' \rightarrow \texttt{add}(z, u) :: \texttt{addstream}(l, l')$$

Then this (merging) program is friendly by taking $\theta^*(l) = L$, $\theta(\texttt{add})(X, Y) = X + Y$, $\theta^*(x :: l) = \theta^*(x) + L + 1$ and $\omega_{\texttt{addstream}}(X, Y) = X + Y$. Thus a variant of theorem 2 holds. The variation comes from the fact that it would be non-sense to consider streams as inputs, since the size of a stream is unbounded. Consequently, the inputs are chosen to be a restricted number of stream heads. In the same way, every mapping program over streams of the shape:

$$\texttt{f}(x) = \textbf{Case } x \text{ of } z :: l \rightarrow \texttt{g}(z) :: \texttt{f}(l)$$

is friendly if **g** represents a friendly program. Thus the variant of theorem 2 also applies. Moreover for all these programs we know that the values computed in the output streams (i.e. in the heads of right-hand side definition) are polynomially bounded in the size of some of the inputs (heads) since the computations involve only friendly functions over non-stream datas (else some parts of the program will never be evaluated). Finally an example of non-friendly program is:

$$\texttt{f}(x) = \textbf{Case } x \text{ of } z :: l \rightarrow \texttt{f}(z :: z :: l)$$

In fact, this program does not fit our requirements since it adds infinitely the head of the stream to its argument, computing thus an unbounded value.

7 Conclusion and Perspectives

The notion of sup-interpretation allows to check that the size of the outputs of a friendly program is bounded polynomially by the size of it inputs. It allows to capture algorithms admitting no quasi-interpretations (division, logarithm, gcd . . .). So, our experiments show that is not too difficult to find sup-interpretations for the following reasons. First, we have to guess sup-interpretations and weights of only some, and not all, symbols. Second, a quasi-interpretations for those symbol works pretty well in most of the cases. And so we can use tools to synthesize quasi-interpretations [1, 9]. Our works is related to semi-automatic procedure to analyse complexity, see for example Benzinger [6] for programs extracted from Nuprl or Debray et al. for logic programs [12].

Sup-interpretation should be easier to synthesize than quasi-interpretations since we have to find fewer assignments. Moreover it is not so hard to find a sup-interpretation, since quasi-interpretation often defines a sup-interpretation, except in the case of additive contexts. Indeed, consider the program $f(c(x, y)) = c(f(x), f(y))$ defined over binary trees. It admits the identity function as quasi-interpretation. However it does not admit a sup-interpretation since its context should have an additive sup-interpretation. Which is clearly impossible in the friendly criteria. Hopefully this drawback only relies on the friendly criteria and not on the sup-interpretation itself. We are currently working on a more general criteria which should be able to capture such programs and whose aim is to capture entirely the class of programs admitting a quasi-interpretation. As a consequence every quasi-interpretation satisfying the friendly criteria is a sup-interpretation. A programmer is also interested in bounding the total number of stack frames. This issue is partially tackled in the full paper by showing that cycles of the call-tree corresponding to friendly programs with strict inequalities in the friendly criteria have a number of occurrences bounded by a polynomial in the size of the inputs. Since every occurence of a cycle is composed of a bounded number of states (which depends directly on the size of the program) and since every cycle occurs a polynomial number of times, we know that the corresponding call-tree will have a number of states bounded polynomially in the size of the inputs. Consequently, for such programs, both stack frame sizes and the number of stack-frames are polynomially bounded by the size of the inputs. The corresponding termination result strongly inherits in a natural way from the dependency pairs method of Arts and Giesl [4]. However, it differs in the sense that the monotonicity of the quasi-ordering and the inequalities over definitions (rules) of a program are replaced by the notion of sup-interpretation combined to weights. Consequently, it shares the same advantages and disadvantages than the dependency pairs method compared to termination methods such as size-change principle by Jones et al. [19], failing on programs admitting no polynomial orderings (Ackermann function, for example), and managing to prove termination on programs where the size-change principle fails. For a more detailed comparison between both termination criteria see [23]. Finally, an open question concerns characterization of time complexity classes with the use of such a tool, particularly, the characterization of polynomial time by determining a restriction on sup-interpretations.

References

1. R. Amadio. Max-plus quasi-interpretations. In Martin Hofmann, editor, *Typed Lambda Calculi and Applications, 6th International Conference, TLCA 2003, Valencia, Spain, June 10-12, 2003, Proceedings*, volume 2701 of *Lecture Notes in Computer Science*, pages 31–45. Springer, 2003.

2. R. Amadio, S. Coupet-Grimal, S. Dal-Zilio, and L. Jakubiec. A functional scenario for bytecode verification of resource bounds. In Jerzy Marcinkowski and Andrzej Tarlecki, editors, *Computer Science Logic, 18th International Workshop, CSL 13th Annual Conference of the EACSL, Karpacz, Poland*, volume 3210 of *Lecture Notes in Computer Science*, pages 265–279. Springer, 2004.

3. R. Amadio and S. Dal Zilio. Resource control for synchronous cooperative threads. Research Report LIF.

4. T. Arts and J. Giesl. Termination of term rewriting using dependency pairs. *Theoretical Computer Science*, 236:133–178, 2000.

5. D. Aspinall and A. Compagnoni. Heap bounded assembly language. *Journal of Automated Reasoning (Special Issue on Proof-Carrying Code)*, 31:261–302, 2003.

6. R. Benzinger. Automated higher-order complexity analysis. *Theoretical Computer Science*, 318(1-2):79–103, 2004.

7. M. Blum. A machine-independent theory of the complexity of recursive functions. *Journal of the Association for Computing Machinery*, 14:322–336, 1967.

8. G. Bonfante, A. Cichon, J.-Y. Marion, and H. Touzet. Algorithms with polynomial interpretation termination proof. *Journal of Functional Programming*, 11(1):33–53, 2001.

9. G. Bonfante, J.-Y. Moyen J.-Y. Marion, and R. Péchoux. Synthesis of quasi-interpretations. *Workshop on Logic and Complexity in Computer Science, LCC2005, Chicago*, 2005. http://www.loria/~pechoux.

10. G. Bonfante, J.-Y. Marion, and J.-Y. Moyen. On lexicographic termination ordering with space bound certifications. In Dines Bjørner, Manfred Broy, and Alexandre V. Zamulin, editors, *Perspectives of System Informatics, 4th International Andrei Ershov Memorial Conference, PSI 2001, Akademgorodok, Novosibirsk, Russia, Ershov Memorial Conference*, volume 2244 of *Lecture Notes in Computer Science*. Springer, Jul 2001.

11. G. Bonfante, J.-Y. Marion, and J.-Y. Moyen. Quasi-interpretation a way to control resources. *Submitted to Theoretical Computer Science*, 2005. http://www.loria.fr/~moyen/appsemTCS.ps.

12. S.K. Debray and N.W. Lin. Cost analysis of logic programs. *ACM Transactions on Programming Languages and Systems*, 15(5):826–875, 1993.

13. N. Dershowitz. Termination of rewriting. *Journal of Symbolic Computation*, pages 69–115, 1987.

14. S.G. Frankau and A. Mycroft. Stream processing hardware from functional language specifications. In Martin Hofmann, editor, *36th Hawai'i International Conference on System Sciences (HICSS 36)*. IEEE, 2003.

15. M. Hofmann. Linear types and non-size-increasing polynomial time computation. In *Proceedings of the Fourteenth IEEE Symposium on Logic in Computer Science (LICS'99)*, pages 464–473, 1999.

16. M. Hofmann. A type system for bounded space and functional in-place update. In *European Symposium on Programming, ESOP'00*, volume 1782 of *Lecture Notes in Computer Science*, pages 165–179, 2000.

17. A. Hugh and S.C. Khoo. Affined-based size-change termination. *APLAS 2003, Beijing*, 2003.
18. D.S. Lankford. On proving term rewriting systems are noetherien. Technical report, 1979.
19. Chin Soon Lee, Neil D. Jones, and Amir M. Ben-Amram. The size-change principle for program termination. In *Symposium on Principles of Programming Languages*, volume 28, pages 81–92. ACM press, january 2001.
20. S. Lucas. Polynomials over the reals in proofs of termination: from theory to practice. *RAIRO Theoretical Informatics and Applications*, 39(3):547–586, 2005.
21. J.-Y. Marion and J.-Y. Moyen. Efficient first order functional program interpreter with time bound certifications. In Michel Parigot and Andrei Voronkov, editors, *Logic for Programming and Automated Reasoning, 7th International Conference, LPAR 2000, Reunion Island, France*, volume 1955 of *Lecture Notes in Computer Science*, pages 25–42. Springer, Nov 2000.
22. J. Regehr. Say no to stack overflow. 2004. `http://www.embedded.com`.
23. R. Thiemann and J. Giesl. Size-change termination for term rewriting. In *14th International Conference on Rewriting Techniques and Applications*, Lecture Notes in Computer Science, Valencia, Spain, 2003. Springer.

Lazy Set-Sharing Analysis

Xuan Li[1], Andy King[2], and Lunjin Lu[1]

[1] Oakland University Rochester, MI 48309, USA
{x2li, l2lu}@oakland.edu
[2] University of Kent, Canterbury, UK
a.m.king@kent.ac.uk

Abstract. Sharing analysis is widely deployed in the optimisation, specialisation and parallelisation of logic programs. Each abstract unification operation over the classic Jacobs and Langen domain involves the calculation of a closure operation that has exponential worst-case complexity. This paper explores a new tactic for improving performance: laziness. The idea is to compute partial sharing information eagerly and recover full sharing information lazily. The net result is an analysis that runs in a fraction of the time of the classic analysis and yet has comparable precision.

1 Introduction

Sharing analysis is one of the most well-studied analyses within logic programming. Two variables are said to share if they are bound to terms that contain a common variable; otherwise they are independent. Independence information has many applications in logic programming that include occurs-check reduction [24, 10], automatic parallelisation [11] and finite-tree analysis [2]. Set-sharing analysis [17, 18], as opposed to pair-sharing analysis [24], has particularly attracted much attention. This is because researchers have been repeatedly drawn to the algebraic properties of the domain since these offer tantalising opportunities for implementation [3, 7, 8, 12].

The reoccurring problem with the set-sharing domain is the closure under union operation that lies at the heart of the abstract unification ($amgu$) operation [18]. A sharing abstraction is constructed from a set of sharing groups each of which is a set of program variables. Closure under union operation repeatedly unions together sets of sharing groups, drawn from a given sharing abstraction, until no new sharing group can be obtained. This operation is exponential, hence the interest in different, and possibly more tractable, encodings of set-sharing [7, 8]. One approach to curbing the problem of closure is to schedule the solving of a sequence of equations so as to first apply $amgu$ to equations that involve ground terms [21]. To this end, Muthukumar and Hermenegildo [22] detail an queueing/dequeueing mechanism for maximally propagating groundness among systems of equations. This tactic exploits the commutativity of the $amgu$ operation [13, 21][Lemma 62]. A refinement of this idea is to schedule the $amgu$ operations using an estimate of the cost of a closure. The $amgu$ operations are applied in

M. Hagiya and P. Wadler (Eds.): FLOPS 2006, LNCS 3945, pp. 177–191, 2006.
© Springer-Verlag Berlin Heidelberg 2006

order of increasing closure cost and then widening is invoked [25, 21][Section 4.3]
when the application of a closure becomes prohibitively expensive. To support
widening, the set-sharing domain has been extended [25, 21][Section 4.3] from a
set of sharing groups, to a pair of sets of sharing groups. A sharing group in the
first component (that is called a clique [25]) is then reinterpreted as representing
all sharing groups that are contained within it.

This paper addresses the question of whether closure calculation is actually
required at all. It shows that cliques can be reinterpreted as pending closure
operations. Under this reinterpretation, the complexity of $amgu$ can be reduced
to a quadratic time operation on sharing groups and a constant time operation on
cliques. If necessary, a classic set-sharing abstraction can be recovered using the
cliques without incurring a precision loss by applying a closure operation for the
groups that are relevant to each clique. Quite apart from being rather surprising,
this reinterpretation of cliques can avoid computing closures all together in some
circumstances. Firstly, if one clique is contained within another, then the smaller
clique is redundant as is its associated closure operation. Secondly, if a clique
contains those variables that appear in a call, then it can be passed from one
procedure to another without applying closure. Thirdly, if closure is prohibitively
expensive, then it can be retained as clique, albeit incurring a possible loss of
precision in the projection and merge operations. This leads to an analysis that
is parameterised by a cost threshold k: a clique is only created if the resulting
number of sharing groups exceed k. The resulting analysis is polynomial and
benchmarking suggests that it realises a good tradeoff between precision and
efficiency.

This paper is organised as follows. Section 2 contains basic concepts and
recalls the *Sharing* domain. Section 3 informally introduces the motivation via
examples. Sections 4-7 present the abstract domain and abstract operators in
details. Section 8 discusses an experimental implementation. Section 9 discusses
related work and section 10 concludes.

2   Preliminaries

Let $\mathcal{V}$ denote a denumerable universe of variables. Let $var(o)$ be the set of
variables in the syntactic object o. If S is a set then $|S|$ is its cardinality and
$\wp(S)$ is the powerset of S. The (classic) set-sharing domain *Sharing* is defined
by $Sharing = \{S \in \wp(\wp(\mathcal{V})) \mid \emptyset \in S\}$. We call a set of variables $G \subseteq \mathcal{V}$ a sharing
group and a set $S \in Sharing$ a sharing abstraction. The restriction $G \upharpoonright V$ is
defined by $G \upharpoonright V = G \cap V$ where $V \subseteq \mathcal{V}$. Moreover, if $S \in Sharing$ then $S \upharpoonright V$
is defined by $S \upharpoonright V = \{G \upharpoonright V \mid G \in S\}$. The function $max : \wp(\wp(\mathcal{V})) \to \wp(\wp(\mathcal{V}))$
is defined by $max(S) = \{G \in S \mid \forall H \in S.G \subseteq H \to G = H\}$.

The most important operator in *Sharing* is the abstract unification operator
$amgu_{x=t}$ where x is a variable and t is a term not containing x. The operator
$amgu_{x=t}$ is defined in terms of three auxiliary operations. The closure under
union of a sharing abstraction S, denoted by S^*, is the smallest superset of S
satisfying if $X \in S^*$ and $Y \in S^*$ then $X \cup Y \in S^*$. The set of sharing groups in

S that are relevant to a syntactic object o is $rel(o, S) = \{G \in S \mid var(o) \cap G \neq \emptyset\}$. We say that a sharing abstraction $S \in Sharing$ is relevant to a term t iff $rel(t, S) \neq \emptyset$. The cross union of two sharing abstractions S_1 and S_2 is defined by $S_1 \uplus S_2 = \{G \cup H \mid G \in S_1 \wedge H \in S_2\}$. The following definition of the abstract unification is adapted from [8] that is equivalent to classic definition in [17, 18].

Definition 1. $amgu_{x=t}(S) = S \setminus rel(x, S) \setminus rel(t, S) \cup (rel(x, S) \uplus rel(t, S))^*$ where $\setminus$ is the set minus operator.

The set of all clique-sets CL [25] is defined by $CL = \wp(\{G \in \wp(\mathcal{V}) \mid G \neq \emptyset\})$. A clique is an element of a clique-set. In this paper, a clique is the abstraction of an equation of the e where e takes the form $x = t$.

3   Motivation Example

This section informally introduces the basic idea using several examples. We demonstrate how to use cliques and part of sharing abstraction to represent the whole sharing abstraction.

Example 1. Suppose $S = \{\emptyset, \{X_1\}, \{X_2\}, \{X_3\}, \{X_4\}, \{X_5\}, \{X_6\}, \{X_7\}\}$ and equation e is $X_1 = f(X_2, X_3, X_4, X_5, X_6, X_7)$. If we apply the classical abstract unification $amgu$, we obtain

$$amgu_e(S) = \{\emptyset\} \cup \left\{ \begin{array}{l} \{X_1, X_2\}, \{X_1, X_3\}, \{X_1, X_4\}, \\ \{X_1, X_5\}, \{X_1, X_6\}, \{X_1, X_7\} \end{array} \right\}^*$$

There are 63 groups in $amgu_e(S) \setminus \{\emptyset\}$ in all. Note that we only list 6 groups instead of enumerating all 63 groups for the sake of saving space. We shall refer to these 6 groups as the basis of the 63 groups because the whole closure (the 63 groups) can be recovered from the basis (the 6 groups) by applying closure under union operator to the basis. In other words, we can use the basis to represent the whole closure. The intuition behind the analysis is to record which groups participate in the closure under union and avoid computing closure under union operation until it is called for. We record which groups participate in closure under union by keeping a record of the set of variables that are contained within the equation e. Moreover, we only consider the equations that contain at least one variable and thus we can use a clique [25] to represent these variable sets. Therefore we use a pair $\langle E, S \rangle \in CL \times Sharing$ to represent a sharing abstraction: the first component is the set of cliques; the second component is the partially computed sharing information. In this way, we can avoid closure under union operation during analysis.

Example 2. Continuing with example 1, the state of sharing after abstract unification is expressed as

$$\left\langle \begin{array}{l} \{\{X_1, X_2, X_3, X_4, X_5, X_6, X_7\}\}, \\ \{\emptyset, \{X_1, X_2\}, \{X_1, X_3\}, \{X_1, X_4\}, \{X_1, X_5\}, \{X_1, X_6\}, \{X_1, X_7\}\} \end{array} \right\rangle$$

In this example, this part of sharing information is $S \setminus rel(x = t, S) \cup rel(x, S) \uplus rel(t, S)$. We will show that this is not a coincident in the later sections.

When we need to recover full sharing information, we can just apply the closure under union to those groups that are relevant to each clique.

Example 3. Continuing with example 2, there is only one clique in first components. If we denote $\{X_1, X_2, X_3, X_4, X_5, X_6, X_7\}$ by e and $\{\emptyset, \{X_1, X_2\}, \{X_1, X_3\}, \{X_1, X_4\}, \{X_1, X_5\}, \{X_1, X_6\}, \{X_1, X_7\}\}$ by S, then the full sharing information is obtained by

$$S \cup rel(e, S)^* = \{\emptyset\} \cup \left\{ \begin{array}{l} \{X_1, X_2\}, \{X_1, X_3\}, \{X_1, X_4\}, \\ \{X_1, X_5\}, \{X_1, X_6\}, \{X_1, X_7\} \end{array} \right\}^*$$

which coincides with the sharing information derived in example 1.

If there is more than one clique, then sharing is recovered by considering each clique in turn.

Example 4. Consider $\langle\{e_1, e_2\}, S\rangle$ where $e_1 = \{X, Y\}$, $e_2 = \{Y, Z\}$ and $S = \{\emptyset, \{X\}, \{Y\}, \{Z\}\}$. First, applying e_1, we obtain $S_1 = S \cup rel(e_1, S)^* = \{\emptyset, \{X\}, \{Y\}, \{Z\}, \{X, Y\}\}$. Next applying e_2, we have $S_1 \cup rel(e_2, S_1)^* = \{\emptyset, \{X\}, \{Y\}, \{Z\}, \{X, Y\}, \{Y, Z\}, \{X, Y, Z\}\}$. In fact, as is shown latter, the order in which the cliques are consider is incidental.

Although we call closure under union operator when we recover full sharing information, we only apply it on demand. Even if the client wants to get full sharing information at every program point, a lazy evaluation strategy is still better because we avoid redundant computation during analysis. For an instance, when clique e_1 is a subset of e_2, we can disregard e_1 because the effect of e_1 is subsumed by that of e_2. Moreover, the number of groups involved in least fixed point computation is much less than the number of groups involved in classical *Sharing* because only part of closure is involved.

In summary, we only compute part of sharing information at each program point during analysis and can recover full sharing information on demand after analysis. As a result, the closure under union operator is avoided for abstract unification. In following sections, we will present this new domain formally.

4   Abstract Domain

Reducing the input data size and improving the efficiency of operators over the domain are two ways to improve the efficiency of an analysis. Recall definition 1:

$$amgu_{x=t}(S) = S \setminus rel(x, S) \setminus rel(t, S) \cup (rel(x, S) \uplus rel(t, S))^*$$

For the ensuing discussion, denote $rel(x, S) \uplus rel(t, S)$ by S_b. Rather than directly compute S_b^* and use this closure to calculate $amgu_{x=t}(S)$, we compute the partial sharing information $S \setminus rel(x, S) \setminus rel(t, S) \cup S_b$ and record information that enables S_b^* to be computed on demand. The size of the partial sharing information inferred using this strategy is never more, and is often significantly less, than that inferred using full sharing. The key issue is to resolve which groups belong to S_b so that we can recover S_b^* on demand. One way to deduce S_b, and hence S_b^*, is to save the equation $x = t$ because if $G \in S \setminus rel(x, S) \setminus rel(t, S) \cup S_b$ then $G \in S_b$ iff $rel(x = t, G) \neq \emptyset$. Since only variables in the equation actually matter in $rel(x = t, G)$, it is sufficient to record the clique $var(x = t)$ to recover S_b and thereby derive full sharing. To summarise, the computational domain of *Sharing* is replaced with pairs of the form $\langle E, S \rangle \in CL \times Sharing$ where each clique in the first component is an abstraction of an equation and is used to recover the full sharing information that $\langle E, S \rangle$ describes. The following function formalises this idea since it maps each abstract values in $CL \times Sharing$ to the sharing abstractions they describe:

Definition 2. $\langle E, S \rangle \propto S'$ iff $r(\langle E, S \rangle) = S'$ where $r(\langle E, S \rangle)$ is defined as follows:

$$r(\langle \emptyset, S \rangle) = S$$

$$r(\langle \{e\} \cup E', S \rangle) = S'' \cup rel(e, S'')^*$$

where $e \in E$, $E' = E \setminus \{e\}$ and $S'' = r(\langle E', S \rangle)$.

This function is called the recovery function. Although this recovery function calls closure under union operator, the recovery function is itself only called on demand. Henceforth, we abbreviate $r(\langle E, S \rangle)$ by $r(E, S)$.

Example 5. Let $\langle E, S \rangle = \langle \{e_1, e_2, e_3\}, S \rangle$, where $e_1 = \{X, Y\}$, $e_2 = \{Y, Z\}$, $e_3 = \{Y, W\}$ and $S = \{\emptyset, \{X\}, \{Y\}, \{Z\}, \{W\}\}$. Thus we can recover the full sharing information S' that $\langle E, S \rangle$ describes by unfolding definition 2 in the following fashion:

$$S' = r(\{e_1, e_2, e_3\}, S) = r(\{e_3\}, r(\{e_1, e_2\}, S)) = r(\{e_3\}, r(\{e_2\}, r(\{e_1\}, S)))$$

$$S_1 = r(\{e_1\}, S) = S \cup rel(e_1, S)^* = \{\emptyset, \{X\}, \{Y\}, \{Z\}, \{W\}, \{X, Y\}\}$$

$$S_2 = r(\{e_2\}, S_1) = S_1 \cup rel(e_2, S_1)^* = \left\{ \begin{array}{l} \emptyset, \{X\}, \{Y\}, \{Z\}, \{W\}, \\ \{X, Y\}, \{Y, Z\}, \{X, Y, Z\} \end{array} \right\}$$

$$S' = r(\{e_3\}, S_2) = S_2 \cup rel(e_3, S_2)^* = \left\{ \begin{array}{l} \emptyset, \{X\}, \{Y\}, \{Z\}, \{W\}, \{X, Y\}, \\ \{Y, Z\}, \{X, Y, Z\}, \{Y, W\}, \\ \{X, Y, W\}, \{Y, Z, W\}, \{X, Y, Z, W\} \end{array} \right\}$$

One natural question is whether the order in which cliques are considered in the recovery process actually matters. The following lemma is a partial answer to this question: it shows that the ordering does not matter when there are only two cliques in the first component.

Lemma 1

$$S \cup rel(e_1, S)^* \cup rel(e_2, S \cup rel(e_1, S)^*)^* = S \cup rel(e_2, S)^* \cup rel(e_1, S \cup rel(e_2, S)^*)^*$$

The following proposition lifts this result to an arbitrary number of cliques; it also means that the recovery function satisfies the diamond property.

Proposition 1. $r(E, S) = r(P, S)$ whenever P is a permutation of E.

The abstract domain $CL \times Sharing$ is a non-canonical representation because different pairs $\langle E_1, S_1 \rangle \neq \langle E_2, S_2 \rangle$ can map to the same sharing abstraction during recovery. To obtain a partially ordered domain, it is necessary to induce an equivalence relation on $CL \times Sharing$. We therefore define $\langle E_1, S_1 \rangle \equiv \langle E_2, S_2 \rangle$ iff $r(E_1, S_1) = r(E_2, S_2)$ and consider the abstract domain $XSharing = (CL \times Sharing)_\equiv$, that is, the computational domain of sets of equivalence classes induced by $\equiv$. The partial ordering over $XSharing$, denoted by $\sqsubseteq$, can then by defined as $\langle E_1, S_1 \rangle \sqsubseteq \langle E_2, S_2 \rangle$ iff $r(E_1, S_1) \subseteq r(E_2, S_2)$. It then follows that $\langle XSharing, \sqsubseteq \rangle$ is a complete lattice.

For notational simplicity, we blur the distinction between elements of $XSharing$ and the elements of $CL \times Sharing$ and interpret the pair $\langle E_1, S_1 \rangle \in CL \times Sharing$ as representing the equivalence class $[\langle E_1, S_1 \rangle]_\equiv \in XSharing$. For example, the recovery function over $XSharing$ is the natural lifting of this function to the domain of equivalence classes.

5   Abstract Unification

The rationale for our work is to avoid applying the calculating closure under union operator in abstract unification. In the following definition, we detail how to avoid the closures by instead creating cliques in the first component. An important consequence of this scheme, is that the operator is polynomial in the number of groups. In what follows, we prove that this new notion of abstract unification is both sound and precise.

Definition 3

$$xamgu_{x=t}(\langle E, S \rangle) = \left\langle \begin{array}{c} max(E \cup \{var(x = t)\}), \\ (S \setminus rel(x = t, S)) \cup (rel(x, S) \uplus rel(t, S)) \end{array} \right\rangle$$

Henceforth, we abbreviate $xamgu_{x=t}(\langle E, S \rangle)$ by $xamgu_{x=t}(E, S)$. Note that we only need to maintain maximal cliques in the first component because the effect of a smaller clique is subsumed by that of a larger one (one that strictly contains it). Therefore, we say a clique e_i is redundant in $E \in CL$ if there exists $e_j \in E$ such that $e_i \subseteq e_j$. In that this is just one way of detecting redundancy: other more sophisticated ways are also possible.

Example 6. Consider $\langle E, S \rangle$ where $E = \{\{X, Y, Z\}\}$ and $S = \{\emptyset, \{X, Y\}, \{X, Z\}, \{Z, W\}\}$. Then $xamgu_{Y=Z}(E, S) = \langle \{\{X, Y, Z\}\}, \{\emptyset, \{X, Y, Z\}, \{X, Y, Z, W\}\} \rangle$

Lemma 2 explains how $xamgu$ coincides with $amgu$ when there is no clique in the first component.

Lemma 2. $r(xamgu_{x=t}(\emptyset, S)) = amgu_{x=t}(S)$.

Proposition 2 also builds towards the main correctness theorem by showing the equivalence of of two instances of abstract unification that operate on pairs whose clique sets differ by just one clique.

Proposition 2. $r(xamgu_{x=t}(E,S)) = r(xamgu_{x=t}(E \setminus \{e\}, r(\{e\}, S)))$ where $e \in E$.

By applying proposition 2 inductively, it follows that $r(xamgu_{x=t}(E,S)) = r(xamgu_{x=t}(\emptyset, r(E,S)))$, that is, the result of applying $xamgu$ to $\langle E, S \rangle$ coincides with the sharing abstraction obtained by applying $xamgu$ to $\langle \emptyset, r(E,S) \rangle$. This result leads into Theorem 1 which states that $xamgu$ neither compromises correctness not precision with respect to the classic approach of set-sharing.

Theorem 1. $r(xamgu_{x=t}(E,S)) = amgu_{x=t}(r(E,S))$.

Example 7. Recall from example 6 that $xamgu_{Y=Z}(E,S) = \langle\{\{X,Y,\ Z\}\}, \{\emptyset, \{X,Y,Z\}, \{X,Y,Z,W\}\}\rangle$. By applying r to the $\langle E, S \rangle$ pair we obtain $r(E,S) = \{\emptyset, \{X,Y\}, \{X,Z\}, \{Z,W\}, \{X,Y,Z\}, \{X,Y,Z,W\}, \{X,Z,W\}\}$. Then applying $amgu$ to $r(E,S)$ yields $amgu_{Y=Z}(r(E,S)) = \{\emptyset, \{X,Y,Z\}, \{X,Y,Z,W\}\}$. Observe $r(xamgu_{Y=Z}(E,S)) = amgu_{Y=Z}(r(E,S))$ as predicted by the theorem.

6 Projection

Projection on *Sharing* is relatively simple. In our proposal, projection is not straightforward as one might think. If projection was defined as $\langle E, S \rangle \upharpoonright\upharpoonright V = \langle E \upharpoonright V, S \upharpoonright V \rangle$, then cliques would be possibly lost by projection which could affect recovery and can possibly compromise the soundness of the analysis as a whole. For example, suppose $\langle E, S \rangle = \langle\{\{X,Y\}\}, \{\emptyset, \{Z,X\}, \{Y,W\}\}\rangle$ and $V = \{Z, W\}$. Then $\langle E \upharpoonright V, S \upharpoonright V \rangle = \langle\emptyset, \{\emptyset, \{Z\}, \{W\}\}\rangle$ and hence we lose the information that Z and W could possibly share. In our projection operator, we divide the cliques into three classes. We need to apply a polynomial transformation for all cliques in the first class before applying the classical projection operator $\upharpoonright$. It is easy to do projection for the cliques in the second class. No projection is needed for the cliques in the third class.

6.1 First Class

Let $V \subseteq \mathcal{V}$ be a set of variables of interest. Every clique e such that $e \cap V = \emptyset$ is in the first class and it will be totally projected away. Usually the first class cliques are generated by renaming. One way to keep the effect of a clique e in the first class is applying the recovery function. This is precise but inefficient because of the closure under union operator in the recovery function. To avoid this, we maintain the effect of e by replacing e with a new clique e' that simulates the effect of e. This guarantees soundness but could lose precision. First, we define two auxiliary functions.

Observe that if we use $\cup rel(e, S)$ to replace e, we will ensure $rel(e, S)$ is selected because $rel(e, S) \subseteq rel(\cup rel(e, S), S)$.

Definition 4. Function $Replace : CL \times Sharing \rightarrow CL$ is defined by

$$Replace(E, S) = max(\{\cup rel(e, S) | e \in E\})$$

We say that two cliques e_1 and e_2 are related with respect to a sharing abstraction S if $rel(e_2, rel(e_1, S)) \neq \emptyset$. We also say e_i and e_j are related with respect to S if e_i is related to e_l with respect to S and e_l is related to e_j with respect to S. We say E is related with respect to S if every $e \in E$ is related to each other with respect to S.

Definition 5. Let E_1 be a set of cliques in the first class. We define a rewriting rule $\Longrightarrow_S$ by $E_1 \Longrightarrow_S E_2$ if $e_1, e_2 \in E_1 \wedge rel(e_2, rel(e_1, S)) \neq \emptyset \wedge E_2 = E_1 \setminus \{e_1, e_2\} \cup \{e_1 \cup e_2\}$; otherwise $E_1 \Longrightarrow_S E_1$.

We write $E \Longrightarrow_S^* E'$ if there exist $E_1, E_2, \ldots, E_n$ with $E_1 = E, E_n = E'$, $E_i \Longrightarrow_S E_{i+1}$ for $0 \leq i \leq n - 1$ and $E' \Longrightarrow_S E'$. That is we apply $\Longrightarrow_S$ repeatedly until all the related cliques are combined into one. In other words, there are no two cliques that are related with respect to S in E'. Once we have E', we can apply the *Replace* function to replace all the cliques in E'. Note that the order in which cliques are considered and combined does not effect the final result. Thus this definition satisfies the diamond property and is well-defined.

Let $E \Longrightarrow_S^* E'$. Then here exists $E_1, E_2, \ldots, E_n$ with $E_1 = E, E_n = E'$, $E_i \Longrightarrow_S E_{i+1}$ for $0 \leq i \leq n-1$. Note that n is bounded by the number of groups. Each combination of two related cliques is polynomial. Thus the transformation is polynomial in the number of groups too.

Example 8. Let $E = \{\{X_5, X_8\}, \{X_5, X_6\}\}$, $S = \{\emptyset, \{X_1, X_6, X_8\}, \{X_4, X_8\}, \{X_5\}, \{X_2, X_6\}\}$ and $V = \{X_1, X_2, X_3, X_4\}$. Then $E' = \{\{X_5, X_6, X_8\}\}$ where $E \Longrightarrow_S^* E'$.

Every $e \in E$ is replaced by a corresponding $e' \in Replace(E', S)$ where $E \Longrightarrow_S^* E'$. There exists $e'' \in E'$ such that $e' = \cup rel(e'', S)$. Observe that $e \subseteq e''$ follows from the definition of $\Longrightarrow_S^*$. Thus $rel(e, S) \subseteq rel(e'', S)$ and $\cup rel(e, S) \subseteq \cup rel(e'', S) = e'$. Thus e' actually includes the effect of e. If e' is not relevant to V then it says nothing about V and hence it does not matter at all. Therefore we can delete all the cliques that are not relevant to V in $Replace(E', S)$ where $E \Longrightarrow_S^* E'$.

Definition 6. Let E be a set of cliques in the first class and V is a set of variables. The function $T : CL \times Sharing \rightarrow CL$ is defined by $T(E, S) = Replace(E', S) \setminus E''$ where $E \Longrightarrow_S^* E'$, $E'' = \{e' \in Replace(E', S) | e' \cap V = \emptyset\}$.

Note that $T(\emptyset, S) = \emptyset$.

Example 9. Continuing with example 8, observe that $Replace(E', S) = \{\{X_1, X_2, X_4, X_5, X_6, X_8\}\}$ where $E \Longrightarrow_S^* E'$. Hence $Replace(E', S) \setminus E'' = Replace(E', S)$ because $E'' = \emptyset$. Thus, $T(E, S) = \{\{X_1, X_2, X_4, X_5, X_6, X_8\}\}$.

Proposition 3. (Soundness)
Let E be a set of cliques in the first class and $E' = T(E, S)$. Then

$$r(E, S) \upharpoonright V \subseteq r(E' \upharpoonright V, S \upharpoonright V)$$

6.2   Second Class and Third Class

Let V be a set of variables, $\langle E, S \rangle \in XSharing$ and $e \in E$. If $e \cap V \neq \emptyset$ and $e \not\subseteq V$, we say that the clique e is in the second class. If the clique e is a subset of V then we say it is in the third class.

Proposition 4. Let V be a set of variables. If $rel(e, S) = rel(e \upharpoonright V, S)$ for each $e \in E$ then $r(E, S) \upharpoonright V = r(E \upharpoonright V, S \upharpoonright V)$.

Example 10. Let $\langle E, S \rangle = \langle \{\{X, Y\}, \{Z, W\}\}, \{\emptyset, \{X, Y, Z\}, \{Z, W\}\} \rangle$ and $V = \{X, Z\}$. Then $r(E, S) = \{\emptyset, \{X, Y, Z\}, \{Z, W\}, \{X, Y, Z, W\}\}$ and hence $r(E, S) \upharpoonright V = \{\emptyset, \{X, Z\}, \{Z\}\}$. On the other hand, $\langle E \upharpoonright V, S \upharpoonright V \rangle = \langle \{\{X\}, \{Z\}\}, \{\emptyset, \{X, Z\}, \{Z\}\} \rangle$. Therefore $r(E, S) \upharpoonright V = r(E \upharpoonright V, S \upharpoonright V)$.

Lemma 3. If a clique e is in second class then $rel(e, S) = rel(e \upharpoonright V, S)$.

According to lemma 3 and proposition 4, we can directly project those cliques in the second class without losing soundness and precision. It is obvious that $rel(e, S) = rel(e \upharpoonright V, S)$ is true for each clique in the third class. Note that the second class and the third class are both relevant to V while the first class is not. Thus we can conclude that we can directly apply classical projection to all those cliques that are relevant to V. This is useful for implementation.

6.3   Projection

Therefore, we define the projection as following.

Definition 7. Let $\mathcal{V}$ be the set of all variables and $V \in \wp(\mathcal{V})$. The projection function $\upharpoonright\upharpoonright$: $XSharing \times \wp(\mathcal{V}) \rightarrow XSharing$ is defined as $\langle E, S \rangle \upharpoonright\upharpoonright V = \langle (T(E_1, S) \cup E_2 \cup E_3) \upharpoonright V, S \upharpoonright V \rangle$ where E_1 contains the first class cliques in E, E_2 contains the second class cliques in E and E_3 contains the third class cliques in E.

Theorem 2. (Soundness)
Let V be a set of variables and $\langle E, S \rangle \in XSharing$. Then $r(E, S) \upharpoonright V \subseteq r(\langle E, S \rangle \upharpoonright\upharpoonright V)$.

Although the projection operator needs to transform the first class cliques, it is still faster than applying the recovery function because T is polynomial in the number of groups.

7   Other Operations and Parameter Throughout

The design of the analysis is completed by defining other operators that are required by an analysis engine. The initial state is $\langle \emptyset, init(\varepsilon) \rangle$ where $init(\varepsilon)$ describes the empty substitution [18]. The renaming operator $Rename : XSharing \rightarrow XSharing$ is defined by $Rename(\langle E, S \rangle) = \langle tag(E), tag(S) \rangle$ where tag is classical tagging function defined in [18]. The join operator $\sqcup : XSharing \times$

$XSharing \rightarrow XSharing$ is defined by $\langle E_1, S_1 \rangle \sqcup \langle E_2, S_2 \rangle = \langle E', S' \rangle$ where $r(E', S') = r(E_1, S_1) \cup r(E_2, S_2)$. In practice, we use $\langle E_1, S_1 \rangle \sqcup \langle E_2, S_2 \rangle = \langle max(E_1 \cup E_2), S_1 \cup S_2 \rangle$ as an approximation. Observe $r(E_1, S_1) \cup r(E_2, S_2) \subseteq r(max(E_1 \cup E_2), S_1 \cup S_2)$. Thus it is sound but may lose precision.

Example 11. Let $e_1 = \{x, y\}$, $e_2 = \{y, z\}$, $S_1 = \{\emptyset, \{x, y\}, \{z\}\}$ and $S_2 = \{\emptyset, \{y, z\}, \{x\}\}$. Then $r(\{e_1\}, S_1) \cup r(\{e_2\}, S_2) = \{\emptyset, \{x\}, \{z\}, \{x, y\}, \{y, z\}\}$ while $r(\{e_1, e_2\}, S_1 \cup S_2) = \{\emptyset, \{x\}, \{z\}, \{x, y\}, \{y, z\}, \{x, y, z\}\}$. This is not precise because it says variables x, y, z share a variable.

Basically, more cliques mean more efficiency and less cliques mean more precision. In fact, we can think *Sharing* is the most precise case of *XSharing* because it saves no clique in first component. We can control the complexity/precision ratio in two way:

- When do we create clique? The analysis is parameterised by a cost threshold k: a clique is only created if the resulting number of sharing groups exceed a predefined threshold k.
- Which clique do we create or remove? A practical analyser requires a grounding operator whose effect is to ground given set of variables in a state. To this end, a grounding operator $ground : XSharing \times \mathcal{V} \rightarrow XSharing$ is introducing that is defined by

$$ground(\langle E, S \rangle, x) = \langle E \setminus rel(x, E), r(rel(x, E), S) \setminus rel(x, r(rel(x, E), S)) \rangle$$

Observe that cliques are possibly removed from first component and that the overall size of the abstraction is not increased by this operator. This operator is applied to model the effect of a built-in predicate such as $>/2$. The effect of $>/2$ is to ground the variables associated with this operator. For instance, the effect of $X > Y$ is to ground both X and Y.

8 Implementation

We have implemented the new abstract domain and incorporated it to a top down framework which is based on Nilsson [23]. The implementation is written in C++. To obtain a credible experimental comparison, both the classical *Sharing* and *XSharing* are implemented using the same language, the same framework, the same data structure and the same primitive operators. Table 1 compares *Sharing* and *XSharing* on cost and precision using some standard benchmark programs. The first column and the fifth column list the names of programs. The second column, the third column, the sixth column and the seventh column are time performance for *XSharing* and *Sharing* respectively. The fourth and the last column are the loss of precision in percentage considering pair sharing information. Suppose there are n program points in a program. For program point i, the pair sharing information computed by *Sharing* is PS_i while *XSharing* computes XPS_i. Pair-sharing PS_i must be a subset of XPS_i since *XSharing* is approximate. It follows that $|XPS_i| \geq |PS_i|$. Then pair sharing precision lost at program point i can be defined by $(|XPS_i| - |PS_i|)/|PS_i|$. The pair sharing precision lost for whole program is $\sum_{i=1}^{n}((|XPS_i| - |PS_i|)/|PS_i|)/n$.

Benchmarks are divided into two groups in table 1. *XSharing* and *Sharing* are both acceptable for the programs in the first group. For the programs in the second group, *XSharing* is much faster. Classical *Sharing* takes hundreds seconds for *peepl.pl, sdda.pl, ga.pl* and *read.pl* while *XSharing* only takes several seconds. This is not a surprise because all key operators are polynomial.

Table 1. Time Performance Considering Effects of Built-in Predicates; k=0

CPU: Intel(R) Pentium(R) 4 CPU 2.40GHz. Operating System: Windows XP							
	XSharing	Sharing	Precision		XSharing	Sharing	Precision
Program	Time	Time	Pair lose	Program	Time	Time	Pair lose
append.pl	0.008	0.016	0	qsort.pl	0.008	0.015	0
merge.pl	0.015	0.016	0	path.pl	0.008	0.008	0
zebra.pl	0.031	0.016	0	life.pl	0.016	0.041	0
disj_r.pl	0.015	0.015	0	queens.pl	0.008	0.047	0
browse.pl	0.032	0.047	0	gabriel.pl	0.016	0.031	0
treesort.pl	0.015	0.172	0.5	dnf.pl	0.11	0.062	11
boyer.pl	0.047	0.062	0	tsp.pl	0.047	0.032	5
peephole.pl	0.078	0.125	0	kalah.pl	0.047	0.281	0
aiakl.pl	0.094	0.468	3	treeorder.pl	0.14	1.172	0
cs_r.pl	0.078	1.187	0	boyer.pl	1.547	7.86	0
peep.pl	1.86	137.797	0	read.pl	2.469	129.859	0
sdda.pl	5.453	151.68	0	ga.pl	0.281	209.687	0

There are 24 programs in table 1. The pair sharing information computed by *XSharing* is exactly same as *Sharing* for 20 programs. For the programs *peepl.pl, sdda.pl, ga.pl* and *read.pl*, the performance is remarkably improved while we have exactly same pair sharing information. There is loss of precision for 4 programs. This is caused by ordering, join and projection operators. For program *treesort.pl*, the precision loss is 0.5% that is almost equal to zero. An interesting program is *dnf.pl*. We lost 11% precision for this program while *Sharing* is faster than *XSharing*. This is a negative result for our analysis. We investigated this program and found out that there are many variables that are ground and thus closure under union operations are applied on small sets. This explains why *Sharing* is actually faster. Therefore, in our opinion, our analysis is more suitable for complex programs that involve many variables and closure under union operations.

We can adjust the threshold k to control the complexity/precision ratio of the system. The threshold is 0 for all programs in table 1 and there are four programs that lose precision. We can find the minimal k that guarantees these programs do not lose precision. The minimal k are listed in the last column in table 2. The other columns are same as table 1.

Table 2. The Minimal Threshold without Losing Precision

	XSharing	Sharing	Precision	Threshold
Program	Time	Time	Pair lose	k
treesort.pl	0.328	0.172	0	16
dnf.pl	0.047	0.062	0	16
aiakl.pl	0.483	0.468	0	171
tsp.pl	0.020	0.032	0	23

There are many built-in predicates in a real program and it is important to consider the effect of them. Thus we have supported all built-in predicates in the benchmark programs. For example, we have considered built-in predicates such as $=/2$ and $sort/2$ whose effect is to apply abstract unification. We also processed built-in predicates such as $>/2$ and $ground/1$ whose effect is to ground variables. Other control built-in predicates such as $;/2$ and $\rightarrow/2$ are also processed. Note that considering the effect of built-in predicates with grounding effect can improve the efficiency significantly because many groups are removed.

9   Related Work

There have been much research in sharing analysis of logic programs [17, 24, 4, 20, 8, 19, 9, 22, 14, 5] that have attempted to tame the computational aspects of this domain without compromising too much precision. One approach is reducing the number of groups that can possibly arise is due to Fecht [12] and Zaffanella et al. [25] who use maximal elements to represent downward closed powersets of variables. In fact Zaffanella et al. [25] apply a pair of sharing abstractions, which is almost same as our proposal. The key difference is interpretation. In [25], a clique represents all sharing groups that contained within it. In this paper, a clique is used to select the basis of a closure.

Bagnara et al. [3] also argue that $Sharing$ is redundant for pair-sharing based on the following assumption: that the goal of sharing analysis for logic program is to detect which pairs of variables are definitely independent. A group G is redundant with respect to a sharing abstraction S if S already contains the pair sharing information that G contains. Thus they obtain a simpler domain and, perhaps more importantly, reduce complexity of abstract unification. That is, closure under union is not needed. This simpler domain is as precise as $Sharing$ on pair-sharing. On the other hand, Bueno et al. [6] argue that the assumption in [3] is not always valid. First, there are applications that use $Sharing$ other than retrieving sharing information between pairs of variables. Second, $Sharing$ is more precise when combined with other source of information. In this paper, we consider a group is redundant if it can be regenerated using the cliques saved in first component. Moreover, the redundant concept is applied to cliques.

Howe and King [16] present three optimisations for $Sharing$. These optimisations can be used when combine $Sharing$ with freeness and linearity. One principle in [16] is that the number of sharing groups should be minimised. This principle is also used in our approach, though we do not seek to exploit either freeness or linearity.

Another thread of work is in the use different encodings of the *Sharing* domain. In [8], Codish et al. show that *Sharing* is isomorphic to the domain of positive Boolean functions [1]. The closure under union operator over *Sharing* corresponds to downward closure operator ↓ over *Pos* that maps a positive Boolean function to a definite Boolean function. A definite Boolean function thus corresponds to a sharing that is closed under union. This domain is efficient because of efficient data structure of Boolean function. Howe et al. propose a downward closure operator ↓ in [15]. Codish et al. [7] also propose an algebraic approach to the sharing analysis using set logic programs. This domain is isomorphic to *Sharing* and leads to intuitive definitions for abstract operators.

10   Conclusion

This paper presents a new domain for sharing analysis based on a new efficient representation for *Sharing*. All key operators are polynomial with respect to the number of groups and soundness proofs are given. Moreover, by remembering the cliques, we provide a scheme to reason about the relationship between cliques such as finding redundant cliques. Lastly, there is a parameter to control the complexity/precision ratio of the system. For the future work, we will devote more efforts on the precision and find more redundant cliques. It looks promising to explore how a pair can be recovered to non-redundancy sharing [3] by changing the representation of first component too.

Acknowledgments. This work was funded, in part, by NSF grants CCR-0131862 and INT-0327760, the EPSRC grant EP/C015517. We would like to thank the anonymous referees for their insightful comments for this paper.

References

1. Tania Armstrong, Kim Marriott, Peter Schachte, and Harald Søndergaard. Two Classes of Boolean Functions for Dependency Analysis. *Science of Computer Programming*, 31(1):3–45, 1998.
2. Roberto Bagnara, Roberta Gori, Patricia M. Hill, and Enea Zaffanella. Finite-Tree Analysis for Constraint Logic-Based Languages. *Information and Computation*, 193(2):84–116, 2004.
3. Roberto Bagnara, Patricia M. Hill, and Enea Zaffanella. Set-Sharing is Redundant for Pair-Sharing. *Theoretical Computer Science*, 277(1-2):3–46, 2002.
4. Roberto Bagnara, Enea Zaffanella, and Patricia M. Hill. Enhanced Sharing Analysis Techniques: A Comprehensive Evaluation. *Theory and Practice of Logic Programming*, 5(1&2):1–43, 2005.
5. Maurice Bruynooghe, Bart Demoen, Dmitri Boulanger, Marc Denecker, and Anne Mulkers. A Freeness and Sharing Analysis of Logic Programs Based on A Pre-interpretation. In Radhia Cousot and David A. Schmidt, editors, *Proceedings of the Third International Symposium on Static Analysis*, volume 1145 of *Lecture Notes in Computer Science*, pages 128–142, London, UK, 1996. Springer-Verlag.

6. Francisco Bueno and Maria J. García de la Banda. Set-Sharing Is Not Always Redundant for Pair-Sharing. In Yukiyoshi Kameyama and Peter J. Stuckey, editors, *Proceedings of 7th International Symposium on Functional and Logic Programming*, volume 2998 of *Lecture Notes in Computer Science*, pages 117–131. Springer, 2004.

7. Michael Codish, Vitaly Lagoon, and Francisco Bueno. An Algebraic Approach to Sharing Analysis of Logic Programs. *Journal of Logic Programming*, 42(2):111–149, 2000.

8. Michael Codish, Harald Søndergaard, and Peter J. Stuckey. Sharing and Groundness Dependencies in Logic Programs. *ACM Transactions on Programming Languages and Systems*, 21(5):948–976, 1999.

9. Agostino Cortesi and Gilberto Filé. Sharing Is Optimal. *Journal of Logic Programming*, 38(3):371–386, 1999.

10. Lobel Crnogorac, Andrew D. Kelly, and Harald Sondergaard. A Comparison of Three Occur-Check Analysers. In Radhia Cousot and David A. Schmidt, editors, *Proceedings of Third International Symposium on Static Analysis*, volume 1145 of *Lecture Notes in Computer Science*, pages 159–173. Springer, 1996.

11. Jacques Chassin de Kergommeaux and Philippe Codognet. Parallel Logic Programming Systems. *ACM Computing Surveys*, 26(3):295–336, 1994.

12. Christian Fecht. An Efficient and Precise Sharing Domain for Logic Programs. In Herbert Kuchen and S. Doaitse Swierstra, editors, *Proceedings of the 8th International Symposium on Programming Languages: Implementations, Logics, and Programs*, volume 1140 of *Lecture Notes in Computer Science*, pages 469–470. Springer, 1996.

13. Patricia M. Hill, Roberto Bagnara, and Enea Zaffanella. Soundness, Idempotence and Commutativity of Set-Sharing. *Theory and Practice of Logic Programming*, 2(2):155–201, 2002.

14. Patricia M. Hill, Enea Zaffanella, and Roberto Bagnara. A Correct, Precise and Efficient Integration of Set-Sharing, Freeness and Linearity for The Analysis of Finite and Rational Tree Languages. *Theory and Practice of Logic Programming*, 4(3):289–323, 2004.

15. J. M. Howe and A. King. Efficient Groundness Analysis in Prolog. *Theory and Practice of Logic Programming*, 3(1):95–124, January 2003.

16. Jacob M. Howe and Andy King. Three Optimisations for Sharing. *Theory and Practice of Logic Programming*, 3(2):243–257, 2003.

17. Dean Jacobs and Anno Langen. Accurate and Efficient Approximation of Variable Aliasing in Logic Programs. In Ross A. Overbeek Ewing L. Lusk, editor, *Proceedings of the North American Conference on Logic Programming*, pages 154–165. MIT Press, 1989.

18. Dean Jacobs and Anno Langen. Static Analysis of Logic Programs for Independent And-Parallelism. *Journal of Logic Programming*, 13(2&3):291–314, 1992.

19. Andy King. Pair-Sharing over Rational Trees. *Journal of Logic Programming*, 46(1-2):139–155, 2000.

20. Vitaly Lagoon and Peter J. Stuckey. Precise Pair-Sharing Analysis of Logic Programs. In *Proceedings of the 4th ACM SIGPLAN International Conference on Principles and Practice of Declarative Programming*, pages 99–108. ACM Press, 2002.

21. Anno Langen. *Advanced Techniques for Approximating Variables Aliasing in Logic Programs*. PhD thesis, 1991.

22. Kalyan Muthukumar and Manuel V. Hermenegildo. Compile-Time Derivation of Variable Dependency Using Abstract Interpretation. *Journal of Logic Programming*, 13(2-3):315–347, 1992.

23. Ulf Nilsson. Towards a Framework for the Abstract Interpretation of Logic Programs. In Pierre Deransart, Bernard Lorho, and Jan Maluszynski, editors, *Proceedings of the Programming Language Implementation and Logic Programming*, volume 348 of *Lecture Notes in Computer Science*, pages 68–82. Springer, 1989.
24. Harald Søndergaard. An Application of Abstract Interpretation of Logic Programs: Occur Check Reduction. In Bernard Robinet and Reinhard Wilhelm, editors, *Proceedings of the 1st European Symposium on Programming*, volume 213 of *Lecture Notes in Computer Science*, pages 327–338. Springer, 1986.
25. Enea Zaffanella, Roberto Bagnara, and Patricia M. Hill. Widening Sharing. In Gopalan Nadathur, editor, *Proceedings of the International Conference on Principles and Practice of Declarative Programming*, volume 1702 of *Lecture Notes in Computer Science*, pages 414–432, London, UK, 1999. Springer-Verlag.

Size-Change Termination and Bound Analysis

James Avery

Dep. of Computer Science,
University of Copenhagen (DIKU)
avery@diku.dk

Abstract. Despite its simplicity, the size-change termination principle, presented by Lee, Jones and Ben-Amram in [LJB01], is surprisingly strong and is able to show termination for a large class of programs. A significant limitation for its use, however, is the fact that the SCT requires data types to be well-founded, and that all mechanisms used to determine termination must involve decreases in these global, well-founded partial orders.

Following is an extension of the size-change principle that allows for non-well founded data types, and a realization of this principle for integer data types. The extended size-change principle is realized through combining abstract interpretation over the domain of convex polyhedra with the use of size-change graphs. In the cases when data types *are* well founded, the method handles every case that is handled by LJB size-change termination.

The method has been implemented in a subject language independent shared library, libesct (available at [Ave05a]), as well as for the ANSI C specializer C-Mix$_{II}$, handling a subset of its internal language Core-C.

1 Introduction

The question of program termination is one of the classical undecidable problems. This notwithstanding, termination can be proved in quite many cases, either by constructing programming languages in such a way that only a certain class of terminating programs are expressible, or in a fuller language, by reasoning about the semantics of individual programs. [LJB01] presents a practical technique for the latter approach by reasoning about data flow combined with well founded partial orders on the domains of data types.

For C, besides the issue of data types not being well founded, there is the challenge that imperative programs rarely terminate for reasons expressible by a global order on the data type (as is illustrated by the example in section 1.1), thus making size-change termination analysis difficult. As it turns out, both these issues can be addressed by replacing the requirement of well foundedness by the existence of local bounds on program state.

Current work has two foci: The development of a mathematically sound foundation for an extended size-change termination principle and practical work implementing efficient and extensible incarnations of the methods.

M. Hagiya and P. Wadler (Eds.): FLOPS 2006, LNCS 3945, pp. 192–207, 2006.

1.1   Extending SCT to Non-well Founded Types

Although much more powerful than its simplicity suggests, the size-change termination principle is limited in applicability by its requirement that data types must be well-founded.

Of course, any data type with values representable on a computer can be made well-founded by an appropriate ordering, since the domain is inherently countable and so can be bijectively mapped to $\mathbb{N}$. A possible strategy when one wishes to implement SCT for a particular language is then to look for usable well-ordering relations for each type in the language, along with operations that decrease the ranks of elements within these orderings.

However, it isn't at all obvious that such an ordering will correspond very well with the mechanisms that make programs terminate. Rather, it would seem somewhat unlikely. Types such as e.g. trees and lists induce "natural" norms, and this property is used consciously by programmers to make algorithms terminate. But if no natural well-founded partial order arises, trying to find one that renders a significant class of programs size-change terminating seems like an exercise in futility.

An alternate course of action is to attempt to replace the need for well-founded data types with a less restrictive property that still allows an extended size-change analysis to prove termination.

1.2   Rough Overview

The basic idea presented in this paper is to replace the requirement of well-founded data types, a property of the language, by discovering bounds on program state. These should not only be specific to an individual program, but also specific to the program points. With these in hand, one detects through size-change analysis the property that any infinite computation must violate such a bound. This has the added benefit that even when data types are well founded, a larger class of programs size-change terminate under the new condition, since relations among variables are taken into account.

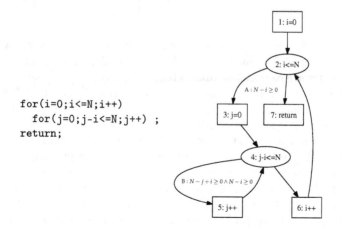

```
for(i=0;i<=N;i++)
    for(j=0;j-i<=N;j++) ;
return;
```

Fig. 1. Simple double-loop

Before delving into the details of how one actually goes about performing such an analysis, let us first take an informal look at a small example in order to build some intuition for the methods presented in the following sections. Consider the tiny C program snippet in figure 1: a simple double loop with two designated program points, A (the arc $2 \to 3$) and B (the arc $4 \to 5$):

Despite its simplicity, no ordering of $\mathbb{Z}$ would seem to make this program size-change terminate. But we immediately see that the inner loop terminates because $N - j + i$ is bounded from below, and this expression is decreased in each iteration. Similarly for $N - i$ in the outer loop.

Let us attempt to discover this property through size-change analysis. We break the analysis into three pieces:

1. **Obtain constraints that hold at each program point.** In this example, we only look at arcs A and B, and we derive the inequalities in fig. 1 directly from the branch-tests.

2. **Construct size-change graphs for the basic blocks that change memory.** The basic blocks that alter the store in the example are the blocks labeled 1, 3, 5 and 6 in figure 1. Their size-change graphs (SCGs) are:

$$
\begin{array}{cccc}
\overline{\begin{array}{c} g_1 \\ N \xrightarrow{\ } N \\ i \quad\ \ i \\ j \xrightarrow{\ } j \end{array}}
&
\overline{\begin{array}{c} g_3 \\ N \xrightarrow{\ } N \\ i \quad\ \ i \\ j \quad\ \ j \end{array}}
&
\overline{\begin{array}{c} g_5 \\ N \xrightarrow{\ } N \\ i \xrightarrow{\ } i \\ j \xrightarrow{\downarrow} j \end{array}}
&
\overline{\begin{array}{c} g_6 \\ N \xrightarrow{\ } N \\ i \xrightarrow{\downarrow} i \\ j \xrightarrow{\ } j \end{array}}
\end{array}
\tag{1}
$$

3. **Combine this information to show no infinite computation paths exist.** Let $\mathcal{S}$ be the transitive closure of size-change graphs for all finite computation paths. The subsets of graphs that go from point A back to A, and from B to B, have these data-flow relations:

$$
\mathcal{S}_A = \left\{ \overline{\begin{array}{c} g_3 : g_6 \\ N \xrightarrow{\ } N \\ i \xrightarrow{\downarrow} i \\ j \quad\ \ j \end{array}} \right\}, \quad
\mathcal{S}_B = \left\{ \overline{\begin{array}{c} g_5 \\ N \xrightarrow{\ } N \\ i \xrightarrow{\ } i \\ j \xrightarrow{\downarrow} j \end{array}}, \ \overline{\begin{array}{c} g_5 : g_6 : g_3 \\ N \xrightarrow{\ } N \\ i \xrightarrow{\downarrow} i \\ j \quad\ \ j \end{array}} \right\}
\tag{2}
$$

The SCG in $\mathcal{S}_A$ represents paths of the form $(234(54)^*6)^+$, and the SCGs in $\mathcal{S}_B$ represents paths $(45)^+$ and $((45)^*4623)^+$ respectively. Thus, any time a computation executes in a path leading from A back to A, N is preserved and i is increased. The net result is a decrease of the expression $N - i$, which is bounded from below. Similarly, any finite computation path going from B back to B will either decrease the expression $N - i$ or decrease $N - j + i$, and both are non-negative.

Now, because the paths that decrease $N - j + i$ at the same time increase $N - i$, one would intuitively suspect that an infinite computation path might possibly fail to decrease either of the expressions infinitely - i.e., although every finite computation path $B \to B$ decreases one or the other, in an infinite computation path they could cancel out. We prove in theorem 2.8 that this can never happen. This implies that A and B can only be visited finitely many times during any computation. Therefore, after a certain point in the path, any allegedly infinite computation path must run entirely within the graph with the arcs A and B removed:

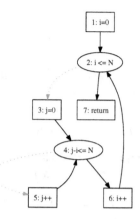

But removing A and B from the program's flow-graph has left a graph with no strongly connected components, and thus no cycles. Consequently, the program as a whole must terminate.

The remainder of this paper develops a formal framework for an extension of the Size-change Termination Principle, forming the mathematical foundation underpinning the intuitive reasoning above.

2   Semantic Foundations

The subject language used in the following is imperative and without function calls, stack or dynamic memory. All variable values are integers.

Definition 2.1.

1. A store *is a tuple* $x \in \mathbb{Z}^N$, *where* N *is the number of program variables.* $V = \{x_1, \ldots, x_N\}$ *is the set of variable names.*
2. *A basic block is a sequence of assignments followed by a jump or a return.*
3. *A program point* p *is the transition between two basic blocks* b *and* b', *corresponding to the arc from* b *to* b' *in the programs flow-graph. The program entry point is denoted* p_0.
4. *A state is a pair* (p, x) *of program point* p *and store* x.
5. *The one-step state transition relation has the form* $(p, x) \rightarrow (p', x')$.
6. *A finite computation path is a finite program point sequence*

$$\pi = p_1, p_2, \ldots, p_m$$

   following program control. We will also write $\pi : p_1 \overset{*}{\twoheadrightarrow} p_m$, *and* $\pi : p_1 \overset{+}{\twoheadrightarrow} p_m$ *if* $m > 0$. *In the case when* $m = 2$, *i.e.* $\pi = p_1, p_2$ *is a single transition, we write* $\pi : p_1 \rightarrow p_2$.
7. *An infinite computation path is a sequence* $\pi = (p_i)_N$ *following program control.*
8. *For a finite computation path* $\pi : p_1 \overset{*}{\twoheadrightarrow} p_m$, *define its store transformation by*

$$\pi \vdash x_1 \overset{*}{\twoheadrightarrow} x_m$$

iff

$$(p_1, \boldsymbol{x}_1) \rightarrow (p_2, \boldsymbol{x}_2) \rightarrow \cdots \rightarrow (p_m, \boldsymbol{x}_m)$$

It is a partial function $\mathbb{Z}^N \rightarrow \mathbb{Z}^N$.

9. *A store* $\boldsymbol{x}$ *is reachable at p iff there exists an initial store* $\boldsymbol{x}_0$ *and a finite computation path* $\pi : p_0 \overset{*}{\rightarrow} p$ *such that*

$$\pi \vdash \boldsymbol{x}_0 \overset{*}{\rightarrow} \boldsymbol{x}$$

We write $Reach(p)$ *for the set of all stores reachable at p.*

Definition 2.2 (Finite Computation Paths as Functions). *For notational convenience, we will write* $\pi(\boldsymbol{x}) = \boldsymbol{x}'$ *iff* $\pi \vdash \boldsymbol{x} \overset{*}{\rightarrow} \boldsymbol{x}'$. *We define the* domain *of* π *as*

$$D(\pi) := \left\{ \boldsymbol{x} \in \mathbb{Z}^N \mid \exists \boldsymbol{x}' \in \mathbb{Z}^N : \pi \vdash \boldsymbol{x} \overset{*}{\rightarrow} \boldsymbol{x}' \right\}$$

and the range *as*

$$R(\pi) := \left\{ \boldsymbol{x}' \in \mathbb{Z}^N \mid \exists \boldsymbol{x} \in \mathbb{Z}^N : \pi \vdash \boldsymbol{x} \overset{*}{\rightarrow} \boldsymbol{x}' \right\} = \pi(D(\pi))$$

It is clear that $\pi : D(\pi) \rightarrow R(\pi)$ *is well defined as a function, in that for each* $\boldsymbol{x} \in D(\pi)$ *there is precisely one* $y \in R(\pi)$ *such that* $y = \pi(\boldsymbol{x})$.

For an infinite computation path $\pi = (p_i)_{\mathbb{N}}$, *define the domain as*

$$D(\pi) := \left\{ \boldsymbol{x} \in \mathbb{Z}^N \mid \forall k \in \mathbb{N} \exists \boldsymbol{x}' \in \mathbb{Z}^N : \pi_k \vdash \boldsymbol{x} \overset{*}{\rightarrow} \boldsymbol{x}' \right\}$$

where $\pi_k = p_0, \ldots, p_k$ *is the length-k prefix of* π.

Definition 2.3 (Realizable). *A (finite or infinite) computation path* π *is* realizable *if and only if* $D(\pi) \neq \emptyset$, *i.e. if there exists some store that will cause* π *to be taken.*

Definition 2.4. *An* assertion *is a relation* $\rho \subseteq \mathbb{Z}^N$. *We write "*$\rho(\boldsymbol{x})$ *holds" or simply "*$\rho(\boldsymbol{x})$*" when* $\boldsymbol{x} \in \rho$. *An assertion holds at program point p iff for any stores* $\boldsymbol{x}_0, \boldsymbol{x}$

$$(p_0, \boldsymbol{x}_0) \overset{*}{\rightarrow} (p, \boldsymbol{x}) \quad \text{implies } \rho(\boldsymbol{x})$$

or, put differently, iff $Reach(p) \subseteq \rho$.

Definition 2.5. *We call an inequality of the form* $f(\boldsymbol{x}) \geq 0$ *with* $f : \mathbb{Z}^N \rightarrow \mathbb{Z}$ *a* functional inequality.

Note, that if a functional inequality $f(\boldsymbol{x}) \geq 0$ *holds at program point p, then the restriction of f to* $Reach(p)$ *maps into the naturals, i.e.*

$$f|_{Reach(p)} : Reach(p) \rightarrow \mathbb{N} \tag{3}$$

Definition 2.6 (decreasing). *A finite computation path* $\pi : p \overset{+}{\rightarrow} p$ *is called* decreasing *iff there exists a functional inequality* $f(\boldsymbol{x}) \geq 0$ *holding at p such that*

$$\forall \boldsymbol{x} \in D(\pi) : f(\boldsymbol{x}) > f(\pi \boldsymbol{x})$$

If the above is true for some given f, we say that π *decreases f.*

2.1 Termination

We now have in place the tools needed to formulate a general termination principle based on inequality assertions and size change. We follow the philosophy of the example in section 1.2. Put simply: Find expressions that are bounded from below, then show them decreasing and finally use this information to show that certain program points are never passed infinitely many times. If the flow-graph remaining after removing these points has no strongly connected components, the program terminates. In the opposite case, we have localized the pieces of the program that may cause non-termination: the remaining strongly connected components.

Definition 2.7 (Safe). *A program point p is called* safe *iff any realizable computation path visits p at most finitely many times.*

Theorem 2.8. *If there exists a finite set $I(p)$ of functional inequalities all holding at program point p, such that any $\pi : p \xrightarrow{+} p$ decreases at least one $f \in I(p)$, then p is safe.*

Proof. Assume, for the sake of contradiction, that the condition holds at p and that $\pi = (p_i)_{\mathbb{N}}$ is a realizable computation path that passes p an infinite number of times. Define correspondingly π_{ij} as the finite computation sub-path of π going from the i'th to the j'th occurrence of p in π, i.e.:

$$\pi : p_0 \xrightarrow{*} p \xrightarrow{\pm} p \xrightarrow{\pm} p \xrightarrow{\pm} p \cdots$$

For each pair $(i, j) \in \mathbb{N}^2$ with $i < j$, define a "color"

$$c(i,j) := \{f \in I(p) \mid \pi_{ij} \text{ decreases } f\}$$

As $c(i,j) \subseteq I(p)$, the cardinality $|c(i,j)|$ is finite and bounded from above for all i, j by $|I(p)|$. Also, from the assumption, $c(i,j) \neq \emptyset$. Now, for each c in the power set $\wp(I(p))$, define the class P_c as

$$P_c := \{(i,j) \in \mathbb{N}^2 \mid i < j \text{ and } c(i,j) = c\}$$

The set $\{P_c \mid c \in \wp(I(p))\}$ is obviously finite and the classes $P_{c'}, P_c$ with $c' \neq c$ are mutually disjoint. By Ramsey's theorem, there is an infinite subset $J \subseteq \mathbb{N}$ and a "color" c_0 such that for any two $i, j \in J$ with $i < j$, we have $c(i,j) = c_0$.

Enumerate J in ascending order as $\{j_1, j_2, \ldots\}$. Then, specifically, $c(j_i, j_{i+1}) = c_0$ for all $i \in \mathbb{N}$. Set π_i to be the finite computation path from p_0 to the j_i'th occurrence of p in π:

$$\pi : p_0 \xrightarrow{*} p \xrightarrow{*} p \xrightarrow{\pm} p \xrightarrow{\pm} p \xrightarrow{\pm} \cdots$$

Choose any $f \in c_0$. Certainly for any $i, j \in \mathbb{N}$ with $i < j$, the computation path $\pi_{j_i j_j}$ decreases f. We now have for any $x_0 \in D(\pi)$:

1. $f(\pi_1 x_0) > f(\pi_{j_1 j_2}(\pi_1 x_0)) = f(\pi_2 x_0)$
2. For $n \geq 2$: $f(\pi_n x_0) > f(\pi_{j_{n+1} j_{n+2}}(\pi_n x_0)) = f(\pi_{n+1} x_0)$

And so the sequence $(f(\pi_k x_0))_{k \in \mathbb{N}}$ is a strictly decreasing sequence. But by the assumption, we have $f(Reach(p)) \subseteq \mathbb{N}$, and for all k we have $\pi_k x_0 \in Reach(p)$. Since there exist no infinitely decreasing sequences in $\mathbb{N}$, our assumption that π visits p an infinite number of times is false; there can exist no such computation path. □

Definition 2.9 (Safety of cycles and subgraphs). *We say that a* cycle γ *in the programs flow-graph* F, *i.e. a closed path visiting no program point more than once, is* safe *iff it contains a program point* p *that is safe.*

We say that a sub-graph F' *of the flow-graph is* safe *if each cycle* γ *in* F' *is safe, i.e. contains at least one safe program point* p. *Equivalently: it is safe if the graph*

$$F' \setminus \{p \in F' \mid p \text{ is safe}\}$$

remaining after removing all safe program points from F' *contains no strongly connected components. In general we'll call this remaining graph the* residual *of* F'.

Theorem 2.10. *If a sub-graph* F' *of the flow-graph* F *is safe, then there exist no infinite realizable computation path lying entirely within* F'.

Proof. Assume that F' is safe and that such an infinite computation path π exists, consisting only of program points within F'. Since the number of cycles in F' is finite, there must exist a cycle $\gamma \subseteq F'$ such that γ appears infinitely many times in π. But since F' is safe, γ contains a safe program point p. Since p cannot appear infinitely many times in π, certainly neither can γ. Thus there can exist no infinite realizable computation path in F'. □

Corollary 2.11. *If the entire flow-graph* F *of a program* P *is safe, in the sense of def. 2.9, then* P *terminates.*

Proof. Any infinite computation on P must correspond to some infinite computation path π in F. If F is safe, then per Theorem 2.10 there exists no such computation paths within F. Thus P must terminate on all input. □

Corollary 2.11 is of considerable interest when dealing directly with program termination. When using the size-change principle as an aid in performing e.g. bounded anchoring analysis (as described by Glenstrup and Jones in [GJ03]), or in other program analyses, we will in general want theorem 2.10.

In the next section, we learn how one can discover certain functional inequalities – the first requirement in theorem 2.8.

3   Invariant Relations Analysis

Even when a program has no explicit interdependence among variables, one may still find correlations and relations among them that hold for all the possible values they may assume. Consider figure 2, which illustrates the reachable stores for some program with two integer variables, x and y. Any particular program store corresponds to a point in $\mathbb{Z}^2$, and the reachable stores that the program can assume at some program point p is a subset $Reach(p) \subseteq \mathbb{Z}^2$.

The nature of this set may be extremely complicated, yet we may still be successful in extracting from it neat relations among the variables that hold for all elements of $Reach(p)$. The aim is to find some approximation that is easily and efficiently expressed and manipulated, and that is safe in the sense that any reachable program store is always contained in the approximation.

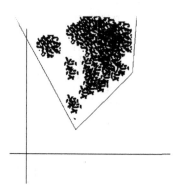

Fig. 2. Linear over-approximation of the set of reachable program stores

In their 78 paper [CH78], Halbwachs and Cousot introduced a very powerful framework for approximating state. The method accomplishes automatic discovery of *invariant linear relations* among program variables by abstractly interpreting programs over the domain of convex polyhedra. For each of the subject language's constructs, they approximated its effect on a convex polyhedron enclosing the program store. The method is able to discover invariants that are not explicit in the program text, and that are often non-obvious. The following small example is given as an appetizer:

Table 1 shows a small function that computes and returns $x - y$ if $x, y > 0$. However, there is no direct flow to z from x or from y. Figure 3 is output by our implementation of [CH78], building on [ea05], when run on subxy.c. As can be seen by inspecting the annotations of the arc to the return statement in block 7, we still find that $z = x - y$ when the function returns - along with quite a few other linear relations that are not easily discovered by hand.

Convex polyhedra. A convex polyhedron of dimension n over the integers is a subset $P \subseteq \mathbb{Z}^n$ that is the intersection of a finite number of affine half-spaces of $\mathbb{Z}^n$. This corresponds to a finite conjunction of linear inequalities.[1] We will write $\mathbb{P}_n$ for the set of convex polyhedra with dimension n. Two important features are worth noticing:

---

[1] We arbitrarily restrict our attention to closed polyhedra, which correspond to conjunctions of weak inequalities. This affects no loss of generality, since on $\mathbb{Z}^n$ the open and closed subsets are the same. For example, $x > 0 \iff x \geq 1$ on $\mathbb{Z}$.

Table 1. Small function that computes $x - y$ (for $x, y > 0$) in a roundabout way

```
int subxy(int x, int y)
{
    int z;
    int i;
```

```
int subxy(int x, int y)          L1:
{                                      z = 0;
    int z,i;                           i = x;
    z = 0;                             if (y <= 0 || x <= 0) goto L2; else goto L3;
    i = x;                         L3:
    if(y<=0 || x<= 0) return 0;        if (i > 0) goto L4; else goto L5;
                                   L5:
    while (i >0){                      if (i < y) goto L6; else goto L7;
        i--;                       L7:
        z++;                           return z;
    }                              L6:
    while (i<y){                       i = i + 1;
        i++;                           z = z - 1;
        z--;                           goto L5;
    }                              L4:
    return z;                          i = i - 1;
}                                      z = z + 1;
                                       goto L3;
                                   L2:
                                       return 0;
}
```

Fig. 3. Linear relations discovered by abstractly interpreting `subxy.c` over the domain of convex polyhedra. Note that non-obvious relations are discovered. Specifically, at the return in block 7, we find that $z = x - y$, although x and y have no direct flow to z.

- The **convex hull** of p and q is the smallest convex polyhedron r such that $r \supseteq p \cup q$. It can be shown that this exists and is unique given p and q. When equipped with set inclusion as its partial order, intersection as the *meet* operation and *convex hull* as its *join*, $\mathbb{P}_n$ forms a lattice with $\emptyset$ as its smallest element, and $\mathbb{Z}^n$ as its largest. This important property allows us to look at increasing sequences $(p_k)_{\mathbb{N}} \subseteq \mathbb{P}_n$ of polyhedra in which each element p_k in the sequence is contained by its successor p_{k+1}, and know that they will have a least upper bound.

- The second important virtue of $\mathbb{P}_n$ is the existence of well-defined **widening-operators** $\nabla : \mathbb{P}_n \times \mathbb{P}_n \rightarrow \mathbb{P}_n$, defined on any $p, q \in \mathbb{P}_n$ such that $p \subseteq q$. A widening-operator by definition satisfies two properties
  1. $p \subseteq p\nabla q$ and $q \subseteq p\nabla q$. (i.e. $Hull(p, q) \subseteq p\nabla q$).
  2. For any increasing chain $q_0 \subseteq q_1 \subseteq q_2 \subseteq \cdots$, the increasing chain $p_0 \subseteq p_1 \subseteq p_2 \cdots$ defined by $p_0 := q_0$ and $p_{k+1} := p_k\nabla q_{k+1}$ has at most a finite number of strict increases.

The second property ensures that any sequence of widening operations converges to an upper bound in a finite number of steps. Specifically, although a sequence of increasingly lax constraints may give rise to an infinite strictly increasing sequence $(q_k)_\mathbb{N}$ of polyhedra, we can utilize the widening operator to find a finite (in the sense that it reaches its upper bound) sequence $(p_k)_\mathbb{N}$ such that $q_k \subseteq p_k$. In particular, the maximal element of the widened sequence contains the upper bound of $(q_k)_\mathbb{N}$. This allows us to iteratively propagate linear invariants throughout the program, finding in a finite number of steps a conjunction of linear equations for each program point, that are known to always hold at that point.

The method of abstract interpretation over the lattice of convex polyhedra is well described in the literature; our own programs are a straightforward implementation of [CH78], using the *Parma Polyhedral Library* [ea05] by Bagnara et al. for widening and basic operations on polyhedra.

4   Size-Change Graphs

Definition 4.1. *Let* $V = \{x_1, \ldots, x_N\}$ *be the set of program variables. In the following, a* size-change graph *is a pair* $g = (g^\downarrow, g^\uparrow)$ *of bipartite graphs from* V *to* V *with labeled arcs:*

$$g^\downarrow \subseteq V \times \{\downarrow, \overline{\top}\} \times V$$
$$g^\uparrow \subseteq V \times \{\uparrow, \underline{\bot}\} \times V \tag{4}$$

where $[x_i \xrightarrow{\downarrow} x_j]$ *and* $[x_i \xrightarrow{\top} x_j]$ *or* $[x_i \xrightarrow{\top} x_j]$ *and* $[x_i \xrightarrow{\downarrow} x_j]$ *are not in the same graph.*

A size-change graph is used to capture definite information about a finite computation path, as is apparent from the following definition:

Definition 4.2 (Approximation of finite computation paths). *A* size-change graph $g = (g^\downarrow, g^\uparrow)$ *is said to* approximate π *iff for each edge* $[x_i \xrightarrow{\downarrow} x_j] \in g^\downarrow$ *we have* $\pi \vdash x \xrightarrow{*} x'$ *implies* $x'_j < x_i$, *for each edge* $[x_i \xrightarrow{\top} x_j] \in g^\downarrow$ *we have* $\pi \vdash x \xrightarrow{*} x'$ *implies* $x'_j \leq x_i$, *and the analogous statements hold true for* $g^\uparrow$.

That is, the graphs are "must-decrease" and "must-increase" graphs, in the sense that the relations they capture must always hold.

Definition 4.3 (SCG Composition). *Let* $g : p \rightarrow p'$ *and* $h : p' \rightarrow p''$ *be size-change graphs. The* composite $q = g; h$ *is the size-change graph* $q : p \rightarrow p''$ *with edges:*

1. $[x_i \xrightarrow{} x_j] \in q^{\downarrow}$ if and only if $\exists k : [x_i \xrightarrow{\delta_1} x_k] \in g^{\downarrow}$ and $[x_k \xrightarrow{\delta_2} x_j] \in h^{\downarrow}$ with $\delta_1, \delta_2 \in \{\top, \downarrow\}$ and $\delta_1 = \downarrow$ or $\delta_2 = \downarrow$.
2. $[x_i \xrightarrow{\top} x_j] \in q^{\downarrow}$ if and only if 1. does not apply, and $\exists k : [x_i \xrightarrow{\top} x_k] \in g^{\downarrow}$ and $[x_k \xrightarrow{\top} x_j] \in h^{\downarrow}$.

and such that the analogous statements hold for $q^{\uparrow}$.

Lemma 4.4 (SCG Composition is Sound). If $\pi : p \xRightarrow{} p'$ and $\tau : p' \xRightarrow{} p''$ are finite computation paths approximated by g and h respectively, then by transitivity of $<, \leq, >$ and $\geq$ the composite graph $g; h$ approximates the finite computation path $\pi\tau : p \xRightarrow{} p''$.

Definition 4.5 (Transitive closure). Let $\mathcal{G}$ be a set of size-change graphs. The transitive closure $\mathcal{S} = \overline{\mathcal{G}}$ over composition is the smallest set $\mathcal{S}$ that fulfills

$$\mathcal{G} \subseteq \mathcal{S} \text{ and } \{g; h \mid g : p \to p' \in \mathcal{S} \wedge h : p \to p' \in \mathcal{S}\} \subseteq \mathcal{S} \tag{5}$$

This set exists and is finite, because the number of different size-change graphs over N variables is finite.

Let $\mathcal{G}$ be a set of size-change graphs that approximate the one-step transitions of a program. Then the closure $\mathcal{S} = \overline{\mathcal{G}}$ over composition summarizes path effects. By induction over lemma 4.4, any realizable finite computation path $\pi : p \to p'$ is approximated by at least one graph $g : p \to p' \in \mathcal{S}$, giving us a *finite* description of all computation paths. The closure is computable by standard methods, e.g. as described in [AHU75].

Let $A^2 := \{0, \top, \downarrow\} \times \{0, \updownarrow, \uparrow\}$ (with A standing for "arrow"). With appropriately defined addition and multiplication ([Ave05b]), A^2 is a continuous semiring. By the mapping in the following definition, $\mathbb{M}_{N \times N}(A^2)$ equipped with standard matrix addition and multiplication over A^2 similarly becomes an idempotent continuous semiring that is isomorphic to the semiring of size-change graphs with union and composition:

Definition 4.6 (SCGs as matrices). Let $g = (g^{\downarrow}, g^{\uparrow})$, and define

$$g_{ij} := (g^{\downarrow}_{ij}, g^{\uparrow}_{ij})$$

$$g^{\downarrow}_{ij} := \begin{cases} \downarrow \text{ if } [x_i \xrightarrow{} x_j] \in g^{\downarrow} \\ \top \text{ if } [x_i \xrightarrow{\top} x_j] \in g^{\downarrow} \\ 0 \text{ otherwise} \end{cases} \quad g^{\uparrow}_{ij} := \begin{cases} \uparrow \text{ if } [x_i \xrightarrow{} x_j] \in g^{\uparrow} \\ \updownarrow \text{ if } [x_i \xrightarrow{\updownarrow} x_j] \in g^{\uparrow} \\ 0 \text{ otherwise} \end{cases} \tag{6}$$

This particular representation is convenient for two reasons: First, it allows for very neat and orderly algebraic analysis. Second, the operations that we perform on SCGs are expressed in terms of very machine-close bitwise operations, and benefit from machine-word bit parallelism. We refer to [Ave05b] for details.

5   Size-Change Termination with Polyhedra and Idempotent SCGs

We are now almost ready to introduce an extended size-change termination principle based on theorem 2.8, but allowing for straightforward computation using size-change graphs and convex polyhedra. The idea is, for each program point p, to find a polyhedron $P \supseteq Reach(p)$ using the method of section 3, and then by way of size-change analysis show that any computation visiting p infinitely many times must leave P and therefore also $Reach(p)$ – thus proving that p is visited at most finitely many times.

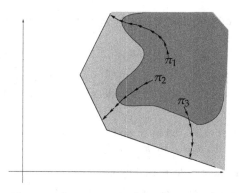

Fig. 4. General strategy: Given a polyhedron P enclosing all reachable stores (indicated above by the dark gray area) show that any infinite computation must at some point leave P

A note on the representation of convex polyhedra. It is customary to compute with a dual representation of convex polyhedra, since some operations are best suited for one representation, and some more efficiently implemented with the other. The first representation is a conjunction of constraints, each of the form

$$c_0 + \sum_{k=1}^{n} c_k x_k \bowtie 0 \tag{7}$$

where $\bowtie$ is one of $\{=, \geq, >\}$. The other is a set of *points, closure points, rays* and *lines*. These are called, under one, *generators* of P, and a set full enough to describe P is called a *generating system* for P. Informally, the points of a minimal generating system used to represent a polyhedron are its vertices, and rays and lines describe its unbounded parts. Most operations needed for abstract interpretation in the style of [CH78] requires the generator representation. For the size-change termination analysis, we'll want the constraint-form. Specifically, we will assume that a polyhedron is of the form

$$P = \left\{ x \in \mathbb{Z}^N \mid f_1(x) \geq 0 \wedge \cdots \wedge f_m(x) \geq 0 \right\} \tag{8}$$

(with each $f_i(x) = c_0^i + \sum_{k=1}^{N} c_k^i x_k$) and we also write, abusing notation slightly,

$$P = \{f_1, \ldots, f_m\} \tag{9}$$

Definition 5.1 (Effect on linear expressions). *Let g be a size-change graph and $f(x) = c_0 + \sum_{k=1}^{N} c_k x_k$. Then we say that g decreases f iff the following hold*

$$1. \forall k : \begin{array}{l} c_k > 0 \text{ implies } g_{kk}^{\downarrow} = \overline{\top} \text{ or } g_{kk}^{\downarrow} = \downarrow \\ c_k < 0 \text{ implies } g_{kk}^{\uparrow} = \underline{\bot} \text{ or } g_{kk}^{\uparrow} = \uparrow \end{array} \tag{10}$$

$$2. \exists k : \begin{array}{l} c_k > 0 \text{ and } g_{kk}^{\downarrow} = \downarrow \text{ or} \\ c_k < 0 \text{ and } g_{kk}^{\uparrow} = \uparrow \end{array}$$

Lemma 5.2 (SCG Effect on a Linear Expression is Sound). *Let $\pi : p \overset{+}{\Rightarrow} p'$ be a finite computation path and g a size-change graph approximating π. If g decreases f*

as in def. 5.1, then π also decreases f as in def. 2.6. In other words, "g decreases f" implies for any $x \in D(\pi)$:

$$f(\pi x) < f(x)$$

Proof. Let there be given $f(x) = c_0 + \sum_{k=1}^{N} c_k x_k$, finite computation path π and size-change graph g approximating π. If g decreases f as in def. 5.1, then, recalling definition 4.2, we note that

- no term $c_k x_k$ is ever increased by π, and
- at least one term is decreased by π.

Consequently, f as a whole is decreased by π. □

Termination: Idempotent Graphs. Let in the following $I(p) := \{f_1, \ldots, f_m\}$ be a finite set of linear expressions such that for any $x \in Reach(p)$,

$$f_1(x) \geq 0 \wedge \cdots \wedge f_m(x) \geq 0 \tag{11}$$

The rôle of the f's will be the same as in section 2.1, but their form is restricted to linear combinations. Further, let $\mathcal{G}$ be a set of SCGs that approximate the program's one-step transitions, and let $\mathcal{S} = \overline{\mathcal{G}}$ be its closure under composition as described in definition 4.5.

Theorem 5.3. *If each $g : p \to p \in \mathcal{S}$ with $g = g; g$ decreases some $f \in I(p)$, then p is safe.*

Proof. The proof is similar to that of theorem 2.8. Assume the left hand side of the theorem to be true. Let $\pi = (p_i)_\mathbb{N}$ be a realizable computation path passing p infinitely many times, and enumerate the occurrences of p in π as α_i, i.e. $\forall i \in \mathbb{N} : p_{\alpha_i} = p$. Define $g_{ij} := g_{p_i}; \cdots ; g_{p_j-1}$, and let the class P_g be defined as

$$P_g := \{(i,j) \in \mathbb{N}^2 \mid i < j \text{ and } g = g_{\alpha_i \alpha_j}\} \tag{12}$$

The set $\{P_g \mid g : p \to p \in \mathcal{S}\}$ is finite (since $\mathcal{S}$ is finite) and the classes are mutually disjoint. By Ramsey's theorem it then follows that there exists an infinite subset $J = (j_i)_\mathbb{N}$ of $\mathbb{N}$ and a size-change graph $g_0 : p \to p \in \mathcal{S}$ such that for any two $i < j$ in J, $g_{\alpha_i \alpha_j} = g_0$. If we now take $i < j < k$ from J, we get

$$g_0 = g_{\alpha_i \alpha_k} = g_{\alpha_i \alpha_j}; g_{\alpha_j \alpha_k} = g_0; g_0 \tag{13}$$

Because of the assumption, g_0 decreases some $f \in I(p)$. Define:

$$\pi : \underbrace{\underbrace{p_0 \xrightarrow{*} p \xrightarrow{*} p}_{\pi_1} \overbrace{\xrightarrow{+} p}^{\pi_{\alpha_{j_1} \alpha_{j_2}}} \overbrace{\xrightarrow{+} p}^{\pi_{\alpha_{j_2} \alpha_{j_3}}} \xrightarrow{+} \cdots}_{\pi_2}$$
$$\underbrace{\phantom{p_0 \xrightarrow{*} p \xrightarrow{*} p \xrightarrow{+} p \xrightarrow{+} p}}_{\pi_3}$$

Then for any initial store x_0, the sequence $(f(\pi_k x_0))_{k \in \mathbb{N}}$ is strictly decreasing. But because $f \in I(p)$, and $\pi_k x_0 \in Reach(p)$, each $f(\pi_k x_0) \geq 0$. Therefore the assumption that π passes p infinitely many times must be false. Consequently, p must be safe. □

6   Algorithm

The algorithm is given in much greater detail - both in pseudo-code and actual working code - in [AS04], [Ave05b] and at [Ave05a]. Here we'll be content with outlining the steps:

1. Find invariants using abstract interpretation, resulting in a polyhedron $\mathcal{P}[p]$ for each program point p, such that $\mathcal{P}[p] \supseteq Reach(p)$.
2. Generate size-change graphs for each program point p as $\mathcal{G}[p]$.
3. Compute the transitive closure $\mathcal{S}$ of $\mathcal{G}$.
4. For each program point p, let $\mathcal{I}[p] \subseteq \mathcal{S}$ be the idempotent size-change graphs $g : p \to p$ in the closure $\mathcal{S}$.
5. Construct residual flow-graph F' containing the program points p that are not safe:
   (a) For each $g \in \mathcal{I}[p]$:
       – Let $\mathcal{P}[p] = \{f_1(\boldsymbol{x}) \geq 0 \wedge \cdots \wedge f_m(\boldsymbol{x}) \geq 0\}$.
       – If g decreases no f_k (def. 5.1) for $1 \leq k \leq m$, then p is not safe.
6. If F' contains no strongly connected components, then P terminates. If any strongly connected components do remain, P may not terminate, and they are the cyclic parts that risk looping forever.

7   Concluding Remarks

We present an extension of the size-change termination principle of [LJB01] to programs with integer valued data types. The extended size-change termination principle is realized through a combination of polyhedral bounds on program state, discovered by abstract interpretation, with size-change analysis. The method has been implemented in a subject language independent shared library, libesct, as well as in the C specializer C-Mix$_{\mathrm{II}}$ for a subset of its internal language Core-C. This subset corresponds to C programs without function calls, pointer aliasing, flat memory and dynamic allocation. It is planned to extend the implementation to handle a useful subset of C, as well as applying it to a first order functional language. The programs are available for download at [Ave05a].

7.1   Related Work

Some work by Henny Sipma and co-workers, as well as recent work by Siau-Cheng Khoo and Hugh Anderson, is very close in spirit to the methods presented here. Both their strategies for determining termination involve finding decreases in linear expressions that are bounded from below.

Sipma and Colon ([SC02]) perform automatic discovery of bounded and decreasing linear expressions, leading to termination. This is accomplished through iterative forward propagation of invariants in the form of polyhedral cones. Rather than describing size-change by a finite approximation (as is the case with size-change graphs), they rely on widening operations to give results in a finite number of steps.

Khoo and Anderson ([KA05]) extend the notion of size-change graphs to *affine graphs*, which are conjunctions of linear interparameter inequalities. Graphs are augmented by *guards*, which are bounds on program state. Then it is shown that infinite compositions of the affine graphs will violate one of these guards. Termination of the analysis is ensured by reducing affine graphs to abstract graphs, which are basically size-change graphs.

7.2 Ideas for Future Work

- In [Lee02] and [BAL04], C.S. Lee and Amir Ben-Amram devise a cubic time approximation to SCT. Correspondence with Lee and Ben-Amram has indicated that their methods may be adaptable, with modifications, to the extended size-change termination principle presented here.
- It should be fairly easy to extend the theorems presented in this paper to allow constraints to be disjunctions of conjunctions of linear inequalities. Constraints of this form can be discovered by using e.g. Presburger arithmetic or interpreting over the power set $\wp(\mathbb{P}_N)$ of polyhedra.
- Another way of determining size-change is by interpretation over the domain of polyhedral cones, which are $2N$-dimensional polyhedra linearly relating state before and after execution of a finite computation path. This is the method being used for termination analysis in [SC02]. It would be interesting to compare the classes of programs handled by this method to those handled by the extended SCT. The differences are subtle: In one respect, polyhedral cones capture more information than size-change graphs, because linear intervariable relations are taken into account. In another respect, they capture less: where two distinct paths can give rise to two distinct size-change graphs, the polyhedral method must yield a single convex hull large enough to contain both.
- Often program termination relies on implicit assumptions about the form of input. An idea was recently suggested by Dr. W.N. Chin that would allow extending the presented method to automatically find safe preconditions on input for which a program size-change terminates.
- The presented methods seem well suited to current work by Carl Christian Frederiksen at U. of Tokyo that employs SCT for automatic proof of liveness properties – for example proving the absence of deadlocks, et cetera. Frederiksen's work is based in part on Podelski's in, among other, [PR05].

References

[AHU75] Alfred V. Aho, John E. Hopcroft, and Jeffrey D. Ullman. *The Design and Analysis of Computer Algorithms*. Addison-Wesley Publishing Company, 1975.

[AS04]   James Avery and Stefan Schou. Stopping C-Mix: PE-termination ensuring binding-time division. Project at Roskilde Universitetscenter, 2004.

[Ave05a] James Avery.   ESCT - The Extended Size-Change Termination Library. http://esct.kvante.org, November 2005.

[Ave05b] James Avery. Size-change termination and bound analysis for an imperative language with integer data types. Report at Datalogisk Instutut, Københavns Universitet (DIKU), July 2005.

[BAL04] Amir Ben-Amram and Chin Soo Lee. A quadratic-time program termination analysis. Under preparation at MPI für Informatik, Saarbrücken, Germany, 2004.

[CH78]   Patrick Cousot and Nicolas Halbwachs.   Automatic discovery of linear restraints among variables of a program.   In *Conference Record of the Fifth Annual ACM SIGPLAN-SIGACT Symposium on Principles of Programming Languages*, pages 84–97, Tucson, Arizona, 1978. ACM Press, New York, NY.

[ea05]   Roberto Bagnara et al. The parma polyhedra library, 2000-2005. University of Parma, http://www.cs.unipr.it/ppl/.

[GJ03]   Arne J. Glenstrup and Neil D. Jones. Termination analysis and specialization-point insertion in off-line partial evaluation. In *ACM Transactions on Programming Languages and Systems*. Department of Computer Science, University of Copenhagen, 2003. Preprint.

[KA05]   Sian-Cheng Khoo and Hugh Anderson. Bounded size-change termination (draft). School of Computing, National University of Singapore, 2005.

[Lee02]   Chin Soon Lee. Program termination analysis in polynomial time. *Generative Programming and Component Engineering '02*, LNCS 2487, October 2002.

[LJB01]   Chin Soon Lee, Neil D. Jones, and Amir M. BenAmram. The size-change principle for program termination. *ACM SIGPLAN Notices*, 36(3):81–92, 2001.

[PR05]   Andreas Podelski and Andrey Rybalchenko. Transition predicate abstraction and fair termination. In *Principles of Programming Languages (POPL)*, 2005.

[SC02]   Henny Sipma and Michael Colon. Practical methods for proving program termination. In *14th International Conference on Computer Aided Verification*, volume LNCS 2404, pages 442–454. Springer Verlag, 2002.

Typed Contracts for Functional Programming

Ralf Hinze[1], Johan Jeuring[2], and Andres Löh[1]

[1] Institut für Informatik III, Universität Bonn,
Römerstraße 164, 53117 Bonn, Germany
{ralf, loeh}@informatik.uni-bonn.de
[2] Institute of Information and Computing Sciences, Utrecht University,
P.O. Box 80.089, 3508 TB Utrecht, The Netherlands
johanj@cs.uu.nl

Abstract. A robust software component fulfills a contract: it expects data satisfying a certain property and promises to return data satisfying another property. The object-oriented community uses the design-by-contract approach extensively. Proposals for language extensions that add contracts to higher-order functional programming have appeared recently. In this paper we propose an embedded domain-specific language for typed, higher-order and first-class contracts, which is both more expressive than previous proposals, and allows for a more informative blame assignment. We take some first steps towards an algebra of contracts, and we show how to define a generic contract combinator for arbitrary algebraic data types. The contract language is implemented as a library in Haskell using the concept of generalised algebraic data types.

1 Introduction

Are you familiar with the following situation?

> You are staring at the computer screen. The run of the program you are developing unexpectedly terminated with a `Prelude.head: empty list` message. A quick `grep` yields a total of 102 calls to *head* in your program. It is all very well that the run wasn't aborted with a `core dumped` notification, but the error message provided isn't very helpful either: which of the many calls to *head* is to blame?

If this sounds familiar to you, then you might be interested in *contracts*. A contract between software components is much like a contract in business, with obligations and benefits for both parties. In our scenario, the components are simply functions: the function *head* and the function that calls *head*. Here is a possible contract between the two parties (from *head*'s perspective): if you pass me a non-empty list, then I shall return its first element. The contract implies obligations and benefits: the caller is obliged to supply a non-empty list and has the benefit of receiving the first element without further ado. The restriction on the input is a benefit for *head*: it need not deal with the case for the empty list. If it receives a non-empty list, however, *head* is obliged to return its first element.

M. Hagiya and P. Wadler (Eds.): FLOPS 2006, LNCS 3945, pp. 208–225, 2006.

As in business, contracts may be violated. In this case the contract specifies who is to blame: the one who falls short of its promises. Thus, if *head* is called with an empty list, then the call site is to blame. In practical terms, this means that the program execution is aborted with an error message that points to the location of the caller, just what we needed above.

The underlying design methodology [1], developing programs on the basis of contracts, was popularised by Bertrand Meyer, the designer of Eiffel [2]. In fact, contracts are an integral part of Eiffel. Findler and Felleisen [3] later adapted the approach to higher-order functional languages. Their work has been the major inspiration of the present paper, which extends and revises their approach.

In particular, we make the following contributions:

- we develop a small embedded domain-specific language for contracts with a handful of basic combinators and a number of derived ones,
- we show how to define a generic contract combinator for algebraic data types,
- we present a novel approach to blame assignment that additionally tracks the cause of contract violations,
- as a proof of concept we provide a complete implementation of the approach; the implementation makes use of *generalised algebraic data types*,
- we take the first steps towards an algebra of contracts.

The rest of the paper is structured as follows. Sec. 2 introduces the basic contract language, Sec. 3 then shows how blame is assigned in the case of a contract violation. We tackle the implementation in Sec. 4 and 5 (without and with blame assignment). Sec. 6 provides further examples and defines several derived contract combinators. The algebra of contracts is studied in Sec. 7. Finally, Sec. 8 reviews related work and Sec. 9 concludes.

We use Haskell [4] notation throughout the paper. In fact, the source of the paper constitutes a legal Haskell program that can be executed using the Glasgow Haskell Compiler [5]. For the proofs it is, however, easier to pretend that we are working in a strict setting. The subtleties of lazy evaluation are then addressed in Sec. 7. Finally, we deviate from Haskell syntax in that we typeset 'x has type τ' as $x : \tau$ and 'a is consed to the list as' as $a :: as$ (as in Standard ML).

2   Contracts

This section introduces the main building blocks of the contract language.

A contract specifies a desired property of an expression. A simple contract is, for instance, $\{\, i \mid i \geqslant 0 \,\}$ which restricts the value of an integer expression to the natural numbers. In general, if x is a variable of type σ and e is a Boolean expression, then $\{\, x \mid e \,\}$ is a contract of type *Contract* σ, a so-called *contract comprehension*. The variable x is bound by the construct and scopes over e.

Contracts are first-class citizens: they can be passed to functions or returned as results, and most importantly they can be given a name.

$$nat \;:\; Contract\ Int$$
$$nat = \{\, i \mid i \geqslant 0 \,\}$$

As a second example, here is a contract over the list data type that admits only non-empty lists.

$nonempty\ :\ Contract\ [\alpha]$
$nonempty = \{\,x \mid not\ (null\ x)\,\}$

The two most extreme contracts are

$false, true : Contract\ \alpha$
$false = \{\,x \mid False\,\}$
$true\ \ = \{\,x \mid True\,\}$

The contract *false* is very demanding, in fact, too demanding as it cannot be satisfied by any value. By contrast, *true* is very liberal: it admits every value.

Using contract comprehensions we can define contracts for values of arbitrary types, including function types. The contract $\{\,f \mid f\ 0 == 0\,\}$, for instance, specifies that 0 is a fixed point of a function-valued expression of type $Int \rightarrow Int$. However, sometimes contract comprehensions are not expressive enough. Since a comprehension is constrained by a Haskell Boolean expression, we *cannot* state, for example, that a function maps natural numbers to natural numbers: $\{\,f \mid \forall n : Int\,.\,n \geqslant 0 \Rightarrow f\ n \geqslant 0\,\}$. We consciously restrict the formula to the right of the bar to Haskell expressions so that checking of contracts remains feasible. As a compensation, we introduce a new contract combinator that allows us to explicitly specify domain and codomain of a function: $nat \rightarrowtail nat$ is the desired contract that restricts functions to those that take naturals to naturals.

Unfortunately, the new combinator is still too weak. Often we want to relate the argument to the result, expressing, for instance, that the result is greater than the argument. To this end we generalise $e_1 \rightarrowtail e_2$ to the *dependent function contract* $(x : e_1) \rightarrowtail e_2$. The idea is that x, which scopes over e_2, represents the argument to the function. The above constraint is now straightforward to express: $(n : nat) \rightarrowtail \{\,r \mid n < r\,\}$. In general, if x is a variable of type σ_1, and e_1 and e_2 are contracts of type $Contract\ \sigma_1$ and $Contract\ \sigma_2$ respectively, then $(x : e_1) \rightarrowtail e_2$ is a contract of type $Contract\ (\sigma_1 \rightarrow \sigma_2)$. Note that like $\{\,x \mid e\,\}$, the dependent function contract $(x : e_1) \rightarrowtail e_2$ is a binding construct.

Many properties over data types such as the pair or the list data type can be expressed using contract comprehensions. However, it is also convenient to be

$$\frac{\Gamma, x : \sigma \vdash e : Bool}{\Gamma \vdash \{\,x \mid e\,\} : Contract\ \sigma} \qquad \frac{\Gamma \vdash e_1 : Contract\ \sigma_1 \quad \Gamma, x : \sigma_1 \vdash e_2 : Contract\ \sigma_2}{\Gamma \vdash (x : e_1) \rightarrowtail e_2 : Contract\ (\sigma_1 \rightarrow \sigma_2)}$$

$$\frac{\Gamma \vdash e : Contract\ \sigma}{\Gamma \vdash [e] : Contract\ [\sigma]} \qquad \frac{\Gamma \vdash e_1 : Contract\ \sigma_1 \quad \Gamma, x : \sigma_1 \vdash e_2 : Contract\ \sigma_2}{\Gamma \vdash (x : e_1) \times e_2 : Contract\ (\sigma_1, \sigma_2)}$$

$$\frac{\Gamma \vdash e_1 : Contract\ \sigma \quad \Gamma \vdash e_2 : Contract\ \sigma}{\Gamma \vdash e_1\ \&\ e_2 : Contract\ \sigma}$$

Fig. 1. Typing rules for contract combinators

able to construct contracts in a compositional manner. To this end we provide a pair combinator that takes two contracts and yields a contract on pairs: $nat \times nat$, for instance, constrains pairs to pairs of natural numbers.

We also offer a *dependent product contract* $(x\!:\!e_1) \times e_2$ with scoping and typing rules similar to the dependent function contract. As an example, the contract $(n : nat) \times (\{\, i \mid i \leqslant n \,\} \twoheadrightarrow true)$ of type $Contract\ (Int, Int \rightarrow \alpha)$ constrains the domain of the function in the second component using the value of the first component. While the dependent product contract is a logically compelling counterpart of the dependent function contract, we expect the former to be less useful in practice. The reason is simply that properties of pairs that do *not* contain functions can be easily formulated using contract comprehensions. As a simple example, consider $\{\, (x_1, x_2) \mid x_1 \leqslant x_2 \,\}$.

In general, we need a contract combinator for every parametric data type. For the main bulk of the paper, we confine ourselves to the list data type: the *list contract combinator* takes a contract on elements to a contract on lists. For instance, $[\,nat\,]$ constrains integer lists to lists of natural numbers. Like $c_1 \times c_2$, the list combinator captures only *independent properties*; it cannot relate elements of a list. For this purpose, we have to use contract comprehensions—which, on the other hand, cannot express the contract $[\,nat \twoheadrightarrow nat\,]$.

Finally, contracts may be combined using conjunction: c_1 & c_2 holds if both c_1 and c_2 hold. However, we neither offer disjunction nor negation for reasons to be explained later (Sec. 4). Fig. 1 summarises the contract language.

3   Blame Assignment

A contract is attached to an expression using *assert*:

$head'\ :\ [\alpha] \rightarrow \alpha$
$head' = assert\ (nonempty \twoheadrightarrow true)\ (\lambda x \rightarrow head\ x)$

The attached contract specifies that the predefined function *head* requires its argument to be non-empty and that it ensures nothing. In more conventional terms, *nonempty* is the *precondition* and *true* is the *postcondition*. Here and in what follows we adopt the convention that the 'contracted' version of the identifier x is written x'.

Attaching a contract to an expression causes the contract to be dynamically monitored at run-time. If the contract is violated, the evaluation is aborted with an informative error message. If the contract is fulfilled, then *assert* acts as the identity. Consequently, *assert* has type

$assert : Contract\ \alpha \rightarrow (\alpha \rightarrow \alpha)$

Contracts range from very specific to very liberal. The contract of *head*, *nonempty* $\twoheadrightarrow$ *true*, is very liberal: many functions require a non-empty argument. On the other hand, a contract may uniquely determine a value. Consider in this respect the function *isqrt*, which is supposed to calculate the integer square root.

$$isqrt \quad : Int \rightarrow Int$$
$$isqrt \; n = loop \; 0 \; 3 \; 1$$
$$\textbf{where} \; loop \; i \; k \; s \mid s \leqslant n \quad = loop \; (i+1) \; (k+2) \; (s+k)$$
$$\mid otherwise = i$$

It is not immediately obvious that this definition actually meets its specification, so we add a contract.

$$isqrt' \; : Int \rightarrow Int$$
$$isqrt' = assert \; ((n : nat) \rightarrow \{ \, r \mid r \geqslant 0 \land r^2 \leqslant n < (r+1)^2 \, \}) \; (\lambda n \rightarrow isqrt \; n)$$

Here the postcondition precisely captures the intended semantics of *isqrt*.

Now that we got acquainted with the contract language, it is time to see contracts in action. When a *contract comprehension* is violated, the error message points to the expression to which the contract is attached. Let us assume for the purposes of this paper that the expression is bound to a name which we can then use for error reporting (in the implementation we refer to the source location instead). As an example, given the definitions *five* = *assert nat* 5 and *mfive* = *assert nat* (−5), we get the following results in an interactive session.

Contracts⟩ *five*
5
Contracts⟩ *mfive*
*** contract failed: the expression '*mfive*' is to blame.

The number −5 is not a natural; consequently the *nat* contract sounds alarm.

If a *dependent function contract* is violated, then either the function is applied to the wrong argument, or the function itself is wrong. In the first case, the precondition sends the alarm, in the second case the postcondition. Consider the functions *inc* and *dec*, which increase, respectively decrease, a number.

$$inc, dec : Int \rightarrow Int$$
$$inc = assert \; (nat \rightarrow nat) \; (\lambda n \rightarrow n + 1)$$
$$dec = assert \; (nat \rightarrow nat) \; (\lambda n \rightarrow n - 1)$$

Here are some example applications of these functions in an interactive session:

Contracts⟩ *inc* $_{\langle 1 \rangle}$5
6
Contracts⟩ *inc* $_{\langle 2 \rangle}$(−5)
*** contract failed: the expression labelled '2' is to blame.
Contracts⟩ *dec* $_{\langle 3 \rangle}$5
4
Contracts⟩ *dec* $_{\langle 4 \rangle}$0
*** contract failed: the expression *dec* is to blame.

In the session we put labels in front of the function arguments, $_{\langle i \rangle}e$, so that we can refer to them in error messages (again, in the implementation we refer to the source location). The first contract violation is caused by passing a negative value to *inc*: its precondition is violated, hence the argument is to blame. In the last call, *dec* falls short of its promise to deliver a natural number, hence *dec* itself is to blame.

It is important to note that contract checking and detection of violations are tied to program runs: *dec* obviously does not satisfy its contract $nat \to nat$, but this is not detected until *dec* is applied to 0. In other words, contracts do not give any static guarantees ('*dec* takes naturals to naturals'), they only make dynamic assertions about particular program runs ('*dec* always received and always delivered a natural number during this run').

This characteristic becomes even more prominent when we consider higher-order functions.

$$codom \ : \ (Int \to Int) \to [Int]$$
$$codom = assert \ ((nat \to nat) \to [nat]) \ (\lambda f \to [f \ _{\langle 5 \rangle} \ n \mid n \leftarrow [1 \mathinner{\ldotp\ldotp} 9]])$$

The function *codom* takes a function argument of type $Int \to Int$. We cannot expect that a contract violation is detected the very moment *codom* is applied to a function—as we cannot expect that a contract violation is detected the very moment we attach a contract to $\lambda n \to n - 1$ in *dec*. Rather, violations are discovered when the function argument f is later applied in the body of *codom*. In the extreme case where the parameter does not appear in the body, we never get alarmed, unless, of course, the result is negative. Consider the following interactive session:

$Contracts \rangle \ codom \ _{\langle 6 \rangle} (\lambda x \to x - 1)$
$[0, 1, 2, 3, 4, 5, 6, 7, 8]$
$Contracts \rangle \ codom \ _{\langle 7 \rangle} (\lambda x \to x - 2)$
*** contract failed: the expression labelled '7' is to blame.

An error is only detected in the second call, though the first call is also wrong. The error message points to the correct location: the argument is to blame.

The following example has been adapted from the paper by Blume and McAllester [6].

$$g \ : \ (Int \to Int) \to (Int \to Int)$$
$$g = assert \ ((nat \to nat) \to true) \ (\lambda f \to \lambda x \to f \ _{\langle 8 \rangle} \ x)$$

The higher-order function g expects a function satisfying $nat \to nat$. Again, we cannot expect that the function contract is checked immediately; rather, it is tested when the function argument is applied.

$Contracts \rangle \ g \ _{\langle 9 \rangle} (\lambda x \to x - 1) \ _{\langle 10 \rangle} 1$
0
$Contracts \rangle \ g \ _{\langle 11 \rangle} (\lambda x \to x - 1) \ _{\langle 12 \rangle} 0$
*** contract failed: the expression labelled '11' is to blame.
$Contracts \rangle \ g \ _{\langle 13 \rangle} (\lambda x \to x) \ _{\langle 14 \rangle} (-7)$
*** contract failed: the expression 'g' is to blame (the violation was caused by the expression(s) labelled '8').

The last call shows that g is blamed for a contract violation even though g's postcondition is *true*. This is because g must also take care that its argument is called correctly and it obviously does not take sufficient measurements. The error message additionally points to the location within g that *caused* the contract violation. This information is not available in the Findler and Felleisen approach [3] (see also Sec. 5). Since g returns a function, the cause is not necessarily located in g's body. As a simple example, consider the η-reduced variant of g.

$$g = assert \ ((nat \twoheadrightarrow nat) \twoheadrightarrow true) \ (\lambda f \to f)$$

Now the second argument is identified as the cause of the contract violation:

Contracts⟩ g $_{\langle 15 \rangle}(\lambda x \to x)$ $_{\langle 16 \rangle}(-7)$
*** contract failed: the expression 'g' is to blame (the violation was caused by the expression(s) labelled '16').

4   Implementing Contracts

In Sec. 2 we have seen several ways to construct contracts. The syntax we have used for contracts may seem to suggest that we need an extension of Haskell to implement contracts. However, using Generalised Algebraic Data Types (GADTs) [7, 8, 9], we can model contracts directly in Haskell. Fig. 2 shows how the concrete syntax translates to Haskell. Note that the binding constructs of the concrete syntax are realized using functional components (higher-order abstract syntax). If we translate the typing rules listed in Fig. 1 to the abstract representation of contracts, we obtain the following GADT.

data *Contract* : $* \to *$ **where**
   Prop   : $(\alpha \to Bool) \to Contract \ \alpha$
   Function : $Contract \ \alpha \to (\alpha \to Contract \ \beta) \to Contract \ (\alpha \to \beta)$
   Pair   : $Contract \ \alpha \to (\alpha \to Contract \ \beta) \to Contract \ (\alpha, \beta)$
   List   : $Contract \ \alpha \to Contract \ [\alpha]$
   And   : $Contract \ \alpha \to Contract \ \alpha \to Contract \ \alpha$

Given this data type we can define *assert* by a simple case analysis.

concrete syntax	Haskell syntax
$\{ \ x \mid p \ x \ \}$	*Prop* $(\lambda x \to p \ x)$
$c_1 \twoheadrightarrow c_2$	*Function* $c_1 \ (const \ c_2)$
$(x : c_1) \twoheadrightarrow c_2 \ x$	*Function* $c_1 \ (\lambda x \to c_2 \ x)$
$c_1 \times c_2$	*Pair* $c_1 \ (const \ c_2)$
$(x : c_1) \times c_2 \ x$	*Pair* $c_1 \ (\lambda x \to c_2 \ x)$
$[c]$	*List* c
$c_1 \ \& \ c_2$	*And* $c_1 \ c_2$

Fig. 2. Concrete and abstract syntax of contracts

$$
\begin{aligned}
assert & \quad : Contract\ \alpha \to (\alpha \to \alpha) \\
assert\ (Prop\ p) \quad a & = \mathbf{if}\ p\ a\ \mathbf{then}\ a\ \mathbf{else}\ error\ \texttt{"contract failed"} \\
assert\ (Function\ c_1\ c_2)\ f & = (\lambda x' \to (assert\ (c_2\ x') \cdot f)\ x') \cdot assert\ c_1 \\
assert\ (Pair\ c_1\ c_2)\ (a_1, a_2) & = (\lambda a_1' \to (a_1', assert\ (c_2\ a_1')\ a_2))\ (assert\ c_1\ a_1) \\
assert\ (List\ c) \quad\ as & = map\ (assert\ c)\ as \\
assert\ (And\ c_1\ c_2)\ a & = (assert\ c_2 \cdot assert\ c_1)\ a
\end{aligned}
$$

The definition makes explicit that only contract comprehensions are checked immediately. In the remaining cases, the contract is taken apart and its constituents are attached to the corresponding constituents of the value to be checked. Note that in the *Function* case the *checked argument* x' is propagated to the codomain contract c_2 (ditto in the *Pair* case). There is a choice here: alternatively, we could pass the original, unchecked argument. If we chose this variant, however, we would sacrifice the idempotence of '&'. Furthermore, in a lazy setting the unchecked argument could provoke a runtime error in the postcondition, consider, for instance, $(x : nonempty) \to \{ y \mid y \leqslant head\ x \}$.

A moment's reflection reveals that the checking of *independent properties* boils down to an application of the *mapping function* for the type in question. In particular, we have

$$
\begin{aligned}
assert\ (Function\ c_1\ (const\ c_2))\ f & = assert\ c_2 \cdot f \cdot assert\ c_1 \\
assert\ (Pair\ c_1\ (const\ c_2)) \quad (a_1, a_2) & = (assert\ c_1\ a_1, assert\ c_2\ a_2)
\end{aligned}
$$

This immediately suggests how to generalise contracts and contract checking to arbitrary container types: we map the constituent contracts over the container.

$$
assert\ (T\ c_1\ \ldots\ c_n) = mapT\ (assert\ c_1)\ \ldots\ (assert\ c_n)
$$

Note that mapping functions can be defined completely generically for arbitrary Haskell 98 data types [10]. In the next section we will show that we can do without the GADT; then the contract combinator for an algebraic data type is just its mapping function.

It remains to explain the equation for *And*: the conjunction *And* c_1 c_2 is tested by first checking c_1 and then checking c_2, that is, conjunction is implemented by functional composition. This seems odd at first sight: we expect conjunction to be commutative; composition is, however, not commutative in general. We shall return to this issue in Sec. 7. Also, note that we offer conjunction but neither disjunction nor negation. To implement disjunction we would need some kind of exception handling: if the first contract fails, then the second is tried. Exception handling is, however, not available in Haskell (at least not in the pure, non-*IO* part). For similar reasons, we shy away from negation.

Although *assert* implements the main ideas behind contracts, the fact that it returns an uninformative error message makes this implementation rather useless for practical purposes. In the following section we will show how to return the precise location of a contract violation.

Nonetheless, we can use the simple definition of *assert* to *optimise* contracted functions. Re-consider the definition of *inc* repeated below.

$$inc = assert \ (nat \rightarrow nat) \ (\lambda n \rightarrow n + 1)$$

Intuitively, inc satisfies its contract, so we can optimize the definition by leaving out the postcondition. Formally, we have to prove that

$$assert \ (nat \rightarrow nat) \ (\lambda n \rightarrow n + 1) = assert \ (nat \rightarrow true) \ (\lambda n \rightarrow n + 1)$$

Note that we must keep the precondition to ensure that inc is called correctly: the equation $assert \ (nat \rightarrow nat) \ (\lambda n \rightarrow n + 1) = \lambda n \rightarrow n + 1$ does not hold. Now, unfolding the definition of $assert$ the equation above rewrites to

$$assert \ nat \cdot (\lambda n \rightarrow n + 1) \cdot assert \ nat = (\lambda n \rightarrow n + 1) \cdot assert \ nat$$

which can be proved using a simple case analysis.

In general, we say that f *satisfies the contract* c iff

$$assert \ c \ f = assert \ c^+ \ f$$

where c^+ is obtained from c by replacing all sub-contracts at positive positions by $true$:

$$
\begin{aligned}
&(\cdot)^+ : Contract \ \alpha \rightarrow Contract \ \alpha \\
&(Prop \ p)^+ \qquad = true \\
&(Function \ c_1 \ c_2)^+ = Function \ c_1^- \ (\lambda x \rightarrow (c_2 \ x)^+) \\
&(\cdot)^- : Contract \ \alpha \rightarrow Contract \ \alpha \\
&(Prop \ p)^- \qquad = Prop \ p \\
&(Function \ c_1 \ c_2)^- = Function \ c_1^+ \ (\lambda x \rightarrow (c_2 \ x)^-)
\end{aligned}
$$

In the remaining cases, $(\cdot)^+$ and $(\cdot)^-$ are just propagated to the components. As an example, $\lambda n \rightarrow n + 1$ satisfies $nat \rightarrow nat$, whereas $\lambda n \rightarrow n - 1$ does not. The higher-order function g of Sec. 3 also does not satisfy its contract $(nat \rightarrow nat) \rightarrow nat$. As an aside, note that $(\cdot)^+$ and $(\cdot)^-$ are executable Haskell functions. Here, the GADT proves its worth: contracts are data that can be as easily manipulated as, say, lists.

5   Implementing Blame Assignment

To correctly assign blame in the case of contract violations, we pass program locations to both $assert$ and to the contracted functions themselves. For the purposes of this paper, we keep the type Loc of source locations abstract. We have seen in Sec. 3 that blame assignment involves at least one location. In the case of function contracts two locations are involved: if the precondition fails, then the argument is to blame; if the postcondition fails, then the function itself is to blame. For the former case, we need to get hold of the location of the argument. To this end, we extend the function by an extra parameter, which is the location of the 'ordinary' parameter.

infixr $\rightarrow$
newtype $\alpha \rightarrow \beta = Fun\{ app : Locs \rightarrow \alpha \rightarrow \beta \}$

In fact, we take a slightly more general approach: we allow to pass a data structure of type $Locs$ containing one or more locations. We shall provide two implementations of $Locs$, one that realizes blame assignment in the style of Findler & Felleisen and one that additionally provides information about the causers of a contract violation. We postpone the details until the end of this section and remark that $Locs$ records at least the locations of the parties involved in a contract.

The type $\alpha \twoheadrightarrow \beta$ is the type of *contracted functions*: abstractions of this type, $Fun\ (\lambda \ell s \rightarrow \lambda x \rightarrow e)$, additionally take locations; applications, $app\ e_1\ \ell s\ e_2$, additionally pass locations. We abbreviate $Fun\ (\lambda \ell s \rightarrow \lambda x \rightarrow e)$ by $\lambda x \twoheadrightarrow e$ if ℓs does not appear free in e (which is the norm for user-defined functions). Furthermore, $app\ e_1\ \ell s\ e_2$ is written $e_1\ _{\ell s} e_2$. In the actual program source, the arguments of $assert$ and of the contracted functions are always single locations, written $\langle \ell \rangle$, which explains the notation used in Sec. 3.

Since contracted functions have a distinguished type, we must adapt the type of the $Function$ constructor.

$$Function : Contract\ \alpha \rightarrow (\alpha \rightarrow Contract\ \beta) \rightarrow Contract\ (\alpha \twoheadrightarrow \beta)$$

Given these prerequisites, we can finally implement contract checking with proper blame assignment.

$$
\begin{aligned}
&assert : Contract\ \alpha \rightarrow (Locs \rightarrow \alpha \rightarrow \alpha) \\
&assert\ (Prop\ p) \quad \ell s\ a \\
&\quad = \textbf{if}\ p\ a\ \textbf{then}\ a\ \textbf{else}\ error\ (\texttt{"contract failed: "} \mathbin{+\!\!+} blame\ \ell s) \\
&assert\ (Function\ c_1\ c_2)\ \ell s_f\ f \\
&\quad = Fun\ (\lambda \ell_x \rightarrow (\lambda x' \rightarrow (assert\ (c_2\ x')\ \ell s_f \cdot app\ f\ \ell_x)\ x') \cdot assert\ c_1\ (\ell s_f \rhd \ell_x)) \\
&assert\ (Pair\ c_1\ c_2)\ \ell s\ (a_1, a_2) = (\lambda a_1' \rightarrow (a_1', assert\ (c_2\ a_1')\ \ell s\ a_2))\ (assert\ c_1\ \ell s\ a_1) \\
&assert\ (List\ c) \qquad \ell s\ as \quad = map\ (assert\ c\ \ell s)\ as \\
&assert\ (And\ c_1\ c_2)\ \ell s\ a \quad = (assert\ c_2\ \ell s \cdot assert\ c_1\ \ell s)\ a
\end{aligned}
$$

The $Function$ case merits careful study. Note that ℓs_f are the locations involved in f's contract and that ℓ_x is *the* location of its argument (ℓ_x has type $Locs$ but it is always a single location of the form $\langle \ell \rangle$). First, the precondition c_1 is checked possibly blaming ℓs_f or ℓ_x. The single location ℓ_x is then passed to f, whose evaluation may involve further checking. Finally, the postcondition $c_2\ x'$ is checked possibly blaming a location in ℓs_f. Note that c_2 receives the checked argument, not the unchecked one.

It may seem surprising at first that $assert\ c_1$ adds ℓs_f to its file of suspects: can f be blamed if the precondition fails? If f is a first-order function, then this is impossible. However, if f takes a function as an argument, then f must take care that this argument is called correctly (see the discussion about g at the end of Sec. 3). If f does not to ensure this, then f is to blame.

In essence, $assert$ turns a contract of type $Contract\ \alpha$ into a contracted function of type $\alpha \twoheadrightarrow \alpha$. If we re-phrase $assert$ in terms of this type, we obtain the implementation listed in Fig. 3. Note that the elements of $\alpha \twoheadrightarrow \beta$ form the arrows of a category, the Kleisli category of a comonad, with $\lambda x \twoheadrightarrow x$ as the identity and

$$assert \qquad\qquad\quad : Contract\ \alpha \rightarrow (\alpha \twoheadrightarrow \alpha)$$
$$assert\ (Prop\ p) \qquad\ = prop\ p$$
$$assert\ (Function\ c_1\ c_2) = fun\ (assert\ c_1)\ (assert \cdot c_2)$$
$$assert\ (Pair\ c_1\ c_2) \qquad = pair\ (assert\ c_1)\ (assert \cdot c_2)$$
$$assert\ (List\ c) \qquad\quad = list\ (assert\ c)$$
$$assert\ (And\ c_1\ c_2) \qquad = assert\ c_2 \diamond assert\ c_1$$

$$prop \qquad : (\alpha \rightarrow Bool) \rightarrow (\alpha \twoheadrightarrow \alpha)$$
$$prop\ p \ \ = Fun\ (\lambda\ell s\ a \rightarrow \textbf{if}\ p\ a\ \textbf{then}\ a\ \textbf{else}\ error\ (\texttt{"contract failed: "} +\!\!+ blame\ \ell s))$$

$$fun \qquad : (\alpha_1 \twoheadrightarrow \beta_1) \rightarrow (\beta_1 \rightarrow \alpha_2 \twoheadrightarrow \beta_2) \rightarrow ((\beta_1 \twoheadrightarrow \alpha_2) \twoheadrightarrow (\alpha_1 \twoheadrightarrow \beta_2))$$
$$fun\ g\ h\ = Fun\ (\lambda\ell s_f\ f \rightarrow Fun\ (\lambda\ell_x \rightarrow$$
$$(\lambda x' \rightarrow (app\ (h\ x')\ \ell s_f \cdot app\ f\ \ell_x)\ x') \cdot app\ g\ (\ell s_f \rhd \ell_x)))$$

$$pair \qquad : (\alpha_1 \twoheadrightarrow \beta_1) \rightarrow (\beta_1 \rightarrow \alpha_2 \twoheadrightarrow \beta_2) \rightarrow ((\alpha_1, \alpha_2) \twoheadrightarrow (\beta_1, \beta_2))$$
$$pair\ g\ h = Fun\ (\lambda\ell s\ (a_1, a_2) \rightarrow (\lambda a_1' \rightarrow (a_1', app\ (h\ a_1')\ \ell s\ a_2))\ (app\ g\ \ell s\ a_1))$$

$$list \qquad : (\alpha \twoheadrightarrow \beta) \rightarrow ([\alpha] \twoheadrightarrow [\beta])$$
$$list\ g \quad = Fun\ (\lambda\ell s \rightarrow map\ (app\ g\ \ell s))$$

$$(\diamond) \qquad : (\beta \twoheadrightarrow \gamma) \rightarrow (\alpha \twoheadrightarrow \beta) \rightarrow (\alpha \twoheadrightarrow \gamma)$$
$$g \diamond h \quad = Fun\ (\lambda\ell s \rightarrow app\ g\ \ell s \cdot app\ h\ \ell s)$$

Fig. 3. Contract checking with proper blame assignment

data $Locs = NegPos\{neg : [Loc], pos : [Loc]\}$

$$blame \qquad : Locs \rightarrow String$$
$$blame\ \ell s = \texttt{"the expression "} +\!\!+ show\ (head\ (pos\ \ell s)) +\!\!+ \texttt{" is to blame"}$$
$$+\!\!+ (\textbf{case}\ tail\ (pos\ \ell s)\ \textbf{of}$$
$$[\,] \rightarrow \texttt{"."}$$
$$\ell s' \rightarrow \texttt{" (the violation was caused by the expression(s) "} +\!\!+$$
$$concat\ (interleave\ \texttt{", "}\ (map\ show\ \ell s')) +\!\!+ \texttt{")."})$$

$$\langle\cdot\rangle \ :\ Loc \rightarrow Locs$$
$$\langle\ell\rangle = NegPos\ [\,]\ [\ell]$$

$$(\rhd) : Locs \rightarrow Locs \rightarrow Locs$$
$$NegPos\ ns\ ps \rhd NegPos\ ns'\ ps' = NegPos\ (ps +\!\!+ ns')\ (ns +\!\!+ ps')$$

Fig. 4. Extended blame assignment

'$\diamond$' acting as composition. Furthermore, *list* is the mapping function of the list functor. The implementation also makes clear that we can do without the GADT provided *assert* is the only operation on the data type *Contract*: the combinators of the contract library can be implemented directly in terms of *prop*, *fun*, *pair*, *list* and '$\diamond$'. Then *assert* is just the identity.

It remains to implement the data type *Locs* and the associated functions. Let us start with a simple version that supports blame assignment in the style of Findler & Felleisen. A contract either involves one or two parties.

data $Locs = Pos\{pos : Loc\} \mid NegPos\{neg : Loc, pos : Loc\}$

We distinguish between positive and negative locations corresponding to function and argument locations. Blame is always assigned to the positive location.

$$\begin{aligned}&blame \quad : Locs \rightarrow String \\ &blame \; \ell s = \text{"the expression "} + show \; (pos \; \ell s) + \text{" is to blame."}\end{aligned}$$

The actual locations in the source are positive.

$$\langle \ell \rangle = Pos \; \ell$$

The magic lies in the implementation of '$\rhd$', which combines two elements of type *Locs*.

$$\begin{aligned}&(\rhd) : Locs \rightarrow Locs \rightarrow Locs \\ &Pos \; \ell \qquad \rhd Pos \; \ell' = NegPos \; \ell \; \ell' \\ &NegPos \; \ell' \; \ell \rhd \_ \quad = NegPos \; \ell \; \ell'\end{aligned}$$

Two single locations are merged into a double location; if the first argument is already a double location, then the second argument is ignored. Furthermore, positive and negative occurrences are interchanged in the second case. This is vital for functions of order 2 or higher. Re-consider the function g of Sec. 3.

$$\begin{aligned}&g = assert \; ((nat \rightarrow nat) \rightarrow true) \; _{\langle 0 \rangle} (\lambda f \rightarrow \lambda x \rightarrow f \; _{\langle 2 \rangle} x) \\ &\dots g \; _{\langle 1 \rangle} (\lambda x \rightarrow x) \; _{\langle 3 \rangle} (-7) \dots\end{aligned}$$

The precondition of g, $nat \rightarrow nat$, and the postcondition of g's argument f, nat, are checked using $Pos \; 0 \rhd Pos \; 1 = NegPos \; 0 \; 1$. The precondition of f, however, is checked using $NegPos \; 0 \; 1 \rhd Pos \; 2 = NegPos \; 1 \; 0$. Thus, if f's precondition fails, g itself is blamed.

It is apparent that '$\rhd$' throws away information: location 2, which possibly causes the contract violation is ignored. We can provide a more informative error message if we keep track of all the locations involved. To this end we turn *Locs* into a pair of stacks, see Fig. 4. Blame is assigned to the top-most element of the stack of positive locations; the remaining entries if any detail the cause of the contract violation. The new version of '$\rhd$' simply concatenates the stacks after swapping the two stacks of its first argument. Just in case you wonder: the total length of the stacks is equal to the order of the contracted function plus one. Thus, the stacks seldom contain more than 2 or 3 elements.

6   Examples

In this section we give further examples of the use of contracts. Besides, we shall introduce a number of derived contract combinators.

6.1   Sorting

An *invariant* is a property that appears both as a pre- and postcondition. To illustrate the use of invariants, consider the implementation of insertion sort:

$$insert\text{-}sort \; : \; (Ord \; \alpha) \Rightarrow [\alpha] \to [\alpha]$$
$$insert\text{-}sort = foldr \; insert \; [\,]$$
$$insert : (Ord \; \alpha) \Rightarrow \alpha \to [\alpha] \to [\alpha]$$
$$insert \; a \; [\,] \qquad\qquad\qquad = [a]$$
$$insert \; a_1 \; (a_2 :: as) \mid a_1 \leqslant a_2 \quad = a_1 :: a_2 :: as$$
$$\qquad\qquad\qquad \mid otherwise = a_2 :: insert \; a_1 \; as$$

The helper function *insert* takes an element a and an ordered list, and inserts the element at the right, according to the order, position in the list. In other words, *insert a* takes an ordered list to an ordered list.

$$insert' \; : \; (Ord \; \alpha) \Rightarrow \alpha \rightarrowtail [\alpha] \rightarrowtail [\alpha]$$
$$insert' = assert \; (true \rightarrowtail ord \rightarrowtail ord) \; (\lambda a \rightarrowtail \lambda x \rightarrowtail insert \; a \; x)$$

The contract *ord* for ordered lists is defined as follows:

$$ord \; : \; (Ord \; \alpha) \Rightarrow Contract \; [\alpha]$$
$$ord = \{\, x \mid ordered \; x \,\}$$
$$ordered \qquad\qquad\qquad : \; (Ord \; \alpha) \Rightarrow [\alpha] \to Bool$$
$$ordered \; [\,] \qquad\qquad\quad = True$$
$$ordered \; [a] \qquad\qquad\quad = True$$
$$ordered \; (a_1 :: a_2 :: as) = a_1 \leqslant a_2 \wedge ordered \; (a_2 :: as)$$

The type 'ordered list' can be seen as an abstract data type (it is concrete here, but it could easily be made abstract), whose invariant is given by *ord*. Other ADTs such as heaps, search trees etc can be handled in an analogous manner.

For completeness, here is the contracted version of *insertion-sort*:

$$insertion\text{-}sort' \; : \; (Ord \; \alpha) \Rightarrow [\alpha] \rightarrowtail [\alpha]$$
$$insertion\text{-}sort' = assert \; (true \rightarrowtail ord) \; (\lambda x \rightarrowtail insertion\text{-}sort \; x)$$

Note that we did not specify that the output list is a permutation of the input list. Assuming a function $bag : (Ord \; \alpha) \Rightarrow [\alpha] \to \lbrace\!\lbrace \alpha \rbrace\!\rbrace$ that turns a list into a bag, we can fully specify sorting: $(x : true) \rightarrowtail ord \; \& \; \{\, s \mid bag \; x \; {==} \; bag \; s \,\}$. Loosely speaking, sorting preserves the 'baginess' of the input list. Formally, $g : \sigma \to \sigma$ preserves the function $f : \sigma \to \tau$ iff $f \; x \; {==} \; f \; (g \; x)$ for all x. Again, we can single out this idiom as a contract combinator.

$$preserves \quad : \; (Eq \; \beta) \Rightarrow (\alpha \to \beta) \to Contract \; (\alpha \rightarrowtail \alpha)$$
$$preserves \; f = (x : true) \rightarrowtail \{\, y \mid f \; x \; {==} \; f \; y \,\}$$

Using this combinator the sort contract now reads $(true \rightarrowtail ord) \; \& \; preserves \; bag$. Of course, either *bag* or the equality test for bags is an expensive operation (it almost certainly involves sorting), so we may content ourselves with a weaker property, for instance, that *insertion-sort* preserves the length of the input list: $(true \rightarrowtail ord) \; \& \; preserves \; length$.

The example of sorting shows that the programmer or library writer has a choice as to how precise contracts are. The fact that contracts are first-class citizens renders it possible to abstract out common idioms. As a final twist on this topic, assume that you already have a trusted sorting function at hand. Then you could simply specify that your new sorting routine is extensionally equal to the trusted one. We introduce the *is* contract combinator for this purpose.

$$is \quad : (Eq\ \beta) \Rightarrow (\alpha \to \beta) \to Contract\ (\alpha \to \beta)$$
$$is\ f = (x : true) \rightarrowtail \{\ y \mid y == f\ x\ \}$$
$$insertion\text{-}sort'' = assert\ (is\ sort)\ (\lambda x \rightarrowtail insertion\text{-}sort\ x)$$

6.2   Recursion Schemes

The function *insertion-sort* is defined in terms of *foldr*, the catamorphism of the list data type. An intriguing question is whether we can also attach a contract to *foldr* itself?

$$foldr \qquad\qquad : (\alpha \to \beta \to \beta) \to \beta \to [\alpha] \to \beta$$
$$foldr\ f\ e\ [] \qquad = e$$
$$foldr\ f\ e\ (a :: as) = f\ a\ (foldr\ f\ e\ as)$$

The application to sorting gives $(true \rightarrowtail ord \rightarrowtail ord) \rightarrowtail ord \rightarrowtail true \rightarrowtail ord$ as a contract, but this one is, of course, way too specific. The idea suggests itself to abstract from the invariant, that is, to pass the invariant as an argument.

$$foldr' : Contract\ \beta \to (\alpha \rightarrowtail \beta \rightarrowtail \beta) \rightarrowtail \beta \rightarrowtail [\alpha] \rightarrowtail \beta$$
$$foldr'\ inv = assert\ ((true \rightarrowtail inv \rightarrowtail inv) \rightarrowtail inv \rightarrowtail true \rightarrowtail inv)$$
$$(\lambda f \to \lambda e \to \lambda x \to foldr\ (\lambda a \to \lambda b \to f\ \langle 17 \rangle\ a\ \langle 18 \rangle\ b)\ e\ x)$$

Again, the fact that contracts are first-class citizens proves its worth. Higher-order functions that implement general recursion schemes or control constructs typically take contracts as arguments.

Interestingly, we can optimize *foldr'* as it satisfies its contract:

$$assert\ ((true \rightarrowtail inv \rightarrowtail inv) \rightarrowtail inv \rightarrowtail true \rightarrowtail inv)\ \overline{foldr}$$
$$= assert\ ((true \rightarrowtail true \rightarrowtail inv) \rightarrowtail inv \rightarrowtail true \rightarrowtail true)\ \overline{foldr}$$

where $\overline{foldr} = \lambda f \to \lambda e \to \lambda x \to foldr\ (\lambda a \to \lambda b \to f\ \langle 17 \rangle\ a\ \langle 18 \rangle\ b)\ e\ x$ is the contracted version of *foldr*. If we unfold the definition of *assert*, the equation simplifies to

$$assert\ inv \cdot foldr\ \bar{f}\ \bar{e} = foldr\ \hat{f}\ \bar{e} \tag{1}$$

where $\bar{f} = assert\ (true \rightarrowtail inv \rightarrowtail inv)\ f$, $\hat{f} = assert\ (true \rightarrowtail true \rightarrowtail inv)\ f$, and $\bar{e} = assert\ inv\ e$. Equation (1) can be shown either by a simple appeal to *foldr*'s fusion law [11] or using parametricity [12]. In both cases, it remains to prove that

$$assert\ inv\ \bar{e} \qquad = \bar{e}$$
$$assert\ inv\ (\bar{f}\ a\ as) = \hat{f}\ a\ (assert\ inv\ as)$$

Both parts follow immediately from the idempotence of conjunction: $c\ \&\ c = c$ or more verbosely *assert* $c \cdot assert\ c = assert\ c$, see Sec. 7.

7   Properties of Contracts

In this section we study the algebra of contracts. The algebraic properties can be used, for instance, to optimize contracts: we shall see that $[c_1] \& [c_2]$ is the same as $[c_1 \& c_2]$, but the latter contract is more efficient. The properties are also helpful for showing that a function satisfies its contract: we have seen that the 'correctness' of $foldr'$ relies on $c \& c = c$.

$$false \& c = false \qquad\qquad c_1 \& (c_2 \& c_3) = (c_1 \& c_2) \& c_3$$
$$c \& false = false \qquad\qquad c_1 \& c_2 = c_2 \& c_1 \qquad\qquad (\dagger)$$
$$true \& c = c \qquad\qquad\qquad c \& c = c \qquad\qquad\qquad (\dagger)$$
$$c \& true = c \qquad\qquad \{\, x \mid p_1 \,\} \& \{\, x \mid p_2 \,\} = \{\, x \mid p_1\ x \wedge p_2\ x \,\}$$

$$true \twoheadrightarrow true = true$$
$$(c_1 \twoheadrightarrow d_1) \& (c_2 \twoheadrightarrow d_2) = (c_2 \& c_1) \twoheadrightarrow (d_1 \& d_2)$$
$$true \times true = true$$
$$(c_1 \times d_1) \& (c_2 \times d_2) = (c_1 \& c_2) \times (d_1 \& d_2)$$
$$[true] = true$$
$$[c_1 \& c_2] = [c_1] \& [c_2]$$

Fig. 5. Properties of contracts

Up to now we have pretended to work in a strict languiage: we did not consider bottom in the proofs in the previous section. Let us now switch back to Haskell's non-strict semantics in order to study the algebra of contracts in a more general setting.

It is easy to show that $assert\ c$ is less than or equal to $assert\ true$:

$c \preccurlyeq true$

where '$\preccurlyeq$' denotes the standard information ordering. This property implies, in particular, that $assert\ c$ is strict. Note that, for brevity, we abbreviate the law $assert\ c_1 \preccurlyeq assert\ c_2$ by $c_1 \preccurlyeq c_2$ (ditto for equations).

Now, what happens if we apply the same contract twice; is the result the same as applying it once? In other words, is '$\&$' idempotent? One can show that idempotence holds if '$\&$' is commutative (the other cases go through easily). Since '$\&$' is implemented by function composition, commutativity is somewhat doubtful and, indeed, it does not hold in general as the following example shows: let $c_1 = \{\, x \mid sum\ x == 0 \,\}$ and $c_2 = [false]$, then

Contracts⟩ $length\ (assert\ (c_1 \& c_2)\ [-2,2])$
2
Contracts⟩ $length\ (assert\ (c_2 \& c_1)\ [-2,2])$
*** contract failedthe expression '$[-2,2]$' is to blame.
Contracts⟩ $length\ (assert\ ((c_1 \& c_2) \& (c_1 \& c_2))\ [-2,2])$
*** contract failed: the expression '$[-2,2]$' is to blame.

The reason is that $[false]$ is not the same as $false$ in a lazy setting: the first contract returns a lazy list of contract violations, the second is a contract violation. In a strict setting, commutativity holds trivially as $assert\ c\ x \in \{\bot, x\}$.

The first and the last call demonstrate that idempotence of '&' does not hold for contracts that involve conjunctions, that is, these contracts are not *projections*.

Fig. 5 summarises the properties of conjunctions. Equations that are marked with a (†) only hold in a strict setting. The list combinator and the *independent* variants of '→' and '×' are implemented in terms of mapping functions. The remaining laws listed in Fig. 5 are immediate consequences of the well-known functor laws for these maps (bearing in mind that *true* corresponds to *id* and '&' to composition).

8 Related Work

Contracts are widely used in procedural and object-oriented (first-order) programming languages [2]. The work on higher-order contracts by Findler and Felleisen [13, 3] has been the main inspiration for this paper. Blume and McAllester [6, 14] describe a sound and complete model for F&F contracts, which proves that the contract checker discovers all violations, and always assigns blame properly. They show how by restricting the predicate contracts in the F&F language mixing semantics and soundness is avoided, and they show how to regain the expressiveness of the original F&F language by adding general recursive contracts. Furthermore, Findler, Blume, and Felleisen [15] prove many properties about contracts, for example, that contracts are a special kind of *projections* (which have been used to give a meaning to types), and that contracts only modify the behaviour of a program to assign blame. We have implemented contracts as a library in Haskell, using generalised algebraic data types, giving a strongly typed approach to contracts. Our approach allows for a more informative blame assignment. We provide contract constructors for pairs, lists and algebraic data types and a combinator for conjunction. Conjunctions greatly increase the usability of the contract language: they allow the programmer to specify independent properties separately. However, conjunctions also have a disturbing effect on the algebra: in a lazy setting, contracts that include conjunctions are not necessarily projections.

Stating and verifying properties of software is one of the central themes in computer science. The properties of interest range from simple properties like 'this function takes an integer and returns an integer' to complex properties that precisely describe the behaviour of a function like the contract for *insertion-sort* given in Sec. 6.1. Relatively simple properties like Hindley-Milner types can be statically checked by a compiler. To statically prove a complex property for a function it is usually necessary to resort to theorem provers or interactive type-checking tools. Contracts also allow the specification of complex properties; their checking, however, is relegated to run-time. The design space is summarised in the table below.

	static checking	dynamic checking
simple properties	static type checking	dynamic type checking
complex properties	theorem proving	contract checking

Contracts look a bit like types, but they are not. Contracts are dynamic instead of static, and they dynamically change the program. Contracts also differ from dependent types [16]. A dependent type may depend on a value, and may take a different form depending on a value. A contract refines a type (besides changing the behaviour as explained above). Dependently typed programs contain a proof of the fact that the program satisfies the property specified in the type. A contract is only checked, and might fail.

As a characteristic property, contracts are attached to program points, which suggests that they cannot capture general *algebraic properties* such as associativity or distributivity. These properties typically involve several functions or several calls to the same function, which makes it hard to attach them to *one* program point. Furthermore, they do not follow the type structure as required by contracts. As a borderline example, an algebraic property that can be formulated as a contract, since it can be written in a type-directed fashion, is idempotence of a function:

$$f' = assert\ (true \rightarrow \{\, y \mid y == f\ y \,\})\ (\lambda x \rightarrow f\ x)$$

In general, however, algebraic properties differ from properties that can be expressed using contracts. In practice, we expect that contract checking is largely complementary to tools that support expressing and testing general algebraic properties such as Quickcheck [17]. We may even observe a synergy: Quickcheck can possibly be a lot more effective in a program that has good contracts.

GHC [5], one of the larger compilers for Haskell, provides *assertions* for expressions: *assert x* returns *x* only if *p* evaluates to *True*. The function *assert* is a strict function. Chitil et al. [18] show how to define *assert* lazily. In contrast to contracts, assertions do not assign blame: if the precondition of a function is not satisfied, the function is blamed. Furthermore, contracts are type directed, whereas an assertion roughly corresponds to a contract comprehension.

9   Conclusion

We have introduced an embedded domain-specific language for typed, higher-order and first-class contracts, which is both more expressive than previous proposals, and allows for a more informative blame assignment. The contract language is implemented as a library in Haskell using the concept of generalised algebraic data types. We have taken some first steps towards an algebra of contracts, and we have shown how to define a generic contract combinator for arbitrary algebraic data types.

We left a couple of topics for future work. We intend to take an existing debugger or tracer for Haskell, and use the available information about source locations to let blaming point to real source locations, instead of user-supplied locations as supported by the implementation described in this paper. Furthermore, we want to turn the algebra for contracts into a more or less complete set of laws for contracts.

Acknowledgements. We are grateful to Matthias Blume, Matthias Felleisen, Robby Findler and the five anonymous referees for valuable suggestions regarding content and presentation. Special thanks go to Matthias Blume and referee #5 for pointing out infelicities in the previous implementation of blame assignment.

References

1. Meyer, B.: Applying 'design by contract'. IEEE Computer **25**(10) (1992) 40–51
2. Meyer, B.: Eiffel: The Language. Prentice Hall (1992)
3. Findler, R.B., Felleisen, M.: Contracts for higher-order functions. ACM SIGPLAN Notices **37**(9) (2002) 48–59
4. Peyton Jones, S.: Haskell 98 Language and Libraries. Cambridge University Press (2003)
5. The GHC Team: The Glorious Glasgow Haskell Compilation System User's Guide, Version 6.4.1. (2005) Available from http://www.haskell.org/ghc/.
6. Blume, M., McAllester, D.: A sound (and complete) model of contracts. ACM SIGPLAN Notices **39**(9) (2004) 189–200
7. Xi, H., Chen, C., Chen, G.: Guarded recursive datatype constructors. In: POPL '03, ACM Press (2003) 224–235
8. Hinze, R.: Fun with phantom types. In Gibbons, J., de Moor, O., eds.: The Fun of Programming. Palgrave Macmillan (2003) 245–262 ISBN 1-4039-0772-2 hardback, ISBN 0-333-99285-7 paperback.
9. Peyton Jones, S., Washburn, G., Weirich, S.: Wobbly types: Type inference for generalised algebraic data types. Technical Report MS-CIS-05-26, University of Pennsylvania (2005)
10. Hinze, R.: Polytypic values possess polykinded types. Science of Computer Programming **43** (2002) 129–159
11. Hutton, G.: A tutorial on the universality and expressiveness of fold. Journal of Functional Programming **9**(4) (1999) 355–372
12. Wadler, P.: Theorems for free! In: The Fourth International Conference on Functional Programming Languages and Computer Architecture (FPCA'89), London, UK, Addison-Wesley Publishing Company (1989) 347–359
13. Findler, R.B.: Behavioral software contracts (dissertation). Technical Report TR02-402, Department of Computer Science, Rice University (2002)
14. Blume, M., McAllester, D.: Sound and complete models of contracts. Journal of Functional Programming (2006) to appear.
15. Findler, R.B., Blume, M., Felleisen, M.: An investigation of contracts as projections. Technical Report TR-2004-02, The University of Chicago (2004)
16. Nordström, B., Petersson, K., Smith, J.: Programming in Martin-Löf's Type Theory. Oxford University Press (1990)
17. Claessen, K., Runciman, C., Chitil, O., Hughes, J., Wallace, M.: Testing and tracing lazy functional programs using Quickcheck and Hat. In Jeuring, J., Peyton Jones, S., eds.: Advanced Functional programming. Volume 2638 of Lecture Notes in Computer Science., Springer-Verlag (2003)
18. Chitil, O., McNeill, D., Runciman, C.: Lazy assertions. In Trinder, P., Michaelson, G., Peña, R., eds.: Implementation of Functional Languages: 15th International Workshop, IFL 2003, Edinburgh, UK, September 8–11, 2003. Volume 3145 of Lecture Notes in Computer Science., Springer-Verlag (2004) 1–19

Contracts as Pairs of Projections

Robert Bruce Findler[1] and Matthias Blume[2]

[1] University of Chicago
[2] Toyota Technological Institute at Chicago

Abstract. Assertion-based contracts provide a powerful mechanism for stating invariants at module boundaries and for enforcing them uniformly. In 2002, Findler and Felleisen showed how to add contracts to higher-order functional languages, allowing programmers to assert invariants about functions as values. Following up in 2004, Blume and McAllester provided a quotient model for contracts. Roughly speaking, their model equates a contract with the set of values that cannot violate the contract. Their studies raised interesting questions about the nature of contracts and, in particular, the nature of the *any* contract.

In this paper, we develop a model for software contracts that follows Dana Scott's program by interpreting contracts as projections. The model has already improved our implementation of contracts. We also demonstrate how it increases our understanding of contract-oriented programming and design. In particular, our work provides a definitive answer to the questions raised by Blume and McAllester's work. The key insight from our model that resolves those questions is that a contract that puts no obligation on either party is not the same as the most permissive contract for just one of the parties.

1 A Tour of Contracts

Assertion-based contracts play an important role in the construction of robust software. They give programmers a technique to express program invariants in a familiar notation with familiar semantics. Contracts are expressed as program expressions of type boolean. When the expression's value is true, the contract holds and the program continues. When the expression's value is false, the contract fails, the contract checker aborts the program, and hopefully, it identifies the violation and the violator. Identifying the faulty part of the system helps programmers narrow down the cause of the violation and, in a component-oriented programming setting, exposes culpable component producers.

The idea of software contracts dates back to the 1970s [31]. In the 1980s, Meyer developed an entire philosophy of software design based on contracts, embodied in his object-oriented programming language Eiffel [30]. Nowadays, contracts are available in one form or another for many programming languages (*e.g.*, C [37], C++ [33], C# [29], Java [1, 4, 7, 20, 22, 24, 26], Perl [5], Python [32], Scheme [14, 35], and Smalltalk [3]). Contracts are currently the third most requested addition to Java.[1] In C code, assert statements are particularly popular, even though they do not have enough information to properly assign blame and thus are a degenerate form of contracts. In fact, 60% of

---

[1] http://bugs.sun.com/bugdatabase/top25_rfes.do as of 1/20/2006

M. Hagiya and P. Wadler (Eds.): FLOPS 2006, LNCS 3945, pp. 226–241, 2006.

the C and C++ entries to the 2005 ICFP programming contest [10] used assertions, despite the fact that the software was produced for only a single run and was ignored afterwards.

The "hello world" program of contract research is:

```
float sqrt(float x) { ... }
// @pre{ x >= 0 }
// @post{ @ret >= 0 && abs(x - @ret * @ret) <= 0.01 }
```

The pre-condition for sqrt indicates that it only receives positive numbers, and its post-condition indicates that its result is positive and within 0.01 of the square root of its input. If the pre-condition contract is violated, the blame is assigned to the caller of sqrt, but if the post-condition is violated, the blame is assigned to sqrt itself.

Until relatively recently, functional languages have not been able to benefit from contract checking, and with what might seem to be a good reason. Because functional languages permit functions to be used as values, contract checking must cope with assertions on the behavior of functions, *i.e.*, objects with infinite behavior. For example, this contract restricts f's argument to functions on even integers:

let f(g : (int{even} → int{even})) : int = ... g(2) ...

But what can it mean for a function to only accept functions on even numbers? According to Rice's theorem, this property is not decidable.[2]

Rather than try to check a function's behavior when we first encounter it, we can — in keeping with the spirit of dynamically enforced contracts — wait until each function is called with or returns simple values and only at that point check to see if the values match the contract.[3]

Once contract checking is delayed, blame assignment becomes subtle. In general, the blame for a contract violation lies with the party supplying the value at the point where the contract violation occurs. In a first-order setting, the caller first supplies a value to a function and it responds with another value. Thus the caller is responsible for the entire contract on the input and the function is responsible for entire contract on the result. In the higher-order function world, however, this reasoning is too simplistic.

Consider the situation where f (as above) is called with the function $\lambda x.x+1$, and f, as shown, calls its argument with the number 2. At this point, a contract violation occurs, because 3 is produced, but 3 is not an even integer. Clearly, the blame for the contract violation cannot lie with f, because f called its argument with a valid input. Instead, the blame for the violation must lie with f's caller, because it did not provide a suitable function. In a similar fashion, if f had supplied 3 to its argument, f would be to blame.

To generalize from the first-order setting, we need to observe that all of the negative positions in the contract (those positions that occur to the left of an odd number of

---

[2] Object-oriented programming languages share this problem with higher-order functional languages. In particular, it is impossible to check whether a contract concerning behavioral subtyping holds until the classes are instantiated and the relevant methods are invoked [13, 16]. We focus here on the functional setting because it is simpler than the object-oriented one.

[3] And thus, in answer to the age-old question, no: the tree does not make a sound if no one is there to hear it fall. In fact, it didn't even fall until someone sees it on the ground.

arrows) are points at which the context is supplying values and therefore the context must be blamed for any violations of those parts of the contract. Similarly, all of the positive positions in the contract (those that occur to the left of an even number of arrows) are points where the function supplies values to its context and thus the function must be blamed for any violations of those parts of the contract. In our running example, f is responsible for the inputs to the function it receives, and f's caller is responsible for the results of that function.

In the first order setting, the negative and positive positions of the contract match the pre- and post-conditions for a function, making traditional pre- and post-condition checking a natural specialization of higher-order contract checking.

The remainder of this paper explores models of higher-order contracts. The next section introduces the formal setting for the paper. Section 3 shows how our original contract checker is in fact a disguised version of projections. Section 4 introduces projections and discusses orderings on projections. Section 5 relates projections to Blume and McAllester's model of contracts. Equipped with this background, section 6 revisits Blume and McAllester's motivating example, and section 7 concludes.

2   Modeling Scheme and Contracts

For the rest of this paper, we focus on an idealized, pure version of Scheme [17, 21, 27], and source programs that contain a single contract between two parties in the program. The syntax and semantics for this language is given in figure 1. A program consists of a series of definitions followed by a single expression (ellipses in the figure indicate (zero or more) repeated elements of whatever precedes the ellipsis). Definitions associate variables with expressions and expressions consist of λ expressions, applications, variables, symbolic constants (written as a single quote followed by a variable name), integers, booleans, **if** expressions, primitives for cons pairs, the three primitive predicates, procedure? integer?, and pair?, and an expression to assign blame.

The operational semantics is defined by a context-sensitive rewriting system in the spirit of Felleisen and Hieb [9]. Contexts are non-terminals with capital letters (P, D, E) and allow evaluation in definitions, from left-to-right in applications, in the test position of **if** expressions, and in **blame** expressions. The evaluation rules are standard: β_v for function application, the predicates procedure?, integer?, and pair? recognize λs, integers, and cons pairs respectively, car and cdr extract the pieces of a cons pair, and **if** chooses between its second and third arguments (unlike in standard Scheme, our **if** requires the test to be a boolean). Variables bound by **define** are replaced with their values, and finally **blame** aborts the program and identifies its argument as faulty.

The syntactic shorthands allow us to write examples later in the paper in a clear manner, but without cluttering the language and it's semantics unduly. The composition operator, in particular, is defined to evaluate its arguments before performing the composition in order to match a standard functional definition, to avoid variable capture and associated machinery [8, 23], and to make later computations simpler.

Contracts belong on module boundaries, mediating the interaction between coherent parts of a program. Rather than build a proper module system into our calculus, however, we divide the program into two parts: an arbitrary context (not just an eval-

syntax

```
p = d ... e
d = (define x e)
e = (λ (x ...) e) | (e e ...) | x | 'x | i | #t | #f | (if e e e)
  | cons | car | cdr | procedure? | integer? | pair? | (blame e)

P = dv ... D d ... e | dv ... E
D = (define x E)
E = (v ... E e ...) | (if E e e) | (blame E) | □

dv = (define x v)
v = (λ (x ...) e) | (cons v v) | 'x | i | #t | #f
  | cons | car | cdr | procedure? | integer? | pair?
i = integers
x = variables
```

operational semantics

```
P[((λ (x ...) e) v ...)] ⟶ P[{x/v ...}e] ;; #x = #v
P[(integer? i)] ⟶ P[#t]
P[(integer? v)] ⟶ P[#f] ;; v not an integer
P[(procedure? (λ (x ..) e))] ⟶ P[#t]
P[(procedure? v)] ⟶ P[#f] ;; v not a λ expression
P[(pair? (cons v₁ v₂))] ⟶ P[#t]
P[(pair? v)] ⟶ P[#f] ;; v not a cons pair
P[(car (cons v₁ v₂))] ⟶ P[v₁]
P[(cdr (cons v₁ v₂))] ⟶ P[v₂]
P[(if #t e₁ e₂)] ⟶ P[e₁]
P[(if #f e₁ e₂)] ⟶ P[e₂]
P[x] ⟶ P[v] ;; where (define x v) is in P
P[(blame 'x)] ⟶ x violated the contract
```

syntactic shorthands

```
(define (f x ...) e) = (define f (λ (x ...) e))
(let ([x e₁] ...) e₂) = ((λ (x ...) e₂) e₁ ...)
(cond [e₁ e₂] [e₃ e₄] ...) = (if e₁ e₂ (cond [e₃ e₄] ...))
(cond) = #f
(e₁ ∘ e₂) = (let ([x₁ e₁][x₂ e₂]) (λ (y) (x₁ (x₂ y))))
```

Fig. 1. Syntax and semantics for a core Scheme

uation context) and a closed expression in the hole of the context, with a contract at the boundary. We call the context the client and the expression the server; the contract governs the interaction between the client and the server. Separating the program in this manner is, in some sense, the simplest possible model of a module language. Although it does not capture the rich module systems available today, it does provide us with a simple setting in which to effectively study contracts and contract checking.

As examples, consider the following clients, contracts, and servers:

Client	**Contract**	**Server**
(□ 2)	odd → odd	(λ (y) y)
(□ 3)	odd → odd	(λ (y) (− (* y y) y))
(□ (λ (x) (+ x 2)))	(odd → odd) → even	(λ (f) (f 1))

The first contract says that the server must be a function that produces odd numbers and that the client must supply odd numbers, but when plugging the server expression into the hole (□) in the client context, the client calls the server function with 2, so it is blamed for the contract violation. In the second line, the client correctly supplies an odd number, but the server produces an even number, and so must be blamed. In the third line, the client supplies a function on odd numbers to the server. The server applies the function to 1, obeying the contract. The server then receives 3 from the client, discharging the client's obligation to produce odd numbers, but the server returns that 3, which is not an even number and thus violates the contract; this time, the server broke the contract and is blamed for the violation.

3   Re-functionalizing the Contract Checker

A specification of contracts for a language with atomic values and single-argument functions boils down to three functions:

$$\text{flat} : (\alpha \rightarrow \text{boolean}) \rightarrow \text{contract } \alpha$$
$$\text{ho} : \text{contract } \alpha \times \text{contract } \beta \rightarrow \text{contract } (\alpha \rightarrow \beta)$$
$$\text{guard} : \text{contract } \alpha \times \alpha \times \text{symbol} \times \text{symbol} \rightarrow \alpha$$

The flat and ho functions are combinators that build contracts. The function flat consumes a predicate and builds a contract that tests the predicate. Usually, flat is applied to predicates on flat types, like numbers or booleans. In languages that have richer function types, e.g., multi-arity functions or keyword arguments, flat can be used to construct contracts that test flat properties of functions, such as the arity or which keywords the function accepts. The function ho builds a contract for a function, given a contract for the domain and a contract for the the range. As an example, (ho (flat odd?) (flat odd?)) is the contract from the first example in section 2, given a suitable definition of odd?. To enforce a contract, guard is placed into the hole in the client context, around the server expression. Its first argument is the contract (built using flat and ho). Its second argument is the server, and its last two arguments name the server and the client, and are used to assign blame. When fully assembled, the first example from section 2 becomes:

```
((guard (ho (flat odd?) (flat odd?))
        (λ (y) y)
        'server 'client)
  2)
```

In earlier work [14], we provided the first implementation of that interface. In that implementation, the contract construction functions were just record constructors and the interesting code was in the guard function, as shown in figure 2. The flat_1 and ho_1 functions collect their arguments. The guard_1 function is defined in cases based on the

```
;; data Contract₁ α where
;;    Flat :: (α → Bool) → Contract α
;;    Ho :: Contract α → Contract β → Contract (α → β)

(define (flat₁ p) p)
(define (ho₁ dom rng) (cons dom rng))

(define (guard₁ ctc val pos neg)
  (cond
    [(procedure? ctc)
     (if (ctc val) val (blame pos)))]
    [(pair? ctc)
     (let ([dom (car ctc)]
           [rng (cdr ctc)])
       (if (procedure? val)
           (λ (x)
             (guard₁ rng
                     (val (guard₁ dom x neg pos))
                     pos
                     neg))
           (blame pos)))]))
```

Fig. 2. Original contract library implementation

structure of the contract. If the contract is a flat contract, the corresponding predicate is applied and either blame is assigned immediately, or the value is just returned. If the contract is a higher-order function contract, the value is tested to make sure it is a procedure; if so, another function is constructed that will, when applied, ensure that the inputs and outputs of the function behave according to the domain and range contracts. The last two arguments to $guard_1$ are reversed in the recursive call for the domain contract, but remain in the same order in the recursive call for the range contract. This reversal ensures proper blame assignment for the negative and positive positions of the contract.

Without types, we can represent a higher-order function contract as a pair of contracts and a flat contract as the corresponding predicate, but written in this manner, the program would not type-check in SML or Haskell. It does type-check, however, if we use the generalized abstract datatype [19, 42] $Contract_1$, shown as a comment in figure 2.

The $Contract_1$ datatype constructors can be viewed as two defunctionalized functions [36], and $guard_1$ as the defunctionalized version of apply.[4] To re-functionalize the program, we can move the code in the first **cond** clause of $guard_1$ to a function in the body of the flat contract combinator, move the code from the second **cond** clause to a function in the body of the higher-order contract combinator, and replace the body of $guard_1$ by a function application. The new type for contracts is thus a function that accepts all of the arguments that $guard_1$ accepts (except the contract itself), and produces the same result that $guard_1$ produces. If we clean up that implementation a little bit by currying contracts and then lifting out partial applications in the body of ho, we get the code in figure 3.

---

[4] Yang [43] and Danvy & Nielsen [6] have also explored similar transformations, in more detail.

```
;; type Contract₂ α = symbol × symbol → α → α

(define (flat₂ pred?)
  (λ (pos neg)
    (λ (val)
      (if (pred? val) val (blame pos)))))

(define (ho₂ dom rng)
  (λ (pos neg)
    (let ([dom-p (dom neg pos)]
          [rng-p (rng pos neg)])
      (λ (val)
        (if (procedure? val)
            (λ (x) (rng-p (val (dom-p x))))
            (blame pos))))))

(define (guard₂ ctc val pos neg) ((ctc pos neg) val))
```

Fig. 3. Re-functionalized, cleaned up contract implementation

These two transformations lead to a significantly improved implementation, for two reasons:

– The new implementation is more efficient. PLT Scheme comes with a full featured contract checking library that includes over 60 contract combinators and several different ways to apply contracts to values [35, Chapter 13]. We changed PLT Scheme's contract library from an implementation based on the code in figure 2 to one based on the code in figure 3 and checking a simple higher-order contract in a tight loop runs three times faster than it did before the change. Of course, PLT Scheme does not contain a sophisticated compiler, and the performance improvement for such a implementations is likely to be less dramatic. For example, in ghc-6.4.1 [40] on a 1.25 GHz PowerPC G4, the figure 3 version of a toy contract library is 25% faster than a version similar to the one in figure 2, but written with pattern matching.

– The new implementation is easier to extend. Adding contracts for compound data like pairs and lists is simply a matter of writing additional combinators. For example, a combinator for immutable cons pairs can be defined without changing the existing code:

```
;; pair/c : contract α × contract β → contract (α × β)
(define (pair/c lhs rhs)
  (λ (pos neg)
    (let ([lhs-p (lhs pos neg)]
          [rhs-p (rhs pos neg)])
      (λ (x) (if (pair? x)
                 (cons (lhs-p (car x)) (rhs-p (cdr x)))
                 (blame pos))))))
```

4   Contracts as Pairs of Error Projections

Even more striking than the implementation improvements is that the text of the body of the ho_2 contract combinator is identical to Scott's function space retract and the text of the body of the `pair/c` contract combinator is identical to his retract for pairs [39]. The correspondence between our contracts and Scott projections is not mere syntactic coincidence; there is a semantic connection and the rest of this paper explores that connection in depth.

Scott defined projections (p) as functions (technically, elements in the domain $\mathbf{P}_\omega$) that have two properties:

1. $p = p \circ p$
2. $p \sqsubseteq 1$

The first, called the retract property, states that projections are idempotent on their range. The second says that the result of a projection contains no more information than its input. The equations also make intuitive sense for contracts. The first means that it suffices to apply a contract once; the second means that a contract cannot add behavior to a value. The second rule is not quite right for a contract checker, however, because the contract must be free to identify erroneous programs by signaling errors. Instead, we insist on a slightly different property, namely that the only behavior that a contract adds are such errors, and otherwise the contract leaves its input untouched. We call such functions error projections. The ho contract combinator always produces error projections from error projections and `flat` produces error projections for first-order inputs and produces error projections when its predicate does not explore the higher-order behavior of its argument (as we showed in earlier work [12]).

Retracts have a natural ordering, as defined by Scott [39]

$$a \propto b \text{ if and only if } a = a \circ b$$

When viewed as an ordering on contracts, it relates two retracts a and b if a signals a contract violation at least as often as b, but perhaps more. Intuitively, it captures the strength of the contract. A contract that ignores its argument and always signals an error is the smallest contract (*i.e.*, it likes the fewest values), and the identity function is the largest contract (*i.e.*, it likes the most values).

Given this ordering and the ho_2 contract combinator, it is natural to ask if the ordering is contra-variant in the domain and co-variant in the range of ho_2, analogous to conventional type systems. Disappointingly, as noted by Scott, it is co-variant in the domain.

Theorem 1. *(Scott [39]) For any retracts, d_1, d_2, and r, if $d_1 \propto d_2$, then (ho_2 d_1 r) $\propto$ (ho_2 d_2 r).*

Proof. Assume that $d_1 \propto d_2$, and consider the composition of (ho_2 d_1 r) and (ho_2 d_2 r)

```
  (ho₂ d₁ r) ∘ (ho₂ d₂ r)
= (λ (f) (λ (x) (r (f (d₁ x))))) ∘        ;; definition of ho₂
  (λ (f) (λ (x) (r (f (d₂ x))))) 
= (λ (f) ((λ (f) (λ (x) (r (f (d₁ x))))) ;; definition of
             ((λ (f) (λ (x) (r (f (d₂ x)))))  ;;   composition & let,
              f)))                            ;;   and βᵥ
= (λ (f) ((λ (f) (λ (x) (r (f (d₁ x))))) ;; βᵥ
            (λ (x) (r (f (d₂ x))))))))
= λ (f) (λ (x) (r ((λ (x) (r (f (d₂ x))))  ;; βᵥ
                     (d₁ x))))
= (λ (f) (λ (x) (r (r (f (d₂ (d₁ x)))))))) ;; βω [38]
= (λ (f)                                    ;; apply retract law,
    (λ (x) (r (f (d₂ (d₁ x))))))            ;;   to eliminate one r
= (λ (f) (λ (x) (r (f (d₁ x)))))           ;; by assumption & lemma (below)
= (ho₂ d₁ r)                                ;; definition of ho₂
```

The steps above use the lemma that for retracts a and b, $a = a \circ b$ implies $a = b \circ a$. □

Thus, because functions are naturally contra-variant in their arguments, this ordering fails to properly capture the ordinary reasoning rules about functions. Inspecting the analogy between contracts and error projections, we see that the Scott ordering ignores the blame associated with contracts. To cope with blame, we must first separate each contract into two projections: one that assigns blame to the client and one that assigns blame to the server, and then we can compare the projections separately. A violation of the first projection in the pair indicates the server is to blame and a violation of the second indicates the client is to blame.

Concretely, we represent contracts as pairs of error projections that are parameterized over the guilty party. We assume, however, that the parameterized projection does not dispatch on the symbol, and when it does assign blame, it always assigns blame to the symbol is received as an argument. Figure 4 shows the new implementation of the contract combinators.

As before, the sense of the blame is reversed for the domain side of a function contract. This reversal is captured in this version of the combinators by using the client's part of the domain (ac) in the server part of ho's result (the car position) and using the server's part of the domain (as) in the client part in the result (the cdr position).

To show that the new higher-order contract combinator checks the contracts in the same manner as the one in figure 3, we can construct suitable inputs for both combinators from a single set of error projections, and show that they produce the same higher-order projection.

Theorem 2. *For any values* a, b, c, d : symbol $\rightarrow \alpha \rightarrow \alpha$

```
(ho₂ (λ (pos neg) ((a pos) ∘ (b neg)))
     (λ (pos neg) ((c pos) ∘ (d neg))))

=

(let ([pr (ho₃ (cons a b)
               (cons c d))])
  (λ (pos neg)
    ((car pr) pos) ∘ ((cdr pr) neg)))
```

```
;; type Contract₃ α = (symbol → α → α) × (symbol → α → α)

(define (flat₃ f)
  (cons (λ (s) (λ (x) (if (f x) (blame s) x)))
        (λ (s) (λ (x) x))))

(define (ho₃ a b)
  (cons (λ (s)
          (let ([ac ((cdr a) s)]
                [bs ((car b) s)])
            (λ (val)
              (if (procedure? val)
                  (λ (x) (bs (val (ac x))))
                  (blame s)))))
        (λ (s)
          (let ([bc ((cdr b) s)]
                [as ((car a) s)])
            (λ (val)
              (if (procedure? val)
                  (λ (x) (bc (val (as x))))
                  val))))))

(define (guard₃ ctc val pos neg)
  (let ([server-proj ((car ctc) pos)]
        [client-proj ((cdr ctc) neg)])
    (client-proj (server-proj val))))
```

Fig. 4. Contract combinators for contracts as pairs of projections

Proof (sketch). The proof is an algebraic manipulation in Sabry and Felleisen's equational theory $\lambda\beta_v X$ [34, 38] (without η_v) extended with δ rules for **if** [28]. For details, see the accompanying tech report [11].   □

To define a blame-sensitive ordering, we must take into account the difference between contracts that blame the client and contracts that blame the server. In particular, assigning blame more often to the client means that *more* servers are allowed, whereas assigning blame less often to the client means *fewer* servers are allowed.

Definition 1 (≪)

$$(\text{cons } a_s \, a_c) \ll (\text{cons } b_s \, b_c)$$
$$\textit{if and only if}$$
$$(a_s \, \text{s}) \ll (b_s \, \text{s}) \quad \textit{and} \quad (b_c \, \text{s}) \ll (a_c \, \text{s}) \quad \textit{for any symbol } \text{s}.$$

Theorem 3. *The relation ≪ is a partial order.*

Proof. Follows directly from the fact that ≪ is a partial order (Scott [39]).   □

Theorem 4. *For any error projections,* d_1, d_2, *and* r, *and symbol* s,

$$d_1 \lll d_2 \ \textit{implies} \ (\text{ho}_3 \ d_2 \ r) \lll (\text{ho}_3 \ d_1 \ r).$$

Proof (sketch). This proof is an algebraic manipulation using the equations in the proof of theorem 2 and C_{lift} [9] used for **blame**, plus the lemma that, for any two retracts a and b, if $a = a \circ b$ then $a = b \circ a$. For details, see the accompanying tech report [11]. □

In short, a blame-sensitive ordering provides one that is naturally contra-variant in the domain of the functions.

5   Ordering Contracts in the Blume-McAllester Model

The quotient model of contracts proposed by Blume and McAllester [2] also leads to an ordering on contracts. This section revisits their model and connects the $\lll$ ordering to the ordering in their model.

In Blume and McAllester's work, contracts (c) are either function contracts or predicates that never signal errors, diverge, or get stuck.[5]

$$c = c \rightarrow c \mid (\lambda \ (x) \ e)$$

The meaning of each contract is a set of terms representing values that satisfy the contract. The values inhabiting higher-order function contracts are procedures that, when given an input in the domain contract, produce an output in the range contract or diverge. The values inhabiting flat contracts are the safe values that match the flat contract's predicate. Safe values are either first-order values, or functions that map safe arguments to safe results (or diverge). In other words, safe values can never be the source of an error.

Definition 2. *The set* **Safe** *is the largest subset of the set of values* v *such that each element of* **Safe** *is either:*

1. *an integer,* #t, #f, *or*
2. $(\lambda \ (x) \ e)$ *where, for each value* v_1 *in* **Safe**, *either* $((\lambda \ (x) \ e) \ v_1) \longrightarrow^*$ v_2 *and* v_2 *is in* **Safe**, *or* $((\lambda \ (x) \ e) \ v_1)$ *diverges.*

An expression e diverges if, for all e_2 such that $e \longrightarrow^* e_2$, there exists an e_3 such that $e_2 \longrightarrow e_3$. Blume and McAllester showed that definition 2 is well-formed [2].

Given **Safe**, we can formally define the meaning of contracts.

Definition 3. $[\![\cdot]\!] : c \rightarrow \{v\}$

$$[\![(\lambda \ (x) \ e)]\!] = \{v \in \textbf{\textit{Safe}} \mid ((\lambda \ (x) \ e) \ v) \longrightarrow^* \text{\#t}) \}$$

$$[\![c_1 \rightarrow c_2]\!] = \left\{ (\lambda \ (x) \ e) \ \middle| \begin{array}{l} \forall v_1 \in [\![c_1]\!]. \\ \quad ((\lambda \ (x) \ e) \ v_1) \longrightarrow^* v_2 \ \textit{and} \ v_2 \in [\![c_2]\!] \\ \textit{or} \\ \quad ((\lambda \ (x) \ e) \ v_1) \ \textit{diverges} \end{array} \right\}$$

---

[5] In their work, contracts are formulated differently, but these differences are minor. Their safe is $(\lambda \ (x) \ \text{\#t})$, their int is $(\lambda \ (x) \ (\text{integer? } x))$, and our $(\lambda \ (x) \ e)$ is $\langle \text{safe} \mid \lambda x.e \rangle$.

The subset ordering ($\subseteq$) on the sets of values produced by $[\![\cdot]\!]$ induces an ordering on contracts and we can ask how that ordering relates to $\ll$. To do so, we first map Blume and McAllester's contracts to error projections, via $(\!|\cdot|\!)$.

Definition 4. $(\!|\cdot|\!) : c \rightarrow e$

$$(\!|(\lambda\ (x)\ e)|\!) = (\texttt{flat}_3\ (\lambda\ (x)\ e))$$
$$(\!|c_1 \rightarrow c_2|\!) = (\texttt{ho}_3\ (\!|c_1|\!)\ (\!|c_2|\!))$$

We would like the two ordering relations to be the same but unfortunately $\subseteq$ relates slightly more contracts than $\ll$. First we note that if the error projection ordering relates two contracts, so does the set model's ordering.

Theorem 5. *For any* c, c': $(\!|c|\!) \ll (\!|c'|\!) \;\Rightarrow\; [\![c]\!] \subseteq [\![c']\!]$

Proof (sketch). The proof is a simultaneous induction on the structure of c and c', and is given in the accompanying technical report [11]. $\qquad\square$

The reverse direction does not hold for every pair of contracts. Consider these two contracts in the Blume-McAllester model:

$(\lambda\ (x)\ \texttt{false}) \rightarrow (\lambda\ (x)\ \texttt{false}) \qquad (\lambda\ (x)\ \texttt{false}) \rightarrow (\lambda\ (x)\ \texttt{true})$

In both cases, the range contract is irrelevant, because the domain contract always rejects all values. Accordingly, they both map to the same set of values under $[\![\cdot]\!]$. The corresponding pairs of error projections, however,

```
(define p₁ (ho₃ (flat₃ (λ (x) false)) (flat₃ (λ (x) false))))
(define p₂ (ho₃ (flat₃ (λ (x) false)) (flat₃ (λ (x) true))))
```

are not the same and, in particular, $p_2 \ll p_1$ does not hold.

Still, the two orders are related when we restrict higher-order function contracts in a minor way. In particular, every flat contract that appears as the domain position of a function contract must accept at least one value. In practice, this restriction is minor, because functions that always fail when applied are not generally useful. To express this restriction formally, we define a sub-language of c, called ĉ:

$$\hat{c} = \texttt{ne-c}\ |\ (\lambda\ (x)\ e)$$
$$\texttt{ne-c} = \texttt{ne-c} \rightarrow \hat{c}\ |\ \texttt{non-empty-predicate}$$

where `non-empty-predicate` stands for flat predicates that accept at least one value.

Theorem 6

1. *There exists* c *and* c' *such that* $[\![c]\!] \subseteq [\![c']\!] \;\Rightarrow\; (\!|c|\!) \not\ll (\!|c'|\!)$
2. *For any* ĉ, ĉ': $[\![\hat{c}]\!] \subseteq [\![\hat{c}']\!] \;\Rightarrow\; (\!|\hat{c}|\!) \ll (\!|\hat{c}'|\!)$

Proof (sketch). The first part follows from the example above. The proof of the second part is a simultaneous induction on the structure of ĉ and ĉ', and is given in the accompanying technical report [11]. $\qquad\square$

6   Revisiting the Blume-McAllester Example

Now that we have developed an ordering on contracts and can treat contracts as error projections, we can revisit Blume & McAllester's motivating example [2]:

Client	Contract	Server
(**let** ([invert	(non-zero-num? → num?)	(λ (x) x)
(λ (y) (/ 1 y))])	→	
((□ invert) 0))	any	

According to the contract between the context and the expression, invert must not receive zero as input. But when we put the identity function into the hole of the context, invert is applied to 0. So, someone must be blamed. The key question is whom?

There are two seemingly intuitive answers for this question. Here is the one that Blume & McAllester put forth (paraphrased):

> The (λ (y) (/ 1 y)) flows into the domain contract, non-zero-num? → num? and then back out into any. Clearly, non-zero-num? → num? should be a subcontract of any, because any accepts any value and thus is the highest contract in the subtyping ordering. Accordingly, we cannot blame (λ (x) x).

Here's the one that Findler & Felleisen saw, when they first looked at this expression:

> The expression (λ (x) x) accepts a function with a requirement that it not be abused. It then lets that function flow into a context that may do anything (and thus promises nothing), because its contract is any. So, (λ (x) x) must be blamed for failing to protect its argument.

These two intuitive explanations are clearly in conflict. Surprisingly, both have a correct interpretation in our model of contracts as projections, depending on the meaning of the word "any" and the corresponding choice of the any projection pair.

To see how, we can start by simplifying the program according to the definitions of the contract combinators, as shown in figure 5. The first expression shows the client, contract, and server combined into a single expression. The second expression shows how the domain contract is distributed to invert and the range contract is distributed to the result of the applying (λ (x) x) to invert. The inner guard expression corresponds to the domain part of the original contract, so the arguments to guard are reversed from their original senses, meaning that the client is responsible for results of invert and the server is responsible for the arguments to invert. The third expression shows how the inner guard is distributed into the body of invert. Again, the arguments to guard are reversed for the domain, leaving the server responsible for the value of y. At this point, we are left with the contract any applied to a procedure.

To support Blume & McAllester's answer, we must interpret any as the highest contract in the ≪ ordering,

```
(cons (λ (s) (λ (x) x))
      (λ (s) (λ (x) (blame s))))
```

With this interpretation of any, the client is immediately blamed, as they predict.

```
(((guard ((non-zero-num → num) → any) (λ (x) x) 'server 'client)
   invert)
  0)
= ((guard (any)
          ((λ (x) x) (guard (non-zero-num → num)
                            invert
                            'client 'server))
          'server 'client)
   0)
= ((guard (any)
          (λ (y) (guard (num)
                        (/ 1 (guard (non-zero-num) y 'server 'client))
                        'client 'server))
          'server 'client)
   0)
```

Fig. 5. Distributing the Contracts in the Blume-McAllester Example

To support Findler & Felleisen's answer, we must interpret any as the contract that never assigns blame,

```
(cons (λ (s) (λ (x) x))
      (λ (s) (λ (x) x)))
```

With this any, the outer guard in the last expression of figure 5 simply disappears. Thus, when the context supplies 0 to invert the latent guards assign blame to the server, as they predict.

Now that we have both projection pairs, we can ask which interpretation of any is more useful in practice. While such a judgment call is not supported by the model, it seems clear that the top of the ordering is a less useful contract, because it will always immediately abort the computation with a contract violation. The contract that never assigns blame, however, is useful because it allows us to build contracts that specify some properties, but leave others undetermined.

7   Conclusion

The Blume-McAllester contract example focuses our attention on an important lesson for contract programmers: the contract that never assigns blame is not the most permissive; the contract that always blames someone else is. Of course, finding partners that would agree to such a contract is a Phyrric victory, because it is impossible to achieve a useful goal with a contract that is always violated. As in real life, so too in programming: you've got to give a little to get a little.

Ever since their initial appearance in Scott's work, projections have enjoyed a wide use. Wadler and Hughes used them for strictness analysis [41], Launchbury used them for partial evaluation [25], and in our own work, projections have enabled us to build better models for contracts [12], to use contracts to connect nominal and structural type systems in a single language [15], and to interoperate between Java and Scheme [18]. We believe that this work is just the tip of the iceberg and intend to explore them further.

Acknowledgments. Thanks to Bob Harper for alerting us to the connection between contracts and retracts and to Matthias Felleisen and the FLOPS 2006 reviewers for their comments on this paper.

References

1. Bartetzko, D. Parallelität und Vererbung beim Programmieren mit Vertrag. Diplomarbeit, Universität Oldenburg, April 1999.
2. Blume, M. and D. McAllester. Sound and complete models of contracts. *Journal of Functional Programming*, to appear.
3. Carrillo-Castellon, M., J. Garcia-Molina, E. Pimentel and I. Repiso. Design by contract in Smalltalk. *Journal of Object-Oriented Programming*, 7(9):23–28, 1996.
4. Cheon, Y. A runtime assertion checker for the Java Modelling Language. Technical Report 03-09, Iowa State University Computer Science Department, April 2003.
5. Conway, D. and C. G. Goebel. Class::Contract – design-by-contract OO in Perl. http://search.cpan.org/~ggoebel/Class-Contract-1.14/.
6. Danvy, O. and L. R. Nielsen. Defunctionalization at work. In *International Conference on Principles and Practice of Declarative Programming*, 2001.
7. Duncan, A. and U. Hölzle. Adding contracts to Java with handshake. Technical Report TRCS98-32, The University of California at Santa Barbara, December 1998.
8. Dybvig, R. K., R. Hieb and C. Bruggeman. Syntactic abstraction in Scheme. *Lisp and Symbolic Computation*, 5(4):295–326, December 1993.
9. Felleisen, M. and R. Hieb. The revised report on the syntactic theories of sequential control and state. *Theoretical Computer Science*, pages 235–271, 1992.
10. Findler, Barzilay, Blume, Codik, Felleisen, Flatt, Huang, Matthews, McCarthy, Scott, Press, Rainey, Reppy, Riehl, Spiro, Tucker and Wick. The eighth annual ICFP programming contest. http://icfpc.plt-scheme.org/.
11. Findler, R. B. and M. Blume. Contracts as pairs of projections. Technical Report TR-2006-01, University of Chicago Computer Science Department, 2006. http://www.cs.uchicago.edu/research/publications/techreports/TR-2006-01.
12. Findler, R. B., M. Blume and M. Felleisen. An investigation of contracts as projections. Technical Report TR-2004-02, University of Chicago Computer Science Department, 2004.
13. Findler, R. B. and M. Felleisen. Contract soundness for object-oriented languages. In *Object-Oriented Programming, Systems, Languages, and Applications*, 2001.
14. Findler, R. B. and M. Felleisen. Contracts for higher-order functions. In *Proceedings of ACM SIGPLAN International Conference on Functional Programming*, 2002.
15. Findler, R. B., M. Flatt and M. Felleisen. Semantic casts: Contracts and structural subtyping in a nominal world. In *European Conference on Object-Oriented Programming*, 2004.
16. Findler, R. B., M. Latendresse and M. Felleisen. Behavioral contracts and behavioral subtyping. In *Proceedings of ACM Conference Foundations of Software Engineering*, 2001.
17. Flatt, M. PLT MzScheme: Language manual. Technical Report TR97-280, Rice University, 1997. http://www.mzscheme.org/.
18. Gray, K. E., R. B. Findler and M. Flatt. Fine-grained interoperability through contracts and mirrors. In *Object-Oriented Programming, Systems, Languages, and Applications*, 2005.
19. Jones, S. P., G. Washburn and S. Weirich. Wobbly types: Practical type inference for generalised algebraic dataypes. http://www.cis.upenn.edu/~sweirich/publications.html.

20. Karaorman, M., U. Hölzle and J. Bruno. jContractor: A reflective Java library to support design by contract. In *Proceedings of Meta-Level Architectures and Reflection*, volume 1616 of *lncs*, July 1999.

21. Kelsey, R., W. Clinger and J. Rees (Editors). Revised[5] report of the algorithmic language Scheme. *Higher-Order and Symbolic Computation*, 11(1):7–105, 1998. Also appears in ACM SIGPLAN Notices 33(9), September 1998.

22. Kiniry, J. R. and E. Cheong. JPP: A Java pre-processor. Technical Report CS-TR-98-15, Department of Computer Science, California Institute of Technology, 1998.

23. Kohlbecker, E. E., D. P. Friedman, M. Felleisen and B. F. Duba. Hygienic macro expansion. In *ACM Symposium on Lisp and Functional Programming*, pages 151–161, 1986.

24. Kramer, R. iContract: The Java design by contract tool. In *Technology of Object-Oriented Languages and Systems*, 1998.

25. Launchbury, J. *Projections factorizations in partial evaluation*. Cambridge University Press, 1991.

26. Man Machine Systems. Design by contract for Java using JMSAssert. http://www.mmsindia.com/, 2000.

27. Matthews, J. and R. B. Findler. An operational semantics for R5RS Scheme. In *Workshop on Scheme and Functional Programming*, 2005.

28. McCarthy, J. A basis for a mathematical theory of computation. *Computer Programming and Formal Systems*, 1961. http://www-formal.stanford.edu/jmc/basis/basis.html.

29. McFarlane, K. Design by contract framework. http://www.codeproject.com/csharp/designbycontract.asp.

30. Meyer, B. *Eiffel: The Language*. Prentice Hall, 1992.

31. Parnas, D. L. A technique for software module specification with examples. *Communications of the ACM*, 15(5):330–336, May 1972.

32. Plösch, R. Design by contract for Python. In *IEEE Proceedings of the Joint Asia Pacific Software Engineering Conference*, 1997. http://citeseer.nj.nec.com/257710.html.

33. Plösch, R. and J. Pichler. Contracts: From analysis to C++ implementation. In *Technology of Object-Oriented Languages and Systems*, pages 248–257, 1999.

34. Plotkin, G. D. Call-by-name, call-by-value and the λ-calculus. *Theoretical Computer Science*, 1:125–159, 1975. http://homepages.inf.ed.ac.uk/gdp/publications/cbn_cbv_lambda.pdf.

35. PLT. PLT MzLib: Libraries manual. Technical Report PLT-TR05-4-v300, PLT Scheme Inc., 2005. http://www.plt-scheme.org/techreports/.

36. Reynolds, J. C. Definitional interpreters for higher-order programming languages. *Higher-Order and Symbolic Computation*, 11(4):363–397, 1998. Reprinted from the proceedings of the 25th ACM National Conference (1972), with a foreword.

37. Rosenblum, D. S. A practical approach to programming with assertions. *IEEE Transactions on Software Engineering*, 21(1):19–31, Janurary 1995.

38. Sabry, A. and M. Felleisen. Reasoning about programs in continuation-passing style. *Lisp and Symbolic Computation*, 6(3/4):289–360, 1993.

39. Scott, D. S. Data types as lattices. *Society of Industrial and Applied Mathematics (SIAM) Journal of Computing*, 5(3):522–586, 1976.

40. The GHC Team. Glasgow Haskell compiler. http://www.haskell.org/ghc/.

41. Wadler, P. and R. J. M. Hughes. Projections for Strictness Analysis. In Kahn, G., editor, *Functional Programming Languages and Computer Architecture*, volume 274, pages 385–407, Portland, Oregon, USA, September 14–16, 1987. Springer, Berlin.

42. Xi, H., C. Chen and G. Chen. Guarded recursive datatype constructors. In *Proceedings of the ACM Conference Principles of Programming Languages*, 2003.

43. Yang, Z. Encoding types in ml-like languages. In *Proceedings of ACM SIGPLAN International Conference on Functional Programming*, 1998.

iData for the World Wide Web
Programming Interconnected Web Forms

Rinus Plasmeijer and Peter Achten

Software Technology, Nijmegen Institute for Computing and Information Sciences,
Radboud University Nijmegen, Toernooiveld 1, 6525ED Nijmegen, Netherlands
phone: +31 (0)24 3652644; fax: +31 (0)24 3652525
phone: +31 (0)24 3652483; fax: +31 (0)24 3652525
rinus@cs.ru.nl, P.Achten@cs.ru.nl

Abstract. In this paper we present the iData Toolkit. It allows programmers to create interactive, dynamic web applications with state on a high level of abstraction. The key element of this toolkit is the iData element. An iData element can be regarded as a self-contained object that stores values of a specified type. Generic programming techniques enable the automatic generation of HTML-forms from these types. These forms can be plugged into the web application. The iData elements can be interconnected. Complicated form dependencies can be defined in a pure functional, type safe, declarative programming style. This liberates the programmer from lots of low-level HTML programming and form handling. We illustrate the descriptive power of the toolkit by means of a small, yet complicated example: a project administration. The iData Toolkit is an excellent demonstration of the expressive power of modern generic (poly-typical) programming techniques.

Keywords: server side web programming, web forms, functional programming.

1 Introduction

The World Wide Web is experiencing a rapid growth of web based applications. For many companies their web based services are their only contact with clients. These clients gain access to these applications via a wide variety of browsers. In addition, they tend to use these applications in a browsing style: clients clone windows, move back and forward through visited links, visit different sites, and so on. These aspects impose strong demands on web applications in order to assure correct behavior. It is important that these web applications are constructed in a well-understood way, and are based on solid foundations. In the iData Toolkit project we are working on a framework for these purposes. The main features of the toolkit are:

- The toolkit is based on a single concept, that of *interactive Data*, or iData.
- The web application is a single program (perhaps consisting of several modules) instead of a collection of loosely coupled script pages.

M. Hagiya and P. Wadler (Eds.): FLOPS 2006, LNCS 3945, pp. 242–258, 2006.

- The toolkit is defined in a pure functional programming language, and uses features such as strong typing and expressive type systems.
- The toolkit offers a good separation of concerns. The computational content of the web application is separated from the presentation in a clear way.
- The programmer has fine grained control over the life span of the application's state. State can be stored persistently, session based, or page based.

We focus on two challenges when programming the web: the first is how to program *forms* in a concise, abstract, and well-defined way, and the second is how to *interconnect* these forms. Forms are the interactive parts of web applications. In them, users can enter data, using a variety of interactive elements such as text input fields, (radio) buttons, and pull down menus. An application page generally consists of several forms which content may depend on each others state. We guarantee that user input is always type correct, and that the server side application always receives the correct data.

We meet the above challenges by imposing a typed discipline on the untyped world of web programming in a novel way. In our framework, forms are really *editors of values*. Because we use a strongly typed programming language, these *values have a well-defined type*. We *derive the form automatically from the type* of the value of an editor using *generic programming techniques* [13, 14, 2]. Such an editor is an iData. This results in a powerful abstraction: iData Toolkit programmers do not program forms, but instead design types and values of iData. We have implemented this approach earlier for Graphical User Interfaces [1]. The implementation of the iData Toolkit [20] is both entirely different and a major improvement of the previous work.

Generic programming has been built in in Clean [21, 3] and GenericH∀skell [17]. We use Clean. Clean details are explained in the text. We assume that the reader is familiar with functional and generic programming.

Contributions presented in this paper are:

- We present a single programming concept, the iData, with which dynamically, interconnected, type-safe web applications can be developed.
- We show that iData offer a high level of abstraction because they are programmed in terms of data models. Forms are rendered automatically from the type of these data models.
- iData can be interconnected type-safely, as if they were stateful objects.

This paper is structured as follows. In Sect. 2 we introduce the iData Toolkit by means of a few key examples. We show what steps an iData Toolkit application programmer goes through by discussing a case study of a small, yet complex and realistic example of a web form in Sect. 3. We discuss related work in Sect. 4. Finally, we conclude in Sect. 5.

2   The Concept of iData

An iData element is an object with two major components: (i) a *state*, or *value*, which type is determined by the programmer, and (ii) a *form*, or *rendering*, which is derived automatically by the toolkit from the state and its type.

The programmer manipulates the iData in terms of the state and its type, whereas the application user manipulates the iData in terms of a low-level form. Clearly, the iData Toolkit needs to mediate between these two worlds: every possible type domain has to be automatically mapped to editable forms, and every user action on these forms has to be automatically mapped back to the original type domain, with a possibly different value.

In this section we explain the main concepts of the iData Toolkit by means of a few key examples. Please notice that although the code of these examples has a static flavour, each of these examples are complete interactive web applications. First we discuss the architecture of server side web applications.

2.1 Architecture

The applications that we study reside on web servers. They are launched by the web server whenever a (remote) web browser program sends a request for an HTML page. It is the task of the application to *compute* an HTML page, and then *terminate*. The web server takes care that the generated HTML page is sent back to the web browser program.

In our approach, a web application consists of two parts: the declaration of the interconnected iData elements, and the generation of the HTML page that contains (a subset of) the automatically derived forms of these iData elements.

Interconnection of iData is programmed in a pure functional data dependency style. This gives the program a highly declarative flavor. Yet, the application is started from scratch every time a web form is altered by the user. The current state of the program is completely determined by the iData elements. They are re-created each time the program is started, and are able to recover their current state (possibly changed by the user). To make this possible, the serialized state of an iData is stored either at the server on disk or in the HTML page. All iData elements therefore automatically always contain a type correct value reflecting the latest changes made by a user. For recalculation of a page, and even of a complete web site, the same algorithm can be re-used taking the current iData states as starting point, enabling the highly declarative style of programming.

iData Toolkit applications compute HTML pages. There are many possible approaches to handle this (Sect. 4). This aspect of the iData Toolkit was not our priority We have chosen an approach that fits in our framework, i.e. an approach that uses data types to model output. The HTML that is computed by the application is encoded with algebraic data types, using a *types-as-grammar* approach [25]. This has the following advantages. (1) We get a complete context free grammar for HTML which is convenient for the programmer. (2) The type system eliminates type and typing errors that can occur in plain HTML. (3) Compiling an instance of this data type to HTML code is done by a compact type driven generic function. (4) Such a generic implementation is very robust, future changes of HTML are likely to change the type definitions only. A snapshot of the algebraic data types is:

```
:: Html    = Html   Head Rest
:: Head    = Head   [HeadAttr]  [HeadTag]
:: Rest    = Body   [BodyAttr]  [BodyTag] | Frameset [FramesetAttr] [Frame]
:: Frame   = Frame  [FrameAttr]           | NoFrames [Std_Attr]     [BodyTag]
:: BodyTag = A      [A_Attr]    [BodyTag] | ...
           | H1     [Hnum_Attr] String    | ...
           | Var    [Std_Attr]  String
           | STable [Table_Attr][[BodyTag]] | BodyTag [BodyTag] | EmptyBody
```

The last three data constructors of BodyTag are not part of HTML, but are provided for programming convenience. The data constructor STable generates a 2-dimensional table, the data constructor BodyTag turns a list of body tag elements into a single body tag, and EmptyBody can be used as an empty element.

The code below shows the standard overhead of every iData Toolkit program:

```
module FLOPS2006Examples
import StdEnv, StdHtml                                              1.

Start :: *World → *World                                            2.
Start world = doHtml example world                                 3.
```

The proper library modules need to be imported (line 1). Lines 2–3 declare the main function of every Clean program. The *uniqueness attribute* * just in front of World guarantees that values of this type are always used in a *single threaded manner*. Clean uses *uniqueness typing* [6, 7] to allow destructive updates and side-effects. The opaque type World represents the entire external environment of the program. The iData program is given by the function example :: *HSt → (Html,*HSt). The wrapper function doHtml turns this function into a common Clean program. It initializes the HSt value with all serialized values that can be found in the HTML page, and includes the World as well. This implies that every iData Toolkit application has full access to the external world, and can, for instance, connect to databases and so on. Below, we only show the example*i* functions, and skip the standard overhead.

2.2   iData Have Form

The first example demonstrates the fact that iData elements are type driven. A simple Int iData is created (Fig. 1(a)).

```
example1 :: *HSt → (Html,*HSt)
example1 hst
    ♯ (nrF,hst) = mkEdit (nIDataId "nr") 1 hst
    = mkHtml "Int editor" [ H1 [] "Int editor", BodyTag nrF.form ] hst
```

Passing multiple environments around explicitly is supported syntactically in Clean by means of ♯-definitions. These are non-recursive *let*-definitions, which scope extends to the bottom, but not the right-hand side. This is the standard approach in Clean. Even though the examples in this paper do not exploit the flexibility of multiple environment passing (by for instance connnecting to a database system), we present them in this style. The function mkEdit (Sect. 2.5) declares an iData element `nrF::IData Int` with initial value `1::Int`. The element is identified with the value `(nIDataId "nr")::IDataId` (Sect. 2.5). The `IData` record holds the `form` rendering of the iData, its `value`, and a boolean that states iff this particular iData element has been `changed` by the user:

```
:: IData m = { form::[BodyTag], value::m, changed::Bool }
```

Key features that are illustrated in this small example are the declaration of an iData element (`nrF`) from an identification value and an initial value, and that this iData element has an automatically derived rendering in terms of a form that can be addressed by `nrF.form`. It is a general property of an iData that a user can only enter input that is type-safe. When a user creates wrong input, the previous value (of correct type) is restored. If an initial value of some other type would have been specified as argument of `mkEdit`, a corresponding, yet completely different iData element is generated, with a rendering that allows only input of the appropriate type. Finally, the declaration of iData is robust against ill-typed use: only if the current `HSt` value contains a serialized representation of a value of the correct type, then the iData uses the deserialized value of the correct type; otherwise it relies on its initial value. Hence, all iData declarations with the same label but different type use their own initial value. If the declaration of an iData *updates* the `HSt`, then it may be the case that the type of the reference is modified accordingly. It is the responsibility of the application programmer to use unambiguous names throughout his program. Although this approach is not fail-safe, it is easy to explain to programmers, and problems can be avoided by using separate declaration functions (Sect. 3.2). We are still investigating if better solutions exist or need to be created.

Note that the definition of the web page, given by the function `mkHtml ::` `String [BodyTag] *HSt → (Html,*HSt)`, is cleanly separated from the declaration of the iData. At this spot we can freely mix HTML code that is automatically generated from iData elements with "ordinary" hand-written HTML code.

2.3   iData Have Value

In this example we show that, besides a form, iData also have a value (Fig. 1(**b**)).

```
example2 hst
    # (nrFs,hst) = seqList [mkEdit (sumId nr) nr \\ nr ← [1..5]] hst
    = mkHtml "Numbers" [ H1 [] "Numbers", sumtable nrFs ] hst

sumtable nrFs = STable [] (                [nrF.form    \\ nrF ← nrFs] ++
                          [[toHtml (sum [nrF.value \\ nrF ← nrFs])]])
sumId i       = nIDataId ("sum" <$ i)
```

Five iData elements are activated: `nrFs :: [IData Int]` (`seqList fs st` threads a state value *st* through a list of state transformer functions *fs* and collects their results and the final state). The function `sumtable` places their *forms* in a column, underneath of which the sum of their *values* is displayed. The value of an iData is given by the `value` field of that iData. The library function `toHtml` uses the generic form rendering function we also use for the iData to render values of arbitrary type into HTML. The overloaded operator <\$ appends a String version of its second argument to its first argument.

2.4   iData **Have Sharing**

Repeated use of the same iData declaration refers to a shared iData object. A first advantage of this scheme is that an iData can be seen as a store of a value of a certain, arbitrary type. Where values are actually being stored depends on the kind of iData created (see 2.5). Hence, we do not need to introduce a separate concept to store data. A second advantage is that both the value and rendering of iData can be used arbitrarily many times in a HTML page without causing ambiguity problems. We illustrate the latter by replicating the column of integer iData and their sum in the example below (Fig. 1(c)):

```
example3 hst
    ♯ (nrFs,hst) = seqList [mkEdit (sumId nr) nr \\ nr ← [1..5]] hst
    = mkHtml "Numbers"
         [ H1 [] "Numbers", STable [][[sumtable nrFs],[sumtable nrFs]]] hst
```

Editing any of the iData elements also automatically affect the other iData in the same row. The sum is displayed twice, at the bottom of both columns.

2.5   iData **Have Model-View Separation**

So far we have seen that the rendering one obtains for free from an iData element is completely determined by its type. What if we don't like this particular rendering? Suppose that for this particular example we want to replace the default integer editor boxes by iData elements that are counters. These counters have different self contained behavior: pressing the buttons should increment/decrement the integer value. This warrants good separation between model (integer value) and view (counter). Indeed, in the example code we only have to replace mkEdit by counterIData that we will define later on to obtain the desired program that displays five counters instead of five integer editors (Fig. 1(d)).

```
example4 hst
    ♯ (nrFs,hst) = seqList [counterIData (sumId nr) nr \\ nr ← [1..5]] hst
    = mkHtml "Numbers" [ H1 [] "Numbers", sumtable nrFs ] hst
```

The counter iData ensures that its integer value is incremented/decremented at every corresponding button press. Although we have created an iData element with a completely different behaviour (view), it still returns an integer value to the programmer. The model has not changed, and therefore nothing else in program has to be altered, since iData elements are self contained and fully compositional. But how can a programmer define these counters?

Creating iData **forms.** The one *pivotal* library function mkIData allows the definition of all sorts of iData elements one can imagine. It has type signature:

```
mkIData :: IDataId m (IBimap m v) → IDataFun m
         | gForm{|*|}, gUpd{|*|}, gPrint{|*|}, gParse{|*|} v
:: IDataFun m :== *HSt → (IData m,*HSt)
```

With `mkIData` any model-view mapping can be made. The polymorphic type variable m stands for *model*, and the generically overloaded type variable v stands for *view*. Class restrictions on this generic variable v appear after |. It shows that `mkIData` obtains its power by making use of four generic functions (of kind $\star$):

- `gForm` creates a form from a view type,
- `gUpd` converts any change made by the user with a browser in a form to a corresponding change in the view value,
- `gPrint` serializes values of any type for iData storage, and
- `gParse` de-serializes values of any type for iData recovery.

For the programmer all these generic functions addressed in the context restriction have as small consequence that he has to tell Clean to automatically derive these generic functions (see [2, 3]) for the user defined types that he wants to view. In order to visualize a user defined view type Type, somewhere in the program the programmer has to define

derive gForm Type; **derive gUpd Type**; **derive gPrint Type**; **derive gParse Type**

Clean function types show their *arity* by separating arguments with white-space, Therefore, `mkIData` requires *three* arguments. Let's take a closer look at these arguments. The *first* argument of `mkIData` is of type IDataId.

```
:: IDataId  = { id::String, lifespan::LifeSpan, mode::Mode }
:: LifeSpan = Page | Session | Persistent
:: Mode     = Edit | Display
```

The `id` field of this record type is used to unambiguously identify iData elements. The programmer creates them by making up String identifiers, which is a typical way of identifying forms in web applications. It is the task of the programmer to use names in such a way that every use of (`mkIData id`) refers to the same iData element of some type m. We already saw in the sharing example that one can refer multiple times to the same iData element. The `lifespan` field controls the *life span* of the corresponding iData value: its value is either remembered as long as the same page is being viewed (`lifespan = Page`), or during a browser session (`lifespan = Session`), or independently of sessions (`lifespan = Persistent`). Persistent storage simply means that instead of storing a serialized representation of the value of an iData in the HTML page, the serialized value is written to and read from disk on the server side. Finally, the *edit mode* of iData can be set. This mode is typically editable (`mode = Edit`), but sometimes they should only display constant values (`mode = Display`). For convenience, for any kind of thinkable IDataId combination, a library function is offered {n,s,p}[d]IDataId :: String → IDataId. Here, n, s, p represent the `lifespan` values Page, Session, and Persistent respectively. If d is included, the `mode` is Display, otherwise it is Edit.

The *second* argument of `mkIData` is its initial value. This initial value is used when an iData element is created for the first time or if no matching iData was found in the HSt environment. This happens for instance when a web page is viewed for the first time.

The *third* and final argument of mkIData is the most complicated one because it is used to define the model-view abstraction. This allows the application to work with iData that have state values of type m, but that are *visualized* by means of values of type v. This is a variant of the well-known model(-controller)-view paradigm [16]. What is special about our approach, is that a view is also determined by its data type. The type can be regarded as a model of a view, and hence can be handled generically in exactly the same way! This is clearly expressed in the type signature of mkIData, which states that the generic machinery must be available for the view model v.

The mapping between a model m and its view v has to be given by defining an instance of the following record type IBimap m v:

```
:: IBimap m v = { toView   :: m (Maybe v) → v,  updView   :: Bool v → v
                , fromView :: Bool v → m,        resetView :: Maybe (v → v) }
```

The record contains model-view conversion functions and functions to enable the desired self contained behavior. Model values are transformed to views with toView. It can use the previous view value if available. The self contained behavior of an iData element is handled by updView. Its first argument records if the view has been changed by the user. The same argument is passed to fromView which transforms updated view values back to model values. Finally, resetView is an optional separate normalization of the updated view value.

The *result* of mkIData is an *HSt environment function of type IDataFun m that yields a (IData m) value. The abstract type *HSt is constructed by the iData Toolkit immediately after the application has been restarted and contains the serialized states of all views. The non-persistent view states are stored in the HTML form and transmitted whenever the page is changed. Persistent view states reside on disk on the server side and are read when needed.

Integer as model, Counter as view. Now that we have explained the most important function of the iData Toolkit, we can show how a self contained counter can be defined as a view for an integer model.

First of all, we need some button machinery. In the iData Toolkit, all imaginable input forms, such as labelled buttons, image buttons, radio buttons, and pull down menus, are predefined by specializing types to these input forms. In Sect. 2.6 we show how programmers can use the very same specialization mechanism for their own purposes. As an example we show the predefined type for a pull down menu and a button. Both are used in Sect. 3.

```
:: PullDownMenu = PullDown (Int,Int) (Int,[String])
:: Button       = Pressed | LButton Int String | PButton (Int,Int) String
```

A value (PullDown (v,w) $(i,elts)$) is shown as a pull down menu of width w that displays v elements of *elts*. The index of the selected element is i. A value (LButton w l) creates a w pixels wide button with label l. A value (PButton (w,h) p) creates a button that is w pixels wide and h pixels high, and that has a picture at file path p. Whenever a button is pressed, its iData value is set to Pressed.

Second of all, we need to specify layout. By default, arguments of data constructors are placed in a column, top- and right-aligned with the data constructor. As we have seen in the examples above, tables are useful to specify different layouts. For convenience, we have introduced a number of types to lay out elements in rows and columns. Furthermore, 2,3,4-tuples layout their elements in a row.

Elements such as the above can be used by defining iData of values of these types. A `Counter` for an integer value can be constructed by adding an up and down button to it. This results in the following (synonym) type:

```
:: Counter := (Int,Button,Button)
```

We can now straightforwardly define `counterIData` in terms of `mkIData`. To express the mapping between an integer model and a counter view, we need to define `toView`, `updView`, `fromView`, and `resetView`:

```
counterIData :: IDataId Int → IDataFun Int
counterIData iDataId i        = mkIData iDataId i ibm
where ibm        = { toView    = λn v → useOldView (n,down,up) v
                   , updView   = λ_ v → updCounter v
                   , fromView  = λ_ (n,_,_) → n
                   , resetView = Nothing }
     (up,down) = (LButton (defpixel / 6) "+",LButton (defpixel / 6) "-")

     updCounter :: Counter → Counter
     updCounter (n,Pressed,_) = (n - 1,down,up)
     updCounter (n,_,Pressed) = (n + 1,down,up)
     updCounter noPresses     = noPresses

useOldView :: a (Maybe a) → a
useOldView new (Just old)= old
useOldView new Nothing   = new
```

Frequently Used Views. The function `mkIData` is a very powerful function with which any model-view abstraction can be defined. Frequently used patterns are predefined in the library. Two examples used in this paper are:

```
mkEdit :: IDataId m → IDataFun m | gForm{|*|},gUpd{|*|},gPrint{|*|},gParse{|*|} m
mkEdit iDataId m = mkIData iDataId m { toForm     = useOldView
                                     , updForm    = modeUpd iDataId.mode m
                                     , fromForm   = λ_ v → v
                                     , resetForm = Nothing }
where modeUpd Edit    _    _ newv = newv
      modeUpd Display initm _ _   = initm

mkSelf2:: IDataId m (m → m) → IDataFun m | gForm{|*|},gUpd{|*|},gPrint{|*|},gParse{|*|} m
mkSelf2 iDataId m f = mkIData iDataId m { toForm     = useOldView
                                        , updForm    = λ_ v → f v
                                        , fromForm   = λ_ v → v
                                        , resetForm = Nothing }
```

The `mkEdit` function was used in examples 2.2 and 2.3. It can be used as a 'store' in `Display` mode, or as a straight editor in `Edit` mode. iData can also be used to create an intelligent store with custom behavior. iData that are declared with `mkSelf2` memorize a value, initialized with the second argument of the function. When declared, the iData applies the argument function `f` to its value (by `updForm`). In this way stores can preserve properties: e.g. one can ensure that a stored list is always sorted by defining a sort function as parameter. Because iData can be shared, the programmer is able to parameterize `mkSelf2` with different function arguments. In this way, the stored state can be manipulated from the outside. In combination with the `pdIDataId` function, this results in a persistent memory store which obeys these properties.

2.6 iData Have Specialization

iData can be specialized, just as generic functions can. The generic mechanism can render a value of any type. With specialization one can overwrite the default way this is done. This cannot only be used to create buttons and the like when certain types are being used, but it can also be used to customize the look and feel of any user defined type. By using specialization one can separate the handling of the functionality of the web page (by the programmer) from the way things look (by the designer of a site).

Suppose the designer likes the counters in Sect. 2.5 much better than the default integer editors that were used in Sect. 2.2 and 2.3. Assume that he wants to ensure that, throughout the program, these counters are being used instead of the plain integer boxes. For this purpose he needs to specialize the generic form rendering function `gForm` for the `Int` type. This is done by:

```
gForm{|Int|} iDataId i hst = specialize asCounter iDataId i hst
where asCounter :: IDataId Int → IDataFun Int
      asCounter iDataId i  = λhst
         ♯ (counterF,hst) = counterIData iDataId i hst
      = ( { changed     = counterF.changed
          , value       = fst3 counterF.value
          , form        = counterF.form }, hst )
```

The `asCounter` function that defines the specialization uses `counterIData` as defined in 2.5. The library function

```
specialize :: (IDataId a → IDataFun a) IDataId a → IDataFun a | gUpd{|*|} a
```

is able to 'plug in' the specialization function into any arbitrary other iData structure. Given this specialization for `Integers`, in any place where an iData of an `Integer` value is needed, a counter iData will be made. In such a setting, the programs 2.2, 2.3, and 2.4 all have self contained counters instead of integer boxes without any change to be made in the presented code.

3 Case Study: Project Administration Web Application

As a case study we construct a small, yet complicated form that could be part of a site with which (simple) projects are administrated. It consists of a dynamic

number of interconnected sub-forms. Its size is 250 *loc* (including empty lines):
50% handles the problem domain, 12% specialization, and 38% form programming. The screenshot in Fig. 2 shows the application with all sub-forms active.

3.1   Basic Logic of the Project Administration

We assume that the types and algorithms needed to do the actual project administration have been defined and designed separately, without any knowledge of the web interface that has to be created on top of it. Let's assume that to administrate projects, the following, self-explanatory, types have been defined.

```
:: Project     = { plan ::ProjectPlan, status::Status, members::[Worker] }
:: ProjectPlan = { name ::String, hours ::Int }
:: Status      = { total::Int,    left  ::Int }
:: Worker      = { name ::String, status::Status, work::[Work] }
:: Work        :== (Date,Int)
:: Date        = Date Int Int Int
```

We assume that for the maintenance of the project adminstration, suitable initialization, update, and retrieval functions are defined on these data structures, such as `initProject :: String Int → Project`. Their definitions are straightforward. We use them where needed, but skip their definition for lack of space.

3.2   Designing Forms by Defining Types

The screenshot in Fig. 2 reveals that we have defined at least three iData input forms: one to define a new *project*, one to add a *worker* to an existing project, and one to assign worked *hours* for an existing worker of an existing project. These are located below each other. The details view on the right hand side is not an iData, but just displays all information of one existing project. Clearly, the iData have a strong interconnected behavior: only if a project exists, then workers can be added to it; working hours can be assigned only for workers on projects they participate in. We show how to specify these dependencies.

For each iData we need a corresponding type, since iData's forms are generated type driven. Sometimes, we can use (a combination of) existing types, and sometimes we need to define new types. Because iData can be shared, it is good practice to define a separate declaration function for each of them. In case of straight editors, we use the `mkEdit` function. If we need to be able to impose properties on the state of an iData, we use the `mkSelf2` function. So, for every iData we give the type and define a creation function.

The *project* form can be of type `ProjectPlan`, which is given above. The creation function is `projectIData`. Initially we assume that no projects are planned.

```
projectIData :: IDataFun ProjectPlan
projectIData = mkEdit (nIDataId "project") (initProjectPlan "" 0)
```

For the *worker* form we define a new type `WorkerPlan`. It holds all project names a worker is involved in, the worker's `name`, and the `hours` that should be added to a particular project. The *worker* form must know all projects that have been entered. The function `adjWorkers` :: `[Project]` `WorkerPlan` $\rightarrow$ `WorkerPlan` updates the worker plan with all new project plan names. For this reason, it is a customizable editor created with `mkSelf2`.

```
:: WorkerPlan    = { project::ProjectList, name::String, hours::Int }
:: ProjectList  :== PullDownMenu

workerIData :: (WorkerPlan → WorkerPlan) → IDataFun WorkerPlan
workerIData f
    = mkSelf2 (nIDataId "worker") (initWorkerPlan "" 0 0 initProjects) f
```

For the *hours* form we define the type `DailyWork`. For a given project (in `projectId`), and a given worker (in `myName`), it stores how many hours have been worked on a particular date. Because this form depends on the current list of projects and associated workers, this declaration function is also created with `mkSelf2`. The function `adjDailyWork` :: `[Project]` `DailyWork` $\rightarrow$ `DailyWork` updates the daily work value with all currently registrated project-worker combinations.

```
:: DailyWork   =   { projectId  ::ProjectList, myName::WorkersList
                   , hoursWorked::Int,          date  ::Date }
:: WorkersList :== PullDownMenu

hoursIData :: (DailyWork → DailyWork) → IDataFun DailyWork
hoursIData f
    = mkSelf2 (nIDataId "hours") (initDailyWork 0 0 initProjects) f
```

Of course we need to store the whole project administration of type `[Project]`. This can be achieved by using a persistent iData. Again, we make its declaration function `adminIData` parametrized. By now, the pattern should be clear.

```
adminIData :: ([Project] → [Project]) → IDataFun [Project]
adminIData f = mkSelf2 (pdIDataId "admin") initProjects f
```

Finally, the user manipulates the forms of the application. Changes to the database are committed by pressing one of the buttons to add a *project, worker*, or *hours*. The corresponding actions are given by the functions

```
addNewProject  :: ProjectPlan [Project] → [Project]
addNewWorkplan :: WorkerPlan  [Project] → [Project]
addDailyWork   :: DailyWork   [Project] → [Project]
```

The library function `ListFuncBut` associates $m \rightarrow m$ functions with buttons, and yields an (`IData` $(m \rightarrow m)$) which value is either one of the selected functions or the identity function.

```
ListFuncBut :: Bool IDataId [(Button, m → m)] → IDataFun (m → m)
```

With this function, we can concisely specify the buttons of the application:

```
btnsIData::DailyWork WorkerPlan ProjectPlan → IDataFun ([Project] → [Project])
btnsIData daylog workplan project
  = ListFuncBut False (nIDataId "mybuttons")
```

```
[ (LButton defpixel "addProject", addNewProject  project )
, (LButton defpixel "addWorker",  addNewWorkplan workplan)
, (LButton defpixel "addHours",   addDailyWork   daylog  ) ]
```

3.3 Interconnecting iData

To create the desired web application we need to do two things: we have to
declare and interconnect all iData and we have to deliver an HTML page that
contains the renderings of these iData. We do not discuss the latter aspect: it is
not essentially different from the tiny examples given in Sect. 2. Interconnecting
the iData is what matters:

```
example hst
  # (projectF,hst) = projectIData   hst                              1.
  # (workerF,  hst) = workerIData id hst                             2.
  # (hoursF,   hst) = hoursIData   id hst                            3.
  # (btnsF,    hst) = btnsIData    hoursF.value workerF.value
                                   projectF.value hst                4.
  # (adminF,   hst) = adminIData btnsF.value    hst                  5.
  # (workerF,  hst) = workerIData (adjWorkers    adminF.value) hst   6.
  # (hoursF,   hst) = hoursIData  (adjDailyWork adminF.value) hst    7.
  = mkHtml "projectadmin" [ H1 [] "Project Administration"           8.
              ... /* not shown due to lack of space */ ] hst
```

First, the three user forms, *project*, *worker*, and *hours*, are declared (lines 1-
3). As a result, they recover their possibly altered state. Then the buttons are
declared (line 4). If the user has pressed one of them, then the value of btnsF
is the associated administration update function. This function, btnsF.value, is
then applied in the declaration function of the complete administration (line 5).
Given the new administration, the *worker* and *hours* form need to be updated
with the new project and workers lists (line 6-7). For this reason the latter
two forms occur twice in the code. This is a typical iData Toolkit programming
pattern. The program guarantees that users can only add workers to existing
projects and hours to existing workers.

4 Related Work

iData components are form abstractions. A pioneer project to experiment with
form-based services is Mawl [5]. The <bigwig> project [9] uses Powerforms [8].
Both projects provide *templates* which, roughly speaking, are HTML pages with
holes in which scalar data as well as lists can be plugged in (Mawl), but also other
templates (<bigwig>). Powerforms reside on the client-side of a web application.
The type system is used to filter out illegal user input. They advocate compile-
time systems, just as we do, because this allows one to use type systems and
other static analysis. The main differences are that in our approach *all first
order user types* are admissible in iData, that iData are automatically derived
from these types, and that we can use the expressiveness of the host language
to obtain higher-order forms/pages.

Continuations are a natural means to structure interactive web applications. This has been done by Hughes [15], using his Arrow framework; Queinnec [22], who takes the position that continuations are at the essence of web browsers; Graunke *et al* [11], who have explored continuations as (one of three) functional compilation technique(s) to transform sequential interactive programs to CGI programs. Our approach is simpler because for every page we have a complete (set of) model value(s) that can be stored and retrieved generically in a page. An application is resurrected by recovering its previous state, merging the user modification, if any, and computing the proper next state that is re-rendered.

Many authors have worked on creating and manipulating HTML (XML) pages in a strongly typed setting. Early work is by Wallace and Runciman [26] on XML transformers in Haskell. The Haskell CGI library by Meijer [18] frees the programmer from dealing with CGI printing and parsing. Hanus uses similar types [12] in Curry. Thiemann constructs typed encodings of HTML in extended Haskell in an increasing level of precision for *valid* documents [23,24]. XML transforming programs with GenericH∀skell has been investigated in UUXML [4]. Elsman and Larsen [10] have worked on typed representations of XML in ML [19]. Our *types-as-grammar* approach eliminates all syntactically incorrect programs, but we have not put effort in eradicating all semantically incorrect programs. Our research interest is in the automatic creation of forms from type specifications, and less in the definition of the HTML pages in which they reside.

5   Conclusions and Future Work

In this paper we have presented the iData Toolkit, an innovative toolkit for the construction of server side web applications. The toolkit is founded on a strongly typed, pure, functional programming language with support for generic programming. The key concept of the toolkit is the iData element. A web application is a function that computes an HTML page. Forms in this page are derived automatically by the iData Toolkit from the typed states of the declared iData elements. Each and every iData handles its initialization, state recovery, and rendering. The result is that applications can be defined in a concise and declarative style.

In this paper, we have illustrated the expressiveness of the iData Toolkit by means of several small examples, and one larger case study. To test the suitability of the iData Toolkit for constructing real world applications, we have created all kinds of applications, such as a fully functional CD-shop site. Also for these larger web applications we have observed that they can be defined in the same concise and declarative way as the examples in this paper.

We believe that the conciseness of programs, the use of a single iData concept, and the embedding in a functional programming language, are important factors to enable reasoning about these programs. We think that the iData Toolkit provides a step in the direction of formal reasoning about dynamic, type-safe, server side web applications.

Acknowledgements

Jan Kuper coined the name iData for our editor components. Paul de Mast kindly provided us with a Clean web server application to readily test the toolkit. Javier Pomer Tendillo has been very helpful in setting up the iData Toolkit, and find out the nitty-gritty details of HTML programming. We thank Pieter Koopman and Maarten de Mol for reviewing this paper and help us improving it. Finally, we thank the referees of this paper for their useful comments.

References

1. P. Achten, M. van Eekelen, R. Plasmeijer, and A. van Weelden. GEC: a toolkit for Generic Rapid Prototyping of Type Safe Interactive Applications. In *5th International Summer School on Advanced Functional Programming (AFP 2004)*, volume 3622 of *LNCS*, pages 210–244. Springer, August 14-21 2004.
2. A. Alimarine. *Generic Functional Programming - Conceptual Design, Implementation and Applications*. PhD thesis, University of Nijmegen, The Netherlands, 2005. ISBN 3-540-67658-9.
3. A. Alimarine and R. Plasmeijer. A Generic Programming Extension for Clean. In T. Arts and M. Mohnen, editors, *The 13th International workshop on the Implementation of Functional Languages, IFL'01, Selected Papers*, volume 2312 of *LNCS*, pages 168–186. Älvsjö, Sweden, Springer, Sept. 2002.
4. F. Atanassow, D. Clarke, and J. Jeuring. UUXML: A Type-Preserving XML Schema-Haskell Data Binding. In *International Symposium on Practical Aspects of Declarative Languages (PADL'04)*, volume 3057 of *LNCS*, pages 71–85. Springer-Verlag, June 2004.
5. D. Atkins, T. Ball, M. Benedikt, G. Bruns, K. Cox, P. Mataga, and K. Rehor. Experience with a Domain Specific Language for Form-based Services. In *Usenix Conference on Domain Specific Languages*, Oct. 1997.
6. E. Barendsen and S. Smetsers. Uniqueness typing for functional languages with graph rewriting semantics. In *Mathematical Structures in Computer Science*, volume 6, pages 579–612, 1996.
7. E. Barendsen and S. Smetsers. *Graph Rewriting Aspects of Functional Programming*, chapter 2, pages 63–102. World scientific, 1999.
8. C. Brabrand, A. Møller, M. Ricky, and M. Schwartzbach. Powerforms: Declarative client-side form field validation. *World Wide Web Journal*, 3(4):205–314, 2000.
9. C. Brabrand, A. Møller, and M. Schwartzbach. The <bigwig> Project. In *ACM Transactions on Internet Technology (TOIT)*, 2002.
10. M. Elsman and K. F. Larsen. Typing XHTML Web applications in ML. In *International Symposium on Practical Aspects of Declarative Languages (PADL'04)*, volume 3057 of *LNCS*, pages 224–238. Springer-Verlag, June 2004.
11. P. Graunke, S. Krishnamurthi, R. Bruce Findler, and M. Felleisen. Automatically Restructuring Programs for the Web. In M. Feather and M. Goedicke, editors, *Proceedings 16th IEEE International Conference on Automated Software Engineering (ASE'01)*. IEEE CS Press, Sept. 2001.

12. M. Hanus. High-Level Server Side Web Scripting in Curry. In *Proc. of the Third International Symposium on Practical Aspects of Declarative Languages (PADL'01)*, pages 76–92. Springer LNCS 1990, 2001.

13. R. Hinze. A new approach to generic functional programming. In *The 27th Annual ACM SIGPLAN-SIGACT Symposium on Principles of Programming Languages*, pages 119–132. Boston, Massachusetts, January 2000.

14. R. Hinze and S. Peyton Jones. Derivable Type Classes. In G. Hutton, editor, *2000 ACM SIGPLAN Haskell Workshop*, volume 41(1) of *ENTCS*. Montreal, Canada, Elsevier Science, 2001.

15. J. Hughes. Generalising Monads to Arrows. *Science of Computer Programming*, 37:67–111, May 2000.

16. G. Krasner and S. Pope. A cookbook for using the Model-View-Controller user interface paradigm in Smalltalk-80. *Journal of Object-Oriented Programming*, 1(3):26–49, August 1988.

17. A. Löh, D. Clarke, and J. Jeuring. Dependency-style Generic Haskell. In *Proceedings of the eighth ACM SIGPLAN International Conference on Functional Programming (ICFP'03)*, pages 141–152. ACM Press, 2003.

18. E. Meijer. Server Side Web Scripting in Haskell. *Journal of Functional Programming*, 10(1):1–18, 2000.

19. R. Milner, M. Tofte, R. Harper, and D. MacQueen. *The Definition of Standard ML (Revised)*. MIT Press, 1997.

20. R. Plasmeijer and P. Achten. The Implementation of iData - A Case Study in Generic Programming. In A. Butterfield, editor, *Proceedings Implementation and Application of Functional Languages, 17th International Workshop, IFL05*, Dublin, Ireland, September 19-21 2005. Technical Report No: TCD-CS-2005-60.

21. R. Plasmeijer and M. van Eekelen. *Concurrent CLEAN Language Report (version 2.0)*, December 2001. http://www.cs.ru.nl/~clean/.

22. C. Queinnec. The influence of browsers on evaluators or, continuations to program web servers. In *Proceedings Fifth International Conference on Functional Programming (ICFP'00)*, Sept. 2000.

23. P. Thiemann. WASH/CGI: Server-side Web Scripting with Sessions and Typed, Compositional Forms. In S. Krishnamurthi and C. Ramakrishnan, editors, *Practical Aspects of Declarative Languages: 4th International Symposium, PADL 2002*, volume 2257 of *LNCS*, pages 192–208, Portland, OR, USA, January 19-20 2002. Springer-Verlag.

24. P. Thiemann. A Typed Representation for HTML and XML Documents in Haskell. *Journal of Functional Programming*, 2005. Under consideration for publication.

25. A. van Weelden, S. Smetsers, and R. Plasmeijer. A Generic Approach to Syntax Tree Operations. In A. Butterfield, editor, *Proceedings Implementation and Application of Functional Languages, 17th International Workshop, IFL05*, Dublin, Ireland, September 19-21 2005. Technical Report No: TCD-CS-2005-60.

26. M. Wallace and C. Runciman. Haskell and XML: Generic combinators or type-based translation? In *Proc. of the Fourth ACM SIGPLAN Intnl. Conference on Functional Programming (ICFP'99)*, volume 34-9, pages 148–159, N.Y., 1999. ACM.

Appendix

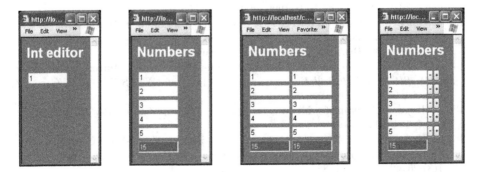

Fig. 1. Screen shots of the initial state of the toy examples in Sect. 2. **(a)** A simple integer iData. **(b)** Summing the value of iData. **(c)** Sharing iData. **(d)** Model-View separation of iData.

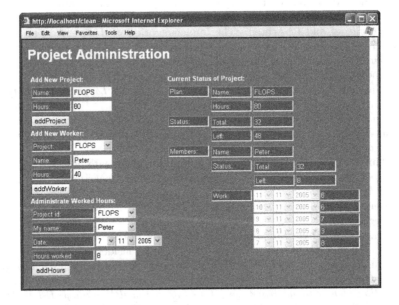

Fig. 2. Screen shot of the project administration case study in Sect. 3

Crossing State Lines:
Adapting Object-Oriented Frameworks
to Functional Reactive Languages*

Daniel Ignatoff, Gregory H. Cooper, and Shriram Krishnamurthi

Computer Science Department,
Brown University
{dignatof, greg, sk}@cs.brown.edu

Abstract. Functional reactive programming integrates dynamic dataflow with functional programming to offer an elegant and powerful model for expressing computations over time-varying values. Developing realistic applications, however, requires access to libraries, such as those for GUIs, that are written in mainstream object-oriented languages. Previous work has developed functional reactive interfaces for GUI toolkits but has not provided an account of the principles underlying the implementation strategy.

In this paper, we investigate this problem by studying the adaptation of the object-oriented toolkit MrEd to the functional reactive language FrTime. The heart of this problem is how to communicate state changes between the application and the toolkit's widget objects. After presenting a basic strategy for adaptation, we discuss abstraction techniques based on mixins and macros that allow us to adapt numerous properties in many widget classes with minimal code duplication. This results in a wrapper for the entire MrEd toolkit in only a few hundred lines of code. We also briefly discuss a spreadsheet developed with the resulting toolkit.

1 Introduction

Functional reactive programming (FRP) extends a general-purpose functional language with abstractions for expressing values that change over time. By combining the features of dataflow and higher-order functional programming, it supports concise, declarative descriptions of reactive and interactive systems. This paper specifically uses the language FrTime [3] (pronounced "father time"), an embedding of FRP in the DrScheme [7] programming environment. FrTime pursues a push-driven evaluation strategy that permits incremental program development (e.g., in a read-eval-print loop) formulated atop the eager semantics of Scheme.

While FRP provides an elegant notation for specifying the computational core of systems, application developers need more: they also must be able to use standard libraries for graphics, user interfaces, networking, and so on. These libraries have several important characteristics. First, they tend to be large and detailed, so it is impractical to rewrite them. Second, they are maintained by third-party developers, so they should

---

* This work is partially supported by NSF grant CCR-0305949.

M. Hagiya and P. Wadler (Eds.): FLOPS 2006, LNCS 3945, pp. 259–276, 2006.

be integrated with a minimum of modification to enable easy upgrading. Third, these libraries—especially for GUIs—are often written in object-oriented (OO) languages. The integration process must therefore handle this style, and ideally exploit it. An important subtlety is that OO and FRP languages have different notions of state: OO *makes state explicit but encapsulates it, whereas state in FRP is hidden from the programmer by the temporal abstractions of the language.* Somehow, these two representations of state must be reconciled.

We have made considerable progress on this integration problem for the specific case of GUIs. The DrScheme environment provides a large and robust GUI library called MrEd [8], based on the wxWindows framework, which is used to build DrScheme's interface itself. The environment is a good representative of a library that meets the characteristics listed above; furthermore, its integration is of immediate practical value. We have discovered several useful abstractions based on *mixins* [2] (classes parameterized over their super-classes) that enable a seamless integration. We have further found that there are patterns to these mixins and abstracted over them using *macros* [10]. As a consequence, the adapter for MrEd is under 400 lines of code.

This paper may appear on the surface to describe work similar to the FranTk [14] and Fruit [4] projects, and in fact the interface we develop for MrEd is similar in spirit to the ones developed for those systems. However, those other systems focus on the design of a programmer's interface for building GUI applications in a functional reactive language. In contrast, our work addresses the lower-level, largely orthogonal issue of importing legacy object-oriented frameworks into an FRP system. Our primary example also happens to be GUI libraries, as these have direct practical applicability and are sufficiently complex to make an interesting case study. However, the ideas we present are not specific to GUI libraries. If anything, adapting other kinds of libraries should be even easier, given the highly imperative nature of GUIs.

This paper is organized as follows. First, we present the implementation of a small GUI application in MrEd, which we use to illustrate some of the difficulties posed by the standard object-oriented GUI programming model. Next we provide a brief overview of FrTime, whose notion of *signals* offers a more natural, declarative mechanism for modeling state. We then discuss the design philosophy that governs our adaptation of MrEd to a signal-based programming interface. The heart of the paper is a description of our implementation of this interface and of the abstractions that capture the essence of the adaptation. We talk briefly about a spreadsheet application built with the adapted toolkit, then discuss related work and provide concluding remarks.

2   GUI Construction with an Object-Oriented Toolkit

We walk through the process of writing a small GUI application in MrEd, the standard GUI library included with the extended object-oriented language supported by DrScheme. MrEd resembles the OO GUI libraries of languages like C++ and Java.

The application we develop is a simple timer; it counts seconds for a user-specified time, displaying the elapsed time both graphically and textually. Figure 1 shows the entire code, which we explain incrementally.

```
(define frame (new frame% [label "Timer"] [height 80] [width 300] [alignment '(left top)]))
(define gauge (new gauge% [parent frame] [label "Elapsed Time"] [range 60]))
(define message (new message% [parent frame] [label "0 s"] [stretchable-width true]))
(define slider
   (new slider% [parent frame] [label "Duration (s)"]
                [min-value 30] [max-value 120] [init-value 60]
                [callback (λ (s e) (send gauge set-range (send slider get-value)))]))
(define button (new button% [parent frame] [label "Reset"]
                             [callback (λ (b e) (set! elapsed 0))]))

(define elapsed 0)
(define (loop)
   (when (< elapsed (send slider get-value))
      (send gauge set-value elapsed)
      (send message set-label (format "~a s" elapsed))
      (sleep/yield 1)
      (set! elapsed (add1 elapsed))
      (loop)))
(send frame show #t)
(loop)
```

Fig. 1. A simple timer application in Scheme with MrEd, with a screenshot at the lower right

First, we create a window. In MrEd, a normal top-level window is called a *frame%*.[1]
A **new** expression constructs an object of a given type with a set of named parameters,
in this case the label, dimensions, and alignment. We next create gauge and message
widgets as children of the window. The gauge is to display the elapsed time as a colored
bar, and the message to present the same information textually.

We then add a slider that lets the user adjust the timer's duration. The slider needs
a parent and a label like the other controls, along with a range. Whenever the user
adjusts the duration through the slider, we need to update the gauge's range accordingly.
The toolkit provides a *callback* for this purpose, which lets the application register a
procedure to be executed whenever the user interacts with a widget.

The last widget is a reset button, which also takes a callback procedure. In this case,
the callback simply resets the elapsed time to 0. After creating the widgets, we tell the
window to display itself (and its contents) by invoking the *show* method. We then write
a loop to count out the duration and keep the gauge and message widgets up to date.

2.1 Evaluating the GUI Coding Style

This simple example gives a sense of the nature of GUI programming. Even in a mostly
functional language like Scheme, the programming style is very imperative. In particular, the need to handle values that change over time forces the programmer to use mutation and other side-effecting operations. The application needs to know when its values
change so it can update the properties of widgets, and it needs to register callbacks so it
can find out when widget properties change and accordingly update its internal state.

---

[1] By convention, class names in DrScheme end with a % sign, suggesting object-orientation.

All these callbacks and imperative operations tend to invert and obscure the system's structure and data dependencies. For example, the contents of the gauge and message depend on the variable *elapsed*, but this relationship is not apparent from the widgets' definitions. Instead, the loop body is responsible for updating the widgets, so we need to examine *it* to understand the behavior of all the widgets. Similarly, the range of the gauge depends on the value of the slider, but gauge's definition does not express this relationship; instead, the slider's callback invokes methods on the gauge to keep it up-to-date. In general, when an object's state depends on external mutation, reasoning about its behavior requires awareness of all invocations that target the object. This *structural inversion* is a serious impediment to understanding and maintaining the code. For example, if a developer adds, modifies, or removes a widget, then he must be sure to identify and properly update all of its referents.

3   FrTime

Much of the complexity of GUI programming arises from the lack of linguistic support for modeling values that change over time. This is what necessitates the use of imperative state, with the resulting inversion of program structure and increase in complexity.

The goal of dataflow programming is to support the modeling of change. Dataflow languages introduce a concept of *signals*, or time-varying values. This idea has been revived in a recent line of work called functional reactive programming (FRP) [6, 13], which merges dataflow with higher-order functional programming. We have developed an implementation of FRP for DrScheme [7] called FrTime [3].

FrTime publishes a signal called *seconds*, which represents the current time as an integral number of seconds. We can project its value at any moment by asking for its **value-now**. This returns the current constant integer value of the signal. We can also use *seconds* to build new signals; for example, (*even? seconds*) alternates between **true** and **false** every second.

We can model the elapsed time in our application by computing the difference between the current value of *seconds* and its value when the count started. We express this in code with (− *seconds* (**value-now** *seconds*)), where (**value-now** *seconds*) returns a constant, and subtracting it from *seconds* yields a new signal that starts at 0 and increments every second. Because we use signals, the language automatically keeps them up-to-date. Otherwise we would need to keep track of the passage of time (e.g., with a timer or *sleep* command) and manually update all the variables that (transitively) depend on it. These tasks are tedious to perform manually and prone to errors.

The signals we've described so far are all examples of *behaviors*, which mean they have a value at every point in time after their creation. Behaviors correspond naturally to the values of many GUI widgets. For example, a gauge renders a time-varying integer, and a message displays a time-varying string. Likewise, a slider lets the user manipulate a time-varying integer, and a text field lets him edit a time-varying string.

Signals may also take the form of *event sources*, which carry streams of discrete values called *occurrences*. For example, FrTime's animation library provides event sources called *mouse-clicks* and *key-strokes*, which carry the mouse clicks and key strokes cap-

```
(define frame (new ft-frame% [label "Timer"] [width 200] [height 80] [visible true]))
(define slider (new ft-slider% [label "Duration"] [min-value 15] [max-value 60]))
(define button (new ft-button% [label "Reset"]))
(define duration (send slider get-value-b) )
(define last-click-time ;; initially holds application's start time
    (hold (map-e (send button get-clicks) (λ (_) (value-now seconds)))
        (value-now seconds)))
(define elapsed (min duration (- seconds last-click-time)))
(define gauge (new ft-gauge% [label "Elapsed time:"] [range duration]
                [parent frame] [value elapsed] ))
(define message (new ft-message% [label (format "~a s" elapsed)]
                [parent frame] [min-width 50]))
```

Fig. 2. Implementation of the timer in FrTime

tured by a given window. FrTime also provides a collection of event-processing combinators that are analogous to list-processing routines. For example, *filter-e* removes unwanted occurrences from an event stream, while *map-e* transforms each value by applying a given function.

FrTime provides several primitives for converting between behaviors and event streams. One is *changes*, which consumes a behavior and returns an event source that emits the new value each time the behavior changes. Conversely, *hold* consumes an event source and returns a behavior that reflects the last event occurrence value; *hold* also takes an optional initial value to use until the first event occurs. For example, if a program applies *hold* to *key-strokes*, the result is a behavior whose value indicates the last key pressed.

Widgets like buttons and menu items support interaction through discrete events rather than manipulation of continuous values. Thus they correspond naturally to FrTime event streams instead of behaviors. We can use standard FrTime operators to construct behaviors from these event streams. For example, from a stream of button clicks, we can define a behavior that reflects the time of the last click. We express this by mapping a procedure that projects the current time over the stream of clicks (ignoring the click event's *void* value); *hold*ing the resulting stream yields the time of the last click. We provide *hold* with the program's start time, which is the value until the first click. The code is as follows:

```
(define last-click-time
    (hold (map-e (send button get-clicks) (λ (_) (value-now seconds)))
        (value-now seconds)))
```

This definition plays an important role in the program shown in Fig. 2, which presents a FrTime implementation of the timer using the ideas of this paper. The new version is free of callbacks and imperative method invocations. Instead, input widgets like the slider and button provide behaviors and events that reflect the user's interactions, and output widgets like the gauge and message allow the application to provide behaviors that specify property values for their entire lifespan. We draw a box around code that participates in the interface between signals and widgets.

4   Adapting MrEd to FrTime

In Sect. 2 we introduced MrEd, an object-oriented toolkit for building GUIs, and presented a simple example to illustrate some of the difficulties imposed by the standard GUI programming model. In Sect. 3 we presented FrTime, a language that extends DrScheme with support for first-class signals, and we showed how this new feature provides a suitable abstraction for modeling change, which is an important problem in interactive GUI applications. In this section, we put the pieces together and show how to adapt MrEd so that its interface is based on FrTime's behaviors and events.

Recall that we are trying to import a large legacy class framework in a manner consistent with the goals set forth in the Introduction. We wish to reuse the existing implementation as much as possible and perform a minimum of manual adaptation. In order to minimize the manual effort, we need to uncover patterns and abstract over them. In this case, the main problem we must address is how to communicate state changes between the object-oriented and functional reactive models.

The functional reactive world represents state implicitly through time-varying values, and the dataflow mechanism is responsible for keeping it consistent. In contrast, the object-oriented world models state with mutable fields, and programmers are responsible for writing methods that keep them consistent. We presume that the toolkit implementors have done this correctly, so our job is simply to translate state changes from the dataflow program into appropriate method invocations. However, since GUI toolkits also mediate changes coming from the user, they provide a callback mechanism by which the application can monitor state changes. The interface between the GUI and FrTime must therefore also translate callbacks into state changes in the dataflow world.

Not surprisingly, the nature of the adaptation depends primarily upon the direction of communication. We classify each widget property according to whether the application or the toolkit changes its state. The most interesting case, naturally, is when both of them can change the state. We now discuss each case separately.

4.1   Application-Mutable Properties

MrEd allows the application to change many of a widget's properties, including its value, label, cursor, margins, minimum dimensions, and stretchability. A widget provides an accessor and mutator method for each of these properties, but the toolkit never changes any of them itself, so we classify these properties as "application-mutable."

In a functional reactive setting, we can manipulate time-varying values directly, so it is natural to model such properties with behaviors. For example, we would use a behavior to specify a gauge's value and range and a message's label. This sort of interface renders accessors and mutators unnecessary, since the property automatically updates whenever the behavior changes, and the application can observe it by reading whatever behavior it used for initialization.

To implement a behavior-based interface to such widget properties, the first step is to derive a subclass from the original MrEd widget. For example, we can define a *ft-gauge%* from the MrEd gauge.

> (**define** *ft-gauge%*
>   (**class** *gauge%* ...))

In the new class, we want to provide constructor arguments that expect behaviors for all of the application-mutable properties. In FrTime, behaviors extend the universe of values, and any constant may be taken as a special case of a behavior (that never changes); i.e., behaviors are supertypes of constants. Thus the application may safely supply constants for any properties that it wishes not to change. Moreover, if we use the same property names as the superclass, then we can construct an *ft-gauge%* exactly as we would construct an ordinary gauge. This respects the principle of contravariance for function subtyping: our extension broadens the types of legal constructor arguments.

In fact, the DrScheme class system allows us to override the superclass's initialization arguments, or **init-fields**. Of course, the superclass still refers to the original fields, so its behavior remains unchanged, but this lets us extend the constructor interface to permit behaviors. The code to add these initialization arguments is as follows:

> (**init-field** *value label range vert-margin horiz-margin min-width* ...)

Next, we need code to enforce consistency between these behavioral fields and the corresponding fields in the superclass. The first step is to perform superclass initialization, using the current values of the new fields as the initial values for the old ones. Although the old and new versions of the fields have the same names, there is no ambiguity in the superclass instantiation expression; in each name/value pair, the name refers to a field in the superclass, and the value expression uses the subclass's scope.

> (**super-instantiate** () [*label* (**value-now** *label*)] [*range* (**value-now** *range*)] ...)
> (**send this** *set-value* (**value-now** *value*))

(Since there is no initial *value* field in the superclass, we need to set it separately after super-class initialization.)

Having set appropriate initial values for the fields, we need to ensure that they stay consistent as the behaviors change. That is, we need to translate changes in state from the dataflow program to the object-oriented "real world." This is a central problem in building an interface between the two models.

The basic idea behind our translation is straightforward: detect changes in a behavior and update the state of the corresponding object through an appropriate method call. We use the FrTime primitive *changes* to detect changes in a behavior and expose them on an event stream. Then we convert the event stream into a series of method invocations. This second step is somewhat unusual, since the methods have side effects, unlike the operations found in a typical dataflow model. However, in this case we are concerned not with *defining* the model but with *communicating* its state to the outside world. The effects are therefore both safe (they do not interfere with the purity of the model) and necessary (there is no other way to tell the rest of the world about the system's changing state).

The invocation of imperative methods is technically trivial. Since FrTime is built atop Scheme, any procedure that updates a signal is free to execute arbitrary Scheme code, including operations with side effects. Of course, we ordinarily avoid the practice of performing side effects in signal processors, since it could lead to the violation of program invariants. As mentioned above, it is safe when the effects are restricted to communication with the outside world (as they are in this case). In particular, we use the primitive *map-e*, passing a procedure that invokes the desired method:

> (*map-e* (λ (*v*) (**send this** *set-value v*)) (*changes value*))
> (*map-e* (λ (*v*) (**send this** *set-label v*)) (*changes label*))
> . . .

Each call above to *map-e* creates a new event stream, whose occurrences all carry the *void* value—the return value of the imperative method call—but are accompanied by the method's side effects. Because the event values are all *void*, they have no meaningful use within a larger dataflow program.

The above expressions are static initializers in the widget classes, so they are evaluated whenever the application constructs a new instance. Using static initializers allows the adapter to automatically forward updates without the developer having to invoke a method to initiate this. Because the code constructs signals, which participate in the dataflow computation, it therefore has a dynamic effect throughout the life of the widget, unlike typical static initializers.

Subtleties Involving Side-Effecting Signals

We have resolved the interface for communicating state changes from the dataflow to the object-oriented model. However, a more serious concern is the mismatch between their notions of *timing*. In a typical object-oriented program, method invocations are synchronous, which fixes the ordering of operations within each thread of control. However, FrTime processes updates according to their data dependencies, which does not necessarily correspond to a sequential evaluation order. This makes it difficult for programmers to reason about when effects occur.

Fortunately, the functional reactive model and interface are designed in such a way as to prevent operations from occurring unpredictably. Most importantly, there is at most one signal associated with any given widget property, so there is no contention over who is responsible for keeping it up-to-date. Secondly, FrTime processes updates in order of data dependencies, so if one property's signal depends on another's, then it will be updated *later*. If the order of updates were significant, then this would seem to be the "safe" order in which to do things, assuming that the application's data dependencies reflect similar dependencies in the toolkit.

There is, however, a problem with the strategy described above that is difficult to diagnose and debug. The symptoms are as follows: at first, the program seems to work just fine. Sometimes it may run successfully to completion. Other times, depending upon what else is happening, it runs for a while, then suddenly and seemingly without explanation the gauge's properties stop updating when the behaviors change. The point at which it stops varies from run to run, but there are never any error messages.

The problem results from an interaction with the memory manager. An ordinary FRP application would use the event source returned by the *map-e*, but in this case we only care about side effects, so we neglect to save the result. Since there are no references to the updating event source, the garbage collector eventually reclaims it, and the gauge stops reacting to changes in the behavior.

To avoid these problems, we define a new abstraction specifically for side-effecting event processors. This abstraction, called *for-each-e!*, works just like *map-e*, except that it ensures its result will not be collected. It also lends itself to a more efficient implementation, since it can throw away the results of the procedure calls instead of enqueuing them on a new event stream.

The *for-each-e!* implementation stores references to the imperative event processors in a hash table, indexed by the objects they update. It is important that this hash table hold its keys with weak references so that, if there are no other references to the widget, both it and the event processor may be reclaimed.

4.2   Toolkit-Mutable Properties

Some widget properties are controlled primarily by the user or the toolkit rather than the application. For example, when the user resizes a window, the toolkit adjusts the locations and dimensions of the widgets inside. Since the application cannot control these properties directly, the widgets provide accessor methods but no mutators. Additionally, the application may want to be notified of changes in a property. For example, when a drawing canvas changes size, the application may need to update its content or recompute parameters for its scrollbars. For such scenarios, accessor methods alone are insufficient, and toolkits provide callback interfaces as described in the previous section. However, we saw that callbacks lead to an imperative programming style with various pitfalls, so we would like to support an alternative approach.

For such "toolkit-mutable" properties, we can remove the dependency on callbacks by adding a method that returns the property's time-varying value as a behavior. For example, instead of allowing registration *on-size* and *on-move* callbacks, the toolkit would provide methods that return behaviors reflecting the properties for all subsequent points in time.

The implementation of such methods is similar to that for application-mutable properties. However, in this case we cannot just override the existing *get-width*, *get-height*, *get-x*, and *get-y* methods and make them return behaviors. Though FrTime allows programmers to use behaviors just like constants, an application may need to pass a widget to a library procedure written in raw Scheme. (For example, the widget may need to invoke methods in its superclass, which is implemented in Scheme.) If a Scheme expression invokes an accessor and receives a behavior, there is nothing FrTime can do to prevent a type-mismatch error. Since behaviors are supertypes of constants, overriding in this manner would violate the principle of covariance for procedure return values.

To preserve type safety, we must define the new signal-aware methods so as not to conflict with the existing ones. We choose the new names by appending *-b* to the existing names, suggesting the behavioral nature of the return values. Again, we derive a subclass of the widget class we want to wrap. For example, continuing with the *ft-gauge%*, we would add methods called *get-width-b get-height-b*, *get-x-b*, and *get-y-b*.

We need to determine how to construct the behaviors returned by these methods. We want these behaviors to change with the corresponding widget properties, and we know that the widget's *on-size* or *on-move* method will be called when the properties change. So, we are now faced with the converse of the previous problem—converting a imperative procedure call into an observable FrTime event.

FrTime provides an interface for achieving this goal, called *make-event-receiver*. This procedure returns two values: an event source e and a unary procedure *send-event$_e$*. Whenever the application executes (*send-event$_e$ v*), the value v occurs on e. In the implementation, *send-event$_e$* sends a message to the FrTime dataflow engine indicating that v should occur on e, which leads to v's being enqueued on the stream of e's occurrences. By overriding the widget's callbacks and calling *make-event-receiver*, we can create an event source carrying changes to the widget's properties:

```
(define-values (width-e send-width) (make-event-receiver))
(define-values (height-e send-height) (make-event-receiver))
(define/override (on-size w h)
  (super on-size w h)
  (send-width w)
  (send-height h))
;; similarly for position
```

Once we have the changes to these properties in the form of FrTime event sources, we convert them to behaviors with *hold*:

```
(define/public (get-width-b) (hold width-e (send this get-width)))
(define/public (get-height-b) (hold height-e (send this get-height)))
. . .
```

4.3   Application- and Toolkit-Mutable Properties

We have discussed how to adapt properties that are mutable by *either* the toolkit or the application, but many properties require mutability by *both* the toolkit and the application. This need usually arises because there are several ways to change the same property, or several views of the same information. For example, a text editor provides scrollbars so the user can navigate a long document, but the user can also navigate with the keyboard, in which case the application needs to update the scrollbars accordingly.

All widgets that allow user input also provide a way to set the value from the application. Several other properties may be set by either the toolkit or the user:

Focus. When the user clicks on a widget, it receives *focus* (meaning that it hears key strokes) and invokes its *on-focus* callback method. This is the common mode of operation, but the application can also explicitly send focus to a widget. For example, when a user makes a choice to enter text, the application may automatically give the text field focus for the user's convenience.

Visibility. The application may hide and show widgets at various stages of an interactive computation. Since *show*ing a widget also shows all of its descendents, the toolkit provides an *on-enable* callback so the application does not need to track ancestry. In addition, the user can affect visibility by, for example, closing a window, which hides all of its children.

Ability. Similar to visibility, the application can selectively enable and disable widgets depending upon their necessity to various kinds of interaction. Enabling also works transitively, so the toolkit invokes the *on-enable* method for all children of a newly-enabled widget.

One might naturally ask, since we have already discussed how to adapt application- and toolkit-mutable properties, why we cannot simply combine the two adaptation strategies for these hybrid properties. The reason is that the application specifies a property's time-varying value through a behavior, which defines the value at every point in the widget's lifespan. This leaves no gaps for another entity to specify the value.

Our solution to this problem is to use event sources in addition to behaviors. Recall that in the implementation of toolkit-mutable properties, we first constructed an event source from callback invocations, then used hold to create a behavior. In this case, both the application and toolkit provide event streams, and instead of holding directly, we merge the streams and hold the result to determine the final value:

```
(init-field app-focus app-enable app-show)
(define-values (user-focus send-focus) (make-event-receiver))
(define/public (has-focus-b?)
   (hold (merge-e app-focus user-focus) (send this has-focus?)))
(define/override (on-focus on?)
   (super on-focus on?)
   (send-focus on?))
 ...
```

This code completely replaces the fragments shown previously for properties that are mutable by only the application or the toolkit.

4.4   Immutable Properties

MrEd does not allow certain properties to change once a widget is created. For example, every non-window widget has a parent, and it cannot be moved from one parent to another. In theory, we could build a library atop MrEd in which we simulated the mutability of these properties. However, this would be a significant change to not only the toolkit's interface but also its functionality, and we would have to implement it ourselves. Since our goal is to reify the existing toolkit through a cleaner interface, we have not attempted to extend the underlying functionality.

5   Automating the Transformation

We have so far discussed how to replace the imperative interface to object-oriented widget classes with a more elegant and declarative one based on behaviors and events. The problem is that there is a large number of such widgets and properties, and dealing with all of them by hand is a time-consuming and tedious task. Thus we look to reduce the manual effort by automating as much as possible of the transformation process.

The reader may have noticed that the code presented in the previous section is highly repetitive. There are actually two sources of repetition. The first is that we need to perform many of the same adaptations for all of the MrEd widget classes, of which there are perhaps a dozen. The second is that the code used to adapt each property is essentially the same from one property to the next. We now discuss how to remedy these two forms of duplication individually, by abstracting first over multiple widget classes, then over multiple properties within each class.

5.1 Parameterized Class Extensions

In Sect. 4 we adapted a collection of widget properties by sub-classing. Since most of the code in the subclasses is essentially the same across the framework, we would like to be able to reuse the common parts without copying code. In other words, we would like a class extension parameterized over its superclass.

The DrScheme object system allows creation of *mixins* [2, 9], which are precisely such parameterized subclasses. We write a mixin to encapsulate the adaptation of each property, then apply the mixins to all classes possessing the properties. For example, instead of defining an *ft-gauge%* like we did before, we define a generic class extension to adapt a particular property, such as the label:

```
(define (adapt-label a-widget)
  (class  a-widget
    (init-field label)
    (super-instantiate () [label (value-now label)])
    (for-each-e! (changes label) (λ (v) (send this set-label v)) this)))
```

In the code snippet above, we box the superclass position of the class definition to highlight that it is a variable rather than the literal name of a class. This parameterization makes it possible to abstract over the base widget class and thus to apply the adaptation to multiple widgets.

We write mixins for other properties in a similar manner. Since there are several properties common to all widget classes, we compose all of them into a single mixin:

```
(define (adapt-common-properties a-widget)
  (foldl (λ (mixin cls) (mixin cls)) a-widget (list adapt-label adapt-enabling ...)))
```

Although this procedure contains no explicit **class** definitions, it is still a mixin: it applies a collection of smaller class extensions to the input class. This *compound* mixin takes a raw MrEd widget class and applies a mixin for each standard property. The resulting class provides a consistent FrTime interface for all of these properties. For example, we can use this mixin to adapt several widget classes:

```
(define pre-gauge% (adapt-common-properties gauge%))
(define pre-message% (adapt-common-properties message%))
...
```

We call the resulting widget classes "pre-" widgets because they still await the adaptation of widget-specific properties. Most importantly, each widget supports manipulation of a particular kind of value (e.g., boolean, integer, string) by either the application or the toolkit, and the various combinations give rise to different programmer interfaces.

5.2   A Second Dimension of Abstraction

Mixins allow us to avoid copying code across multiple classes. However, there is also code duplication across mixins. In Sect. 4, we develop patterns for adaptation that depend on whether the property is mutable by the application, the toolkit, or both. Once we determine the proper pattern, instantiating it only requires identification of the field and method names associated with the pattern. However, in Sect. 4 we duplicated the pattern for each property.

In most programming languages, we would have no choice but to copy code in this situation. This is because languages don't often provide a mechanism for abstracting over field and method names, as these are program syntax, not values. However, Scheme provides a *macro system* [10] with which we can abstract over program syntax. For example, with application-mutable properties we only need to know the name of the field and mutator method, and we can generate an appropriate mixin:

> (**define-syntax adapt-app-mutable-property**
>   (**syntax-rules** ()
>   [(_ *field mutator*)
>   (λ (*widget*)
>   (**class** *widget*
>   (**init-field** *field*)
>   (**super-instantiate** () [*field* (**value-now** *field*)])
>   (*for-each-e!* (*changes field*) (λ (*v*) (**send this** *mutator v*)) **this**)))]))

With this macro, we can generate mixins for the application-mutable properties:

> (**define** *adapt-label* (**adapt-app-mutable-property** *label set-label*))
> (**define** *adapt-vert-margin* (**adapt-app-mutable-property** *vert-margin vert-margin*))
> . . .

Of course, we write similar macros that handle the other two cases of mutability and instantiate them to produce a full set of mixins for all of the properties found in MrEd's widget classes. At this point, we have fully abstracted the principles governing the toolkit's adaptation to a functional reactive interface and captured them concisely in a collection of macros. By instantiating these macros with the appropriate properties, we obtain mixins that adapt the properties for actual widgets. We compose and apply these mixins to the original MrEd widget classes, yielding new widget classes with interfaces based on behaviors and events.

The ability to compose the generated mixins safely depends upon two properties of the toolkit's structure. Firstly, most properties have distinct names for their fields and methods and hence are non-interfering by design. Secondly, in cases where two properties *do* share a common entity (for example, the single callback *on-size* affects the width and height), the disciplined use of inheritance (i.e., always calling **super**) ensures that one adaptation will not conflict with the other.

To save space and streamline the presentation, we have simplified some of the code snippets in this paper. The full implementation has been included with the DrScheme distribution since release version 301. We provide a catalog of adapted widgets in an appendix. The core contains about 80 lines of macro definitions and 300 lines of

Scheme code. This is relatively concise, considering that the MrEd toolkit consists of approximately 10,000 lines of Scheme code, which in turn provides an interface to a 100,000-line C++ library. Moreover, our strategy satisfies the criteria set forth in the Introduction: it is a pure interface extension and does not require modifications to the library.

5.3   Language Dependencies

The abstractions we have presented depend heavily on two features of DrScheme: mixins and macros. These features have analogs in other languages. For instance, Smalltalk has recently seen a series of work on *traits* [15], which are similar to mixins and sufficient for our needs. Similarly, C++ programmers have long used the template facility to parameterize classes [17]. Likewise, hygienic macro systems have been defined for a variety of languages including C [18], Java [1] and Haskell [16]. In addition, the use of macros here could potentially also be simulated using features such as meta-classes.

6   A Spreadsheet Application

To evaluate our adapted version of MrEd, we have applied it to a realistic spreadsheet application. The major challenges in building a spreadsheet, in our experience, are implementing a language with its dataflow semantics and managing a large array of cells. Fortunately, FrTime makes the linguistic problem relatively straightforward, since we can reuse its dataflow mechanism to implement update propagation. This leaves the representation and display of the cell grid.

The core of our spreadsheet user interface is an extension of the MrEd *canvas* widget (which we have not discussed so far). A canvas is a region in which the application can listen to key and mouse events and perform arbitrary drawing operations. We render the cell content into a canvas and process mouse events to perform selection. When the user selects a cell, he can enter a formula into a text field, and the selected cell receives the value of the formula.

The functional reactivity helps greatly, for example, in managing the scrolling of the grid content. The canvas includes a pair of scrollbars, which must be configured with ranges and page sizes. These parameters depend upon the number of cells that fit within the physical canvas, which depends upon the size of the canvas relative to the size of the cells. The cell size depends in turn upon the font and margins used when rendering the text. Since the user can resize the window or change the font, these parameters must be kept up-to-date dynamically. In raw MrEd, we would need to manage all of the recomputation by hand, but with the FrTime adaptation, we simply specify the functional relationships between the time-varying values, and the various widget properties update automatically. As a result, the code is largely a functional specification of the model of the spreadsheet; this is absent in a traditional object-oriented implementation because of the structural inversion introduced by the use of callbacks.

As an illustrative example, consider the following snippet of code, which shows the definition of a text field into which the user can type cell formulas:

```
(define formula
  (new ft-text-field%
    [label "Formula:"]
    [content-e (map-e (λ (addr) (value-now (cell-text (addr→key addr))) )₁
                      select-e))]
    [focus-e select-e] ₂))
```

When the user clicks on a cell, the cell's address appears on an event stream called *select-e*. The occurrence of the selection event affects *formula* in two ways. First, the code in box 1 retrieves the selected cell's text from the spreadsheet; this text becomes *formula*'s new content. Second, the code in box 2 specifies that selection events send focus to *formula*, allowing the user to edit the text. When the user finishes editing and presses the *enter* key, *formula* emits its content on an output event stream; the application processes the event and interprets the associated text (code not shown).

The spreadsheet experiment has proven valuable in several respects. First, by employing a significant fragment of the MrEd framework, it has helped us exercise many of our adapters and establish that the abstractions do not adversely affect performance. Second, as a representative GUI program, it has helped us identify several subtleties of FRP and the adaptation of state, some of which we have discussed in this paper. Finally, the spreadsheet is an interesting application in its own right, since the language of the cells is FrTime itself, enabling the construction of powerful spreadsheet programs.

7 Related Work

The use of dataflow in a GUI toolkit has been well-studied. The Garnet [11] and Amulet [12] projects were two early C++ toolkits that included a notion of dataflow. More recently, the FranTk [14] system adapted the Tk toolkit to a programmer interface based on the notions of behaviors and events in Fran [6]. However, FranTk still had a somewhat imperative feel, especially with regard to creation of cyclic signal networks, which required the use of mutation in the application program. Fruit [4] explored the idea of purely functional user interfaces, implementing a signal-based programming interface atop the Swing [5] toolkit.

All of the previous work is concerned with the problem of designing the dataflow interface for the toolkit, and the emphasis is on the experience for the application programmer. We consider this to be fairly well understood. However, the problem of actually implementing such an interface is less well understood. Though all of these earlier systems have included a working implementation, we understand that their development has been ad hoc, and the subtle interaction between imperative toolkits and declarative dataflow systems has not been explained in the literature. Thus, to the best of our knowledge, ours is the first work to address this problem.

8 Conclusions and Future Work

We have explored the problem of adapting a legacy object-oriented GUI toolkit to an interface based on the concepts of behaviors and events from functional reactive programming. The key to this adaptation is understanding the direction in which various state changes flow: from the application to the toolkit, the toolkit to the application, or both ways. This depends upon the particular widget property that we are adapting.

Since there are many widget properties, many of which are common to many widgets, the implementation would ordinarily require a large amount of code duplication. However, in Scheme, we are able to distill the adaptation to its most abstract essence. We express this as a set of three macros, which are parameterized over the names of the fields and methods that implement the various properties. We instantiate these macros to produce a collection of mixins—class fragments parameterized over their superclasses. By applying these to the base widget classes, we implement the full interface adaptation to our functional reactive language.

There are two main directions for future work, which complement each other. First, we plan to continue developing the spreadsheet beyond its current research-prototype stage and also to pursue different kinds of applications. This will help us to evaluate the FrTime language and our adaptation of the MrEd GUI toolkit. Second, new applications are likely to require the importation of other legacy frameworks, which will serve to validate the techniques presented in this paper and also to suggest refinements to them. As we co-opt more libraries, we expect FrTime to become an increasingly powerful platform for application development.

References

1. J. Bachrach and K. Playford. The Java syntactic extender. In *ACM SIGPLAN Conference on Object-Oriented Programming Systems, Languages & Applications*, pages 31–42, 2001.
2. G. Bracha and W. Cook. Mixin-based inheritance. In *ACM SIGPLAN Conference on Object-Oriented Programming Systems, Languages & Applications*, pages 303–311, 1990.
3. G. H. Cooper and S. Krishnamurthi. Embedding dynamic dataflow in a call-by-value language. In *European Symposium on Programming*, 2006.
4. A. Courtney and C. Elliott. Genuinely functional user interfaces. In *Haskell Workshop*, 2001.
5. R. Eckstein, M. Loy, and D. Wood. *Java Swing*. O'Reilly, 1997.
6. C. Elliott and P. Hudak. Functional reactive animation. In *ACM SIGPLAN International Conference on Functional Programming*, pages 263–277, 1997.
7. R. B. Findler, J. Clements, C. Flanagan, M. Flatt, S. Krishnamurthi, P. Steckler, and M. Felleisen. DrScheme: A programming environment for Scheme. *Journal of Functional Programming*, 12(2):159–182, 2002.
8. M. Flatt, R. B. Findler, S. Krishnamurthi, and M. Felleisen. Programming languages as operating systems (*or*, Revenge of the Son of the Lisp Machine). In *ACM SIGPLAN International Conference on Functional Programming*, pages 138–147, 1999.
9. M. Flatt, S. Krishnamurthi, and M. Felleisen. Classes and mixins. In *ACM SIGPLAN-SIGACT Symposium on Principles of Programming Languages*, pages 171–183, 1998.
10. E. E. Kohlbecker Jr. *Syntactic Extensions in the Programming Language Lisp*. PhD thesis, Indiana University, 1986.
11. B. A. Myers, D. A. Giuse, R. B. Dannenberg, D. S. Kosbie, E. Pervin, A. Mickish, B. V. Zanden, and P. Marchal. Garnet: Comprehensive support for graphical, highly interactive user interfaces. *Computer*, 23(11):71–85, 1990.

12. B. A. Myers, R. G. McDaniel, R. C. Miller, A. S. Ferrency, A. Faulring, B. D. Kyle, A. Mickish, A. Klimovitski, and P. Doane. The Amulet environment: New models for effective user interface software development. *IEEE Transactions on Software Engineering*, 23(6):347–365, 1997.

13. H. Nilsson, A. Courtney, and J. Peterson. Functional reactive programming, continued. In *ACM SIGPLAN Workshop on Haskell*, pages 51–64, 2002.

14. M. Sage. FranTk: A declarative GUI language for Haskell. In *ACM SIGPLAN International Conference on Functional Programming*, pages 106–117, 2000.

15. N. Schärli, S. Ducasse, O. Nierstrasz, and A. P. Black. Traits: Composable units of behavior. In *European Conference on Object-Oriented Programming*, pages 248–274, 2003.

16. T. Sheard and S. P. Jones. Template meta-programming for haskell. In *Proceedings of the ACM SIGPLAN workshop on Haskell*, pages 1–16, 2002.

17. M. VanHilst and D. Notkin. Using C++ templates to implement role-based designs. In *International Symposium on Object Technologies for Advanced Software*, pages 22–37, 1996.

18. D. Weise and R. Crew. Programmable syntax macros. In *ACM SIGPLAN Conference on Programming Language Design and Implementation*, pages 156–165, 1993.

Appendix: Adapted User Interface Widgets

ft-frame%. These objects implement top-level windows. They support all of the standard signal-based property interfaces (label, size, position, focus, visibility, ability, margins, minimum dimensions, stretchability, and mouse and keyboard input). As in the underlying *frame%* objects, the *label* property specifies the window's title.

ft-message%. These objects contain strings of text that are mutable by the application but not editable by the user. They support all of the standard signal-based property interfaces. In this case, the *label* property specifies the content of the message.

ft-menu-item%. These objects represent items in a drop-down or pop-up menu. In addition to the standard properties, each widget exposes an event stream that fires whenever the user chooses the item.

ft-button%. These objects represent clickable buttons. In addition to the standard properties, each widget exposes an event stream that fires each time the user clicks it.

ft-check-box%. These objects represent check-box widgets, whose state toggles between **true** and **false** with each click. In addition to the standard properties, each *ft-check-box%* widget exposes a boolean behavior that reflects its current state. The application may also specify an event stream whose occurrences set the state.

ft-radio-box%. These objects allow the user to select an item from a collection of textual or graphical options. In addition to the standard properties, each *ft-radio-box%* object exposes a numeric behavior indicating the current selection.

ft-choice%. These objects allow the user to select a subset of items from a list of textual options. In addition to the standard properties, each *ft-choice%* object exposes a list behavior containing the currently selected elements.

ft-list-box%. These objects are similar to *ft-choice%*, except that they support an additional, immutable *style* property that can be used to restrict selections to singleton sets or to change the default meaning of clicking on an item. Otherwise, the application's interface is the same as that of *ft-choice%*.

ft-slider%. These objects implement slider widgets, which allow the user to select a number within a given range by dragging an indicator along a track. In addition to the standard properties, each *ft-slider%* object allows the application to specify the range through a time-varying constructor argument called *range*, and it exposes a numeric behavior reflecting the current value selected by the user.

ft-text-field%. These objects implement user-editable text fields. In addition to the standard properties, each widget exposes the content of its text field as a behavior, as well as an event stream carrying the individual edit events. The application can also specify an event stream whose occurrences replace the text field content.

WASH Server Pages

Peter Thiemann

Universität Freiburg, Georges-Köhler-Allee 079,
D-79110 Freiburg, Germany
thiemann@informatik.uni-freiburg.de

Abstract. WASH is a Haskell library for server-side web scripting. It presents a session-based abstraction to the programmer which is implemented through a CGI program running a replay monad.

The present paper introduces a retargetted implementation of the WASH run-time system inside a web server. The run-time system supports uploading of WASH programs in source format to the running web server as well as a more efficient, multi-threaded execution model that eliminates the inefficient replay. In recapitulating the replay monad, we further present new operators that improve the efficiency of its log-based implementation.

1   Introduction

Server-side web programming is traditionally the realm of scripting languages like Perl, Python, and PHP. While it is quick and easy to develop web scripts in these language they tend to offer no static guarantees with respect to the run-time behavior of the scripts. In particular, there is no guarantee that

- the XML output produced by a script is well-formed and valid,
- the names of the input fields in a web form match the names required by the script processing the form,
- the values entered in a form have the types expected by the script, and
- the values stored in a session context are used at the right types and in the correct order.

Furthermore, the overall control flow must be implemented by manually performing a closure conversion [9]. One particularly nasty problem arises because HTTP, the underlying protocol of web applications, is stateless. While statelessness is great for scalability it falls short of supporting a session abstraction which is necessary for implementing interactive web applications. While most web programming systems provide support for sessions in the form of per-client state mappings on the server, there are well-known shortcomings with their usual implementation [6, 13].

These shortcomings have inspired the construction of better behaved systems that offer static guarantees and some sort of session model. Examples for such systems are[1]

---

[1] This list is intended to give an abridged overview of the systems and their features. Please see the WASH paper [13] for an in-depth discussion and comparison of their respective merits.

M. Hagiya and P. Wadler (Eds.): FLOPS 2006, LNCS 3945, pp. 277–293, 2006.
© Springer-Verlag Berlin Heidelberg 2006

- BigWig [1], a stand-alone domain-specific language that guarantees well-formed HTML output and imposes a rigid session discipline that incorporates a session-scoped variables (among other features);
- JWig [3], a reimplementation and retrofitting of BigWig's concepts on top of Java;
- MzScheme's library for interactive web programming [5], which allows for programming web applications with the standard control flow of a Scheme program just by using special I/O primitives; and
- WASH [13], the author's system that supports all features mentioned in the first paragraph (session abstraction, type safety, and field name matching).

The main contribution of the present paper is an implementation of WASH's session abstraction inside a Haskell web server[2]. The original implementation is based on CGI so that the new implementation improves the efficiency of existing WASH applications without requiring changes to their code. The main novelty is the representation of each session as a separate thread in the server. Similar to the run-time system of BigWig [1], this session thread handles the entire interaction with a particular user. The efficiency gain has two reasons. First, the thread implementation avoids the cost of repeated process creation caused by the invocation of a large CGI program (the compiled WASH application). Second, it avoids the cost of the replay monad used to implement sessions in past releases of the WASH system.

A secondary contribution is the exposition of a family of log-control operators that improve the efficiency of the log-based implementation of the replay monad for applications that have a particularly regular structure. These operators improve both the CGI-based and the thread-based implementations of WASH.

The paper starts off with a brief user-level introduction to WASH programming in general and the session abstraction in particular. Next, in Sec.3 it explains the essential differences between an external CGI-based execution model and an internal thread-based one. Section 4 recalls the original implementation of sessions using a replay monad and discusses ways of improving the efficiency of this implementation by providing operators inspired by control operators. Section 5 explains the implementation of sessions using threads and their coordination. Section 6 discusses the idea of having mixed execution models with both dedicated threads and replay. The remaining Sec.7 contains further implementation details, Sec.8 reports measurements, Sec.9 discusses further related work, and Sec.10 concludes.

2   Programming with WASH

Programming a web application with WASH is similar to writing a GUI application with a very simple style of interaction. A GUI application constructs its visual skin by combining widgets into a widget tree. Each widget controls a

---

[2] All software described in this paper is available on `http://www.informatik.uni-freiburg.de/~thiemann/haskell/WASH`

(rectangular) fragment of screen estate. It determines the fragment's visual appearance and the actions taken on GUI events like key presses and mouse clicks inside the fragment. A common approach for defining these action registers callback functions with the fragment. In a standard GUI, these callbacks may be called any time and in arbitrary order and they may result in dynamic changes to the widgets. The callbacks obtain their parameters by reading directly from the widget tree. They have to check their parameters, *e.g.*, for type correctness, before performing the actual computation.

A WASH application constructs its skin by constructing an XHTML document. The XML elements in this document play the role of widgets, but only a few dedicated input widgets may give rise to actions. These actions are registered as callbacks with the input widgets. They obtain their parameters by invoking them on handles of input elements. The invocation only succeeds if the input parses at the expected type; otherwise the WASH system refuses the input.

The main difference to a GUI application is the submit-response-style of interaction in a web (WASH) application. Each WASH program repeats two conceptual phases over and over again:

1. internal computation and
2. interaction with the environment.

The interaction with the environment can take two different forms. First, the program may perform an I/O operation and consume its result. Second, the program may construct an XHTML page, display it, and consume the user input to this page. An end user only perceives this second form of interaction: the program presents an XHTML page, the user submits some inputs to the page and receives a new page in response.

WASH represents such an interaction as a value of a monad, the CGI monad. The prime objective of this monad is to mediate the interaction with the environment. Its minimal interface has four operations:

```
run  :: CGI () -> IO ()
io   :: (Read a, Show a) => IO a -> CGI a
tell :: CGIOutput a => a -> CGI ()
ask  :: WithHTML x CGI a -> CGI ()
```

The function run is the start function of the WASH library to execute all CGI programs. Its type indicates that the CGI monad is implemented on top of the IO monad. The io operator implements lifting for the IO monad and thus supports the first kind of interaction with the environment. It is essential for the correct working of a WASH program that all I/O actions are mediated through this operator (see Sec.4 for the reason). The tell operation takes any value that can be displayed on a web browser (indicated by the type class CGIOutput), transforms it to a format suitable for the browser, sends it to the browser, and terminates the web program. Thus, the tell operation forms the leaves of an interaction. Inner nodes are modeled by the ask operation. Conceptually, ask takes a monadic value which constructs an XHTML page (of type WithHTML x

CGI a, the WithHTML component of the monad deals with XHTML construction and the CGI component indicates that accesses to WASH's base monad are permitted during the construction), performs the construction, displays the page on the browser, intercepts the values submitted through the browser, and invokes the callback action selected by this submission. The callback action must be attached to a suitable submission widget in the XHTML page. The ask operation does not subsume tell because ask is restricted to output XHTML whereas tell can display anything.

Figure 1 contains the initial fragment of a WASH program. Its entry point is mainCGI, which displays a web page with two input fields. The first one, name, creates a field for text entry, whereas the second one (with type="submit") creates a submit button. The body of mainCGI looks very much like a fragment of

```
main = run mainCGI

mainCGI :: CGI ()
mainCGI =
 standardQuery "Multiplication Drill" $
  <p>Hi there! What's your name?
     <input type="text" name="name" />
     <input type="submit"
            WASH:callback="mdrill" WASH:parms="name" />
  </p>

mdrill :: NonEmpty -> CGI ()
mdrill nameNE =
   let name = unNonEmpty nameNE in
   standardQuery "Multiplication" $
   <#>
     <p>Hello <%= name %>!</p>
     <p>Let's exercise some multiplication!</p>
     <p>Give me a multiplier
       <input type="text" value="2" name="mpy" />
     </p>
     <p>Number of exercises
       <input type="text" value="10" name="rpt" />
     </p>
     <input type="submit" value="GO!"
            WASH:callback="firstExercise name" WASH:parms="mpy,rpt" />
   </#>

firstExercise :: String -> (Int, Int) -> CGI ()
firstExercise name (mpy, rpt) =
  runExercises 1 [] []
  where
    -- actual program logic
```

Fig. 1. Multiplication drill in WASH

an XHTML page because WASH has a preprocessor that translates XML nota-tion into monadic values of type `WithHTML x CGI a`. The fragment in `mainCGI` is essentially XHTML up to two important points.

- While the `name="name"` attribute of the first input field is correct XHTML, WASH attaches additional meaning to it by treating it as a variable binding. In the rest of the XHTML fragment, `name` is bound to a *handle to the input field with this name*.
- The submit button has two non-XHTML parameters in the WASH namespace, `WASH:callback` and `WASH:parms`. The attribute `WASH:callback` contains a Haskell expression that serves as the callback which is activated when clicking the submit button. The attribute `WASH:parms` contains a comma-separated list of the handles that a form submission passes to the callback.

Clicking the submit button invokes the callback with the *values* entered in the fields corresponding to the handles in the `WASH:parms` attribute. More accurately, the entries are parsed according to the type of the callback's parameter and the invocation only happens if they parse successfully. Otherwise, the same page is displayed again with an indication where the incorrect input occurred.

The `mdrill` function constructs the second page analogously. It contains two input fields of type `Int` the values of which are passed to the callback `firstExercise name`.

This example shows that programming the web with WASH is fairly natu-ral. The programmer writes a single program which implements the control flow between displayed XHTML pages with callback actions. Compared to GUI pro-gramming, all widget handles are typed and unparsable input to a widget is rejected without intervention of the application program.

3   Execution Models

To appreciate the problems with implementing WASH on different platforms, we take a look at the underlying execution models, CGI and session thread. Each of them has to deal with the statelessness of HTTP and does so in quite different ways.

HTTP is stateless because it has a very simple request-response-style design. The browser opens a connection to the server and sends a request. The server processes the request and generates a response. Browser and server close the connection.[3]

3.1   CGI-Based Execution

When the server receives a request for a CGI program it starts this program as a separate process and forwards its output as the response to the browser. Once the response is complete, the CGI program terminates.

---

[3] Our description fits the logical request-response cycle. The actual design reuses ex-isting connections to improve efficiency.

The termination of the CGI program creates some problems. First, how do we select the callback action? Second, how do we determine the callback point in the program? Third, how do we retain a session state between multiple requests from the same client?

CGI programmers have standard answers to these questions. They select the callback action using a manually programmed dispatch. They define callback points by artificially splitting their application into multiple scripts, and they implement session state by including a session ID[4] in the response and maintaining a mapping from session ID to session state on the server.

3.2 Servlet Execution

When the server receives a request for a servlet it starts a new thread to execute the service code for the request. The servlet generates output with the response which is then sent back to the browser.

The implementation of Java servlets behaves slightly differently because starting a thread is expensive on a JVM. Thus, it maintains a pool of threads and selects one of the threads to service a request.

Logically, there is no essential difference between CGI-based execution and servlet execution. It is only that servlet execution is faster if the startup time for a service thread is smaller than the time to create a new process. However, the servlet execution opens the door for another way of reusing threads which we explain in Sec. 5.

4   Sessions and the Replay Monad

WASH tackles the problems of CGI-based execution using a special feature of the CGI monad. The monad is (among others) a state monad that maintains a log of the results of all interactions of the program with the environment. This log contains the results of all I/O operations and all form inputs processed by the program so far.

4.1 Log-Based Replay

How does the log solve the three problems from Sec.3.1? Each web page created by a WASH program contains the current log in encoded form in a hidden input field. When the user submits an output page generated by WASH, then the server invokes the same WASH program, the program reads the log from the page and appends the new inputs to the end of the log. Now the program starts executing its CGI actions. There are three cases to consider:

- If the expression is a non-monadic expression, it is recomputed and its value will be the same as in the previous run of the program.

---

[4] The management of session IDs may be implemented in several different ways [13].

- An invocation of io first checks if the top of the log is the result of an io operation. If so, it returns the value from the log (which is thus the same as in the previous run of the program). Otherwise it performs the operation, logs the result, and continues.
- An invocation of ask first checks if the top of the log is the result of a form submission. If so, it instantiates the fields according to the form submission and calls the thus selected callback function (which is the same as in the previous run of the program). Otherwise it sends the constructed XHTML (including the current log) to the browser and terminates the program.

Hence, WASH performs the selection of the callback action by replaying the program up to the creation of the page containing the callback. At that point, the log is exhausted and the last set of parameters read from the log comprises the user's entries to the submitted page. The WASH program selects the correct callback from the last set of parameters and continues executing the callback (instead of sending the page to the browser). So the log answers the question for the callback point, too.

The use of the log and the type system guarantee that each replay creates the same intermediate values as the previous execution. The type system ensures that all side effecting operations are logged and thus only executed once: each side effecting operation has an IO type and all IO actions are mediated through the io operator. Hence, replaying also answers the question for the session state because program replay constructs equivalent session states each time.

4.2   Properties of the Replay Monad

The replay technique embeds the log of all previous interactions of the server-side program with its environment in the client page. Essentially, the client page contains the entire state of the session with the server. This choice implies a number of advantages and disadvantages.

The prime advantage of replaying is that the server does not have to maintain any client state. Servers are fully exchangeable as long as they all run the same program. Thus, applications are scalable because new servers can be added easily.

Another advantage is that applications are resistant against browser navigation like cloning windows, using the back button, and even saving web pages and continuing an interaction at any later time. This advantage is also a direct consequence of keeping the session state in the client page.

However, there are also some disadvantages. First, the log grows with each interaction step and after some steps its size can become bigger than the actual content of the web page. It is almost always bigger than the fixed size of a session ID as used for implementing CGI sessions.

Second, the growth of the log causes the time for replaying to increase. The replay time is negligible for short interactions but it can lead to a noticeable lag in long interactions. Also, performing the replay puts extra, unproductive load on the server. It can be argued that this extra load impedes scalability.

Section 8 presents some concrete measurements on the impact of the log on performance.

4.3   Log Operators

One approach to avoid building up long logs is to compress multiple log entries into one entry. WASH's log operator

```
once :: (Read a, Show a) => CGI a -> CGI a
```

implements such a compression. The expression once *act* runs the CGI action *act* and replaces all the log entries corresponding to the execution of *act* by one summary entry that contains the return value of *act*.

In particular, an invocation of once *act* first checks if the top of the log is a summary entry. If that is the case, it returns the value from the log entry. Otherwise, it makes sure that the top of the log is a mark and starts executing *act*.

The execution of *act* may lead to two different outcomes. Either some ask inside of *act* stops the program because it requires a user interaction, or all CGI actions inside of *act* can run from the log so that *act* terminates returning some value. The first case, replay works just as before. In the second case, once picks up the returned value, prunes the log up to and including the mark, puts a summary entry with the value on top, and continues.

A typical use of once is the implementation of menu-based interactions. Such interactions present a menu for choosing some function, execute the function, and then always return to the menu. Here is the code snippet for such a menu selection pattern:

```
menu = once selectAFunction >> menu
```

With this definition each trip around the menu results in exactly one log entry.

The log operator

```
forever :: CGI () -> CGI ()
```

is a direct implementation of the recursive menu selection pattern for once. The direct implementation elides the extra log entry and thus implements menu-based interactions that require constant space for the log. The implementation is very similar to the one for once. The only difference is at the end, when forever *act* picks up the returned value, it prunes the log up to the mark, leaves the mark on top, and starts *act* again (instead of continuing with the rest of the program).

However, once and forever are not suitable for maintaining state across the functions selected in the menu. As an example for this kind of state, consider the implementation of a message board where topics are ordered hierarchically and the messages are threaded. The current state in such a system would be the current position in the topic hierarchy, the current thread, and perhaps even the position within the thread. Although the interaction with the system returns to the same view all the time, the underlying state changes from view to view. This kind of systems call for the operator

```
callWithCurrentHistory ::
        (Read a, Show a) =>
        ((a -> CGI ()) -> a -> CGI ()) -> a -> CGI ()
```

```
mainCGI =
  callWithCurrentHistory counter 0

counter backto counterValue =
  standardQuery "Counter" $ p $
    do text "Current counter value "
       text (show counterValue)
       br empty
       submit0 (backto (counterValue+1)) (fieldVALUE "Increment")
       submit0 (backto (counterValue-1)) (fieldVALUE "Decrement")
```

Fig. 2. A counter implementation with callWithCurrentHistory

The operator works similar to a prompt, a control operator that delimits a continuation. It implements a checkpoint with a defined state of type a and provides a *snap-back function* that returns to this checkpoint with a new state. Its first argument, say f, is a function that takes a snap-back function and the state value for the next execution of f's body. The second argument is the initial value of the state. The snap-back function takes the next value for the state, removes all log entries up to its corresponding call to callWithCurrentHistory, and runs f on the next state value. Figure 2 contains the implementation of a counter that requires only constant space for the log.

4.4 Error Detection

At the end of Sec.2 we mentioned that the system immediately rejects forms with unparsable input. This feature is easy to implement in the replay setting. During replay, the program runs through the entire code for constructing an output page even if it is never shown. During this construction dry-run, each widget can check if its input parses correctly. If the input is unparsable, then the widget sets a flag in the CGI monad that causes the page to be redisplayed (instead of taking a callback action). The erroneous input fields are marked by changing their color (usually to red) and by attaching a callback that puts the error message in the status line.

5 Session Threads

The thread-based implementation of WASH is essentially a reimplementation of WASH's minimal interface, run, io, tell, and ask. The underlying idea of the implementation is to assign one dedicated thread in the server to each interactive session.

5.1 Implementation of the Operators

The run operator is no longer necessary in WASH server pages because the web server runs CGI actions directly. However, this change is due to the different run-time environment (servlet instead of CGI), rather than the use of a thread-based implementation.

The io wrapper operator becomes just the monadic lift operation from IO to CGI. Its type restriction to Readable and Showable types could be lifted but we refrained from doing so because we did not want to change the API.

The tell operator remains unchanged because it has no dealings with the session state.

However, the ask operator requires extensive changes. While the log-based implementation terminates after sending its generated form to the browser, the thread-based ask operator must keep its thread alive so that it can continue the session as soon as the form is submitted. Furthermore, because the processing of the inputs and error checking (see Sec.4.4) is performed in the construction action in the argument to ask, the implementation of ask must be a loop that repeatedly constructs the form, checks the inputs, and then either continues with a callback or sends the form to the browser, obtains the new inputs and reiterates the loop.

The second interesting part is obtaining the new inputs which is essentially an exercise in concurrent programming. A WASH program assigns each interaction step (between interactions with the environment) a unique state ID which is a hash value computed from the previous state ID and the input from the environment (e.g., the form parameters). That is, a session thread always carries with it its current state ID.

The server maintains a mapping from state IDs to table entries. The mapping contains an entry for each state that currently has a thread running. The entry contains (among others fields) the timeout value for this interaction step and an mvar, a kind of synchronizing variable provided by concurrent Haskell [12]. The mvar holds a list of mvars each of which is capable of holding a set of form parameters and an output handle.

Now, let's see what table entries are good for. After sending its output to the browser, the session thread creates a new empty mvar, puts this mvar into the threads list belonging to the mapping entry of its state ID, and finally suspends itself by waiting for the mvar to receive a value (using takeMVar). At the same time it starts another thread which sleeps for the time specified by the timeout field, then kills the session thread and removes its mvar. If another thread fills the mvar with form parameters and an output handle before the timeout, then these values are returned to the next iteration of the ask loop.

Filling the mvar is the job of incoming HTTP request caused by form submissions. Each form submission carries with it the state ID of the thread that created the form. The server consults the mapping and obtains a table entry of this state ID. Then it removes one of the mvars from its threads field and fills the mvar with the form's parameters and the handle of the current connection's socket (this value may change for each connection). If the threads field is empty, then all session threads for this state ID have timed out and the server produces an error message.

The implementation requires some additional complications to create the table, create initial table entries, and so on. We elide the details because they do not yield additional insight.

5.2   Properties of Session Threads

The advantage of the session-thread implementation is the faster response time. The reaction time of the application remains virtually constant regardless of the length of the interaction.

However, the improved latency comes at a considerable cost. One disadvantage of this implementation is reduced scalability. Because the session thread lives on a particular server, the entire interaction has to run on this server and cannot easily be moved to another.

Another disadvantage is that browser navigation is now restricted to moving forwards. Using other means of navigation results in an error message, most of the time.

A final disadvantage is the timeout on sessions. If a user does not respond within the timeout period, then the session is lost.

To summarize, the adoption of the session-thread implementation improves on the latency but succumbs to the usual, generally accepted problems of server-side programming models with sessions: timeouts and restricted navigation.

6   Variations

Up to now, we have told a black-and-white story. On one side, there is the log-based replaying implementation and on the other side, there is the session thread-based implementation. In reality, there is a spectrum of possibilities with intriguing features between both.

6.1   Client Log and Server State

One possible combination stores the log **and** the state ID on each client page. When the page is submitted, the server first looks for a thread for the state ID. If such a thread exists, it continues to serve the session as described in Sec. 5. If no such thread exists, then the session is replayed from the log in a new thread and this thread is stored in the mapping for later use.

This combination yields an efficient design which is at the same time extremely robust and versatile.

- As long as a session proceeds in the standard way, *i.e.*, forward within the timeout of each step, the application reacts as quickly as with the session thread-based implementation.
- Browser navigation works without restriction because the submission of an "unexpected" state ID either picks up an existing thread by accident or it creates a new thread by replaying.
- Scalability is improved with respect to pure session threads because requests for a specific server can be redirected to another at the price of one replay.
- The server state is soft [7] in the sense that it improves efficiency when it is present, but it is not necessary for correct execution. That is, when threads time out or even when the server crashes, the session can still continue. Also, the server may kill threads at will if it temporarily runs out of resources, without compromising any session.

In short, the standard way of using the application is very efficient. All conceivable other ways are possible, but at the price of reduced efficiency. The only drawback of this combination is the space required to store the log in the client page (as well as the time to read and write it and to send it over the network).

6.2   Server Log and Server State

Another variation stores the log in the state ID mapping on the server. To this end, each table entry must also contain the state ID of the parent step in the interaction and the form parameters provided in this step. If a given state ID has a table entry but cannot be mapped to a thread (because it timed out, for instance), then the server can reconstruct the log by obtaining the log for the parent's ID (recursively) and appending the form parameters of the last step. The recursion stops at the initial state ID which does not have a parent and corresponds to the empty log.

This combination avoids communicating the log between client and server. It is efficient as long as the session proceeds in the standard way. It tolerates browser navigation at the price of replay.

On the downside, scalability is not immediate because the server state is not soft anymore. Also, robustness is decreased unless the state ID mapping is persistent (e.g., in a database). Finally, there is the problem that the state ID mapping grows continuously and without bounds. Such growth is undesirable and must be avoided by considering the mapping as a cache and removing entries according to a cache replacement policy.

7   Implementation

WASH server pages are implemented as an extension of the author's WASH system. The starting point of the implementation is Simon Marlow's Haskell web server (HWS) [8].

Porting the CGI-based implementation of WASH to HWS mainly requires abstracting the code over the run-time environment CGIEnv. With this abstraction in place, a WASH program can run with the environment initialized according to the CGI standard or directly from the request data inside HWS. The environment also abstracts from the handle on which the program produces its output. In the CGI instance, this handle is stdout and in HWS it is the handle to the socket that connects to the browser. The CGIEnv also provides the place to exchange the handle as required in the session thread implementation. Overall the changes required in the WASH library itself are quite localized and affect only a handful of modules.

The server dynamically compiles and loads WASH programs at run time. This feature is a standard application of the hs-plugins library [11]. The server administration is through a web interface which facilitates experimentation with the loaded WASH programs. For example, it is possible to switch between different implementation schemes for sessions while the server is running.

The code includes the following session implementations:

- the original log-based implementation (LogOnly, see Sec.4),
- the pure session thread implementation (StateIDOnly, see Sec.5), and
- the mixed implementation described in Sec.6.1 (LogAndState).

The remaining alternative (Sec.6.2) is not fully implemented.

8   Measurements

We have performed measurements to quantify two parameters affected by this work, the impact of moving from a CGI-based implementation to the servlet-based implementation and the impact of log-based replay.

We are currently relying on a micro benchmark which uses one particular WASH program, the CalcFix program from the WASH distribution, for all measurements. In Sec.8.3, we explain why we believe that the results are relevant despite the small size of the benchmark suite.

All measurements are performed on a Linux machine running kernel version 2.6.8 with 1 GB of main memory and a 1.7 GHz Pentium M processor. The benchmarking environment is the Apache Jakarta JMeter tool[5], a Java desktop application designed to load test the functional behavior and measure the performance of web applications. The benchmarking software runs on the same machine as the servers so that access to the servers is through the localhost interface. The Haskell software is WSP version 0.1.4 compiled with -O2 and WASH version 2.5.7 (for both CGI and servlet).

Table 1. Response times and throughput (Apache-CGI)

requests #	probes #	average (ms)	throughput (min^{-1})
1	10000	7	7350
10	1000	78	7511
25	400	177	8266
50	200	371	7871
75	150	564	7733
100	100	757	7504

Table 2. Response times and throughput (HWS-servlet)

requests #	probes #	average (ms)	throughput (min^{-1})
1	10000	4	12511
10	1000	48	11727
25	400	127	9988
50	200	259	10668
75	150	376	10812
100	100	440	10885

8.1   CGI vs. Haskell-Servlet

This part of the benchmark compares the startup performance of CalcFix between a WASH-CGI program invoked by Apache/2.0.54 and the same program run as a servlet in LogOnly mode. Tables 1 and 2 contain the results. The first two columns indicate the test configuration: the number of threads that generate requests concurrently and the number of times each thread is run. One thread

---

[5] http://jakarta.apache.org/jmeter/

performs exactly one request so that each configuration generates about 10000 requests. The result columns "average" and "throughput" contain the average time for a request and the number of requests per minute.

The table indicates that HWS serves the servlet roughly 42% faster than Apache+CGI and obtains 45% more throughput. However, it turns out that 90% of the Apache+CGI time results from the process creation involved with starting the CGI program.

The tables also indicate that both servers scale gracefully under load. In fact, during the measurements both servers were running in main memory. We have repeated the same measurements with different WASH programs and obtained roughly the same numbers.

8.2   Log vs. State ID

For this benchmark, JMeter simulates a client for `CalcFix`, an implementation of a desktop calculator. The client is programmed to perform 301 requests in which it repeatedly performs the computation `123+456=` and then clears the display. This application is written naively so that it generates a non-trivial, growing log.

Figure 3 contains the results for the three session implementations. It plots the response of a request against the length of the interaction sequence. The figure shows that the response times of the implementations involving the log (LogOnly, LogAndState) grow linearly with the length of the session. The StateI-DOnly implementation runs essentially in constant time. The StateIDOnly implementation has an average response time of 17ms, whereas LogOnly finishes at 596ms and LogAndState finishes at 162ms.

In a final experiment, we replace the naive implementation of the calculator by a more clever implementation `CalcHistory` which makes use of the

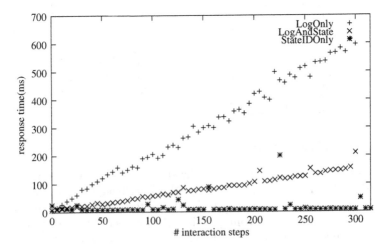

Fig. 3. Response times for `CalcFix`

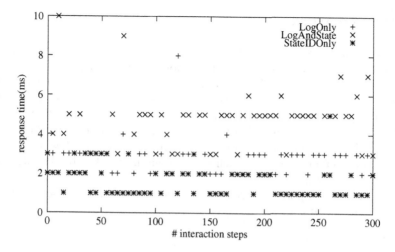

Fig. 4. Response times for `CalcHistory`

`callWithCurrentHistory` operator introduced in Sec.4. The result in Fig.4 shows that the response times are now constant for all execution models. However, the times comprise almost entirely the computation of log or stateID, respectively, because the computation of the application itself is trivial. Still, StateIDOnly is roughly two times faster than LogOnly, whereas the overhead for LogAndState seems to be larger than the sum of both.

8.3   Assessment

The benchmark setup could (and should) be improved by moving the servers to a separate machine.

Our conclusion from Sec.8.1 is that moving from a CGI-based implementation to a servlet-based one is a win mainly because it avoids the costly process creation. The results are meaningful because we are only interested in program startup time; the runtime of the rest of the WASH program is identical for both implementations.

The results in Sec.8.2 clearly demonstrate the cost of log-based replay and the speed advantage of the session thread implementation. They further give some indication that the mixed LogAndState implementation has viable performance and thus represents a good compromise. However, it would be dangerous to draw quantitative conclusions like "30% of the replaying overhead is due to reading and writing the log". Such a conclusion would not be valid because the computation performed by `CalcFix` is quite simple and it is not clear if this application is typical in this respect. However, the LogAndState performance can be considered typical because it only depends on the length of the log.

Finally, the second experiment gives some indication that the log operators are well worth the effort. It is encouraging news because the log operators also apply to the CGI-based implementation.

9   Related Work

Apart from the work already discussed in the introduction, there are two other published implementations of server pages for functional languages.

Haskell server pages (HSP) [10] have been proposed and have finally been put into practice [2]. HSP mirrors the page-centric model of Java ServerPages (JSP). It requires one source file for each displayed page and compiles this source file dynamically on demand. However, it only implements the standard session support of JSP. In contrast, the contribution of the present work is to obtain the efficiency of a server pages approach while retaining the flexible WASH session programming model.

SMLserver [4] supports a notion of ML server pages which also seems to be quite close to the JSP idea.

10   Conclusion

This paper demonstrates the viability of a session thread-based implementation of WASH's session abstraction. It reports on its implementation and presents measurements that demonstrate the performance improvements caused by this new implementation.

References

1. Claus Brabrand, Anders M°ller, and Michael Schwartzbach. The <bigwig> Project. *ACM Transactions on Internet Technology*, 2(2):79–114, 2002.
2. Niklas Broberg. Haskell server pages through dynamic loading. In Daan Leijen, editor, *Proceedings of the 2005 ACM SIGPLAN Haskell Workshop*, pages 39–48, Tallinn, Estland, September 2005.
3. Aske Simon Christensen, Anders M°ller, and Michael I. Schwartzbach. Extending Java for high-level Web service construction. *ACM Transactions on Programming Languages and Systems*, 25(6):814–875, 2003.
4. Martin Elsman and Niels Hallenberg. Web programming with SMLserver. In *Practical Aspects of Declarative Languages, Proceedings of the Fifth International Symposium, PADL'03*, number 2562 in Lecture Notes in Computer Science, pages 74–91, New Orleans, LA, USA, January 2003. Springer-Verlag.
5. Matthias Felleisen. Developing interactive web programs. In *Advanced Functional Programming*, number 2638 in Lecture Notes in Computer Science, pages 100–128, 2002.
6. Paul T. Graunke, Robert Bruce Findler, Shriram Krishnamurthi, and Matthias Felleisen. Modeling Web interactions. In *Proc. 12th European Symposium on Programming*, Lecture Notes in Computer Science, Warsaw, Poland, April 2003. Springer-Verlag.
7. Ping Ji, Zihui Ge, Jim Kurose, and Don Towsley. A comparison of hard-state and soft-state signaling protocols. In *Proceedings of ACM SIGCOMM 2003*, Karlsruhe, Germany, August 2003.
8. Simon Marlow. Developing a high-performance Web server in Concurrent Haskell. *Journal of Functional Programming*, 12(4&5):359–374, July 2002.

9. Jacob Matthews, Robert Bruce Findler, Paul Graunke, Shriram Krishnamurthi, and Matthias Felleisen. Automatically restructuring programs for the web. *Automated Software Engineering*, 11(4):337–364, 2004.

10. Erik Meijer and Danny van Velzen. Haskell Server Pages, functional programming and the battle for the middle tier. In *Draft proceedings of the 2000 ACM SIGPLAN Haskell Workshop*, pages 23–33, Montreal, Canada, September 2000.

11. AndrT Pang, Don Stewart, Sean Seefried, and Manuel M. T. Chakravarty. Plugging Haskell in. In Henrik Nilsson, editor, *Proceedings of the 2004 ACM SIGPLAN Haskell Workshop*, pages 10–21, Snowbird, Utah, USA, September 2004.

12. Simon Peyton Jones, Andrew Gordon, and Sigbj°rn Finne. Concurrent Haskell. In *Proceedings of the 1996 ACM SIGPLAN Symposium on Principles of Programming Languages*, pages 295–308, St. Petersburg Beach, Florida, USA, January 1996. ACM Press.

13. Peter Thiemann. An embedded domain-specific language for type-safe server-side Web-scripting. *ACM Transactions on Internet Technology*, 5(1):1–46, 2005.

Author Index

Lecture Notes in Computer Science

For information about Vols. 1–3840

please contact your bookseller or Springer